Engendering International Health

Basic Bioethics

Glenn McGee and Arthur Caplan, series editors

Pricing Life: Why It's Time for Health Care Rationing
Peter A. Ubel

Bioethics: Ancient Themes in Contemporary Issues
edited by Mark G. Kuczewski and Ronald Polansky

The Human Embryonic Stem Cell Debate: Science, Ethics, and Public Policy
edited by Suzanne Holland, Laurie Zoloth, and Karen Lebacqz

Engendering International Health: The Challenge of Equity
edited by Gita Sen, Asha George, and Piroska Östlin

Engendering International Health
The Challenge of Equity

edited by Gita Sen, Asha George, and Piroska Östlin

A Bradford Book
The MIT Press
Cambridge, Massachusetts
London, England

This book was set in Sabon by Achorn Graphic Services, Inc. and was printed and bound in the United States of America.

Library of Congress Cataloging-in-Publication Data

Engendering international health : the challenge of equity / edited by Gita Sen, Asha George, and Piroska Ostlin.
    p. cm. — (Basic bioethics)
  Includes bibliographical references and index.
  ISBN 0-262-19469-4 (hc. : alk. paper) — ISBN 0-262-69273-2 (pbk. : alk. paper)
  1. World health. 2. Health—Sex differences. 3. Social medicine. 4. Sexism in medicine. I. Sen, Gita. II. George, Asha. III. Östlin, Piroska, 1958- IV. Series.
RA441.E544 2002
362.1—dc21

                                                                2001055808

10 9 8 7 6 5 4 3 2

Contents

Series Foreword   vii

Preface   ix

1   Engendering Health Equity: A Review of Research and Policy   1
    Gita Sen, Asha George, and Piroska Östlin

I   Key Health Areas   35

2   Communicable Diseases: Outstanding Commitments to Gender
    and Poverty   37
    Pamela Hartigan, Janet Price, and Rachel Tolhurst

3   Examining Work and Its Effects on Health   63
    Piroska Östlin

4   Reproductive Health: Conceptual Mapping and Evidence   83
    Jane Cottingham and Cynthia Myntti

5   Violence Against Women: Consolidating a Public Health
    Agenda   111
    Claudia García-Moreno

6   Mental Health: Gender Bias, Social Position, and
    Depression   143
    Jill Astbury

7   Reorienting Public Health: Exploring Differentials in Hip
    Fracture   167
    Rachel Snow

8 Health and Environment: Moving Beyond Conventional
   Paradigms   195
   Jacqueline Sims and Maureen Butter

II Research and Policy   221

9 Social Discrimination and Health: Gender, Race, and Class in the
   United States   223
   Nancy Breen

10 Policy Environments: Macroeconomics, Programming, and
    Participation   257
    Maggie Bangser

11 Class, Gender, and Health Equity: Lessons from Liberalizing
    India   281
    Gita Sen, Aditi Iyer, and Asha George

12 Measuring Up: Gender, Burden of Disease, and Priority
    Setting   313
    Kara Hanson

13 Frameworks for Understanding Health Sector Reform   347
    Hilary Standing

References   373
Contributors   439
Index   443

Series Foreword

We are pleased to present the fourth volume in the series Basic Bioethics. The series presents innovative book-length manuscripts in bioethics to a broad audience and introduces seminal scholarly manuscripts, state-of-the-art reference works, and textbooks. Such broad areas as the philosophy of medicine, advancing genetics and biotechnology, end of life care, health and social policy, and empirical study of biomedical life will be engaged.

Glenn McGee
Arthur Caplan

Basic Bioethics Series Editorial Board
Tod S. Chambers
Carl Elliot
Susan Dorr Goold
Mark Kuczewski
Herman Saatkamp

Preface

The last century saw notable improvements in human health, including longer average life expectancies and fewer infant and child deaths. At the same time, deep economic inequalities and social injustices continue to deny good health to many and persist as obstacles to continued health gains worldwide. Since the 1980s in particular, the question of how policy changes affect health equity has become ever more pressing. Macroeconomic structural reforms exacerbated already existing inequalities and negatively affected the ability of health systems to provide accessible and affordable health care for all. As inequality widens, health achievements are endangered. A central premise of this volume is that unless public health changes its course along some significant dimensions, it cannot effectively address the needs of the poor and the marginalized, many of whom are women.

The volume brings together the work of leading researchers working on the question of gender equity in international health. It traces its origins to a brainstorming workshop and a bibliographic search undertaken in 1997, which revealed that although gender analysis of health has emerged from its infancy, it has yet to mature into a perspective that influences mainstream thinking in international health. Deep-seated gender biases in health research and in policy institutions combine with the lack of well-articulated and accessible evidence to create a vicious circle that downgrades the importance and value of gender perspectives in health.

Two public events, however, generated new interest in these issues within academic, activist, and policy communities. Critical conceptual advances and political commitments made at the United Nations Cairo and Beijing conferences of the mid-1990s on population and women, respectively, provided new ideas and promising opportunities for change. The former event transformed the discourse on population and established the field of reproductive health supported by the social equality and rights of women. Following in close succession, the latter laid out comprehensive policy frameworks for gender equality in all spheres of life.

This book builds on the momentum generated by these conferences. It brings together in one place evidence, conceptual analysis, and historical perspectives spanning both high- and low-income countries. We hope it will serve as a resource to broaden participation in the networks and institutions that define approaches to international health. By doing so, it will challenge current contours of international health research, policy, and practice.

The book goes beyond the scope of many previous publications by:

• Providing a gender and health analysis cross-cut by concern for other markers of social inequity, such as class and race.

• Detailing approaches and agendas that incorporate, but go beyond, commonly acknowledged issues relating to women's health.

• Expanding the debates on global health equity to gender and health issues of concern to both high- and low-income countries.

• Bringing gender and equity analysis into the heart of the debates that dominate international health policy.

The chapters in the first section focus on specific areas within international public health. They detail how poverty, unequal access to resources, discrimination in work, and violence lead to gender disparities in communicable diseases, occupational health, environmental health, mental health, and reproductive health. The second section reviews implications of key policies such as health sector reform, privatization, and economic liberalization for gender equity in health. Some chapters focus particularly on how gender interacts with other social discriminators, such as economic class and race, to influence health access and status. Other contributions discuss the consequences for research and policy of excluding a gender equity analysis.

Together the authors in both sections examine and critique criteria by which health differences between women and men are evaluated and how priorities are set in international policy and research. They analyze the history of public health, as well as its current practice, in order to understand the roots of its biases. They examine women's and men's different social and biologic risks and exposures to disease, access to health and social resources, consequences of ill health for themselves and for their families, and ability to exercise their rights to health and well-being.

Three workshops on "Gender and Health Equity" at the Harvard Center for Population and Development Studies (HCPDS) helped shape this volume. The editors also benefited from interaction with colleagues from the Global Health Equity Initiative at meetings in China, the United States, Kenya, and Bangladesh. In addition, several editorial meetings were held in Cambridge at HCPDS, at the National Institute for Public Health in Stockholm, and at the Indian Institute of Management in Bangalore.

In addition to this volume, HCPDS sought to generate and disseminate knowledge about gender and health equity through various activities. A number of the papers presented at the workshops were distributed to a wider audience of public health professionals as HCPDS working papers and posted on the worldwide web through the Global Reproductive Health Forum at the Harvard School of Public Health. A few of these papers were selected by the Women, Health, and Development Office of the Pan American Health Organization for publication in Spanish. In collaboration with Harvard University Press, HCPDS published an English edition of *Gender Inequalities in Health: A Swedish Perspective* (originally known as *Kön och Ohälsa*), edited by Piroska Östlin, Maria Danielsson, Finn Diderichsen, Annika Härenstam, and Gudrun Lindberg.

We are grateful for the generous support provided by both the Rockefeller Foundation and the Swedish International Development Agency that enabled us to undertake these endeavors. We are also thankful for the general project support provided by the staff of HCPDS and the Institute of Development Studies, in particular, Mark Bailey, Jan Boyes, Christopher Cahill, Suzanne Carlson, Winifred Fitzgerald, Danielle Smith, and Sheryl Stine. In preparing the manuscript we were assisted by Eliane Baume, Surabhi Kukke, and Brian Milder. We very much appreciate the support provided by Carolyn Gray Anderson, Clay Morgan, and Katherine Almeida at The MIT Press, as well as by our four anonymous reviewers.

Most important, we express our gratitude for the collective patience and expertise generously offered by the authors involved in this volume. We are also indebted to our colleagues from the larger Gender and Health Equity Working Group, who generously provided their insights into the working papers and enthusiastically participated in workshops held in Cambridge: Judith Bruce, Sarah Costa, Lesley Doyal, Timothy Evans, Adrienne Germain, Elsa Gómez, Sofia Gruskin, Kris Heggenhougen, Nancy Krieger, Gunilla Krantz, Mercedes Juarez, Ellen Marshall, Pascoal Mocumbi, Florence Muli-Musiime, Fabienne Peter, Michael Reich, Don Sabo, Ami Shah, Carol Vlassoff, Corinne Whitaker, Meg Wirth, and George Zeidenstein.

Engendering International Health

1

Engendering Health Equity: A Review of Research and Policy[1]

Gita Sen, Asha George, and Piroska Östlin

Modern epidemiology is oriented to explaining and quantifying the bobbing of corks on the surface of waters, while largely disregarding the stronger undercurrents that determine where, on average, the cluster of corks ends up along the shoreline of risk.
—McMichael (1995 cited in Farmer 1996)

Why is gender important to a consideration of the causes and consequences of inequity in health? Health sciences have been concerned about health inequity at least since the early part of the nineteenth century, when distinctions between the health status of rich and poor were recognized to be pervasive (Farr 1839; Rosen 1958). Such distinctions are also seen to be causally interactive with other determinants of inequality, such as race and caste (Williams 1997). Yet attention to health equity, on the basis of economic class, caste, or race, has not spilled over to an effective consideration of gender. There is still a need for health professions at large to recognize widespread and profound implications of gender-based inequities in health. With this in mind, this chapter introduces the book by combining our insights with those of our colleagues detailed in subsequent chapters. Together we draw out the implications of a gender approach to health equity.

One sound empirical reason for paying attention to health differences between women and men is that such differences clearly exist even where the socioeconomic gradient may not be strong. For example, in Sweden, a country that is known for more class equality, the risk for becoming depressed at any time before age 80 years is 28% for men and 49% for women (Rorsman et al. 1990).

Furthermore health differences between women and men in any given socioeconomic group (class, caste, or race) can be significant. Patterns of tuberculosis infection and illness vary between poor women and men (Hudelson 1996; Diwan et al. 1998), as do those for coronary heart disease between richer women and men (Östlin et al. 1998). Various studies of inequalities in health showed that even though class may be the main determinant of health inequalities, significant differences in health outcomes by race and gender remain within each class level (Lillie-Blanton et al. 1993; Krieger et al. 1993; Sen et al. this volume).

These differences may not be uniform or even move in the same direction. Although expected differences between polar extremes of social gradients, between rich white men on the one hand, and poor, colored women on the other, are largely confirmed through health research (Breen this volume), no obvious or linear pattern emerges as one moves along the social gradient. In the United States, for example, welfare policies are targeted to poor women with dependent children. In the absence of general unemployment benefits, this leads to worse health access for poor men than for poor women (Breen this volume). It is precisely because of these complex and nonlinear patterns that health research and policy have to pay them greater attention.

Despite these empirical differences and growing attention to health inequity generally, it has taken much longer for gender to be recognized as a contributing social factor than, say, socioeconomic class, race, or caste. In part this is because of the still common fallacy of conflating gender with biological difference. The distinction between sex (as determined biologically) and gender (as constructed socially)[2] has been used extensively in the last quarter-century of research. Particularly developed in the social sciences, the distinction allows researchers to distinguish and comprehend the social bases of differences between women and men. It makes it possible to dig beneath the seeming obviousness of biological difference to the deeper social bases of power and inequality.

Doing this in the health field poses two challenges:

• Health, unlike say education, has a biologic base or at least biological referents. No one would seriously believe that educational differences between races, castes, or genders have a biological basis.[3] But in the field of health, biology cannot simply be wished away as bias. We are forced therefore to analyze the complex ways in which biology and social factors interact when attempting to understand health-related differences between women and men.

• In health sciences, differences between men and women are more influenced by biology than differences between rich and poor or between caste groups. Even race-based differences are probably more similar to class or caste in this regard than to sex, despite the known influence of genetics in particular diseases that are racially differentiated.

Nevertheless, social factors and processes can be just as important for female-male differences as for other differences. For example, it is important to note that apart from being biologically more vulnerable due to pregnancy (Diwan et al. 1998), poor women are also more vulnerable to morbidity from malaria than both rich women and poor men due to poorer access to quality health care services and adequate nutrition. Thus social determinants exacerbate biological vulnerabilities. In fact in many circumstances social disadvantages are prime determinants of unfair health outcomes. For example, women's lower social autonomy and structural disadvantage exacerbate their biological susceptibility to infection with the human immunodeficiency virus (HIV) (Zierler and Krieger 1997; Weiss and Rao Gupta 1998). Rarely does biology act alone to determine health inequities.

Distinguishing between possible biological and social factors is important for analyzing not only health differences but also similarities between women and men. For instance, similar death rates from coronary heart disease should be a source of grave concern, considering that women are supposed to be better protected from heart disease due to higher levels of estrogen (McKinlay 1996). This similarity, despite a protective biological factor, may well indicate the presence of counteracting social disadvantage or discrimination.

Gender bias can also affect our understanding of biological differences and processes. The field of sociobiology is rife with attempts to trace the roots of different female and male behaviors to presumed biological origins without attempts to interrogate either the presumed "naturalness" of such behaviors, or examine their anthropological and historical variability. Thus such theories adduce the numerical scarcity of eggs as a reason for women's "natural" predisposition toward maternal nurturing roles, whereas men, due to their larger production of sperm, can afford to be careless in reproduction (Hubbard 1995). Obviously such "objective" biological theories are innocent of any recognition that male and female roles in nurturing and reproduction are not as rigid as they presume. Anthropologists provide plenty of evidence of societies where nurturing is not confined to one sex and neither is reproductive "carelessness."

In a related manner, Western medicine often legitimizes the association of disease and weakness with women's biological characteristics. Consequently, women's experiences of menstruation and menopause are described as being processes of wasted production and signs of biological decay (Martin 1990). These perceptions not only remove women's control and discretion from their own bodies, they sanction explicit and implicit discrimination against women's active participation in society (Lupton 1994). For example, anthropological evidence details how the salience of premenstrual syndrome grew parallel to women's claims for full participation in public domains (Rittenhouse 1991).

This trend can be traced historically to the treatment of women's nervous systems in Western medicine. Historians of medicine and anthropologists document how the diagnosis of hysteria offered women a legitimate venue for their social frustrations. However, the medicalization of women's social status also reinforced perceptions that women were biologically weaker, delicate, and more susceptible to being invalid (Lupton 1994; Johannisson 1995). As a result, women were discouraged from engaging in various activities on the basis of their fragile constitution and delicate nerves.

For example, a chairman of the Harvard School of Medicine believed that allowing women to enroll in exclusively male educational institutions would be detrimental to their health, not because men were superior to women, but because they were different from women. Women were fully capable of doing all the things that men were entitled to do. "But she cannot do all this, and retain uninjured health and a future secured from neuralgia, uterine disease, hysteria, and other derangements of the nervous systems if she follows the same method that boys are trained in" (Clarke 1874 quoted in Hubbard 1995). It is important to note that women of color or from lower classes were traditionally excluded from such paternalistic concerns about their biological frailty (Krieger and Fee 1994).

The infiltration of discriminatory gender norms into medical knowledge is not, however, a Western monopoly. Much more research is required to explore how traditional medical systems treat gender (Vlassoff 1994). The following example documents bias. It is believed in the highlands of Peru that wind- or air-borne factors related to the supernatural environment (*wayras*) are the principal causes of sickness. As a result, women are considered to be disadvantaged and weak because of their more "open" physiology and because they lose bodily fluids and blood during menstruation and pregnancy. These "handicaps" restrict women from engaging in hard work (*ruway*) that ironically would expel such illness and impurity. Not only are they restricted from traveling to the lowlands where they would be able to engage more directly in the cash economy and in the lucrative gold mining industry, but their own domestic work is devalued as being light work (Larme 1998).

Such research shows that knowledge of the body, health, and illness in various societies and historical periods is culturally constructed and contextually contingent (Lock and Gordon 1998; Lock and Scheper-Hughes 1990). "Power is a key dimension in the cultural construction of medical knowledge. Medical systems frequently reproduce inequalities and hierarchies in a society by naturalizing and normalizing inequalities through facts and images about the body" (Larme 1998). Hence when considering biological differences or special needs in health, it is necessary to be aware that biological givens are often gendered constructions. Moreover these social constructions support gender norms and perceptions that sanction social discrimination that in turn perpetuates health inequities.

Understanding the way in which biological and social factors interact in different aspects of health becomes central to our understanding of how gender operates in health. This has consequences not only for women's health but also for men's. High rates of fatalities and injuries due to traffic accidents among men, for example, may be a consequence of the gendered phenomenon of who drives and who owns cars, and may also reflect a promotion of risk taking through the marketing of maleness (Snow this volume).

If it is true, as we maintain, that many health outcomes are not the result of natural biological pressures but are due to societal influences, they can and ought to be changed through health and social policy. Thus a gendered approach to health, one that distinguishes biological and social factors while exploring their interactions and one that is sensitive to how inequality affects health experiences, provides guidance to identifying appropriate responses from the health care system and from public policy more generally, as we argue in the final section.

Viewing Health through a Gender Lens

Gender refers to structural inequalities marked by unequal access for women and men to material and nonmaterial resources. This in turn forms the basis for defining and distinguishing male and female behaviors, expectations, and roles as well as relations between and among women and men (Rathgeber and Vlassoff 1993). As a social phenomenon, gender enforces unequal relations of power between men and women through symbolic cultural norms and values. In addition, it permeates social institutions as it refers not only to relations between the sexes at the individual level, but also to a complex array of structures, practices, and behaviors that define the organizational systems that constitute human societies. It is thus an organizing principle of social life (West 1993 cited in Hartigan et al. this volume)

Conventional research often defines gender simply as a set of social roles. Yet it is interesting that research on race or class dynamics does not speak in terms of class or race roles. "The reliance on roles as an analytical concept surfaces primarily in relation to gender (rather than race or class) and testifies to a tendency within policy circles to treat gender in isolation from the structural perspectives that inform the analysis of these other forms of social inequality" (Kabeer 1994). Apart from isolating gender analysis from other areas in social policy, exclusive or excessive emphasis on roles leads to a focus on behavior change at the individual level, rather than on policy change at the societal level. This understanding has particular implications for the health field. It reinforces the need to infuse our understanding of health-related behavior, which may be linked on the surface to differences in women's and men's roles, with an analysis of the structural gender inequalities that may underpin such roles and behavior (Stronks et al. 1996).

Unequal relations of power also define the public debate on policies across a range of fields including health. Socially subordinate groups are often victimized or blamed for their own disadvantaged situations, and this applies to women as well. Rape victims are all too often accused of promiscuity and teenage mothers are blamed for irresponsibility. Working women are presumed to be neglectful mothers and thus responsible for the ill health of their children. These generalizations, based as they are on a superficial analysis of social roles rather than on underlying structural inequalities, legitimate and present the daily realities of women (and men) as being the result of their own behavior rather than of interactions between gender structures and behavior.

This problem is not exclusive to gender. Factors such as economic class, race, caste, ethnicity, and sexual orientation have not fared much better in this regard. Health research in practice often does not adequately clarify or critically analyze social constructions of race, class, or sexual orientation just as it does not effectively analyze gender. By not exploring the range of potential underlying factors that may contribute to social inequalities in health along different dimensions, the perception is reinforced that current ill health is inherent in the individual or social group under observation (Lillie-Blanton and LaVeist 1996). At best this results in narrow policy and missed opportunities that lead us down "conceptual paths that have little or no relevance to the way people actually live, and hence inevitably to strategies and policies that have no relevance to prevention" (Clatts 1995). At worst, by obscuring the relations of power that provide the foundation for discrimination, we depoliticize and perpetuate these "monotonous" realities (Farmer 1997a).

Gender, like other social stratifiers, does not operate in isolation (Baca Zinn and Thorton Dill 1998). It is a distinct and powerful form of stratification that interacts with other social markers such as class, race, and sexual orientation. Just as research and policy initiatives have to devise adequate methodologies to deal with disease interactions (e.g., heart disease with hypertension, anemia with malaria, physical violence with depression), they also must recognize the importance of social interactions (e.g., gender with class, race, and/or sexual orientation). These interactions between social determinants may be either additive or multiplicative. In other words, emphasizing gender's distinct yet interactive nature highlights the fact that other social factors can deepen or counteract the effect of gender on health outcomes.

For example, gender and poverty often combine to create multiple barriers to women's well-being. Seventy percent of the poor in the world are women (UNDP 1995). Not only are women more materially disadvantaged than men, they also encounter gender discrimination that often further exacerbates their poverty. It is well recognized that women work just as much or even more than men do; however, their work is largely not valued and therefore not visible in standard labor statistics or regulations (Östlin this volume). Moreover women often have little control over the nature of their work. As a result they often face high opportunity costs when they fall ill, have to seek care, or have to care for someone else. Women also tend to have less decision-making power when it comes to allocation of household and community resources (Hartigan et al. this volume). Consequently, allocation of food, rest, and health care within households and provision of appropriate public infrastructure in communities are often biased against women (Sims and Butter this volume).

Gender Bias, Equality, and Equity

Defining gender as relations of power that interact with biology to generate differences in needs, capabilities, and treatment requires us to focus systematically on the forms that bias takes and the inequality and injustice that result. In doing this in fields other than health, feminist analysts prefer to use the concept of gender *equality* as the foundation for notions of gender justice or *equity*.[4] This is based on the presumption that, being the product of social relations and hierarchies, inequalities between women and men are likely to be inherently biased and unfair. An empirical finding of gender inequality or differences in treatment or outcomes is thus taken as a marker for probable gender inequity as well. Achieving gender equity is therefore viewed as resulting from focusing on gender equality.

Such a position is less tenable in the health field because of the confounding influence of biology. Even when biology is scrutinized through a gender lens, as we proposed earlier, this clearly does not eliminate all of the biological differences between women and men. Absence of difference or gender equality as such cannot therefore be the uniform foundation for gender justice in health. Furthermore equality of health outcomes can in some instances be a marker for gender injustice because it may indicate that women's particular biology-dependent needs or abilities are not adequately recognized.

Gender equity in health must stand therefore on its own foundation: absence of bias. But not being able to draw on a simple universal principle such as equality complicates our task in the health field, because it necessitates an even more careful interrogation of where bias is present and how it works.[5] In particular we have to start with careful scrutiny of the content of gender equity itself to ensure that bias does not masquerade as "natural" biological difference.

Such bias operates at many levels. Within households, girls and boys, women and men often do not receive equal recognition or treatment with regard to nutrition and health care (Das Gupta 1987; Booth and Verma 1992; Lane and Meleis 1991). These biases are deeply ingrained and reproduced by economic differences in property and inheritance, as well as divisions of labor within households and communities. Gender biases that put girls' and women's health at risk are often reinforced by community norms and values regarding women's and men's sexuality, reproduction, and rights (Cottingham and Myntti this volume; Hartigan et al. this volume). Health providers and health service systems often compound these biases by not recognizing their existence or the need for countervailing measures (Standing this volume). And health policies tend to remain insensitive to the implications of such biases unless systematically transformed through public advocacy.

Our approach and that of other authors in this volume is based on the following principles:

1. Where genuine biological difference clearly interacts with social determinants to define different needs and experiences for women and men in health, gender equity may require qualitatively different treatment that is sensitive to these needs.

2. Where no plausible biological reason exists for different health outcomes, social discrimination should be considered a prime suspect for

causing unreasonable health outcomes. Here, recognition that differences are maintained by social discrimination requires that health equity measures focus on policies that encourage equal outcomes. This may require different treatment to overcome historical discrimination.

These two principles provide the basis for deliberating the fairness of an approach or intervention on the basis of its ability to promote health and protect rights to social well-being. This point is crucial to underline. *A gender and health equity analysis insists that, although differences in health needs between women and men do exist in relation to biological and historical differences, this does not "naturally" lead or justify different or unequal social status or rights in just societies.*

Gender thus affects both how we think about health and what we do about it in families, communities, and societies, local, national, and global. Effectively incorporating gender analysis in our understanding of health involves changing our conceptual approaches, questions, and methods, and these are likely to change our research and policy conclusions. Gender appears to affect the risks of mortality and morbidity through different exposure and vulnerability; the severity and consequences of illness; access to resources for health promotion and for the prevention, diagnosis, and treatment of illness; health-related behaviors; experience and implications of ill health; and responses of the health sector.

Consequences of Not Taking Gender Seriously

Resounding Silences

One way in which gender bias manifests in health is through slow recognition of health problems that particularly affect women. One not so distant and well-known example is the case of reproductive tract infections (RTIs), particularly among poor women in developing countries. Despite over fifty years of globally and nationally supported family planning programs and extensive related research into contraceptive behavior, it is only since the 1990s that serious research into the prevalence of RTIs has occurred (Germain et al. 1992).

Another example is domestic violence, its prevalence, and its consequences for women's physical and mental health. New research in this area points to wide prevalence, a range of social causes, and consequences across a wide spectrum of health outcomes (Garcia Moreno this volume).

In both of these problems, the World Health Organization (WHO) and many other agencies and researchers have supported a considerable amount of work. Although these problems are being addressed, they do not exhaust the possible list of such silences. For instance, adequate and equal recognition of breast cancer, a prime cause of female deaths and illness from cancer, has been all too recent (Breen this volume). It is useful to remember that, when speaking about poorly acknowledged health problems, it is possible by definition to speak only about what we have already learned! What is striking in relation to the problems mentioned here is how widespread they are, how significant their effects, and of course how long it has taken the health professions to recognize them.

Misdirected or Partial Approaches

Lack of acknowledgement of women's health problems is only one way in which gender distortions affect research. Misdirected or partial approaches include some of the widest problems across a broad range of health subfields.

In the field of environmental health, air-pollution standards and testing long ignored the problem of indoor air pollution and smoke-filled kitchens that are critical to the health of large numbers of poor women in developing countries. It was generally presumed that, as far as air pollution is concerned, rural areas are cleaner than urban areas and that, since the problem is caused by industry and road traffic in urban areas, it does not discriminate between women and men. This is a classic example of a partial approach that missed a major source of environmental risk for women because it did not start from an awareness as to where women and men spend large parts of their working day. Evidence suggests that indoor air pollution may not only be associated with cardiovascular morbidity in women, but may also be associated with high risks of tuberculosis, high levels of blindness, and inhibited nutrient uptake (Östlin this volume; Sims and Butter this volume).

Occupational health was similarly shortsighted in recognizing the consequences of differences in women's and men's work locations and responsibilities. For instance, occupational stress has different causes and patterns due to women's and men's different roles and their ability to combine work inside and outside the home. A Swedish study found that, toward the end of the paid work day, stress levels of male managers tend to decline whereas those of female managers tend to increase sharply in anticipation of domestic work requirements (Östlin this volume). Furthermore, overtime for men leads to a lower incidence of heart attack, but for women it increases the risk (Alfredsson et al. 1985 cited in Östlin this volume).

Such evidence attests to the argument that determinants of health inequity may be different from those of aggregate health (Whitehead et al. 2001). The example is working conditions in Sweden, which, since they are relatively good on average, do not have much explanatory power for aggregate morbidity, but do explain quite a lot of the differences between economic groups. When gender is added as a stratifier and when work is taken to include both paid and unpaid work, this argument clearly acquires even greater force.

Indeed women's occupations generally have received less attention in terms of measurement of health implications than men's, despite considerable evidence of the persistence of occupational segregation that attests to the fact that, by and large, women and men simply do not do the same kind of work (Anker 1998). Thus we know very little about the health impact of women's work as agricultural workers or in the large number of small and medium-size factories and enterprises (the so-called informal sector) where the overwhelming majority of women are employed in many regions of the world. Where domestic work is concerned, it is typically presumed to be more leisurely, slower paced, and under the control of women. Growing evidence suggests that the reality is rather different. The health implications involve an as yet poorly researched combination of stress and depression (Östlin this volume).

As is well known, early beliefs in the field of mental health traced women's problems to their reproductive biology, as the very word hysteria attests. Such unsubstantiated and almost axiomatic presumptions are not as far behind us as we might suppose or wish. Research continues to focus on the hypothesized relationship between reproductive-related events, such as menstruation, pregnancy, and menopause, and women's higher rates of depression. However, none of these events by itself explains the gender difference in depression (Astbury this volume). Instead, research on postnatal depression identified partner and social support, life events, the experience of motherhood, and infant temperament as critical risk factors (Small et al. 1994 cited in Astbury this volume). Not only did such bias neglect the role of reproduction on men's mental health, it also led to delay in discovering nonreproductive aspects of women's experience of depression, such as their higher risk for cardiovascular morbidity (Musselman et al. 1998 cited in Astbury this volume).

Perhaps no subfield of health research is as replete with contradiction when viewed through a gender lens as reproductive health. Contraceptive acceptability research until very recently (and perhaps even continuing today) tended to presume that women's complaints about discomfort or pain were imaginary and could be ignored. Thus the discovery of the wide prevalence of RTIs was long delayed, although women's weak acceptance of intrauterine devices (IUDs) should have served as an early warning signal if it had not been dismissed by family planning researchers as irrational or psychosomatic (Germain et al. 1992).

Ironically, while women's reproductive biology was being linked in questionable ways to their behavior and mental health, the real implications of gender power relations around sexuality and reproduction for violence and depression were ignored. Continuing research on domestic violence suggests strong links between physical and emotional or psychologic abuse on the one hand and depression on the other through a powerful mix of humiliation and entrapment (Astbury this volume; Garcia-Moreno this volume).

Poor Recognition of Causally Interactive Pathways
Causal interactions affecting health work in two distinct ways: comorbidity among diseases and interactions among social factors. Comorbidity, the simultaneous existence of different diseases in a person, is one of the confounding features of ill health that particularly tests the skills and experience of practicing physicians. Although it is not inherently a sex-differentiated phenomenon (except insofar as reproductive health is concerned), closer examination reveals particular aspects that are of concern from a gender perspective.

For example, malaria increases the risk of anemia in pregnancy, as mentioned earlier. Schistosomiasis is associated with risks of infertility, abortion, and vulnerability to HIV infection (Feldmeier et al. 1993 cited in Hartigan et al. this volume). Although both these are well known at the level of research and general policy recommendations, little has been done actually to devise or test strategies for addressing them in the field. Lack of adequate operations research to test alternative approaches may be part of the larger difficulty posed by weak funding of research into gender and infectious diseases.

This is also where the previously cited problem regarding lack of clinical trials among women of reproductive age becomes a major problem yet again. In the absence of reliable data drawn from trials it is difficult to proceed with treatment. Nonetheless, even in these cases, not all policy is drug dependent. Focusing on reducing malaria risk for reproductive-age women in particular, and reducing anemia among girls and women in general are approaches that do not require new clinical trials, but are predicated on a more women-friendly approach to health programs.

The other source of interactions is interplay among social factors. As discussed above, gender as a social determinant of health does not act alone but is usually interactive with other social stratifiers. Human papilloma virus (HPV) risk (and the resultant elevated risk of cervical lesions and cancer) is greatest for women who are poor, have had several births, and who have themselves had or whose partners have had multiple sexual partners (Thomas et al. 1996 cited in Hartigan et al. this volume). Similarly, the complex mix of social and biological factors in the incidence of HIV and the fact that these are profoundly gender related is only too well known. Whereas male to female transmission of the HIV virus is biologically easier, the growing burden of infection among girls and women is clearly associated with gender power relations. This operates either through women's difficulties in insisting on safe sex practices by their male partners, or through the economic power differences cross-cutting age and gender power in the phenomenon of "sugar daddies" and adolescent girls (Males 1997).

Gwatkin and Guillot (2000) point out that among the poorest 20% of people in the world, communicable, maternal, perinatal, and nutritional conditions are responsible for a relatively larger proportion of female than male ill health (7.5% more deaths, 11.4% more disability life-adjusted years (DALYs). When maternal conditions are excluded from this calculation the higher levels of female ill health persist (6.3% more deaths, 7.5% more DALYs). Of interest, the report also shows that where previously at an aggregate level men were seen to suffer more from non-communicable diseases than women, when cross-cut by class, it is rich women who do (5.4% more deaths, 7.8% more DALYs).[6]

Are such differences due to the interaction of poverty and sex or poverty and gender? We must find ways of sorting out the influences. Existing data suggest that female-male differences in mortality and morbidity from specific infectious diseases vary globally, and point to a mix of economic, social, and environmental gender factors in their epidemiology. Clearly the possible synergy between risk factors has to be better understood so that we can explain, for instance, why after the start of adolescence men are more likely to be infected with tuberculosis but women are more likely to present with the disease (Dolin 1998 cited in Hartigan et al. this volume).

Given the unequal nature of gender relations, a gender approach often tends to uncover health inequity as it particularly affects women. But it can also work to men's disadvantage in health, as we see in the next section.

Relative Vulnerabilities and the Gender Paradox in Health

Across the world, the risk of premature death among people age fifteen to fifty-nine years is higher for nonpoor men than for nonpoor women (WHO 1999c).[7] This led some to maintain that it is men, not women, whose health is more vulnerable. However, the pattern of higher mortality risk is not reflected among the poor, for whom the picture is more mixed across countries. In some countries (India, South Africa) poor men in this age group appear to be at higher risk of dying prematurely than poor women. In others (Egypt, Niger, Nicaragua) there is hardly any gender difference among the poor, whereas in still others (Sri Lanka, China, Poland, Czech Republic) poor women fare worse than poor men. According to the *World Health Report 1999*, countries in which poor women fare worse than poor men also have the fewest people living under absolute poverty (Sri Lanka 4%, Poland 7%, Czech Republic 3%) and have higher life expectancy overall compared with other countries. These results clearly indicate the need for further investigation into links between poverty and gender equity in health.[8]

Social context influences poorer male outcomes where they occur through certain environments and behaviors that are more common among men than women (e.g., smoking, heavy drinking, violence, risk-taking in traffic or sports). These influences on male mortality and morbidity show strong socioeconomic class determinants. From age fifteen to twenty-four, lower-class Dutch males were three times more likely to have a trauma diagnosis than higher-class males of the same age (Gijsbers van Wijk et al. 1995). Poor African-American men in the United States have lower survival curves than men in Bangladesh (Polych and Sabo 1995).

An equally dramatic example is that of male life expectancy in Russia. Between 1989 and 1994 life expectancy at birth decreased by 6.5 years for men and 3.5 years for women due to a striking increase in adult mortality. As a result, in 1994 women in Russia could expect to live 13.5 years longer than men (Shkolnikov 1997). Many men try to cope with stresses through health-damaging behaviors, for example, heavy drinking, and these have effects on accidents and cardiovascular disease as well as crime (Walberg et al. 1998).

A substantial part of this gender gap reflects extraordinary pressures from a rapidly changing society, particularly on the disadvantaged. Research details that socioeconomic differences in mortality were greater in women than in men in Moscow. Hence, although mortality rates remained lower among women than men, women of lower social status suffered disproportionately (Chenet 2000). More research is required to explain how men and women from different classes react heterogeneously to dynamic changes in society.

Following such an agenda, a study comparing gendered health outcomes in East and West Germany showed that men's health fared better than women's in the East (Lüschen et al. 1997). The authors hypothesized that despite insecure jobs and difficult work situations, East German men may experience unification positively in sociopolitical terms and perceive themselves to have better social status than East German women.[9] Obviously more research is necessary to sort out these trends.

Moving beyond mortality, considerable attention has focused on the gender paradox in health in the United States and in western Europe. This refers to the general phenomenon of women being sicker but living longer than men. Women report more physical and psychological symptoms, more chronic illness and disability, take more medication and visit physicians more often. In contrast, men suffer more from life-threatening diseases that cause more permanent disability and earlier death (Verbrugge 1976a, 1985; Nathanson 1987). One can argue that although higher rates of male mortality tend to capture the public imagination, the larger burden of female morbidity is less spectacular and hence less in the public eye (Verbrugge 1985). To put it more bluntly, men die of their illnesses whereas women have to live with theirs (Thorslund et al. 1993).

Conventional wisdom attributes women's higher morbidity to their reproductive health needs. This is certainly true for some countries outside North America and Western Europe. In low-income countries, reproductive problems may play a larger role in explaining gender differences in health (Cottingham and Myntti this volume) and women may have less access to health care services than men in developing countries (Vlassoff 1994; Puentes-Markides 1992; Thaddeus and Maine 1994). However, a Dutch study showed that 60% of women's health problems are not caused by reproductive morbidity (Gijsbers van Wijk et al. 1995). Even though reproductive health issues account for some female excess morbidity, women who do not report such problems still have worse health than men (Popay et al. 1993).

Women's higher mental and physical morbidity also was hypothesized as being caused by their greater sensitivity to bodily cues and to social acceptability of sick roles. It was suggested that women experience more vague symptoms that doctors tend to label as being psychiatric because they are unable to diagnose them without a biological base. However, according to one study based on doctors' reporting of primary health care patients, less than 20% of women's health problems were due to symptoms without diagnosable disease. Moreover, few sex differences were seen in this category, suggesting that women do not have lower thresholds for perceiving and reporting symptoms (Gijsbers van Wijk et al. 1995). Other authors found that women did report more "sick building symptoms" than men did and that through clinical examinations this excess prevalence was real rather than a reporting artifact (Stenberg and Wall 1995).

Even though women use more medication and health services than men, a large part of this can be attributed to women's use of preventive services for contraceptives, cervical screening, and other diagnostic tests (Gijsbers van Wijk et al. 1995). Indeed, it was hypothesized that this contributes to women's higher chronic morbidity, as preventive care diminishes the severity of their health problems. Declining mortality rates since the late 1960s coupled with earlier medical diagnosis of chronic disease has led to ill people living longer. As a result, management of health problems rather than their cure has become the reality for many elderly. Considering that most of the elderly are women, these trends are especially important for them (Verbrugge 1985). Initial research that compares health outcomes of the elderly across a range of developing and industrialized countries seems to prove excess female morbidity. The degree and specific pattern of this excess vary by country even after controlling for women's greater longevity (Rahman et al. 1994).

Some researchers are skeptical about the uniformity of the gender paradox in health. Although they find a general pattern of higher female morbidity, they note a lack of predicted female excess in specific instances (Kandrack et al. 1991). A study of Scandinavian countries found no universal pattern in gender health differences. Instead, excess female morbidity varied by each cultural context (Haavio-Manila 1986). Other investigators highlight the complexity and subtlety of the pattern of gender differences. The "direction and magnitude of sex differences in health vary according to the particular symptom or condition in question and according to the phase of the life cycle. Female excess is only consistently found across the life span for psychological distress and is far less apparent, or reversed, for a number of physical symptoms and conditions" (Macintyre et al. 1996).

"While morbidity and mortality rates and health services utilization patterns are apparently interrelated, it is extremely difficult to establish the causal connection between these factors" (Kandrack et al. 1991). Moreover the conclusions one draws often depends heavily on the health measure used (Arber 1997). Such evidence and the questions they spur underline the caution with which generalizations about gender differences in health can be made and the importance of finding the underlying causes that explain them.

This discussion suggests that the so-called gender paradox may be a more complex phenomenon than often tends to be supposed. Higher male mortality is not universal and is qualified by poverty in ways that are not well understood in some countries. Higher female morbidity may also not have uniform or universal explanations within and across societies. Both phenomena require more careful examination. In particular, female and male vulnerability must be contextualized if we are to understand better which social environments prove harmful to their health.

Engendering Health Research

The discussion above points to how little we understand as yet about gender differences even on such broad aggregates as mortality and morbidity. The potential role of health research in filling these gaps and extending our explanations for observed differences in the various subfields of health is central to effective policies and programs.

Data

Although one may tend to think immediately of complex linkages between biomedical and social sciences, the absence of gender analysis is still felt in some simple and unfortunately rather pervasive ways. This includes the fact that health data (in individual research projects, national, regional levels) is still not systematically disaggregated by sex. The sad fact is that data managers and systems are not adequately sensitized to the need for even basic disaggregation by sex, let alone presentation of data in a manner that will allow cross-tabulation and classification between sex and social stratifiers such as socioeconomic class, race, or caste. Without appropriate disaggregated data, it is difficult even to begin a gender analysis. However, collection of such data by individual research projects or through larger data systems is not without cost. Here is where the question of values, political will, and mobilization comes in.

A more difficult problem in relation to data is the question of their reliability both when collected in the home or community and through records of health service providers. In societies where systematic gender biases exist in health-seeking behavior or where social norms for women of "suffering silently" prevail, morbidity data are known to be underestimates whether self-reported or collected from provider records. This is particularly a challenge for problems that are associated with high levels of social stigma, such as violence against women, abortion, and vesico-vaginal fistula (Garcia Moreno this volume, Cottingham and Myntti this volume, Bangser this volume).

Social norms affect data quality for both men and women. Although men have higher rates of substance use disorders and women have higher rates of most affective disorders, biases in social norms exaggerate these differences as men are more averse to a psychiatric label and women are more averse to a drinker label (Allen et al. 1998 cited in Astbury this volume). These data problems urgently require attention because they mean that our analysis of female–male differences in health is seriously hampered even when we have reasons to believe that they may be significant.

Gender-Sensitive Methodologies

Conventional health research methodologies have been challenged to respond to questions of health equity in general. In addition, various biases inhibit them from fully exploring gender and health inequalities in particular (Breen this volume; Hanson this volume). A cautious interpretation of standard statistics and variables used in health research is recommended. As Macintyre (1986) put it, "None of the social positions of interest, or the variables used to represent them, are unproblematic or self-evident in their meaning, measurement or significance."

For example, in Thailand discrepancies in gender differences in the prevalence of malaria were noted depending on different study designs. Data derived from clinics indicated a male female ratio of 6:1, and mobile clinics found a ratio of 4:1. Considering women's greater use of pharmacies and traditional healers, this statistic would most likely narrow even further if a survey based on all providers or a population-based survey were to be carried out (Ettling et al. 1989 cited in Hanson this volume). Another example is provided in estimates of the global burden of disease where the ranking by "experts" of different sources of female morbidity was significantly at odds with that provided by women in the community (Sadana 1998 cited in Hanson this volume).

Apart from questioning methodologies that may be gender biased, the researcher also must be careful about how variables are defined and measured. The fact that women engage in multiple roles led to the study of the health impact of engaging in varying numbers of roles. Later research found role quality to be a more useful variable in predicting health differences between women and men (Dennerstein 1995). Because it is easier to measure the number of roles rather than their quality, however, health research tends to refer to role occupancy more frequently than role quality (Hibbard and Pope 1993). Nonetheless, Annandale and Hunt (2000) concluded that traditional research has moved from a focus on social roles as properties of individuals, to transitional research that stresses the meaning of roles for people's lives, to emerging perspectives that place roles within a structural framework that allows researchers to examine the relations between gender roles.

Similarly there has been considerable discussion about the effect of different approaches to measuring social class for women, principally because researchers are beginning to question the validity of assuming that husbands' income levels can be surrogates for their wives' social class (Arber 1997). Since most occupational classification systems were developed for men, they differentiate poorly between women's jobs. In Sweden, a large proportion of female-dominated office jobs are classified under just three occupational codes. Highly qualified, general, and specialized secretarial work is found under the same occupational code as general office duties and routine typing. Thus the risk is that studies of socioeconomic inequalities in health, by using these limited occupational titles as indicators of social position, may underestimate inequalities among women. Such bias may be contributing to the general pattern of weaker socioeconomic gradients in mortality and morbidity among women compared with men (Östlin 1998).

Furthermore, traditional variables used to measure race, income, and gender may not be adequately sensitive to reveal all mechanisms of social discrimination in health (Krieger and Fee 1994). How people respond to discrimination may affect their health. Black women who responded actively to unfair treatment were less likely to report high blood pressure than those who internalized their responses. Of interest, black women who reported no experiences of racial discrimination were at highest risk for hypertension (Krieger 1990). Similar studies are beginning to explore the effects of race and antigay discrimination on health (Krieger and Sidney 1997).

Clearly what is required is more sophisticated measurement of the risks to health associated with material, social, and psychological environments in which people live. We have to ask why the experience of living on a low income, for example, or of being previously married, or of being in full-time employment would have a different meaning for women than for men and in what ways these experiences might explain gender differences in health outcomes (Popay et al. 1993).

The answer may not lie only in better quantitative methods, variables, and models. Qualitative research results that link women's poor sense of control, social frustration and poverty with their poorer mental health outcomes provide highly suggestive hypotheses (Pearson 1995; Walters and Charles 1997; Astbury this volume). Similarly, qualitative research on the pressures faced by young girls to start smoking and that prevent adult women from quitting smoking point to promising new areas of investigation and intervention (Royce et al. 1997; Michell and Amos 1997).

These examples indicate the limitations and biases of current variables and methodologies and the need to proceed cautiously. This is particularly true when attempting to evaluate the influence of gender on health. In formulating research questions and hypotheses, it is certainly easier to move forward in areas where reproductive biology is unlikely to play a role. However, where it does play a role, a simple but useful guideline is *not* to assume that reproductive biology accounts for all or even the bulk of the differences between women and men. Gender differences in economic access, social power, and behavioral norms must be presumed to operate unless proved otherwise. As stated, the pathways can be complex and interactive but they can be investigated systematically. This may require a range of methods, both quantitative and qualitative, as well as more interdisciplinary and multidisciplinary research across biological and social sciences.

Bias in Clinical and Drugs Research

Medical research and clinical trials for new drugs have been heavily criticized for their general lack of gender perspective (Mastroianni et al. 1994). Health problems that specifically or predominantly affect women receive less attention and funds than those mainly prevalent among men. The lack of research is obvious in areas concerning the menstrual cycle and nonlethal chronic diseases that affect women disproportionally, such as rheumatism, fibromyalgia, and chronic fatigue syndrome (Doyal 1995; Goldman and Hatch 2000). The only exception to this trend is the area of contraceptive research, which historically neglected male methods.

In the field of occupational and environmental health and safety, women are often not included in toxicological studies. When they are considered, two polar extremes result. Either their biological specificity is not noted at all, or only their reproductive potential is focused on (Silbergeld 2000). For example, regulations against lead provide protection only for women of reproductive age (Hansson 1998). This ignores health risks to all other women as well as those—reproductive and otherwise—to men. More attention has to be paid to the implications of nonreproductive biologic differences between women and men. Evidence shows that women have a higher proportion of fat tissue, causing greater risk from fat-soluble chemicals, as well as thinner skin and slower metabolism, causing different rates of absorption, metabolism, and excretion of chemicals (Östlin this volume; Sims and Butter this volume).

An even more serious problem is exclusion of female subjects from medical and drug trials. The reason for such omission is that the menstrual cycle introduces a potentially confounding variable. Additional grounds for excluding women of childbearing age are fears that experimental treatments or drugs may affect their fertility or expose fetuses to unknown risk.

The International Ethical Guidelines for Biomedical Research Involving Human Subjects prepared by the Council for International Organizations of Medical Sciences (CIOMS), in collaboration with WHO bemoaned this as far back as 1993.

Premenopausal women have also been excluded from participation in many research activities, including non-clinical studies, that do not entail administration of drugs or vaccines, in case the physiological changes associated with various phases of the menstrual cycle would complicate interpretation of research data. Consequently, much less is known of women's than of men's normal physiological processes. This too is unjust in that it deprives women as a class of persons of the benefits of such knowledge.

So far so good. But the guidelines do not go on to make any recommendation as to what should be done to correct this problem.[10]

The consequences of interpreting research results based on studies of male models and, without convincing evidence of their applicability to women, continue to be harmful to women (Hammarström et al. 2001). Evidence shows that technology for diagnoses, treatment of diseases, and rehabilitation programs are not adapted to specific characteristics and needs of women in general, let alone to women in various socioeconomic circumstances or cultural backgrounds. The American Psychiatric Association's Diagnostic and Statistical Manual of Mental Disorders (DSM III) defined the criteria for diagnosing schizophrenia based on male symptoms, even though men have earlier onset of symptoms than women. Application of these criteria to WHO data led to the exclusion of 5% of men and 12% of women who actually had schizophrenia (Hambrecht et al. 1992 cited in Astbury this volume).

Research on gender differences in cardiovascular epidemiology reveals serious consequences from applying male-based diagnostic techniques and treatments to women (Gijsbers van Wijk et al. 1996). Symptoms of heart attack differ a great deal between men and women; however, medical textbooks seldom highlight these differences. It is not surprising therefore that among patients arriving at emergency rooms, making the diagnosis takes longer for women than for men. This is mainly because doctors, more familiar with men's symptomatology, do not immediately recognize the diffuse symptoms women may have. Two studies (Green and Raffin 1993; Heston and Lewis 1992) showed that women in the United States have to wait longer than men for an initial electrocardiogram, delaying diagnosis.

Clearly much has to be done to remove inadvertent and intentional gender bias in health research. As long as the current situation holds wherein women in general and feminist health researchers and decision makers in particular are in the minority and less powerful within the health profession, additional safeguards must be established to ensure that gender equity is addressed. Researchers must establish safeguard mechanisms that involve research subjects. This should be done not only at the time of interpreting and understanding research results but at the early stage of study design, when shaping and refining questions and hypotheses. If this had been done in acceptability studies of IUDs in poor populations, for instance, perhaps the wide prevalence of RTIs would have been noted sooner.

Health System Policies

Moving health system policies toward greater gender equity can be viewed from two angles: (1) development of a human rights framework for policies, programs, and services that is predicated on gender equity, and (2) creation of a supportive institutional environment. Here we draw on key elements of previous sections to put forward some guidelines. These elements are:

• Sorting out biological from social determinants of gender inequality

• Recognizing that gender bias and inequity exist and operate along many dimensions such as services, research, and policy itself; in different subfields such as occupational, environmental, reproductive, mental health, and so on; and at different levels, household, community, providers, and health systems

• Addressing the cross-cutting implications of gender inequity with other social stratifiers such as class, race, or caste

Developing a Human Rights Framework

A human rights framework for gender-equitable policies rests on three pillars: acknowledgement of the need to counteract bias at several levels and along different dimensions in health policy generally as well as in different subfields; recognition of gender-differentiated needs and associated constraints and barriers to health for women and men; and commitment to protect and promote rights to health for all. Developing such a framework requires four sets of policy actions:

1. Ensuring adequate public health resources and funding to promote health equity generally and gender equity in health more specifically

2. Creating new knowledge to promote gender equity through research in the biomedical and social sciences

3. Developing incentives and structures to minimize gender bias (and related class, race, or caste bias) in health programs and services

4. Promoting an intersectoral approach that recognizes the influences on health equity that are located outside the health care sector

Adequate Funding and Resources   Despite recognition of considerable cutbacks in health services and their adverse impacts, as a result of public expenditure cuts flowing from macroeconomic structural adjustment programs (Bangser this volume), little has been done actually to improve the situation even in the poorest countries. Women and girls, as among the most socially vulnerable, tend to suffer most in such circumstances unless significant steps are taken to minimize the negative impact (Whiteford 1993; Sen et al. this volume).

Direct effects include decreased access to health services and delays in health-seeking behavior leading to worse health outcomes (Stewart 1992; Kutzin 1995). This may affect women disproportionally as they require more preventive reproductive health care services (Gijsbers van Wijk et al. 1995; Hanson this volume). Women make up the bulk of both formal lower-tier health workers and informal household carers. As a result, cuts in health and social sectors can lead to higher levels of unemployment among women health workers, as well as increases in work burdens involved in informal home caring (Standing this volume).

At the national level some attempts have been made to tackle cost and affordability barriers in health services to women. For example, South Africa and Sri Lanka provide free maternal and infant health services. Flat fee structures that cover not only regular antenatal and postnatal care but also delivery care, including complications, may be one way to ensure that high costs do not prevent families from bringing women in for such services, especially during obstetric emergencies (WHO 1998e). When health insurance schemes are introduced, care should be taken to ensure that poor women are adequately covered (Carrin and Politi 1997). These schemes not only must cover reproductive health needs and maternity leave, but must not discriminate against women who leave the workforce for reasons of child care.

At a broader level, lack of adequate funding for private research in fields that are viewed as inherently less profitable (infectious diseases) or more risky (contraceptive research) remains acute (Fathalla 1994). In these circumstances there may be no alternative to promoting such research than through public funds. One way of improving public funding is through the increasingly discussed tax on global currency transactions[11] that could increase resources for both improved health service and research in neglected areas such as gender equity.

Knowledge Creation and Awareness Building   Support for the generation of new knowledge, both biomedical and social, is crucial, as we already stated. Although awareness of health professionals regarding gender inequity is growing, it is still fragmentary and much remains to be done. Disentangling the many and interactive determinants involved, addressing women-specific health needs that have been poorly addressed to date, and spelling out broad determinants of women-friendly and gender-sensitive policies are essential. We also must specify program and service needs in greater detail. In some areas, as detailed in the discussion on causally interactive pathways, the broad problem has long been known and yet few programs attempted to address them. Sometimes this neglect is due to absence of operations research to investigate what actually does or does not work at the field level.

This translation of broad policy and program level recommendations into practical guidelines for health services is critical, as shown by the attempted transition in the family planning program in India to a broad approach focusing on reproductive and child health (RCH). Whereas considerable agreement exists over broad directions of this more gender-sensitive approach, the foundation of the new policy, community needs assessment, was one with which public service providers were quite unfamiliar. In the absence of effective operations research in this area, the RCH program's implementation has been delayed (Sen et al. 1999).

Creating knowledge through research cannot by itself affect deeply ingrained biases unless supported by effective education and transformation of values and norms. Since gender biases operate at several levels, from households and communities to providers and policy makers, such transformation has to happen at all these levels. Senior policy makers are often willing to acknowledge the need to sensitize junior service personnel, but reluctant to apply this to themselves. Where households and communities are concerned, many programs for gender education focus on improving women's awareness and knowledge. This has to be balanced by effective programs to transform the values and behaviors of men and boys toward greater gender equity as a support for better health for girls and women and also for themselves.

Countering Biases in Programs and Services   How health care professionals interpret symptoms and perceptions of illness is important in order to obtain adequate diagnoses and provide the best possible treatment for patients. It is therefore of grave concern that gender bias in provider-patient relationships continues in both high- and low-income countries (Pittman and Hartigan 1996). In addition, lack of female medical personnel is sometimes a barrier for women to use health care services. Nonetheless both female and male health providers can be gender-biased in their perception of patient preferences, especially if the patient is also poor, old, black, a migrant, or lower caste.

Studies mainly from high-income countries, such as The Netherlands, Sweden, and the United States, highlight gender inequalities in provision of certain technologies or treatments for the same disease. Women with heart disease are less likely than men to undergo coronary bypass surgery. They are also less likely to have organ transplants such as kidneys (Kutner and Brogan 1990; Held et al. 1988). In the case of lung cancer, women are less likely than men to have cytologic tests of sputum (Wells and Feinstein 1988). Delayed diagnosis and treatment might be one important reason (besides the fact that female patients are generally older than men) why women more often than men die from their first heart attack (Lerner and Kannel 1986).

Minimizing gender bias depends in part on systematic approaches to building awareness and transforming values among service providers, but it also requires other steps to improve access, affordability, and appropriateness. Overuse of certain services, such as gynecological interventions, fetal monitoring, and unnecessary surgical procedures, occurs in a number of high-income countries (Gabe and Calnan 1989; Gijsbers van Wijk et al. 1995; Wajcman 1994). Another problem is that medical doctors frequently attribute women's illnesses to psychiatric disorders and prescribe inappropriate drug therapy (WHO 1998b; Loring and Powell 1988). Women are more likely to be diagnosed with depression than men with the same symptoms and more likely to be prescribed mood-altering psychotropic drugs (Stoppe et al. 1999; Simoni-Wastila 2000 cited in Astbury this volume). Such problems are also emerging in a number of low-income countries with growing prominence of unregulated private health services (Pai 2000). These situations must be redressed through more effective regulation and oversight of health care providers. Development of "best practices" guidelines in this regard could make the solutions more context-specific and effective.

Health-promotion strategies can also be inappropriate. Some interventions view women strategically as ideal and willing health care providers in the home. However, in their enthusiasm they often tend to take a rather instrumental view of women, neglecting both women's own social constraints and their health. One example is oral rehydration therapy (ORT), which is undoubtedly effective in treating childhood diarrhea but ignores the time constraints under which women operate (Leslie 1989 cited in Hartigan et al. this volume).

When services are provided to meet women's needs, they are often based on male perspectives that are unable to respond to women's expectations or specific concerns. As a result they tend to focus on women's reproductive functions, neglecting all their other functions (Paolisso and Leslie 1995; Vlassoff 1994). Even then the quality of care provided may leave a lot to be desired. Studies from rural communities in west Africa (Prevention of Maternal Mortality Network 1992) and Chile (Vera 1993; Matamala 1998) show that women are not always treated with respect by health providers. In many societies, women complain about lack of privacy, confidentiality, and information about options and services available (Vlassoff 1994). Efforts to improve quality of care must go beyond focusing on the behavior of health workers and pay attention to the managerial and resource constraints under which they operate (Standing this volume).

Health care workers are often underpaid, overworked, and sometimes simply too biased to give women information regarding side effects of drugs or treatment. It is no surprise that women sometimes prefer traditional providers (healers) because they take time to explain the illness and to communicate in an understandable and sympathetic way (Vlassoff 1994). In Bangladesh only 13% of poor women and men sought treatment from licensed medical doctors (Bhuiya and Ansary 1998). At least one reason could be their reluctance to confront unsympathetic providers.

Supporting a culture of dialogue between researchers and women's groups or representatives on specific issues works. The WHO's Human Reproduction Program (HPR) provides a good example of promoting such dialogue, thereby helping bring women's voices and concerns to the policy table (WHO 1991a). What has been done with researchers can also be done with service providers, and will help make programs and services less biased and also more relevant and effective in addressing real needs. Interesting models for promoting dialogue with a gender perspective among health workers and between health workers and their users, such as Health Workers for Change and the Client-Oriented, Provider-Efficient (COPE) methodology, are being implemented in various low-income countries (Onyango Ouma et al. 2001; Ben Salem and Beattie 1996).

Promoting an Intersectoral Approach to Health Policy   Although much has to occur to ensure that services are not biased, attention also must extend to sectors outside the health care sector if gender and equity are to be achieved in *health*. This is of critical importance, as poor families make significant trade-offs in determining survival strategies, often with negative consequences for women and girls, and do not stay within externally delineated program sectors. Analyses of how families decide on expenditures for health and other social services could "help to identify inter-sectoral priorities for achieving better health status and lead to a better understanding of inter-sectoral dynamics" (Elson and Evers 1998, cited in Bangser this volume).

Successful intersectoral programming, as described by Bangser in this volume, should promote selected partnerships across traditionally parallel sectors. Programs that bring together education, health, and credit can promote several ends with synergistic effects. For example, UNICEF reports that "when micro-credit is linked with access to basic social services and key social development messages, the health and nutrition of borrowers' children, particularly girls, improves; school enrolment increases; safe water and sanitation use broadens." Furthermore, microcredit empowers women by enabling them to make economic decisions and become the source of increased household income (UNICEF 1997 cited in Bangser this volume).

The most successful examples of intersectoral programs are usually implemented by nongovernment organizations, such as the Bangladesh Rural Advancement Committee (BRAC), the Self-Employed Women's Association (SEWA) in India, and Mahila Samakya, also in India. There are fewer examples of such joined up thinking at the level of national policy making and even less with a gender perspective. Sector-Wide Approaches (SWAps) represent an accelerating trend in donor funding in the health sector, which may likely move toward multisectoral funding. However, as mentioned earlier and with the exception of Evers and Kroon (2000), very little gender analysis of such efforts exists (Standing this volume).

Nonetheless various potential avenues for change exist. The multisectoral responsibility for creating sustainable health is recognized by WHO Europe (WHO 1999d) with emphasis on solidarity, equity, and gender sensitivity. Apart from urging decision makers to recognize the benefits to their sectors from investing in health, member states are called on to establish mechanisms for health impact assessments to ensure that all sectors become accountable to health concerns.

This is especially critical for issues of gender, health, and environment. A framework currently used by both high- and low-income countries to promote better health at all socioeconomic levels, and to integrate environment, health, and development concerns, is the "healthy settings" approach. Better defined as social movements or processes rather than specific projects, the activities undertaken are selected by a wide range of stakeholders from public and private sectors. More effort has to focus on securing gender perspectives within such movements (Sims and Butter this volume).

Creating a Supportive Institutional Environment

A number of steps can be taken to create and strengthen the institutional environment for greater gender equity in health. Since the 1980s considerable experience exists with respect to creating specialized gender units versus mainstreaming gender throughout the organization or institution. While the weight of wisdom leans these days toward the latter, it is clear that gender can be mainstreamed into disappearance unless backed by a unit with senior staff and adequate resources (Jahan 1995; Razavi and Miller 1995). Such mainstreaming also does not happen simply by attempts at sporadic gender training but requires guidelines (beyond checklists), clear incentives and disincentives, and audits.

As in other fields, the gender advisory panel or committee can play a valuable role provided it has a broad and flexible mandate, is adequately resourced, and is linked ex officio to other key committees and panels. The WHO Human Reproduction Program effectively used its gender advisory panel in this way, but a number of other institutions simply create such panels and then ignore them. Creation of such bodies is not synonymous with effectiveness unless they are also empowered and the ground is prepared for the organization to take them seriously.

Large organizations should do this not only in different subunits, but in the organization overall to avoid the twin problems of organizational irrelevance and fragmentation. Above all, what happens in institutions, what standards they give themselves, and what examples they set for others depend on effective leadership and structures of governance. Where commitments to gender equity are not kept, experience shows that it is usually because of a combination of poor leadership and inadequate institutional structures. Conversely, sound leadership together with recognition of the need to create incentives and structures to protect and promote gender equity can make all the difference.

Notes

1. This chapter expands on our earlier work (Östlin et al. 2001a), and draws on Gita Sen's keynote address at the International Conference on Health Research for Development, Bangkok, October 11, 2000.

2. More specifically, gender refers to socially constructed distinctions between women and men based on differences in access to resources and knowledge, social roles, divisions of labor and occupational segregation, power relations and hierar-

chies of authority and decision making, and socially sanctioned and enforced norms regarding identity, personhood, and behavior.

3. It is useful to remember, however, that it was not so long ago that scientists believed in differences in brain capacity on the basis of race and gender, as well as innate, inherited ability among social classes (Krieger and Fee 1994). Some popular perceptions still hold girls to be incapable of learning mathematics for similar innate, biologic reasons.

4. We use the terms gender equity and gender justice interchangeably.

5. For example, during the official Beijing Platform for Action of the Fourth World Conference on Women in September 1995, conservative Islamic governments argued in favor of the language of gender *equity* but were unwilling to accept gender *equality*. Their position was premised on their belief that their laws that enshrine differences in women's and men's rights to property and inheritance are eminently fair or just since they flow from "natural" differences rooted in maternity and hence in roles and abilities.

6. Further gender biases in the DALY methodology are discussed in this volume by Hanson.

7. This obviously does not hold for certain indicators such as domestic violence or mental health. The points made in the section on gender silences earlier also must be borne in mind.

8. Data in the *World Health Report 1999* on which these conclusions are based present some anomalies. For instance, the probability of dying among Sri Lankan poor is higher absolutely than that for Indian poor for both women and men. Why should Sri Lankan poor people age 15 to 59 years have higher probabilities of dying than their Indian counterparts? There is no apparent reason, particularly since both overall female and male life expectancies and levels of absolute poverty are better in Sri Lanka. It may indicate a third underlying factor at work (long-term illness?) that may underpin both poverty and higher risk of dying. This is purely a hypothesis, but if long-term illness is at work, it would not only explain the seeming anomaly between the Sri Lankan and Indian data, it would also mean that a woman suffering from such illness has a strong chance of both being poor and dying sooner, in at least some countries where overall life expectancy is quite high. Clearly more investigation is necessary.

9. Most striking was that East German men fared even better than West German men.

10. These guidelines are being carefully scrutinized for their gender content, and one hopes the problem will be redressed.

11. The so-called Tobin tax on currency transactions is increasingly discussed as a possible way to ensure greater global funding for social sectors during a time of continuing declining net official overseas development aid. Agreements at the five-year review of the World Summit for Social Development (Copenhagen plus Five) opened the door for a full investigation into the feasibility and implications of such taxes; discussions also have been held in British, Canadian, and Belgian parliaments (War on Want 2000).

I
Key Health Areas

2

Communicable Diseases: Outstanding Commitments to Gender and Poverty[1]

Pamela Hartigan, Janet Price, and Rachel Tolhurst

Of the 51 million deaths worldwide in 1993, an estimated one-third resulted from infectious and parasitic diseases (WHO 1995). Most occurred in low-income countries. In sub-Saharan Africa in particular, communicable[2] diseases account for over 70% of the burden of ill health, in contrast to about 10% in high-income countries (World Bank 1993). Despite the number of diagnostics, drugs, pesticides, and vaccines developed during the twentieth century, medical researchers and practitioners continue to struggle against not only familiar diseases, such as childhood infections, diarrheal disease, malaria, and tuberculosis, but also an ever-growing number of emerging infectious diseases such as HIV and hepatitis C.

Why is it that despite over a century of efforts we appear unable to sustain a successful response against long-standing, emerging, and re-emerging diseases? In searching for reasons, one that surfaces is that with the growth of germ theory, communicable disease efforts came to be dominated by biomedical and individually focused theories of causation. Today emphasis continues to be on disease processes. Communicable disease experts have difficulty broadening their vision to incorporate an examination of political, social, and economic conditions that explain why a disease occurs in the first place and how it could be managed effectively.

Yet the major structural impediment to the elimination of infectious diseases is poverty, the greatest risk regardless of a person's age, sex, or race. There is little doubt that these diseases exacerbate poverty, creating a vicious circle. Moreover, if one considers that women constitute approximately 70% of the poor (UNDP 1995), the interaction between poverty and gender may represent the most important risk factor to be addressed in efforts to arrest communicable diseases.

Recognition that structural economic and gender inequalities must be addressed will require a sea change in the thinking and practice of medical and social sciences. This will not be an easy shift, for whereas it is increasingly recognized that horizons have to be widened beyond the molecular level to include social, economic, environmental, and behavioral aspects of individuals and population groups, gender is barely acknowledged.

This chapter does not address all infectious diseases in detail, but looks at a variety of different conditions to illustrate the varying nature of the interrelations among gender, equity, and communicable disease.[3]

Definitions

Diseases are called communicable or infectious because their spread involves an infected agent that is transmitted between hosts (people or animals) through a variety of mechanisms. They can be classified as follows:

1. By biological agents that cause them, which include microscopic bacteria, intracellular viruses, and large, structurally complex helminthic parasites

2. By their mode of spread, which includes person-to-person contact, transmission by air or water, insect carriers or vectors, contact with animals and their products, and contact with blood and blood products

3. By changing history, as existing, emerging, or reemerging diseases

Existing diseases are age-old problems such as tuberculosis, malaria, diarrheal, and childhood diseases, which present continuing challenges for management and control. They can also be considered as reemerging diseases as they become renewed public health problems by either becoming more widespread or more resistant than before. For example, drug-resistant disease strains can overcome formerly effective therapeutic interventions, such as chloroquine for malaria and multidrug therapy for tuberculosis. Complex emergencies due to conflict, floods, and drought also lead to highly vulnerable populations with increased susceptibility. Rift Valley fever and yellow fever are examples of reemerging diseases (WHO 1998c).

Emerging diseases result from newly identified and previously unknown infections. New microorganisms capable of causing disease in humans continue to be detected. Whether or not these develop into public health problems depends on factors related to the microorganism and its environment, or the infected human and his or her environment (Cook 1988). The most important of these to date is HIV. Another previously undetected virus, hepatitis C, was identified in 1989. Today it is the most common cause of posttransfusion hepatitis worldwide (WHO 1997c).

How diseases are classified has an influence on how interventions are developed to address them. For example, biomedical approaches tend to focus on the immediate causative agent, leading to a search for solutions with drugs and vaccines. Public health approaches encompass the relationship among host, agent, and mode of spread, seeking to understand what gave rise to the causative agent in the first place. Classifications that are based on the history of the disease may also emphasize the dynamic nature of public health problems and their interrelation with changing socioeconomic and environmental conditions.

Health Burden

Four-fifths of the gap in health status between the poorest and richest 20% of the world's population consists of communicable diseases. The major infectious causes of deaths and disability-adjusted life years (DALYs) lost among the poor are respiratory infections (13.4%), diarrheal diseases (11.3%), and the childhood cluster of infectious diseases[4] (7.8%) (Gwatkin and Guillot 2000). These account for nearly one-third of all deaths among the world's poor and for proportionately more deaths among females than among males. Among the poorest 20% people in the world, infectious diseases are responsible for 6.3% more of all female deaths and 7.5% more of all female DALYs lost compared with men (Gwatkin and Guillot 2000).

Diseases such as tuberculosis, malaria, and HIV infection are of major significance and show marked regional variations. Malaria kills between 1.5 and 2.7 million people and adversely affects a further 300,000 to 500,000 every year, but 90% of these cases occur in Africa (WHO 1998c; table 2.1). This places a major burden on primary health care services, typically involving 20% to 40% of all out-patient diagnoses (Bloom et al. 2000).

Table 2.1

Estimated malaria deaths, incidence, and burden of disease in thousands by age, sex, and region, 1998 (WHO 1999c)

	Males		Females	
	0–14 yrs	15+ yrs	0–14 yrs	15+ yrs
Deaths				
Africa	476	22	438	27
Americas	0	1	0	1
E. Med	24	2	22	3
Europe	0	0	0	0
SE Asia	17	20	15	21
W. Pacific	5	6	4	5
Incidence				
Africa	67,422	51,436	66,597	52,192
Americas	357	681	330	575
E. Med	3,679	3,191	3,624	3,198
Europe	0	0	0	0
SE Asia	2,913	4,949	2,844	5,084
W. Pacific	711	1,232	676	1,133
DALYs				
Africa	17,040	719	15,860	888
Americas	30	37	27	36
E. Med	868	85	809	91
Europe	0	0	0	0
SE Asia	615	479	566	525
W. Pacific	189	126	159	118

DALYs, disability-adjusted life-years.

Most estimated deaths due to malaria occur among young children. The disease kills 3,000 children under five years of age per day, an average of 1 child every 30 seconds.[5] As shown by malaria, infectious diseases are unevenly distributed across age, with infants and children carrying a heavier proportionate burden worldwide. Nearly 70% of all deaths from communicable disease occur in those under age fourteen years, with girls losing a higher proportion of sex-specific DALYs than boys. Diarrhea, acute respiratory infections, malaria, and measles are major child killers in low- and middle-income countries.

In addition to causing death and morbidity in their own right, infectious diseases can also serve as risk factors for noninfectious diseases. For example, various types of human papilloma viruses are implicated as causes of cervical cancer, the first major tumor shown to be virally induced. Cervical cancer is the most common cancer in women in the developing world, causing 300,000 deaths globally each year. About half a million new cases are detected annually and an estimated 2 million women currently live with the invasive disease (WHO 1995).

Global burden of disease (GBD) figures are beginning to be analyzed in ways that provide clearer pictures of patterns of illness and death around the world. However, they continue to underestimate some of the health problems faced by females and the poor (Gwatkin and Guillot 2000; Hanson 1999). Global figures also conceal wide variations in gender differences in specific diseases or disease clusters across different countries and contexts, reflecting the complex intermix of economic, social, and environmental factors influencing infectious disease epidemiology.

Global Dynamics

The motivation to invest talent, time, and financial resources to arrest the spread of infectious diseases is not new. Nonetheless, realization that globalization of the economy is contributing to the rise and spread of these diseases has created a growing sense of urgency to do something about them. Globalization's emphasis on open markets and free trade zones generates a need for mobile and cheap labor, breaking down traditional systems of economic protection, cultural norms, and social support networks. As markets expand and government roles and regulations lessen, social obligations are more likely to be shirked.

Some low-income countries experienced increasing growth of urban areas and slums, as predominantly male agricultural workers migrated to cities in search of better opportunities, or were squeezed out from rural areas by the consolidation of landholdings for large-scale agribusiness. These urban areas and slums often lack protective infrastructure or social services, leading to higher infectious disease risks through contaminated drinking water, airborne pollution, and crowded housing. The changing gendered nature of family relations and domestic and productive work brings about new risks, such as raised rates of sexually transmitted infections (STIs) and tuberculosis in some groups of male migrant laborers. Those left behind in rural areas, often women and children, face not only increasing vulnerability as access to resources diminishes, but also increased exposures to urban health risks (e.g., STIs, tuberculosis) through returning migrant laborer partners and relatives.

Other less obvious forces transcend the boundaries of nation-states to influence efforts to address communicable diseases. One of these is the economic activity of multinational corporations, especially pharmaceutical companies. Their involvement in developing, testing, and marketing new drugs and vaccines against diseases that affect low-income countries has decreased since the late 1970s (Behrman 1980). Treatments for infectious diseases now only account for 2% of global research and development health budgets (Meikle 2000). Companies respond to market forces and these are weakest in the poor communities of disease-endemic countries. Although some companies are involved in drug-donation programs for specific diseases and others in donating excess stocks, new efforts must be supported to revive their involvement (Reich 2000; Angell 2000).

Finally, a powerful force galvanizing global action in communicable diseases is fear. Ease of international travel and dependence on global food processing and distribution seem to erase the borders of our shrinking world. Images in the Western media of the horrors of Ebola virus, the widespread reality of HIV infection and AIDS, and reemergence of mosquito-borne infections in temperate zone countries lend credence to the notion that both rich and poor now find themselves in "a single disease pool" (McNeill 1976). Ironically, although health leaders may use age-old fear tactics to inspire the better-off to contribute to public health efforts to address infectious diseases, it is highly improbable that those who enjoy material comfort and social acceptance will ever die from these diseases. Structural inequality, of which gender is a critical element, is at the heart of the issue of disease emergence and spread.

Looking Through the Past at the Present

In the face of increasing inequalities and changing gender relations, challenges presented by infectious diseases several centuries ago may in retrospect appear far less complex. Yet the foundation for current difficulties in expanding the epidemiology of infectious diseases to include social inequalities lies in the manner in which these diseases were addressed then.

The European quest for economic and political power over 500 years of colonialism both contributed to the spread of infectious disease and drove the expansion of research and development in medicine and public health. Such efforts were not simply objective searches for truth that stood apart from changing social and economic relations. Instead, medicine was a major part of the "civilizing" drive. It served to contain disorder, a central strategy to meet the "enormous responsibilities which a power like Great Britain shoulders when she extends her territories to Africa. She stands in *loco parentis* to the black races, and the first and foremost duty of a parent is to safeguard the health of those who look to him for sustenance and protection" (Balfour and Scott 1924).

The colonies offered new and largely untouched arenas for medical research as European citizens settled in increasing numbers in Africa, Asia, and the Americas. Efforts were initially focused on safeguarding (male) expatriates, traders, civil servants, and the army from high mortality from communicable diseases. "The first concern is the future of the white race . . . [C]an the Europeans persist as an active, healthy, virile race in these uplands, propagating their species and fulfilling their destiny?" (Johnson 1827). In general, women were excluded from consideration as white women's constitutions were initially seen as too delicate and especially susceptible to the "malign influence of great heat and bright light" of the tropics (Balfour and Scott 1924).

It was only later that interventions were directed at ensuring a healthy "human capital" base as colonial economic self-interest depended on workers whose labor produced profits. For Great Britain, as for other European powers, the health of black African or Indian men was "the chief asset of their countries" (Freemantle 1911). Colonizers largely viewed the health needs of indigenous women as separate from direct involvement in the processes of economic production, despite their often major role in industrial and agricultural work. Instead they stressed women's reproductive role as a means to ensure the health of children as future workers (Christie 1876).

Similar perspectives about the people most affected by infectious diseases can also be found during the Industrial Revolution in Britain in the nineteenth century, another significant moment in the history of these diseases. During that period the new science of statistics revealed soaring death rates from diseases such as typhoid, tuberculosis, and childhood fevers in the slums of industrial cities. Gender and class were central to debates about the nature of these patterns. For example, "moral environmentalism" linked rising rates of STIs with working-class people who were considered synonymous with dirt, depravity, and disease. In addition, gendered notions of morality constructed working-class men as semibarbarous, brutalized by their work and their "inherent lack of morality," whereas working class women were "both eroticized and condemned as moral pollutants" (Mort 1987).

Because infectious diseases were associated with dirt, disorder, "uncivilized" lifestyles, and immorality, whether in slums of Europe or in villages of the tropics, improvements in public health were driven by paternalism. High rates of contagious disease spawned by urban living conditions were eventually reduced not by medical means but by broader public health interventions such as environmental initiatives, improved wages, and better nutrition (Anderson 1992; Doyal 1979). Despite these achievements, growing advances of germ theory sidelined these interventions and strengthened the search for disease-causing agents, exemplified by the discovery of the malaria-causing *Plasmodia*.

It is in this context that the turn of the century saw the rise and consolidation of tropical medicine, based on the idea that there were diseases specific to the tropics that required special expertise (Arnold 1996). The economic and political development of colonialism went hand in hand with a narrower focus on a spectrum of tropical diseases, largely parasitic infections and those such as malaria, filariasis, and sleeping sickness, that were transmitted by insect vectors. In the process, common major killers such as diarrheal diseases and acute respiratory infections were neglected.

In the latter half of the twentieth century, as overt imperialism and paternalism dissipated, the public health agenda for communicable diseases evolved. Nonetheless, modern scientific medicine continued to conceptualize the human body in a mechanistic way devoid of social context. Although it is now widely recognized that such approaches are inadequate, thinking beyond disease and about wellness and people, especially male and female people, still marks the struggle between biomedical and public health perspectives.

Policies shifted from single disease-control programs in the immediate postcolonial period to the era of primary health care in the 1980s. In its broadest sense primary health care advocated comprehensive and integrated approaches to infectious diseases, with an emphasis on multisectoralism, community participation, and poverty reduction. This came to be interpreted more selectively, as exemplified by the UNICEF-sponsored GOBI initiative.[6] Most recently reactions against selective interventions led to new single-disease initiatives, classed as social and political movements, such as Roll Back Malaria and Stop TB.[7] Regardless of whether these modern initiatives followed broader environmental and social frameworks or more biomedical selective frameworks, gender remained a largely unacknowledged factor.

In summary, with emergence of the biomedical model and compartmentalization of knowledge, communicable disease experts shied away from grappling with connections between broader risk factors and health outcomes, and thus failed to support adequately policies and programs that address sociostructural causes. Whereas there is safety in specialization and narrow approaches, "effective analyses of emerging diseases must recognize the study of complexity as perhaps the central general scientific problem of our time" (Levins 1995). Part of the complexity that must be addressed involves the interaction among gender, race, social class, and infectious disease.

The Impact of Gender on Communicable Disease and Health Interventions

General Impact on the Risk and Experience of Communicable Disease

Gender intersects with other social categories, such as age, ethnicity, disability, socioeconomic status, and geographic location, to influence:

• Access to social and material resources that ensure and promote well-being
• Access to preventive measures and effective diagnosis and treatment
• Risk of infection
• Severity and consequences of infection
• Experience of ill health in social and economic terms
• Burden due to ill health in both the family and the community

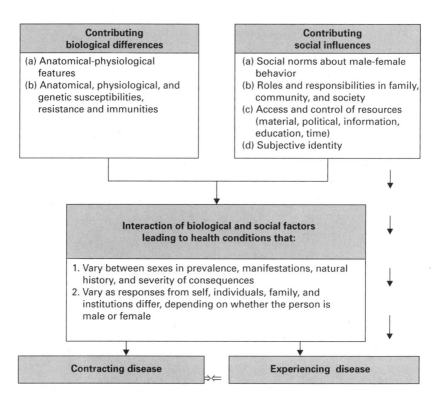

Figure 2.1
Impact of gender on health/illness/care

The model above attempts to capture the complex and dynamic health-disease-care process. While contracting infectious diseases is a function of the interaction of the biological and the social, the experience of the illness or disease is more socially determined.

Biological differences between the sexes affect susceptibility to disease and severity or physical consequences of infection (figure 2.1). For example, pregnancy alters women's acquired immunity to malaria. Malaria during first pregnancy is an important cause of chronic anemia, spontaneous abortion, stillbirth, and maternal mortality in areas of unstable disease transmission (Brabin 1991). Similarly, schistosomiasis in women is associated with infertility, abortion, preterm delivery, and increased vulnerability to HIV infection and life-threatening conditions such as extrauterine pregnancy (Feldmeier et al. 1993).

Whereas most infectious diseases are shared by men and women, to date much of the research conducted on sex-specific aspects of infectious disease focused on women's biological reproductive function, specifically, the fetus or potential fetus she carries. We still have very little knowledge of the sex-specific aspects of infectious diseases other than these. Medical diagnosis and treatment are instead usually based on models of male bodies and their disease manifestations. For example, until quite recently the clinical definition of AIDS was based on male symptoms and ignored some specifically female manifestations (Gilks et al. 1998).

Women may be excluded from biomedical interventions because of their reproductive capacities. An example is the initial administration of ivermectin, which can prevent onchocerciasis with one tablet a year. It was recommended that pregnant women and mothers breastfeeding newborns be excluded from treatment until they were no longer pregnant or breastfeeding, despite confirmatory studies that did not indicate the need for such a measure. In endemic areas this represents up to 30% of women. Women who were excluded for these reasons did not seek treatment once they became eligible for it (Yumkella 1996). Many cited the high cost of transportation, but most noted that they did not know where to get treatment and preferred to wait for the mass campaign. By the time the campaign was undertaken they were again pregnant or breastfeeding. Repeated exclusion from treatment allows these women to become a reservoir for disease transmission.[8]

Whereas biology can aggravate the consequences of disease or often serves as a basis for exclusion from diagnosis and treatment, gender colors the social experience of the health-disease continuum. Gender exercises a powerful influence on identity formation. Both sexes are subject to externally imposed, culturally specific gender norms that constrain what they should or should not do or feel, but most social norms usually place women in a subordinate position in relation to men and set self-imposed limits on their hopes and aspirations (Gilligan 1992). In some societies women are the last to eat, and they serve themselves and their girl children smaller portions compared with what they serve male family members. This can have consequences for their health, as the link between malnutrition and risk and exacerbation of infectious diseases is amply supported in the research literature on diarrheal disease, tuberculosis, malaria, and HIV and AIDS.

The gendered sense of self can also be threatened by certain manifestations of communicable diseases. For example, hydrocele, the genital manifestations of lymphatic filariasis in men, is a chronic swelling of the scrotum. It generally lowers the productivity and wage-earning capacity of those afflicted and is associated with sexual disability. Men may be discouraged from seeking care because these experiences threaten their masculinity.

Gender roles may affect women and men's willingness to admit to ill health or seek care. Men may be unwilling to admit to illness if by so doing they become dependent on family members for whom they have been socialized to care for and sustain (Pittman 1997). Men's perceived role as household providers is often important to their power in the family as well as to their sense of masculinity, so it is likely to be surrendered reluctantly even on a temporary basis to comply with medical directives. Similarly, women may be reluctant to admit to ill health when it disrupts their domestic or caregiving work, when they have no other social supports, or when they perceive that their value relies on their capacity to manage the household. They may therefore continue their activities until they become incapacitated by illness (Hudelson 1996; Rathgeber and Vlassoff 1993).

Women's and men's roles and responsibilities in the family, community, and society can influence risk of infection. Where gender assigns to women the role of washing clothes and fetching water, contact with contaminated water will place them at greater risk for schistosomiasis than men in their communities (Michelson 1993); where men are more exposed, as through fishing, they will be at greater risk (Kaur 1997). Women's higher prevalence of trachoma at all ages reflects their higher risk due to domestic roles as caregivers of children (West et al. 1991).

The value placed on being male or female may have important implications in defining entitlements. The perceived higher value of sons over daughters in many societies often leads to giving priorities to male children where resources for health care are scarce; for example, boys may be more likely than girls to receive health care for diarrheal disease (Rathgeber and Vlassoff 1993) and for trachoma (Lane and Meleis 1991).

In this way, gender affects women and men's ability to use (access) and control resources, such as money, land, tools, time, education, and information. This may affect their ability to protect their health in a range of ways. For example, women most at risk for human papilloma virus infection are those who are poor, with several births, with early sexual activity, and with several sexual partners or men who have multiple sexual unions. In Thai women whose husbands first had sex with a prostitute in their teens and did not use condoms at that time, the risk of cervical cancer was twice that of women whose husbands have never visited a prostitute (Thomas et al. 1996). Within a couple, women often have less power, leading them to be inhibited from inquiring about the sexual habits of their partners, to lack assertiveness to insist on condom use, and to assume men's faithfulness.

Gender norms also influence the impact of suffering from many infectious diseases. For example, women and men are likely to experience different responses to stigmatizing or disfiguring infections, such as tuberculosis, HIV infection, or AIDS, and leprosy by their families and communities. Suffering from these diseases reduces the chances of marriage and increases the likelihood of divorce for women (Hudelson 1996). Women may depend strongly on physical appearance to enhance their prospects for marriage and sustaining a partnership with a man (Rangan and Uplekar 1998).

Specific Gender Dynamics in Infectious Diseases and Interventions

Risk of STIs, HIV Infection, and AIDS   Although global averages show that men are at higher risk than women for these diseases, they do not reflect how these trends are changing. In the early years of the epidemic AIDS was conceived as a largely male disease, but afflicted women now outnumber men in sub-Saharan Africa. Male:female ratios have also been changing in other parts of the world, with the result that men now only outnumber women by about 5% globally (table 2.2; UNAIDS 2000).

In Europe the percentage increase in new AIDS cases among women has exceeded that among men every year since 1984. In the Caribbean, the male:female ratio of HIV infection changed from 5.4:1 in 1983 to

Table 2.2
Estimated number of adults (age 15–49 yrs) living with HIV infection and AIDS, end 1999 (UNAIDS 2000)

	Estimated no. adults with HIV/AIDS	
Region	Female	Male
World	15,700	17,300
Sub-Saharan Africa	12,900	10,500
E. Asia, Pacific	66	464
S., SE Asia	1,900	3,500
E. Europe, C. Asia	110	300
W. Europe	130	390
N. Africa, M. East	42	210
N. America	180	710
Caribbean	130	220
Latin America	300	900

2.1:1 by 1989 (Berer 1993), and now female infection rates exceed male rates among young people in some countries (table 2.3; UNAIDS 2000). In rural Kwazulu-Natal, South Africa, in 1992, a community based cross-sectional seroprevalence survey found that rates of infection were higher among girls and women until age twenty to twenty-four years, whereas they were higher for men age twenty-five to twenty-nine years and above (Karim and Karim 1999). The source of data may affect these ratios. For example, in Uganda a review of reported cases showed almost equal numbers of clinical cases in men and women. In three population-based studies, however, women consistently had a higher infection rate of 1 to 1.4 men to women (Berer 1993).

Interaction between social and biological vulnerabilities leads to gender differences in the risk of HIV infection (Zierler and Krieger 1997). Biologically women, and particularly young women, are at greater risk of infection through heterosexual sex. First, semen is more infectious than vaginal fluids. Second, the vaginal mucous membrane is more vulnerable to infections than the penis. Third, semen remains in the vaginal or rectal tract for longer than vaginal fluids remain on the penis. Women under eighteen and those after menopause are more susceptible than women of reproductive age, as vaginal mucus provides an effective barrier during

Table 2.3
Estimated HIV prevalence rates (%) in young people (age 15–24 yrs), end 1999
(UNAIDS 2000)

Country	Females		Males	
	Low est.	High est.	Low est.	High est.
Botswana	32.55	36.07	13.68	18.00
Congo	5.49	7.43	2.12	4.23
Ethiopia	9.98	13.75	5.96	9.04
Lesotho	23.94	28.85	8.04	16.07
South Africa	22.51	27.13	7.56	15.11
Papua New Guinea	0.16	0.33	0.03	0.13
Cambodia	2.31	4.70	0.94	3.27
India	0.40	0.82	0.14	0.58
Thailand	1.53	3.11	0.47	1.89
Bahamas	2.41	2.93	3.15	4.55
Dominican Republic	2.44	3.11	2.08	3.08
Guyana	2.03	2.58	3.12	4.62
Panama	1.20	1.52	1.33	0.16

the reproductive years (Forrest 1991). Finally, prevalence rates of other STIs are greater in women than in men, which increases the risk of HIV infection through heterosexual relations. Furthermore, in many cases STIs are asymptomatic in women and women often lack information about the symptoms, which impede early detection and timely treatment.

Gender identities, norms, roles, and relations influence women's and men's vulnerability to STIs and HIV infection in different ways by shaping the negotiation of sexual relationships and practices. For example, norms of female sexual passivity and the social value attached to virginity often make it difficult for women, particularly young or unmarried women, to seek information about how to protect themselves against STIs and to raise the issue of protection in a sexual relationship or encounter (UNAIDS 1999). Expectations of male promiscuity place pressure on men to seek many partners. In addition, the value placed on male sexual pleasure and gendered constructions of sexuality discourage men from accepting protective measures such as condom use or nonpenetrative sex (Campbell 1995). Whereas male promiscuity and infidelity are often tacitly accepted, men may be unwilling to admit infidelity to a long-term partner because it may weaken their power in the relationship. This is a barrier to protecting their partners from infection (Welbourn 2000). In addition, knowledge about the risk of HIV infection and AIDS has intensified male preference for younger women due to the assumption that they will be free of infection (Schoepf 1988).

Violence against women, including sexual violence, is a risk factor for HIV. Despite methodological constraints, a preliminary review of associations between violence and HIV infection found that forced sex was indirectly related to HIV risk, intimate partner violence was associated with lack of condom use, and individuals with a history of child sexual abuse were likely to engage in HIV risk-taking behaviors (Maman et al. 2000).

These gender expectations and behaviors often occur in contexts in which women's independent income earning possibilities are fewer than men's (Abrahamsen 1997; Mbizvo 1996) and their socioeconomic status is generally lower (Gupta and Weiss 1993; Schoepf 1988). When women's social and economic positions are threatened by a breakdown in a stable relationship, their ability to refuse sex or insist on protective measures is restricted. For example, despite the fact that 97% of female respondents in an STI study in Zimbabwe cited their husband as the source of their infection, only 7% considered divorce an option (Pitts et al. 1995). The importance of children to women's social and economic security is another factor inhibiting the use of condoms, because of their contraceptive "side effect" (UNAIDS 1999). Many partners and sex in direct or indirect exchange for money, goods, or administrative favors are, in some circumstances, one of few available livelihood strategies for women (Abrahamsen 1997; de Bruyn 1992). The possibilities for women to desist from such relationships or insist on protective measures are therefore limited. Economic policies that encourage gendered labor migration exacerbate these dynamics by leading to prolonged separation of married couples and stimulating both male demand for sex work and incentives for women to supply it.

Thus the intersection of gendered sexual norms with socioeconomic power imbalances leads to a situation of risk for both women and men. Risks to men from STIs and HIV and AIDS often are linked to identities that are associated with stereotypically male behaviors of dominance, aggression, and risk taking. At the same time women face risk because of gender norms and values and may also be restricted in their ability to take actions to protect their own health due to their low socioeconomic positions. The different sources and levels of risk for diverse groups of women and men raise concerns from a gender equity perspective and require different intervention strategies.

Access to Diagnosis and Treatment for Tuberculosis   It is estimated that tuberculosis leads to the deaths of more women and men each year than any other single infectious disease (Murray and Lopez 1996), with the highest prevalence of death and disability in the southeastern Asian region. In 1997 tuberculosis killed approximately 3 million people, around half of whom were women (WHO 1998d). One-third of the world's population (approximately 2,200 million people) are estimated to be infected with the bacterium that causes tuberculosis, but each infected individual only has a 10% lifetime risk of developing the disease (if they are not HIV infected). Most studies find that infection is more likely among men than women after the beginning of adolescence (between 10 and 16 years). Yet it also appears that more women than men of reproductive age are more likely to develop the disease (Dolin 1998). Tuberculosis is responsible for more deaths among women than all direct causes of maternal mortality combined (WHO 1996a).

Every year cases are reported to WHO at a worldwide male:female ratio of 1.5 to 2.1:1 (table 2.4; WHO 1998d). Global estimates of prevalence among women and men should, however, be viewed with some caution. The proportion of female cases identified rises significantly if cases are actively sought out in the community (active case finding), rather than by only reporting those in which individuals have sought care and been diagnosed (passive case finding). For example, a community-based survey in India showed that women suffered from higher morbidity with tuberculosis but requested health services less than men (Kutzin 1993 cited in Hudelson 1996). It is therefore likely that cases among women are underrepresented in statistics due to women's lower access to diagnosis and treatment.

Studies highlighted the relative inaccessibility of diagnosis and treatment under the WHO recommended directly observed treatment short

Table 2.4
Estimated tuberculosis deaths, prevalence, and burden of disease in thousands, by sex and low- and middle-income regions (LI), 1998 (WHO 1999c)

	HIV Positive			HIV Negative		
	All	Males	Females	All	Males	Females
Deaths						
Africa	305	147	158	209	101	108
Americas LI	13	7	6	53	30	23
Eastern Med	3	2	1	139	88	51
Europe LI	1	1	0	53	44	9
SE Asia	35	23	13	682	414	268
W. Pacific LI, China	5	3	2	345	205	139
Prevalence						
Africa	510	246	264	1,047	505	543
Americas LI	22	12	10	378	213	165
Eastern Med	4	3	2	607	384	223
Europe LI	2	2	0	357	295	62
SE Asia	62	39	23	2,940	1,782	1,158
W. Pacific LI, China	8	5	4	1,889	1,124	764
DALYs						
Africa	7,934	3,719	4,215	5,442	2,551	2,891
Americas LI	302	159	143	1,213	638	575
Eastern Med	59	37	22	3,188	2,006	1,182
Europe LI	18	15	3	853	732	122
SE Asia	630	381	249	12,015	7,079	4,935
W. Pacific LI, China	62	35	27	5,337	3,030	2,317

course (DOTS) (Kemp et al. 1996). Diagnosis requires repeated visits to a health facility with appropriate equipment and expertise (often a district hospital) for smear microscopy,[9] and treatment requires drug therapy for a minimum of six months. This therapy should be observed by a health worker or trained volunteer, which usually means visits to the nearest trained provider. The accessibility of diagnosis and treatment for an individual depends on factors such as financial resources, access to transport, and social mobility, all of which clearly have gender dimensions. Vietnamese women said that flexibility in payment type, such as in rice, and timing would be important in allowing them to seek care (Johansson et al. 1999).

Whether or not an individual seeks care involves the ability to take time off work, the opportunity costs of doing so, and the importance of good health for continuing work. These considerations may lead to different and contradictory barriers to care for women and men, and their decision-making power in household deliberations is unlikely to be equal. Study respondents in Bangladesh said that households would generally give priority for tuberculosis treatment to men because, as main income earners, their health was perceived as most important (Fair et al. 1997). However, in Pakistan difficulty taking time from income-generating activities was a major barrier to treatment for men (Liefooghe 1998).

In addition, tuberculosis is a stigmatized disease and the social and economic repercussions of the diagnosis may differ for women and men. The stigma was heightened in recent years by its association with HIV-positive status, which bears its own gender stigma. In Bombay, women and men expressed different fears and described different experiences as a result of the illness. Women feared loss of employment, whereas most men were self-employed and feared lost wages. Married women expressed fears of rejection by their spouses or families, and unmarried women worried about reduced chances of marrying as well as losing their jobs (Nair et al. 1997). Married men and single women perceived a greater level of family support to begin and complete treatment, but married women often tried to hide their symptoms for fear of blame or rejection, and many dropped out of treatment due to the pressure of keeping the illness secret. Fears of responses by families, employers, and the community influence individuals' decisions about whether to seek care for symptoms known to be possibly indicative of tuberculosis such as chronic coughs.

Gendered institutional norms and processes may influence how women and men are treated by the health care system during diagnosis and treatment. For example, Vietnamese women did not receive the diagnosis as quickly as men once they reached health services (Long et al. 1999). The reasons for this difference were not identified, but the mean delay of about two weeks was clinically significant in terms of morbidity for the individual, as well as the rate of transmission. Women in Bangladesh gave the lack of confidentiality offered by formal health services as a reason for preferring to visit traditional healers (Fair et al. 1997). Accessing and completing tuberculosis treatment are clearly influenced by a complex interaction of social, economic, and institutional factors, which are related to gender.

Gender Roles in Communicable Disease Interventions   Infants and children bear a particularly heavy burden of infectious disease in terms of morbidity and mortality. In 1990 in developing countries there were 1,263,000 deaths from diarrheal disease among boys from birth to age four years compared with 191,000 among boys age five years and older. This ratio of roughly 6:1 is also found among females (Murray and Lopez 1996). Although many interventions are targeted at reducing child mortality and morbidity, adults are mobilized to participate in these interventions and their ability to do so is crucially affected by gender roles and relations.

Methods of addressing infectious diseases may be broadly categorized into public health interventions, such as water and sanitation programs; preventive interventions within the biomedical model, such as vaccinations and insecticide-impregnated bed nets; medical interventions such as drug therapy; and promotion of informed care in the home. These approaches tend to operate with gendered assumptions about appropriate targets. For example, water and sanitation programs historically targeted male community members for consultation and involvement, because physical construction work was often involved, and infrastructural issues were considered to relate to the public domain, which was men's sphere. In recent years recognition has been growing that in many communities it is women who are responsible for the daily management of water, so their input is needed in the design and, crucially, management and control of interventions (SIDA 1996).

Conversely, exclusive targeting of women in some instances was a barrier to effective implementation of interventions. Promotion of home care in the "child survival revolution" relied on technical innovations such as oral rehydration therapy (ORT) for diarrhea, which were seen as offering the possibility of dramatic reductions in mortality and morbidity from childhood diseases within a short time frame. These technologies relied on effective implementation by carers of children, who in most cases were mothers. Although mothers were explicitly targeted by health and development agencies in child survival interventions, a review conducted in 1989 found that insufficient attention was paid to the potential demands of these activities on their time (Leslie 1989). Where the burden of communicable disease among children is highest, women are also likely to face the highest demands on their time from both productive and reproductive activities.

Although women stand to benefit from higher rates of child survival in the long term, they experience time constraints in the short term that may well prevent them from reaping these long-term benefits. To be effective, ORT must be given gradually and regularly throughout the diarrheal episode, necessitating the constant presence of the principal carer over three to four days (the average duration of an episode of acute diarrhea). Evaluations of ORT projects found that lack of time and other resources to administer the therapy was a frequent barrier to compliance, which was underestimated by planners. In India, for some mothers giving ORT constituted a significantly heavier child care burden than the usual practice of administering a dose of *goli* (antidiarrheal drug) because the latter could be delegated to another member of the family and because women working in the informal sector did not have enough continuous time available to manage ORT (Balasubrahmanyan 1987 cited in Leslie 1989).

If women's caring burdens are inadvertently increased by health interventions, this may have a negative impact on their socioeconomic positions and health, because it may reduce the time available for productive work or rest. Leslie (1989) commented, "What must be avoided is designing projects as if there were two different groups of low-income women in the Third World, one group with reproductive responsibilities who are the target of health and nutrition projects, and another group with productive responsibilities who are the target of agricultural and income generation projects."

Similarly, preventive health interventions that seek to reduce malaria in endemic areas actively seek out women to ensure that family members, particularly infants and young children, are protected from the disease. As insecticide-impregnated bed nets can effectively protect household members from malaria in endemic areas, control programs focused on women, not men, to wash and impregnate the nets. A study of determinants of permethrin-impregnated bed net use in Benin found that women's income and participation in communal organizations were two of three principal variables that positively correlated with bed net use in households (the other variable was male education level) (Rashed et al. 1999). Because women have the primary responsibility for the health of their families and are aware of children's vulnerability to malaria, they are more inclined than men to want to buy the nets. However, women are less likely than men to have control over household money, so they often have to resort to using their own income, which is considerably lower than men's. Women mentioned lack of access to cash as a reason for not using nets, whereas no men mentioned this reason.

Efforts to train mothers in detection and early intervention of fevers in their children often fail to take into account that women may not control the resources to seek antimalarial drugs or bed nets, or the way in which their position and their relationships with men and senior family members influence their response to children's illness. A study on the Kenyan coast found that a partner's absence was among the reasons given by mothers for a lapse in bringing the child to health services (Mwenesi et al. 1995). In Ghana women consulted the male head of household about treating a child because of the expectation that he would pay for treatment, and his absence could therefore lead to fatal delays in bringing a child to health care services (Livingstone 1995).

The potential outcome of ignoring the multiplicity of tasks women in resource-poor situations juggle is that programs may be ineffective. They may also inadvertently exacerbate gender inequity by adding strain to women's social and health resources and by reinforcing the notion that the only ways women are valued are as mothers and caregivers.

Future Directions and Challenges

Those involved in communicable diseases, whether they work in control of vectors, vaccine and drug development, improvement of surveillance and monitoring systems, or as health care workers in disease-endemic countries, must be mindful that gender structures the way they assess the problem. Gender affects research questions that are asked and the way in which data are examined and analyzed. Traditional biomedical researchers must include their vision the social inequalities that define these diseases. They can no longer exclude such inequalities as being outside their domain.

Basic efforts to be encouraged include disaggregation of data by gender, age, class, and region. In addition, limits of standard data sources should be adjusted for, through measures such as active case finding. More advanced efforts would require social analysis of the information derived and use of new technologies such as geographic information systems to identify correlations between geographic and socioeconomic factors and disease patterns.

Reassessments of policies and interventions in the light of gender analysis can lead to strategies for improving gender equity by emphasizing broader access to treatment and better quality of care for underprivileged groups. Pathways to and payment for diagnosis and treatment can be reviewed to identify ways to make them more accessible to groups of women and men who are underrepresented. For example, the Healthy Women Counselling Guide worked with communities to develop radio health-promotion programs to provide information and stimulate awareness of health and gender issues in the context of rural women's daily lives.[10] It is critical that these interventions be designed in ways that do not reinforce gender norms and stereotypes that assume that women are solely responsible for caring for family members and that they can do so with ease as they "do not work" and have "free time."

Strategies for gender equity also must consider needs specific to marginalized groups. For example, efforts should be made to identify ways to include women in clinical research and treatment regimens without posing harm to them or to fetuses. The design of preventive and curative technologies to diagnose, treat, and prevent communicable diseases must take into account constraints of material poverty, as well as the powerlessness that frames gender, race, and class inequalities. These context-specific social constraints suggest that an emphasis on technologic solutions alone is unlikely to overcome the problems of gender inequality. Attempts to identify universal responses are unlikely to be successful.

Despite existing prophylactics, diagnostics, drugs, or vaccines that can help prevent and control many diseases from which people die, major questions about how to encourage and enable poor men and women to access and use them remain. It is not that efforts have not been made in acknowledging the role of social and behavioral factors. Much has been done and written about the cultural aspects of infectious diseases. But most of the emphasis has been on understanding culture or context so as to find ways of stimulating individual agencies to promote and protect their own or their family's health, without considering structural and relational inequalities such gender and poverty. In most settings where poverty is prevalent, the degree to which individual behavior and health beliefs can be summoned to improve access and compliance are significantly compromised by forces beyond individual control (Farmer 1996). Biomedical interventions that emphasize individual responsibility for health at the expense of structural inequalities conceal the fact that *"Throughout the world, those least likely to comply are those least able to comply* (author's italics) (Farmer 1997b).

The deep-rooted character of the gendered self and the structural nature of gender roles and relations have to be addressed to enable significant improvement in gender equity. Interventions that aim to effect individual behavior change without addressing the power relations that underpin this behavior are likely to meet with limited success. Health-promotion approaches that enable women and men to reflect on gender norms, stereotypes, and relations, such as the Stepping Stones training program developed by Action Aid[11] show that there are possibilities for challenging and beginning to shift power relations that are often considered to be immutable (Welbourn 2000).

Stepping Stones aims to encourage prevention of HIV infection and STIs and uses a participatory adult learning methodologies to explore gender roles, money, attitudes toward sex, sexuality, and death in same-sex peer groups. Impact assessments show that condom use increased, but also that interpersonal communications in relationships improved, domestic violence and alcohol abuse decreased, and young women reported rising levels of self-esteem as well as determination to be economically independent and to become more involved in political life. It is necessary to develop further innovative approaches to shifting gender power relations and to trace their effects on infectious disease.

Finally, communicable diseases are predominantly diseases of poverty. Reduction of poverty and socioeconomic inequality should therefore be at the center of efforts to reduce suffering and death due to these diseases.

Participatory research shows that poor people in both rich and poor countries invariably rate improvements in incomes, housing, food and nutrition, sanitation, and environmental conditions above improvements in health care (Welbourn 1992). Interventions to reduce inequalities in these areas are likely to achieve the most in reducing the burden of communicable disease morbidity and mortality. It is crucial that such interventions be designed with the participation of both poor women and men to ensure that gender needs and priorities are taken into consideration. Gender is more than a variable to be manipulated; it is an organizing principle of society (West 1993).

Notes

1. Ms. Tolhurst's position is funded by the U.K. Department for International Development through Malaria and Health Sector Reform Knowledge Programmes. This chapter draws substantially on gender analyses of infectious disease developed by the gender and health group at the Liverpool School of Tropical Medicine, of which both she and Janet Price are members.

2. Communicable and infectious are used interchangeably.

3. Further details on the epidemiology of specific diseases can be found on the WHO Web site given above.

4. This cluster consists of pertussis, polio, diphtheria, measles, and tetanus.

5. http://www.who.int/health-topics/.

6. Growth monitoring, oral rehydration, breastfeeding, and immunization: a selected package of interventions to reduce childhood infections, the impact of diarrhea, and malnutrition.

7. http://www.who.int/infectious-disease-report/pages/ch4init.html.

8. At the time of this study, twenty-seven women had been treated inadvertently with ivermectin during the first trimester of pregnancy. No negative effects were found on follow-up, and Merck now recommends that the drug be made available to pregnant women during mass treatment campaigns when the risk of complications from untreated onchocerciasis exceeds the potential risk to the fetus from treatment. Similarly, nursing mothers can be given the drug only if the benefits outweigh the potential risk to the infant.

9. Three sputum smears are taken: on the spot at the first visit, one later during the day, and one the next day.

10. http://www.who.int/tdr.

11. http://www.stratshope.org.

3

Examining Work and Its Effects on Health[1]

Piroska Östlin

One of the most striking developments during the late twentieth century was recognition of women's indispensable role in international, national, and household economies. Figures from the World Development Report (World Bank 1995a) reveal that $16 trillion are missing from the global economy each year, representing the value of unpaid work by women and men and underpayment of women's work. Of this $16 trillion, $11 trillion represents the invisible contribution of women.

In almost all regions of the world, in both high- and low-income countries, women's share of the labor force has been rising since the 1970s or 1980s. In the European Union, between 1980 and 1990, women accounted for 7 million of 8 million newly employed. Participation rates of women in many OECD (Organization for Economic Co-operation and Development) countries (e.g., Finland and Sweden) are approximately equal to those of men (Lahelma and Arber 1994).

In low-income countries, women's participation in the labor market has also been rising and accounts on average for 31% of the labor force. This figure should probably be higher, as official statistics in low-income countries often underestimate women's work because of its nonmarket nature, whether as producers in subsistence agriculture, or as workers in the informal sector. Whereas the informal sector in high-income countries often connotes unpaid work, such as volunteerism, in low-income countries it consists of household-based enterprises that may provide employment for family workers or others, but most often only for the proprietor (Stellman and Lucas 2000). In Africa, more than one third of women outside the agricultural sector work in the informal sector;

for example, in Zambia, 72% and in the Gambia, 62%. Proportions are also high in Indonesia (65%) and in Lima, Peru (80%) (Lean Lim 1996).

Women have always played an important role in the economy. However, by focusing on paid work, research obscured their contributions to economies in labor market statistics. Since women's work was mainly (and still is in many countries) performed in the domestic sphere and in the informal sector, it was invisible in the public, economic, and institutional spheres. For this reason, it was viewed as nonproductive and thus often excluded from money transactions. As a result, domestic work and work based in homes entails no direct payments, no protective legislation, and no social security, and is assigned low social status (Hall 1990). Homemakers are not publicly regarded as workers, homes are not regarded as workplaces, and household labor is not considered as work.

Despite these biases, the increasing visibility and importance of women's labor worldwide can no longer be ignored and neglected in policy and research. Highly gendered labor has paramount importance in relation to the hierarchical ordering of society in terms of wealth, power, and prestige. One's occupation and the social position it provides are strongly associated with differences in life chances, freedoms, opportunities, and living conditions, and thereby also significantly influence the possibility of good health. Therefore, the interface between gender and work is a key issue in discussions of social inequalities in general and gender inequalities in health in particular.

The purpose of this chapter is to show how gender inequalities and inequities in health are influenced by gender inequalities in working life, which includes both paid and unpaid work activities.

The General Effect of Work on Gender and Health

Women in general, relative to men, face unequal hiring standards, unequal opportunities for training, unequal pay for equal work, unequal access to productive resources, segregation and concentration in female sectors and occupations, different physical and mental working conditions, unequal participation in economic decisionmaking, and unequal promotion prospects. These factors negatively affect women's status and position in society relative to men, and consequently have an important impact on gender inequalities in health.

In high-income, industrialized countries, despite women's inferior position and discrimination in most arenas and levels of working life, their increased participation in gainful employment not only strengthened their social status and their individual and family's financial situation, but also was beneficial to their health (Waldron et al. 1998). Employment outside the home is an important source of social support and self-esteem, and helps women to be integrated into society and to avoid social isolation in the home. In addition, working outside the home is associated with better mental and physical health of women (Repetti et al. 1989; Walters 1993). Income from work may also reduce women's economic and social dependence on their male partner.[2] In general, a positive relationship was found in a number of studies between many roles and health through greater self-confidence and economic independence. These positive pathways may outweigh the additional stress that comes from the responsibilities of several positions (Barnett and Baruch 1987; Pugliesi 1995). These results may also hold for women from middle- or upper-income households in poorer countries, but we have few actual data to support this.

This general observation obtained mainly from research in high-income countries may, however, not always apply to women in low-income countries, large numbers of whom are exposed to harmful working environments and who often have few choices about whether and where to work. The latter is also often true in higher-income countries, especially for poor women. Little evidence in these circumstances suggests that women who work outside the home are better off.

Thus these women working outside the home are often seen as a negative status symbol by the family, denoting its low economic and social status. In south Asia, for example, whereas women from the poorest households often work outside the home, households are known to withdraw women from such work once their economic status improves.

Nonetheless, even in such situations, poor women who work outside the home evidence greater levels of self-confidence and economic independence, even though they may face hazardous working conditions, stress, and violence (Razavi 2000). In general, however, if the primarily roles assigned to people, such as the breadwinner role for men or the reproductive role in the home for women, are too demanding, additional responsibilities may result in stress and thereby increase the risk of negative health effects (Coser 1974).

Evidence suggests that employment increases the advantage of women over men with respect to life expectancy (Waldron 1991). A cohort study (Vågerö and Lahelma 1998) compared the mortality of Swedish women who took advantage of family-friendly employment policies with those who did not, and found that mortality decreased significantly more among those employed. Positive health selection alone could not account for this difference. Similar evidence from low-income countries is sparse. However, in the Philippines, women's market work improved the quality of their diets and had strong distributional implications, as poor women's diets improved the most (Bisgrove and Popkin 1996).

A large body of literature on unemployment and health indicates that employment is beneficial also for men's survival (Stefansson 1991; Valkonen and Martikainen 1995). There is consensus that unemployment among men is associated with impaired psychologic health and with mortality. It was estimated that in a Finnish male cohort age thirty to fifty-four years, 8% of all deaths and 5% of circulatory deaths could be attributed to the experience of unemployment (Valkonen and Martikainen 1995). The dramatically decreased life expectancy by 6.5 years for Russian men between 1989 and 1994 reflects extraordinary pressures put on them in a rapidly changing society, when many of them lost their jobs and were no longer able to fulfil the role of breadwinner. Some men tackle the stress that arises from this through health-damaging behaviors such as excessive alcohol consumption, smoking, and violence (Shkolnikov 1997).

Although waged employment is proved to be beneficial for both women's and men's health in general, not all working conditions are beneficial. According to Doyal (1995) "the key question is not whether paid work in general is good for all women, but rather which types of work will be harmful or beneficial for which women and under what circumstances." This statement is applicable also to men.

A huge body of occupational health literature shows how work creates exposures to numerous risks and hazards that, regardless of being paid or unpaid, can impair health. These hazards are related to both physical and psychosocial exposures (table 3.1).

Table 3.1
Examples of hazards at work

Physical hazards	Psychosocial hazards
Prolonged physically exerting work	Stress related to:
Heavy lifting and carrying	High mental demand
Unsuitable working postures (bending forward without support of hands, working in twisted postures, working with arms raised, standing for long hours)	Work tempo
	Lack of control over planning of own work
Repetitive and one-sided working movements	Monotonous and repetitive work
Accidents	Lack of social support from superiors and colleagues
Violence	Sexual harassment
Noise	Fear of redundancy, unemployment
Vibration	Fear of accidents, violence, bullying
Heat	Lack of flexible working hours (evening work, night work, alternating or rotating shift work)
Cold	
Poor lighting	
Chemicals (pesticides, oil, cutting fluids, cleaning agents, disinfectants)	
Air pollution	
Organic dusts	
Smoke (passive smoking)	
Ionizing radiation	
Water-borne, blood-borne, airborne infections	

The dose of health-damaging factors varies tremendously among occupations and across countries, as well as between formal- and informal-sector jobs. Some jobs have hardly any hazards, while others are associated with many. These hazards may lead to early death (e.g., accident, suicide, myocardial infarction, cancer) and to chronic or acute disabilities (e.g., injuries, musculoskeletal diseases, skin diseases, poisoning, hearing impairment, infertility, miscarriage, respiratory diseases, infectious diseases, fatigue, burnout). Such adverse health effects may result in absences, early retirement, or unemployment, which in turn may lead to significant decreases in household income, especially in countries without adequate or effective social safety nets.

Gender Segregation of Labor

Gender segregation of work is an important starting point for identifying risks in work environments and understanding gender inequalities in work-related mortality and morbidity. In fact, it is one of the most important and enduring aspects of working life around the world.

It is useful to distinguish between *horizontal* and *vertical* gender segregation. Horizontal segregation describes the concentration of women and men into disproportionately female and male occupations. Shop assistants, hospital orderlies, kitchen assistants, nurses, and secretaries are usually women worldwide, whereas tool makers, miners, professional drivers, and engineers are predominantly men. Vertical segregation is the hierarchical division of power and influence in occupations. Men are found to a greater extent in higher managerial positions and women in lower positions both in male- and female-dominated occupations. In fact, there are systematic differences between genders in the same occupation in terms of grade, pay, authority, and career possibilities.

Allocation of specific tasks to men and to women is extensive and pervasive in all countries, regardless of level of development, wealth, religious orientation, political regime, or degree of gender equality in other domains of society. Extensive cross-country comparisons indicate that social, cultural, and historical factors are of great importance in determining the extent to which occupations are segmented based on workers' gender (Anker 1998). The same study revealed greatly different segregation levels in various regions, with lowest levels in Asia and in Pacific and highest in the Middle East and in North Africa.

Surprisingly high levels of gender segregation were found in Scandinavian countries. This is probably due to extensive employment opportunities open to women in public-sector services such as education, health care, child care, and social services (Melkas and Anker 1998). In many other countries these jobs are undertaken by women outside the labor market without wages, making them invisible in official labor market statistics.

Gender segregation varies not only according to place, but also according to time: construction workers in high-income countries are mainly men, however, in Asian countries they are often women.[3] Jobs that are now seen as men's may historically have been performed by women and vice versa (Bradley 1989; Alvesson and Billing 1997). Before industrialization of the cotton industry, weavers were usually men and spinners were women, but the introduction of power-driven machinery brought a reversal of these roles (Bradley 1989). In general, the division of labor between women and men shifted over time, depending largely on where women's contributions were required (Wikander 1992). However, as discussed later, some of these changes perpetuated discrimination against women.

The gender division of labor is just as obvious in the private world of family and household as in waged employment. In the household, it usually means that most duties—daily tasks of cooking, cleaning the house, doing laundry, and caring for children and sick relatives—are allocated to women, whereas car and household maintenance are men's responsibilities. One important characteristic of women's household work is that it cannot be postponed, and as a result women's leisure time is more fragmented than men's (Frankenhaeuser et al. 1991; Bird and Hill 1992). In high-income countries, women's increased share of paid work in the labor market has not decreased their responsibilities for domestic duties in terms of time spent caring for their families and sick relatives (Moen et al. 1994).

Not only is the division of domestic labor uneven by gender, but social position can further compound this discrimination. In Sweden, women's social position with regard to education level, income, and position at work is associated with the extent of their partner's share of domestic work and child care (Roman 1992; Bejerot and Härenstam 1995). Husbands of women with low qualified work did not increase their part of domestic work to the same extent as other men did during the period of increasing female labor market participation (Nermo 1994).

Gender segregation in both paid and unpaid work may be linked to gender inequities in health in at least two ways. Gender inequities in occupational health may occur, first, if women are working in intrinsically more unhealthy jobs, and second, if certain jobs remain unhealthy because they are female dominated. One finds support for both explanations in the scientific literature.

Evidence suggests that women's unhealthy working conditions and occupational health problems are less likely to be addressed by employers, unions, researchers, and policy makers, which further contributes to inequities in occupational health. The focus was traditionally directed toward health hazards in male-dominated working environments. The historical roots of this concern are probably related to recognition and increased political influence of male-dominated trade unions at the end of the nineteenth century. The heightened power of unions allowed them to negotiate a healthier workplace with employers. While protective legislation on grounds of health and safety led to a healthier workplace for men, the same concerns removed women from better-paid work (Bradley 1989). Health-related arguments of male unionists at that time were particularly instrumental in protecting the industry from female competition.

Male-dominated workplaces are still considered more dangerous in terms of, for example, risk of fatal accidents and chemical health hazards than female-dominated ones. As a result, men's jobs are better paid than women's. In addition, resources allocated for research and policies to improve men's working conditions have been more substantial compared with those allocated for female-dominated work settings. Consequently, success stories from Sweden, for example, include remarkable reduction of fatal accidents and chemical health hazards, which are more common exposures among Swedish men than women (Järvholm 1996). At the same time, however, no improvements are seen with regard to psychosocial work problems, such as negative stress, which is more common among women.

The intrinsically unhealthy nature of women's and men's jobs may have different dimensions along most of the hazards presented in table 3.1. As we will see, women and men are not exposed to the same hazards, or if they are, they are not exposed to the same extent. It is important to note that even if women are exposed to a particular health-damaging factor to the same degree as men, they may experience worse health effects due to both biological and social factors. Furthermore, since neither women nor men are homogeneous categories, huge variations will be seen regarding health-damaging working conditions across different groups of women and different groups of men.

Gender and Work-Related Health Risks

This section contains examples, both from low- and high-income countries, of risk factors most often associated with women's and men's work and how these exposures might affect physical and mental health. In certain cases the same risks have different health outcomes between women and men. We should, however, be aware that what we know about occupational health risks is based primarily on studies concerning men's occupational health, since work is typically considered paid work. Moreover, our knowledge of the health effects of working conditions in low-income countries is extremely sparse due to lack of systematic research.

Work-Related Health Risks in the Household

As mentioned, homemakers are almost exclusively women worldwide. They are neither publicly regarded as workers nor is the home regarded as a workplace. As a result, this work is not included in occupational safety regulations.[4] In general, accidents and diseases related to household work are underestimated, not recorded as occupational, and not compensated by work insurance systems.

This lack of visibility is especially problematic from a gender perspective as women are more prone to work-related injuries at home, whereas men suffer more often from occupational accidents outside the home. In Australia half of all accidents suffered by women happen at home, compared with 21% of those suffered by men (Doyal 1995). Australia does not seem to be different in this respect from other high-income countries (Broom 1986). In many low-income countries, women's daily responsibility for meal preparation using open stoves or fires results in significantly higher incidence of burns (Saleh et al. 1986; Gupta and Srivastava 1988). However, such accidents are not publicly recognized as occupational.

Quantitative measures of health effects of domestic work are very sparse for women and men in high- and low-income countries. As the household is traditionally viewed as the domain of women, studies that focused on these risks looked mainly at women. Hence there is no information about health risks from domestic work for men.

In low-income countries most women still shoulder extremely heavy workloads in the household. Three-fourths of Ghanaian women linked their health problems to their work (Avotri and Walters 1999). Issues of particular concern were gender division of labor, heavy workloads, compulsory nature of work, financial insecurity, and financial responsibility for their children.

Two important responsibilities of women are providing water and fuel for home use (Paulisso and Leslie 1995). These activities involve carrying heavy loads and walking long distances. In addition, the time cost of these activities should not be underestimated. According to estimates from Zimbabwe, mothers' total time spent in fetching water and firewood was 25 hours a week. This alone contributed about 38% of the total household output. Daughters' contribution comes next at 22%, followed by sons' 20% and husbands' at only 13% (Mehretu and Mutambirwa 1992). In addition to musculoskeletal diseases, heavy lifting can lead to miscarriage and stillbirth, prolapsed uterus, menstrual disorders, and functional disability (Prabha 1983; Doty 1987; Doyal 1995). Women's responsibilities for collecting water and washing in rivers expose them to water-borne and water-related diseases and infections such as schistosomiasis (Hartigan 1999), malaria and worms (Kendie 1992).

Women cooking on open stoves not only are at risks of burns, but are also at high risk of illness due to smoke pollution, as was found in India (Mishra et al. 1990). Unacceptable levels of indoor pollution during cooking were indicated by high levels of blood carboxyhemoglobin (Bebera et al. 1991). Such pollution may also have detrimental effects on fetal growth (Dekoning et al. 1985). Fuels commonly used for cooking and other domestic purposes in low-income countries include biomass, kerosene oil, and liquid petroleum gas. Pollutants derived from these fuels include carcinogens and other toxic substances. Furthermore, a relationship was seen between biomass cooking fuels and prevalence of blindness in India (Mishra et al. 2000).

Almost all households in high-income countries have running water, electricity, and basic domestic appliances that remove the worst physical strains and health hazards. However, they are not entirely free from hazards of toxic substances used for cleaning, laundry, car repair, and gardening. These hazards are increasingly present in low-income countries as well. Research to estimate the health effects among men and women of these household chemicals is scarce.

Finally, the risks of mental ill health among full-time homemakers should not be underestimated. As mentioned, housewives are more affected by psychological distress than employed women, probably as a result of isolation. Compared with working women, housewives have more sick days, more limitations in activity, more acute and chronic conditions, less favorable levels of serum cholesterol and lipoproteins, and higher risk of coronary heart disease (Hall 1990). For women in paid employment, household duties may become a considerable source of stress, especially if they work full time and have dependent children (Lundberg 1998). Research regarding health effects of stress among men in similar situations is rare.

Work-Related Health Risks in Waged Employment

Compared with domestic health hazards, knowledge regarding health effects of paid work is more extensive, especially in high-income countries. One finds a number of consequences of the persisting narrow focus on male-dominated health hazards for women's working conditions and health.

Many low-income countries have opportunities for women to earn income in agriculture. The concentration of the female labor force in the agricultural sector is more than 80% in sub-Saharan Africa and at least 50% in Asia (Lean Lim 1996). Subsistence crops, especially in sub-Saharan Africa, are almost exclusively cultivated by women on small farms. The women spend long hours in uncomfortable working postures, which can lead to chronic back pain and other musculoskeletal disorders such as painful neck and shoulders (Paolisso and Leslie 1995).

Cash crop production of, for example, fruits, vegetables, and flowers involves exposure to toxic pesticides. In low-income countries many women work in chemical-laced water when transplanting rice. In addition, they are more involved than men in hand labor, such as weeding, picking, and sorting in fields that have been sprayed, which results in prolonged exposure to pesticides. Men are more involved in fumigating crops, which entails exposure for short periods of time. As a result, extensive use of pesticides constitutes a major health risk for women, and is greater for women than for men (Paolisso and Leslie 1995).

The adverse health effects of pesticide exposure include poisoning, cancer, skin diseases, abortions, premature births, and malformed babies. In Colombia, floriculture workers, made up of 67% women and 33% men, are exposed to 127 different kinds of pesticides (Restrepo et al. 1990). Female workers and wives of male workers had increased risks for congenital malformation, spontaneous abortion, and premature births. The probability of giving birth to malformed babies increased by 30% after the introduction of pesticides and could be as a result of damage to either male or female reproductive organs. Nonetheless in general, as reproduction traditionally is viewed as women's domain, male reproductive health related to toxic contamination has been ignored both in research and protective occupational regulations.

Pesticides and chemicals are also widely used in high-income countries. However, occupational safety regulations and exposure limits for toxic chemicals protect workers from the worst effects. There are reasons to believe that these limits protect women to a significantly lower degree than men. First, studies to determine safe levels of exposure were performed in healthy young men and applied to female workers without convincing evidence of their applicability to women (Messing 1993, 1998). Second, women's greater sensitivity to chemical exposures is often neglected. For example, although women of all ages need stricter protection against lead than men due to biological differences, regulations generally provide stricter protection only for women of reproductive age (Hansson 1998).

Even if men and women were exposed to pesticides and other chemicals to the same degree, the health effects would be worse for women due to their greater biological vulnerability (Messing and Kilbom 1998). Since women have a higher proportion of fat tissue than men, they are at greater risk of harm from exposure to fat-soluble chemicals (Östlin et al. 2001a). Genders differ in the absorption, metabolism, and excretion of fat-soluble chemicals. Women have thinner skin than men, so chemicals can more easily penetrate into their bodies and trigger allergies and eczema. Because women have slower metabolism, chemicals remain in their bodies longer in high concentrations in the blood stream.

Women's greater biological vulnerability to chemicals and segregation in occupations involving exposure to skin allergens, in combination with work where hands are wet for long hours (e.g., cleaning, hairdressing),

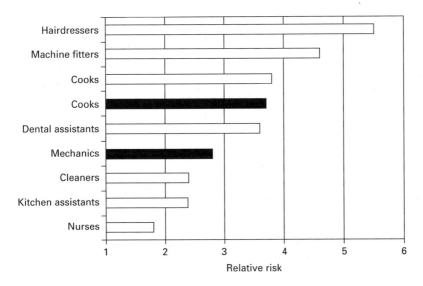

Figure 3.1
Occupational groups with an elevated incidence of reported skin disorders, Sweden, 1990–1991. White bars indicate women, black bars indicate men. (Hedlin et al. 1994, cited in Meding 1998.)

could be part of the explanation behind their elevated incidence of work-related skin disorders. This is in spite of the fact that men in high-income countries are believed to be exposed to chemicals to a higher degree than women. Figure 3.1 shows which occupations in Sweden have the highest number of reported cases of occupational skin disease in relation to the number of individuals employed in each occupation. The results clearly indicate that most cases occur within female occupations involving extensive wet work and handling of chemicals (Meding 1998).

Another area of concern in both low- and high-income countries is the health impact of assembly line production, which has been viewed as particularly suitable for women. Biological explanations concerning size, strength, hormones, and the need for women to be protected for reproductive reasons, which are often used to justify discrimination against employing women, are used in these cases to justify the recruitment of women. Because assembly line production, especially in industries such as toys, garments, or electronics, is considered physically light, it is believed that women are protected from heavy physical strain. Moreover such work is assumed to not require much training, which justifies low wages.

This predominantly female work in factories and processing plants involves working long shifts, monotonous and repetitive work, and exposure to carcinogenic substances (Paolisso and Lesley 1995; Theobald 1999). Repetitive movements made at a fast pace for long hours, combined with fatigue and stress, give rise to musculoskeletal symptoms commonly called repetitive strain injury. This causes considerable pain and discomfort in affected areas, such as hands, wrists, and arms. It can also lead to loss of grip strength in the hands and, over time, to disability that can force permanent cessation of employment (Bird and Hill 1992).

Men more often than women are involved in dynamic work, which usually means that they use different muscle groups doing physically strenuous activity such as lifting or moving heavy loads. Even though each load is heavy, the varying dynamic work causes less damage than static work, which is more common among women and can be characterized by repetitive and one-sided stress on the same muscle fibers for a prolonged period (Joint Work Environment Council for the Government Sector 1997).

If women and men were exposed to the same physical load, it would exert greater physical strain on women than on men. This is because women on average can achieve only 60% or 70% of men's muscular strength as their muscle fibers are more slender and shorter. Women's arm strength is only 50% of men's. Thus, a 20-kilo lift for a woman is equivalent to a 33-kilo lift for a man (Joint Work Environment Council 1997).

In high-income countries most work related fatalities occur in male-dominated occupations. Only 6% of fatal accidents in Sweden between 1987 and 1995 affected women (Kjellberg 1998). This difference is almost entirely due to the fact that men work in environments with greater risk for such exposure (e.g., transportation, mining, fire fighting). In low-income countries men probably are also more affected than women since most accident-prone occupations are male-dominated. Furthermore men in low-income countries, compared with to their counterparts in high-income countries, are more exposed to risks due to weaker safety regulations and safety equipment.

In most industrialized countries more men than women are exposed to noise, vibrations, unfavorable climate, organic solvents, and most other types of conventional physical and chemical risks. Consequently, solvent-related illnesses, hearing loss, and vibration injuries, such as "white fingers," are more common among men. However, work-related musculoskeletal disorders and skin diseases are more common among women (Kjellberg 1998).

Although conventional physical and chemical risks have not disappeared from workplaces, in high-income countries they have been reduced considerably thanks to regulations and preventive measures. As a result, the focus for both policy and research changed toward health hazards associated with psychosocial risk factors, mainly related to the organization of work. This sort of emphasis is found mostly in high-income countries, but there are no reasons to believe that health effects would be different in low-income countries.

One of the most studied risk factors associated with the psychosocial work environment is negative stress, defined as a combination of high psychological demand at work (such as hectic work pace) and low decision latitude (ability to control work tasks) (Karasak 1979). Negative stress is more prevalent in female-dominated occupations and at all levels of the occupational hierarchy measured by socioeconomic status. Negative stress is associated with increased risk of myocardial infarction, mental illness, and musculoskeletal disorders (Karasek and Theorell 1990).

In Sweden, ten hours of overtime a week increased the risk of heart attack in women, whereas men working a similar amount of overtime had a lower incidence than expected (Alfredsson et al. 1985). The different consequences of overtime for women and men, within the same socioeconomic group reflects the higher level of stress put on women because of conflict that may arise between their greater responsibilities for household duties and gainful employment.

The possibilities for control or decision making at work are lower for women than for men, even at the same hierarchical and educational levels (vertical segregation). Women managers have a noticeable accumulation of stress hormones at the end of the working day, when it is time to gear up for domestic duties (Frankenheauser et al. 1989). Women in lower positions did not experience the same increase in hormone levels. Male managers on the other hand showed a sharp reduction of stress hormones after work. Female managers usually enjoy less social support and respect from other managers (mainly men) and also from other women workers (Joint Work Environment Council for the Government Sector 1997).

These two examples show clearly the interaction between gender and other cross-cutting features such as social class. These factors together with race and ethnicity interact with gender when determining power relations in society (Breen 2000). In any given class, women are usually subordinate to men, but the status and power differences between women of different classes can vary from the corresponding class differences between men (Östlin et al. 2001b). The requirements necessary to combine paid employment and household responsibilities exert a greater influence on women's health, given their greater responsibilities in the domestic domain. Whether women of various social classes have possibilities or necessary resources to balance their different roles in the public and domestic domains has a significant impact on inequalities between women and men as well as in different groups of women and different groups of men.

These results indicate also that the structural framework in research and policy has to be complemented by other frameworks, such as the gender role framework, where relations between men and women and the interplay among sex (biological), gender (social), and social status are taken into consideration (Östlin 1997; Annandale and Hunt 2000).

Challenges for Policy and Research

Given the important role gender segregation of labor plays in determining women's (and men's) status and hierarchical position in society and its role in relation to labor market inefficiencies, economic growth, and social justice, reducing sex segregation of work should receive urgent and priority attention by policymakers and researchers (Anker 1998). We do not have to invent new tools. At least in high-income countries, they are already there. National laws and initiatives as well as international conventions and action guides (Lean Lim 1996) are already in place. However, these tools are of little use if the topic is not taken seriously. What we need are new approaches and strategies that would encourage stakeholders to use these tools. In low-income countries, effective workplace health and safety regulations often do not exist, or if they do they are not enforced, especially in the informal sector. There is also reason to believe that in the climate of privatization and economic deregulation of the 1980s and 1990s, the reach and scope of such regulations diminished (Standing 1989).

The primary responsibility for taking measures that ensure employees' health and safety lies with employers, governments, and intergovernmental agencies. The importance of this has become even greater with growing evidence of the shift of so-called dirty industries to low-income countries as health, safety, and environmental regulations become stricter and better enforced in high-income countries.

The new challenge is to find ways in which the traditional divide among policymakers, experts, and those who are the subjects of policy and research can be reduced. "Participatory approaches" in occupational health research, where health and safety professionals collaborate with workers' representatives, were described (Loewenson et al. 1999). Workers in this radical approach are given an active role to ensure that the research being undertaken is relevant to their needs and interests.

Similarly, workers should be given a more active role in developing policies to promote healthier workplaces, and men and women should have an equal place in the process. There is a need to challenge the top-down tendency in policy and research in occupational health and pay more attention to the experiences and perceptions of women and men with different social backgrounds.

General tools and checklists to insert gender considerations into research, policy, and planning can be useful if carefully employed; however, they can also be too prescriptive and lack sensitivity to different national and local needs (Standing 1999). The focus should be on practical problem solving at the workplace and local capacity building involving workers of both sexes, employers, primary or occupational health service providers, and government officials. Negotiating the interests of different stakeholders with varying degrees of power is critical to ensure attention to measures that encourage equal treatment of women and men where they share common needs, as well as recognition that where their needs are different, these differences will be addressed in an equitable manner.

Conclusions

Women's increasing participation in the market economy worldwide has challenged the view of women's and men's socially and culturally determined roles and responsibilities. Occupational health research that traditionally conceptualized work as paid work undertaken by men, and accordingly focused on occupational health risks in male-dominated occupations, can no longer be justified.

However, efforts to include women in occupational health studies by trying to understand their work-related health using solely a structural framework for paid employment also proved not to be adequate. Women's work-related health cannot be understood without complementing the framework based on waged employment with other frameworks related to gender roles and women's work in the domestic sphere.

I have discussed the important role work plays in determining women's and men's position in the social hierarchy in society through the distribution of resources and power and thereby its influence on chances of good health. Strongly gender-segregated labor substantially contributes to the process by which women's inferior position in society, in both the domestic and public spheres, is produced and maintained. The negative consequences of a gender-segregated labor market cannot be observed only in relation to women's wages, career opportunities, working conditions, and health, but should also be viewed in relation to broader societal factors, such as labor market inefficiencies, economic growth, and social justice.

Scrutinizing the gender-segregated labor market is a fruitful starting point for identifying health-damaging and health-promoting factors in women's and men's working environments and understanding gender inequalities in occupational health.

The sphere of working life, in all its forms and domains, is probably the most important arena for action if our objective is to improve the health status of populations in general and to reduce socioeconomic and gender inequalities in health in particular.

Notes

1. I thank Lesley Doyal for her insightful advice on the first outline of this chapter. Furthermore, I express my deepest gratitude to my fellow coeditors, Gita Sen and Asha George, for constructive criticism and excellent editorial suggestions on several drafts.

2. It is important to note that income may be earned in the home through home-based outworking or subcontracting.

3. Gita Sen, personal communication.

4. Safety standards for household appliances contribute, however, to a safer work environment in homes.

4

Reproductive Health: Conceptual Mapping and Evidence[1]

Jane Cottingham and Cynthia Myntti

Although the term "reproductive health" is not new in scientific or activist circles, it emerged as a central concept at the International Conference on Population and Development (ICPD) held in Cairo, Egypt, in 1994 (Caldwell 1996; Cohen and Richards 1994; Dunlop et al. 1996; Hodgson and Cotts Watkins 1997; McIntosh and Finkle 1995; Sen et al. 1994). The Program of Action of the conference rejected coercive approaches to reducing population growth and argued that it is possible to stabilize population growth while meeting the reproductive health needs of women and men and respecting their rights in reproduction. Gender analysis played an important role in creating the ideals around reproductive health established at Cairo and is critical to understanding reproductive health and intervening to improve it.

Gender analysis examines the power relationship between men and women and its consequences on their lives. It questions how the social roles and identities they have been given, as boys and girls, men and women, and fathers and mothers, influence their sexual behavior and their health, including their sexual and reproductive health. Gender analysis further examines how the social system, from public policy and health services to private intimacy, incorporates inequalities of power between women and men. It enables us to examine how women's socially defined roles and relative powerlessness determine their exposure to risk, access to benefits of technology and health care, and realization of their rights. The process also helps us understand the effect on health of how boys are socialized, what cultures define as behavior appropriate to men, and how societies preferentially allocate resources and information to men.

The Evolving Field of Reproductive Health

The ICPD Program of Action contains an entire chapter on gender equality, equity, and empowerment of women. It states that empowerment and autonomy of women and improvement of their political, social, economic, and health status are important ends in themselves, but they are also essential for the long-term success of population programs (United Nations 1995). Whereas this attention by countries of the world to the main objective of feminism is remarkable, it is also quite clear that some confusion remains about what reproductive health means and what gender equality and equity and the empowerment of women have to do with it.

Since Cairo, reproductive health has been used in three ways in academic and development discourse: as a range of physical and psychological conditions, as a principle for organizing a set of health services, and as a paradigm for social change (WHO 1999a). As a spectrum of *conditions,* events, and processes through life, reproductive health integrates the physical and psychological dimensions of health that range from the positive to the negative. Most often, when we say "health" in public health, we mean its opposite: disease or other mental or physical disability. This emphasis on the negative is understandable, as intervening to prevent problems and alleviate suffering is the obvious and compelling response. Yet the discussions that took place around Cairo demanded a broader focus: on concepts of affection, tenderness, pleasure, self-determination, and equity in intimate relations. In other words the Cairo agenda challenged the public health community to incorporate the positive dimensions of health and sexuality, not just morbidity and mortality, into its basic delimitation of the field.

To give a sense of the complexity of reproductive health, it is worth noting that a large and varied list emerges, even when only taking into account biomedically based conditions leading to disability and death related to sexuality and reproduction. An exercise to estimate the burden of reproductive ill health globally (described in more detail below) used six definitions: consequences of sex in adults; consequences of sex in children and adults; conditions of the reproductive organ system; conditions managed through reproductive health services; burden of the reproductive age group; and health problems predominantly affecting the

reproductive age group (Murray and Lopez 1998). Not surprisingly, estimates vary considerably depending on which definition is used, with a
much higher number of estimated deaths using the fourth definition than
the others.

Reproductive health is also often equated with reproductive health *services*. Some effective health services are well defined and include family
planning, safe abortion, cervical cancer screening, skilled attendance in
pregnancy and childbirth, emergency obstetric interventions, and counseling about and prevention and treatment of sexually transmitted infections (STIs) for both women and men. The ICPD challenged programs
to integrate these services so that they are not focused on only one intervention. But it is still unclear what integration actually means. Does it
mean no separate services for adolescents? Is it just adding STI services
into family planning? Evidence to date suggests that different approaches
are probably required in different settings.

Yet to improve reproductive health, interventions other than health
services are also needed. Those that directly affect reproductive health
include laws or policies that, for example, prohibit sexuality education
for young people, restrict free and informed choices regarding fertility
regulation, and reduce public financing of family planning and maternity
care, which in turn affects both coverage and quality of those services
(Cook and Dickens 2000). In contrast, laws and policies that ensure adequate maternity (and paternity) leave, that promote the dissemination of
information about the availability of abortion services, and that recognize
a woman's autonomous power to make decisions about her own fertility
are likely to have a positive impact on reproductive health.

Interventions in other sectors indirectly affect reproductive health by
creating conditions for dignity and choices in daily life. These enabling
conditions include economic policies that maximize basic security and
minimize disparities between people, encourage girls to stay in school
and women to be treated fairly in employment, and support social movements such as zero tolerance for violence and others that push men and
women to question their gender roles (Schuler 1992).

Thus reproductive health, as used in the ICPD document, is also *a paradigm for social change*. It is an approach to analyzing and then responding comprehensively to the needs of women and men in their sexual

relationships and reproduction. This perspective challenges us to look at common approaches in new ways. Take, for instance, one commonly advocated approach to the prevention of HIV infection and AIDS: safe sex. For women to practice safe sex they must be able to refuse unwanted sex, use appropriate protection in wanted sex, and exert some influence over the behavior and risk taking of sexual partners (Dixon-Mueller 1993; Worth 1989). Obviously the social context of unequal gender relationships must be central to any plan to implement an intervention program around safe sex.

Reproductive health as a paradigm for social change addresses questions of rights, equity, and dignity. It demands moving beyond the biomedical model to examine health in its social context, for only when the social determinants, including gender, of health and ill health are understood can interventions be appropriately defined. Heise (1998) uses a similar approach to examining the social ecology of violence against women.

Mapping Reproductive Health

How does gender affect reproductive health? To examine the relationship among gender, power, and reproductive health, we must first map the field of reproductive health, making explicit our assumptions about those processes and events and identifying in a framework determinants and outcomes of interest (Myntti and Cottingham 1998).

The map of reproductive health proposed here consists of a basic framework of processes, events, and outcomes experienced by an individual through time (figure 4.1). This framework seeks to consider sexual and reproductive health outcomes that both men and women experience. In the spirit of the ICPD, it makes explicit reference to positive reproductive health processes and outcomes, not just negative ones. It also seeks to specify time, change, and movement over a life span, incorporating processes such as socialization. Laid over this framework are four levels of social institutions that set the stage for gender analysis in intimate and family relations, in community-level institutions, in the provision of services, and in the formulation of policies and laws directly and indirectly affecting reproductive health.

The Basic Framework

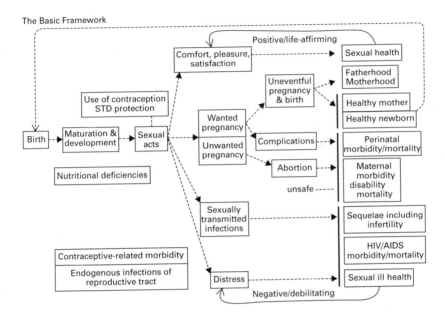

Figure 4.1
Mapping reproductive health.

The layers of our map may be summarized as follows:

The base

• The basic behavioral-biological-psychological framework: processes, events, and outcomes experienced by an individual through time

Social institutional levels

• Intimate and family relationships
• Communities and their institutions: schools, religious institutions, the media, and the market
• Health systems encompassing both preventive and curative services
• State institutions responsible for legislation and policies

Our map is complex because it contains multiple outcomes, some of which are also vaguely defined and poorly developed for measurement at this time. However, we do not want preoccupation with measurement to inhibit us from a fresh conceptualization of reproductive health. Defining indicators, addressing the technicalities of measurement, and creating and refining appropriate models for different contexts should follow our work.

The Basic Behavioral-Biological-Psychological Framework

The framework allows us to visualize an individual moving through time, developing physically and psychologically, engaging in behaviors that have an impact on reproductive health, and learning from that experience. We note the processes of physical and psychological maturation and development, important antecedents for sexual and reproductive health.

These processes encompass many different variances. Outcomes may be social (fatherhood), physical (morbidity and mortality), and psychological (comfort or distress). Psychological outcomes represent two ends of a spectrum of reactions rather than discrete conditions. In addition, some outcomes are also determinants. Pregnancy as an outcome of sexual acts, for instance, may itself determine a range of outcomes from motherhood to death. Sexual acts include all forms of sexual expression, only some of which carry the risks of pregnancy and STI. Contraceptive and gynecological morbidities may occur irrespective of sexual activity.

Social Institutional Levels

Level 1: The Individual in the Context of Intimate and Family Relationships   This is the first level of the social world surrounding an individual, and it has a profound influence on reproductive health. The young person receives his or her first education about identity, self-worth, and relationships from parents and other close relatives at home and grows into social networks and sexual relations (box 4.1).

Norms of interpersonal behavior are learned early. Family relationships themselves can offer good and bad models for children. For example, some research links the violent behavior of adult men to witnessing marital violence as a child, being abused oneself as a child, or having had an absent or rejecting father (Heise 1998). Sexual behavior in adulthood appears to be founded on fundamental values learned at home: of self-worth and respect for others, and understanding that actions have conse-

Box 4.1
Level one: the individual in intimate and familial relationships

Socialization
Role models
Respect for others
Responsibility for one's actions
Self-worth
Entitlements
Social networks
Relationships and their economic basis
Autonomy
Decision-making power
Physical mobility
Control over sexual acts; wanted or unwanted, protected or unprotected
Control of resources
Information
Money
Time
Social support

quences (SIECUS 1991). One reason that adolescence can be a particularly vulnerable time is because family structures and relationships may disempower young people from getting access to the information and services that they need to have safe sexual relationships that often begin in adolescence (WHO, UNPFA, and UNICEF 1997).

Sexual relationships also have a social and economic basis that determines the terms on which sex takes place. The power that women have in intimate relationships will help them determine whether sex is voluntary or not and whether it is protected from unwanted pregnancy and disease (Dixon-Mueller 1993). An economically dependent wife or girlfriend may have greater difficulty negotiating the terms of a sexual act than some sex workers, who may be in a position to reject one paying customer for another (Worth 1989). The power implicit in economic relationships also can lead young boys into exploitative situations with older men.

Some negative reproductive health outcomes, such as pregnancy-related mortality and morbidity, might be avoided if family resources were mobilized to cover costs of emergency care and transportation

Box 4.2
Level two: community institutions: schools, religious institutions, media, and the market

---

Norms and taboos around sexuality
Expectations surrounding personal relationships
Values
Information: ideas and facts

(Prevention of Maternal Mortality Network 1992; Thaddeus and Maine 1994). In every society, economically disadvantaged families may not have resources to spend on any family member. When an obstetric emergency occurs in an impoverished family, that family may have no option but to let the woman die at home. Women may lose out in the competition for scarce resources not only when they are experiencing an acute problem in pregnancy but throughout their lives from the food they eat, to the clothes they wear, to the resources at their disposal for their own health. This is the ultimate example of how gender and poverty work together to the detriment of women, with sometimes fatal consequences.

Level 2: Community Institutions: Schools, Religious Institutions, the Media, and the Market   A wide range of messages that shape both behavior and opportunities with consequences for reproductive health are transmitted through community-level institutions (box 4.2).

The meaning and value given to some of the outcomes in our framework, such as sexual health, sexual dysfunction, satisfaction, distress, motherhood and fatherhood, will always be strongly influenced by dominant cultural norms. Certain practices may be defined as taboo or desirable. The debate surrounding female genital mutilation is a clear example of a practice defined by some societies as desirable (Gruenbaum 1996).

Community norms create powerful ideals of masculinity and femininity and they define what sexual behavior is appropriate for men and for women. They condemn or condone sexual practices and relationships such as having multiple partners and sex outside marriage. That masculine sexuality incorporates elements of self-destructive risk, conquest, and even violence has profound implications for sexual relationships, reproductive health, and gender equality (Figueroa 1998).

The AIDS pandemic underscores the necessity of recognizing that publicly stated norms do not always determine private behavior. For instance, sex workers themselves are enmeshed in a web of intimate, family, and community relationships that privately condone and publicly condemn prostitution. Improvements in information, education, and counseling do not necessarily translate directly into behavior change. Sexual identities (heterosexual, homosexual, or bisexual) may not always correspond with sexual behavior (Parker 1993).

Community values also define how work roles are compensated and for whom the work is appropriate. This affects access to resources and information, which together are necessary for decision making. For instance, communities may or may not view adolescents' work as giving them rights to disposable income and access to services. Similarly, women frequently care for the terminally ill but this is not normally recognized by social services. These situations have broader implications for reproductive health both for the individuals involved and for their communities.

Level 3: Community Institutions: Preventive and Curative Services   An individual moving through time is likely to require health services at different points in his or her life. Some services only women need, since only they become pregnant and give birth. The priority, visibility, and level of resources given to these services say something about the value of women in a society (box 4.3). The services include emergency and other obstetric care, antenatal and postnatal care, abortion services, and repair of pregnancy-related problems such as fistulas and urinary incontinence (WHO 1994a).

But services that both men and women need also reveal how well women's specific needs are understood and addressed. They range from sexuality education to broadly defined sexual and reproductive health care, family planning, diagnosis and treatment of STIs, and care for persons living with AIDS. Do the services respond to specific needs and concerns of men and women and actively seek to empower them by giving them knowledge? Are there different assumptions on the part of service providers about what men and women need? The focus of public sector family planning programs on reducing women's fertility not only ignored the

Box 4.3
Level three: community institutions: preventive and curative services

---

Sexuality education
Adolescent health care
Family planning
Abortion services
Treatment for sexually transmitted infections
Antenatal care
Birthing and newborn care
Counseling for victims of abuse and perpetrators of violence
Infertility counseling and care
Care and repair of pregnancy related disabilities
Care for people living with HIV infection and AIDS

---

fact that men often play a key role in reproductive decision making, but did little to address men's needs in reproduction and sexuality (Greene and Biddlecom 1997; Hawkes 1998).

Level 4: Legislation and Policy: State Responsibility   Not all services required for reproductive health are related to health care provision. State institutions make laws and public policy that create an environment that either enables or constrains reproductive health at different times in life (box 4.4).

Two broad policy areas indirectly affect reproductive health. First are policies that define the economic security of each and every citizen. Certain economic policies create situations that pose substantial risks to reproductive health. For example, countries that follow the path of economic growth with inequality create, through increasing poverty and economic vulnerability, circumstances in which having a safe sex life is not an option for some people.

Second are policies that strengthen the position of women specifically. Policies that require girls to stay in school make it more possible for women to work in fairly compensated jobs and to control their own property. Policies that specifically enhance the economic basis on which women enter into relationships, including sexual relationships, ultimately influence their power to protect their own health (Sen and Batliwala 2000; Worth 1989).

Box 4.4
Level four: Legislation and policy: state responsibility

Directly affecting reproductive health
• Establishing and adequately funding sexuality education for young people
• Devoting resources and creating incentives to offer high-quality reproductive health services and sexual health care for men and women
• Ensuring that safe abortion services exist for all who need them
• Devoting resources to maternity care coverage and quality, including emergency obstetric care
• Prohibiting use of unnecessary birthing technologies
• Restricting use of technology for prenatal sex selection
• Establishing laws and creating programs to aid victims of rape, domestic abuse, prostitution, and sexual coercion
• Creating a legal and economic framework to eradicate female circumcision
• Establishing and enforcing laws prohibiting discrimination against persons with HIV infection and AIDS

Creating the context for reproductive health
• Laws that establish equal rights for women
• Establishing and enforcing laws on the education of girls
• Establishing and enforcing laws that give women the right to control property
• Establishing and enforcing laws that give women the right to wage equity
• Establishing and enforcing laws that establish age of consent for sexual relations
• Creating policies that support working mothers
• Creating policies that promote equity and economic security for all citizens
• Creating laws on child support from noncustodial parents

Many policies and laws directly affect reproductive health. In countries with strongly enforced demographic targets and population control policies, it may be difficult to respect reproductive rights and promote reproductive health. Providers eager to perform well in such a situation may not be able to follow ethical guidelines or respect the human rights of their clients.

The list of other policies directly related to reproductive health includes the legal status of female genital mutilation and adequacy of funding for addressing the problem, provision of services for young people, attention to the quality of care in reproductive health, legal status of abortion and sterilization, coverage and quality of pregnancy and perinatal care, and adequacy of funding for biomedical research on health problems that only women experience or on the way females experience communicable and noncommunicable diseases. Less obvious, although equally direct in their impact on reproductive health, would be public policies and laws on rape and domestic abuse, childcare provision for single and working mothers, the legal status of prostitution, professional guidelines, and policies on appropriate use of birthing technologies.

Gender and Reproductive Health: New Evidence

The map attempts to tease out some of the complexities of reproductive health and points to levels at which a gender analysis must be conducted. Presenting new evidence to elucidate the entire map is beyond the scope of this chapter. Instead we present evidence on a selection of these elements that are grouped into conditions, services, and approaches. Data are not intended to be exhaustive, but rather to highlight the way in which reproductive health is a gendered concept.

Reproductive Health Conditions and the GBD

In the international public health community, the approach that is currently being used to assess the extent of ill health, are the global burden of disease estimates (GBD) (Murray and Lopez 1998). These estimates assess the burden to the world's population from premature mortality and disability by using a combined measure, the disability-adjusted life year (DALY). Estimates are based on available epidemiological data, vital registration data and a complex calculation of disability involving estimates of average duration, age discounting and weighting according to the "value" of the disability.

For reproductive health, conditions included in the GBD exercise are

• Sexually transmitted infections

• Maternal mortality and morbidity directly related to pregnancy and childbirth (antepartum and postpartum hemorrhage, puerperal sepsis and other infections, hypertensive disorders of pregnancy, prolonged and obstructed labor, unsafe abortion, ectopic pregnancy)

• Conditions arising during the perinatal period (low birthweight, birth asphyxia)
• Congenital anomalies
• HIV infection and AIDS
• Unsafe sex as a risk factor

These conditions, although clearly covering some key issues, are far from presenting a complete picture of reproductive health conditions. Furthermore, the calculations take as their starting point the International Classification of Diseases (9th ed.), which means that many conditions such as fistula and incontinence, uterine prolapse, menstrual disorders, nonsexually transmitted reproductive tract infections (RTIs) are not included (AbouZahr and Vaughan 2000). Other conditions not captured at all are female genital mutilation, stillbirth, infertility, reproductive health consequences of sexual abuse and other violence against women, and mental health dimensions of reproductive health. The DALY methodology also excludes all indirect obstetric complications such as those related to malaria, anemia, hepatitis, diabetes, epilepsy, and cardiovascular disease (WHO 1998). These were estimated to contribute to at least 20% of all maternal deaths (WHO 1994a).

In terms of the map, one major missing piece is a measure to capture positive health aspects of reproductive health, or improvements in reproductive health such as those accruing from the benefits of avoiding unwanted pregnancy. This remains one of the challenges for the next decade.

An innovative and gender-sensitive way of looking at the burden of disease represented by reproductive ill health starts with unsafe sex as a risk factor (Berkley 1998). Acknowledging the risks related to pregnancy and childbirth and to STIs, it includes additional sexually transmitted infections such as hepatitis B and lack of access to contraceptives in those wanting to prevent pregnancy. It also points to homicide and violence related to unequal gender relations in sexuality but does not include it for lack of available data.

With this broader definition, calculations show that in 1990 unsafe sexual activity was estimated to have accounted for over 1 million deaths (2% of deaths worldwide) and close to 50 million lost DALYs or about

3.5% of global DALYs lost in that year (table 4.1). It is no surprise that the heaviest burdens occur in women, who account for 71% of the overall disease burden from unsafe sex. In women age fifteen to forty-four years globally 12% of deaths and 15% of DALYs lost are due to conditions related to unsafe sex. The highest proportion is in sub-Saharan Africa where it rises to 26% of deaths and 30% of DALYs lost. In India those percentages are 11% and 20%, respectively, and in Latin America and the Caribbean the figures are 9% and 14%, respectively (Berkley 1998).

The GBD estimates have other serious limitations. For example, the data are based mainly on hospital studies, thus giving little indication of incidence or prevalence of conditions in the population as a whole. However, they still indicate the extent of reproductive ill health at a global level, and they represent a substantial improvement on earlier attempts to quantify the problem (AbouZahr and Vaughan 2000). Reproductive ill health contributed a minimum of 5% to 15% of the GBD. Broken down by sex this becomes 22% for women of reproductive age (15–44 years) compared with only 3% for men (Murray and Lopez 1998).

Gendered Reproductive Health Conditions

The greatest burden of reproductive ill health arises from conditions that affect only women: those related to pregnancy and childbirth. The global burden from these conditions was estimated to be around 15% for women of reproductive age. WHO, UNICEF, and UNFPA estimate that in 1995, 515,000 women across the globe died from pregnancy-related causes (WHO, UNICEF, and UNFPA 2001). While it seems as though these number have decreased slightly from the previous estimates for 1990, the regional breakdown shows a decline only in countries of the Asia region, with figures for Latin America and the Caribbean remaining static, and those for sub-Saharan Africa increasing.

Globally it is estimated that 13% of maternal deaths are from unsafe abortion carried out either by persons lacking necessary skills or in an environment lacking minimal medical standards, or both, and that 20 million of the estimated 46 million abortions annually are unsafe (WHO 1997a). It is important to underline that up to 4.5 million of these abortions are estimated to be in adolescents. It is estimated that between 20% and 30% of unsafe abortion procedures result in reproductive tract infec-

Table 4.1
Percentages of total DALYs lost due to reproductive ill health in women and men age 15–44 years, 1990

| | Total DALYs lost (%) | | | | | | | | |
| | STIs excluding HIV | | HIV | | Maternal conditions | Reproductive tract cancers | | Totals | |
	Women	Men	Women	Men	Women	Women	Men	Women	Men
Established market economies	2.36	0.10	0.99	4.08	2.09	3.18	0.02	8.62	4.20
Former socialist economies	3.52	0.30	0.03	0.09	6.25	2.83	0.03	12.63	0.41
Sub-Saharan Africa	6.31	1.79	8.38	6.29	24.45	0.54	0.02	39.69	8.54
India	6.58	2.49	0.20	0.43	19.19	1.42	0.01	27.40	2.93
China	0.21	0.05	0.00	0.01	6.91	0.99	0.01	8.12	0.06
Other Asia, Pacific Islands	7.00	2.05	0.14	0.24	14.55	1.66	0.01	23.36	2.30
Middle East crescent	1.47	0.32	0.03	0.18	18.70	0.97	0.02	21.17	0.51
Latin America, Caribbean	3.97	0.60	1.06	3.63	9.64	2.14	0.02	16.80	4.25
World	4.23	1.09	1.78	2.02	14.47	1.42	0.01	21.90	3.12

Source: Abou Zahr, C. and P. Vaughan 2000. Assessing the burden & sexual reproductive ill-health. *Bulletin of the World Health Organization*, 78(5): 655–666.

tions, of which between 20% and 40% lead to pelvic inflammatory disease and infertility (WHO 1997a).

Large differences exist in the incidence of and mortality from abortion between regions. In most developing regions there are 20 or more unsafe abortions per 1,000 women of reproductive age. In Latin America and the Caribbean, the rate is as high as 40 unsafe abortions per 1,000 women of reproductive age, although actual mortality is proportionately lower than in other regions (AbouZahr and Ahman 1998).

The GBD calculations on STIs included only chlamydia, gonorrhea, and syphilis. However, a number of studies in different parts of the world showed that bacterial vaginosis is often the most frequent condition (Bhatia et al. 1997) and 1999 estimates of STI incidence among adults globally show that trichomoniasis accounts for 174 million cases in contrast to chlamydia (92 million), gonorrhea (62 million), and syphilis (12 million) (WHO 2001).

The sex differential in the data is very clear. In 1990 STIs accounted for 4.2% of DALYs lost in women and 1.1% lost in men age fifteen to forty-four (see table 4.1). If the definition of STIs is expanded to include HIV, human papilloma virus, and hepatitis B, the burden increases to 6.3% in women and 3.5% in men (Rowley and Berkley 1998). If other complications associated with these three STIs, such as ectopic pregnancy, are included, the burden for women would be even higher. This disease burden is greatest in the developing world and in sub-Saharan Africa in particular, where in 1990 STIs accounted for 6.3% of DALYs lost in women of reproductive age and 1.8% of DALYs lost in men of the same age (Rowley and Berkley 1998).

Why is it that women suffer from a greater burden of disease in this case than men? At the purely biological level, transmission of infections through sexual intercourse is more efficient from male to female than vice versa. This is partly because of prolonged exposure to organisms when infected ejaculate is retained in the vagina, particularly for pathogens that produce discharge or are present in genital secretions, such as gonococci, chlamydia, trichomonads, and HIV (Howson et al. 1996).

A closer look at the women and men who are getting infected reveals the gender dynamics of the situation. In Ethiopia, 88% of sex workers were infected with gonorrhea and 78% with chlamydia, which is perhaps not surprising. But for women who had only one husband and no other sex partners these percentages were as high as 40% for gonorrhea and 54% for chlamydia (Duncan et al. 1994). In Thailand, one of the few studies carried out on men's commercial sexual partnerships found that 50% of married men and 43% of single men had bought sex from women during the study period. The more a situation was unlike a brothel, the less likely men were to feel at personal risk of HIV infection and the less likely they were to use a condom, suggesting that men's perception of risk and their own contribution to transmitting STIs was seriously lacking (Maticka-Tyndale et al. 1997)

At a national level, data on HIV prevalence generally may be biased downward for women because the source of such data is often antenatal clinics. The most recent UNAIDS and WHO update on the HIV-AIDS epidemic indicates that "in many African countries antenatal estimates tend to underestimate the real levels of HIV infection in women" (UN-AIDS and WHO 1999). Results of fifteen studies of HIV prevalence in the general population conducted in various African countries show that infected women progressively become less fertile. The longer the infection progresses, the less likely they are to become pregnant. Because many HIV-infected women are no longer becoming pregnant, they are not showing up at antenatal clinics where blood samples for anonymous HIV testing are taken. Antenatal estimates thus fail to reflect the true extent of HIV infection in the female population as a whole.

On the other hand, population-based studies suggest that HIV infection levels in men are lower than those in pregnant women. Even though in the early stages of the epidemic more men than women tend to be infected, over time the male-female gap is closed and eventually the ratio is reversed. UNAIDS and WHO estimated that at the end of 1999, 12.2 million women and 10.1 million men age fifteen to forty-nine years were living with HIV in sub-Saharan Africa. The report points to the major role played by age differences in the women and men becoming infected. Women tend to become infected far younger than men, partly because girls tend to become sexually active younger than boys and partly because older men, those infected with HIV, tend to coerce girls into sex or buy their favors with "sugar-daddy" gifts. According to studies in several African populations, girls age fifteen to nineteen are five or six times more likely to be HIV-positive than boys their own age (UNAIDS and WHO 1999).

The picture differs in other regions of the world and in different groups of populations. It is worth noting that in eastern Europe and the central Asian region, where injection drug use is currently the principal risk factor for HIV infection, the prevalence of STIs has exploded, making a potentially lethal combination. This is especially true for sex workers who are also injection drug users (UNAIDS and WHO 1999).

A rapid overview of country-based studies gives an idea of the extent of some conditions that are traditionally neglected. The prevalence of urinary incontinence was measured in Turkey among women age eighteen to forty-four who were admitted to an outpatient clinic with various gynecological complaints. It was 25%, with the lowest prevalence in women age eighteen to twenty-four years and the highest in the those age forty to forty-four years. Eighty-five percent of incontinent women had never sought medical help (Turan et al. 1996). The much-cited population-based study in Giza, Egypt, found a 14% prevalence of urinary tract infection (UTI) in women age fourteen to sixty. Fifty-two percent of the women had at least one RTI, including 44% with vaginitis. The infections were also associated with uterine and vaginal prolapse, intrauterine devide use, sexual exposure, and poor personal hygiene (Khattab et al. 1999; Stewart 1994). Twenty-three percent of women in an Indonesian clinic were positive for at least one RTI or STD, 44% of whom tested positive for candidiasis (Cohen and Zazri 1997). Such findings indicate that RTIs and urinary incontinence are undoubtedly significant health problems for women.

Obstetric fistula is the result of prolonged or obstructed labor. It is a condition in which a hole forms in the wall between the vagina and bladder or rectum or both. Data on its prevalence are practically nonexistent. In 1991, WHO reviewed the literature and found scattered and uneven data showing, for example, a prevalence of obstetric fistula of 55 per 100,000 births in Ethiopia, 80 per 100,000 births in Nigeria, 4% of deliveries in Afghan refugees in Pakistan, and 16% of gynecological admissions to a hospital in Khartoum, Sudan (WHO 1991b).

Women who suffer fistula are almost always from poor, rural areas where health services are poor or nonexistent and where means of transport to appropriate services are terribly slow. The women are usually very young (50–80% under 20 years of age in some African studies) and are often primiparous. Most have a stillborn baby as a result of obstructed labor, which in itself is a source of great suffering. In addition, unless the fistula is surgically repaired, women are destined to live with continuous leaking urine and/or feces, causing UTIs, vaginitis, and excoriation of the vulva. This in turn leads to huge social consequences. These women are not allowed to handle food, cook, or pray, not allowed to get on a bus, or do any of the normal tasks and pleasures of daily living. Often they are cast out of their families and/or abandoned by their husbands (WHO 1991).

There are few data on reproductive health-related psychological conditions for either sex. Concerns about sexual performance, premature ejaculation, and inability to maintain an erection are reported to be among the most common psychosexual disorders in men in North America and western Europe, but there are almost no data from elsewhere on these subjects (Collumbien and Hawkes 2000). Slightly more is known about what appears to be quite a common problem for women: postpartum depression. Eighteen percent of women in China, for instance, suffered from this disorder (Yip et al. 1997), yet the full extent of it is not known. Clearly a huge amount of work remains to be done in this area simply to chart the full extent and severity of reproductive ill health both in women and in men.

Reproductive Health Services

The paradigm shift from population control to reproductive health proposed in Cairo in 1994 generated a huge quantity of literature on the importance of integrated reproductive health services that would address the unmet need for contraception, the need for good maternity care, and prevention and treatment of STIs. Even before Cairo, there was a growing call for greater emphasis on quality of care as one way of ensuring that women's rights are protected and gender-sensitive services promoted. At the same time, the stark reality of maternal mortality ratios pointed to the fact that many women in developing countries have no access to even essential and emergency obstetric care, let alone regular access to family planning and STI prevention and treatment services.

Indeed the ICPD +5 document set as its targets for the next five to ten years not reduction in maternal mortality as such (since it is expensive and difficult to measure and not very useful for tracking changes in the short and medium term), but rather the proportion of births assisted by skilled attendants (United Nations 1999). This includes antenatal care, clean and safe delivery whether the delivery takes place at home or in a health facility, and postpartum care for mother and infant (WHO 1997b).

The most recent estimates by WHO on coverage of maternity care show that in the developing world only 66% of women receive any antenatal care, less than 55% of deliveries are attended by skilled personnel, and only 40% of deliveries take place in health institutions. This implies that more than 45 million pregnant women annually do not receive antenatal care and almost 60 million births take place without a skilled attendant present. Between 90 and 100 million women (more than 70% of women in less developed regions) do not receive postpartum care (WHO 1997b). It is worth noting that, although the proportion of women who deliver with trained assistance increased in all regions of the world since 1985, the increase is small, 48% to 55%, for developing regions.

The three subregions with the lowest coverage of care in pregnancy and at delivery (34%) together account for almost half of all deliveries. These subregions, south central Asia with 30% of the world's births and western and eastern Africa with 15%, contribute heavily to the numbers of deliveries taking place without skilled attendance worldwide. However, subregions themselves are not homogeneous, hiding disparities among individual countries. Also these rather broad percentages do not take account of the content and quality of care, frequency of visits, or stage of pregnancy at which care began. Strikingly for most developing countries the proportion of women receiving antenatal care is distinctly higher than the proportion receiving care by skilled personnel at delivery (WHO 1997b).

Work developing indicators to measure whether progress is being made in improving women's reproductive health in this regard elaborated process indicators. These include questions such as are there enough facilities providing essential obstetric care? Are they well distributed? Are enough women using these facilities? Are the right women (those with obstetric complications) using these facilities? Are sufficient quantities of critical services being provided? Is the quality of the services adequate? Answers to these questions will provide new evidence of governments' achieving reproductive health for women in the future (Wardlaw and Maine 1999).

The concept of unmet need for contraception has been heavily criticized by feminists (Dixon-Mueller and Germain 1992) for ignoring the social context in which decisions about sexual relations, contraception, and childbearing take place. Unmet need as commonly used is also problematic for narrowly focusing on married women (rather than all women and also men) and not embracing such concerns as dissatisfaction with present contraceptive methods and inability to use an appropriate method (e.g., because of breastfeeding).

Some demographic and health surveys included samples of unmarried women and men. Data from these surveys indicate, at least in part, the extent to which family planning and reproductive health services are reaching those who need them. Globally, the proportion of married women who are not using contraception but who want to stop or delay childbearing (those with an unmet need) is estimated to be 24%. This translates into 29% for sub-Saharan Africa, 18% for Asia, and 20% for Latin America and the Caribbean. In surveys of unmarried women in 19 African countries, an average of 20% of single (never-in-union) and 31% of formerly married women were estimated to have a need for contraception. Indeed, substantial majorities of sexually active unmarried women in a survey of ten African and nine Latin American and Caribbean countries wished to avoid pregnancy, but were not using contraception (United Nations 1996), indicating a high level of need for contraceptive information and services.

It is worth noting that in all regions, uneducated women and rural women usually have the highest levels of unmet need for contraception (United Nations 1998). This underlines the fact that information and services are still not accessible to considerable proportions of populations. Unmet need for contraception remains a crude measure, but is a basis on which to examine gender roles further and reasons why people still do not have access to means to control their fertility.

To reinforce the point more dramatically, a review of country-based studies on abortion in selected developing countries revealed that between

6% and 33% of women admitted to hospital for abortion complications were under twenty years of age. Up to 98% of them had not used contraception at first intercourse, at the time of conception or at the time of the interview (Bott 2000). Most studies described how adolescents and young unmarried women lacked access to family planning services that generally target (or in some cases are legally restricted to) married adults, despite evidence of early sexual activity in all countries.

In Asia, Latin America, and Europe men's and women's reports of current contraceptive use are usually not far apart; in sub-Saharan African countries, however, men report substantially greater use of contraception. This appears to be mainly due to greater use by men of condoms (presumably outside marriage) and rhythm. In addition, men's ideal family size was larger than women's, and both men's education and extent of communication between partners had a great influence on contraceptive use (Ezeh et al. 1996). Closer examination of women's reasons for not using contraception showed that husband's disapproval was frequently mentioned, confirming the current view that men have to be included in information and education activities related to providing reproductive health services (Bongaarts and Bruce 1996). The most frequently cited reason for nonuse of contraception was fear of health effects. This too indicates a huge lacuna in information and support to women requiring contraception.

The Cairo agenda, however, was explicit about moving away from programs that focused only on reducing fertility through contraceptive use alone. Many developing countries, with the political and financial support of international agencies, installed vertical family planning programs. A reproductive health approach, however, seemed logically to lead to a call for integrating services in such a way that women's reproductive health needs would be addressed in a comprehensive fashion. At very minimum, it was argued, maternal health, family planning, and STI prevention and treatment should be brought together. How to achieve this integration, whether at the same location, on the same or different days, with a referral system, and with what personnel and resources, was the subject of intense debate and production of many guidelines generally based on little evidence.

A review of attempts to integrate STI management into family planning (FP) services highlighted a range of different experiences with this across the globe (Dehne and Snow 1999). The FP projects and programs that experimented with integrating of STI management into their services mostly emphasized prevention rather than care. This is partly because of the cost of laboratory diagnosis. Where preventive management of STIs was integrated, the quality of services and, in particular, providers' attitudes and communication skills improved.

In two experimental studies conducted in FP clinics in Thailand and Vietnam in 1994, twice as many women were satisfied with services where providers had been trained in STI prevention and case management compared with control services where no staff had been trained (Dehne and Snow 1999). This kind of integration also led to increased access and use of services in some countries, but this was due less, the authors suggest, to integration per se but rather to expanded coverage and outreach to men, youth, and other groups not previously the focus of FP services.

Evidence also suggests that integration of STI prevention elements may have enhanced FP objectives more than STI objectives. Documented experience and empirical evidence of public health benefits of integrated STI and FP services are extremely limited, and without this kind of evidence appropriate and effective integration strategies cannot be defined or evaluated (Dehne and Snow 1999).

Quality of services is also a major contributor to people's use or nonuse of reproductive health services, and is believed to influence reproductive health outcomes. In Lebanon, 88% of the births take place in hospitals where many practices and procedures conform neither to women's preferences nor to evidence-based best practices (Kabakian-Khasholian et al. 2000). A review of evidence concerning maternal deaths attributable to service-related factors at various levels of the referral system suggests that a substantial percentage of maternal deaths in over thirteen countries is due to inadequate supplies and equipment or poor client management (Ravindran 1992).

A number of studies even before the Cairo conference revealed an association between quality of care and contraceptive adoption, use, or continuation at the individual level (WHO 2001). Indeed, the quality of care framework was elaborated first for FP services, but was since extended to other aspects of reproductive health. Probably the most important aspects

from a gender perspective are dimensions related to client-provider interaction. Since women use reproductive health services so much more than
men, and since much of reproductive health is still surrounded by myths
and moralistic attitudes about what women should and should not do in
the area of sexuality and reproduction, they often have to confront negative or judgmental attitudes on the part of providers (Gready et al. 1997).
This is particularly true of abortion services, where privacy and confidentiality are highly prized by clients (Gupte et al. 1999).

Reproductive Health as a Framework for Social Change

Perhaps more than any other area of health and illness, reproductive
health is heavily influenced by laws and policies, both those that directly
affect reproductive health such as those related to the provision of safe
abortion, sexuality education for young people, or prohibiting discrimination against persons with HIV infection and AIDS and those that indirectly have an impact. As our map describes, the latter include laws on
the education of girls, those that give women the right to control property
or to have wage equity, and those that establish and enforce an age of
consent for sexual relations.

It has been shown repeatedly that restrictive laws on abortion are a major contributor to maternal mortality from unsafe abortion (Royston and
Armstrong 1989). Most unsafe abortions occur in the developing world
where only a few countries have liberalized their laws since the 1980s and
1990s. However, it must be stressed that laws by themselves, without active and clear policies and regulations for implementation, are a necessary
but not a sufficient condition (Alan Guttmacher Institute 1999). India and
Zambia, where abortion is not against the law, continue to show high
abortion mortality statistics because of many obstacles to putting the law
into practice, including lack of training for providers, failure to authorize
providers and facilities, and lack of resources for and commitment to delivering good services at the primary health care level (Berer 2000).

In South Africa, on the other hand, where a liberal abortion law was
enacted in 1996, huge efforts have been invested in training providers
and ensuring that both they and the general population have information
about the law and women's rights. Even when the law is more restrictive,
most countries allow abortion to save the mother's life and many allow

it for cases of rape and incest and fetal impairment (only three countries, Chile, El Salvador, and Malta, have an absolute prohibition on abortion). Yet many women in these countries do not have access to safe services because of complicated administrative or judicial regulations, untrained providers, or simply lack of information about their rights. The ICPD +5 enjoins governments to train and equip health service providers to offer safe abortions where this is not against the law. An enormous amount of work remain to be done to make this a reality.

Policies that help women, especially poor women, obtain greater access to health services will be in line with the reproductive health approach. It is perhaps not surprising that South Africa again is an example where such a policy was put into place. Because of the extraordinary social change that took place after the abolition of apartheid and the move to democracy, and because of a strong women's health movement, South Africa made bold moves to develop a health sector through policies that are, among other things, sensitive to women's needs (Fonn et al. 1998). Among big changes made was lifting of user fees for basic health services. Examination of the impact of this policy on maternal health services shows an increase in use of existing antenatal and pediatric services, but it does not appear to have influenced the number of deliveries within facilities (Schneider and Gilson 1999). More studies of this kind are required to help identify what does and does not work to improve women's health through greater access to services.

As a result of agreements in ICPD, reproductive rights are classified as an integral part of human rights and therefore subject to international law. Thanks to the efforts of a handful of feminist international human rights lawyers and public health specialists, the body of international law on reproductive and sexual health and rights is growing, reflected in the review and closing comments of the various human rights committees that oversee and monitor the application by countries of the human rights covenants. (Two examples are the International Covenant on Civil and Political Rights, which contains an article on the right to life, and the Covenant on Economic, Social and Cultural Rights, which contains the right to health.)

Thus the Human Rights Committee, which monitors implementation of the Civil and Political Covenant, ruled in 1996 that the Peruvian government's criminal law subjected women to inhumane treatment because it allows criminal prosecution of women who have abortions (Cook 1997). The Committee concluded that "abortion gives rise to a criminal penalty even if a woman is pregnant as a result of rape and that clandestine abortions are the main cause of maternal mortality" (UNHCR 1996). Bringing into law issues related to services that only women need (and therefore if not provided can be classified as discrimination against women) is an extraordinary step forward in bringing gender equity into reproductive health. As with all of the evidence reviewed here, a huge amount of work is yet to be done, but the foundation blocks are being relentlessly put into place.

The concept of reproductive health was born out of a profound and desperate need on the part of women to change the population control approach of development thinkers and actors of the 1960s and 1970s. Population control meant looking at women only as breeders of too many children and constructing programs that would curb their fertility by whatever means available. As a counter-concept reproductive health essentially requires social change. By linking the different aspects of women's and men's lives, their sexuality and their ability or inability to have children, their sexual roles and the power inherent in them, reproductive health demands that we examine the very fabric of society, of social as well as sexual intercourse. Over two decades or so at the international level, the concept has driven change in the discourse about, for instance, adolescents' sexuality, abortion, and gender roles and power in sexual relations. What was earlier seen as relegated to the private sphere became the subject of public debate and, most importantly, an area where women's human rights were recognized.

Policy Conclusions and Recommendations

Gender analysis played a critical role in creating the ideals around reproductive health, but so too must it be an integral part of defining interventions to improve reproductive health worldwide. Reproductive health demands moving beyond the biomedical model to examine health in its social context, for only when the social determinants, *including gender,* of health and ill health are understood can interventions be appropriately defined. Central to that analysis are questions of rights, equity, and dignity. Specifically, recommendations can be made in three areas:

1. **Evidence:** a huge amount of work still must be done to define and then map out the extent of disability and death due to many conditions related to reproductive ill health. The consequences, physical, psychological, social, and economic, of these conditions have to be analyzed for gender differences and integrated into the DALY or other methodologies used to estimate extent of burden of disease and needs for interventions.

2. **Services:** health care must be analyzed in terms of whether it reinforces or weakens gender stereotypes and whether it perpetuates inequalities or promotes equity, and whether it encourages or discourages the exercise of rights (Matamala 1998). This can be done in whatever way services are integrated, and even if they are not. The development and refinement of useable indicators to measure these dimensions would be a major step forward.

3. **Policies and laws:** laws that support reproductive health and rights must be promoted, promulgated, and put into place, and must be shored up with policies that make them meaningful in practice. Apart from the more obvious laws that help populations fulfill their right to the highest attainable standard of health, or their right to the benefits of scientific progress, others related to protecting the right to nondiscrimination (in employment, education, marriage, access to health services) and the right to information and education (especially for adolescents) must be systematically put in place (Cook and Dickens 2000).

Note

1. The views expressed in this paper are those of the authors and do not necessarily reflect the position of the World Health Organization.

5

Violence Against Women: Consolidating a Public Health Agenda[1]

Claudia García-Moreno

. . . women will not be free from violence until there is equality, and equality cannot be achieved until the violence and the threat of violence is eliminated from women's lives.
—Canadian Panel on Violence Against Women (1993)

Violence is widespread and is a growing problem. It takes many forms and occurs in all settings: at work, in the home, in the streets, and the community at large. It affects both males and females of all ages, particularly young people. However, there are important differences in the forms and consequences of violence that women and men experience. Most violence is perpetrated by men, whatever the sex and age of the victim. Most significant, females experience violence primarily at the hands of men they know and within the so-called safe haven of home and family. The response of society to different forms of violence also differs. Whereas street violence is recognized as a crime and state intervention is seen as legitimate, most governments are hesitant when it comes to taking action and legislating on violence against women by their intimate partners. Because it happens in what is considered the private sphere of the home, this kind of violence is harder to document and to prevent, and easier to ignore.

Twenty years of activism on violence against women by women's organizations is slowly changing this. In particular the end of the twenty-first century saw growing recognition of such violence as a legitimate concern. It is now part of the international agenda: initially as a women's human rights issue at the World Conference on Human Rights in Vienna in 1993, as it related to sexual and reproductive health at the International

Conference on Population and Development in Cairo in 1994, and as a critical area requiring a whole chapter in the Platform for Action of the Fourth World Conference on Women in Beijing in 1995. In addition, international organizations such as the World Bank (Heise et al. 1994), World Health Organization (WHO 1996c, 1997), and United Nations Population Fund (UNFPA) among others have taken it up as a public health issue.

Violence against women is a complex and multidimensional problem. Factors at individual, household, and societal levels put women at risk or, alternatively, may help to reduce the risk. This violence is embedded within social and cultural norms that perpetuate inequality between women and men, and condone or even encourage discrimination against women, including chastisement of women by men. Domestic violence in particular is the epitome of unequal power relationships between women and men. This is why it has also been called gender-based violence.

Violence against women or gender-based violence can take many forms. It includes domestic violence by intimate partners; forced sex and other forms of sexual violence; trafficking of women; and forms of violence linked to traditions that are specific to certain countries, such as dowry-related deaths, female genital mutilation, and murder of women by their relatives in the name of family honor (honor killings). It can happen in different locations and situations, such as in the home, in custodial situations (prisons, police), in the community, perpetrated by the state, and in situations of armed conflict, refugees, and displacement.

All of these forms of violence are associated with power inequalities between women and men, between children and their caregivers, as well as growing economic inequalities both within and between countries. Domestic or partner violence and sexual violence are the most common and universal forms, and are the focus of this chapter.[2]

Definition

There is no universally accepted definition of violence against women. Some argue for a broad definition that includes any act or omission that causes harm to women or keeps them in a subordinate position. This would include what is sometimes referred to as structural violence, such as poverty and unequal access to health services and education. The benefit of a broad definition is that it places gender-based violence in a wider social context (Richters 1994) and allows interested parties to bring attention to most breaches of women's human rights under the rubric of violence against women.

The drawback is that by creating far-reaching meanings, a definition's descriptive power is lost. An expert consultation in WHO agreed that issues of structural violence would be dealt with best under discrimination (WHO 1996c). The definition in the United Nations Declaration on the Elimination of Violence Against Women, adopted by the General Assembly in 1993, is "Any act of gender-based violence that results in, or is likely to result in, physical, sexual or mental harm or suffering to women, including threats of such acts, coercion or arbitrary deprivation of liberty, whether occurring in public or in private life" (United Nations 1993). It provides a useful conceptual and advocacy framework, but more specific operational definitions are necessary for research, surveillance, and monitoring.

The cross-cultural applicability of definitions is one issue that arises in the context of international studies and cross-country comparisons. Anthropologists and women's health advocates have highlighted the difficulties of creating international classifications, as concepts of what constitutes violence against women vary profoundly across cultures. Because universal classification systems cannot fully account for this variance, they must be used with caution (WHO 1996c). All societies have forms of violence that are tolerated or at times even encouraged by norms and customs. However, whether socially condoned or not, these acts as well as their effects on women's health and lives, must be recorded. Addressing only culturally unacceptable forms of violence fails to meet the spectrum of women's needs.

Researchers partially overcome this issue by focusing on the measurement of specific behaviors or acts and their effects on women's physical, sexual and emotional well-being. Specific instruments such as the conflict tactics scale (CTS; Straus et al. 1996) were developed along this vein, and a modified version of the CTS in particular, is increasingly used for research in developing countries. The CTS has been criticized for, among other things, failing to address the context in which violence occurs

(Dobash and Dobash 1992; Johnson 1998). Other methodologies are being developed that build on some elements of the CTS but also capture power and control dynamics and other contextual issues (WHO 1999e).

Magnitude of the Problem

A 1994 World Bank discussion paper provided the first global overview of the magnitude of the problem and its health consequences (Heise et al. 1994). Since then, growing numbers of studies from both developing and developed countries documented the prevalence of intimate partner violence (tables 5.1 and 5.2).

It should be noted that these studies, while internally consistent, have different definitions of violence and different methodologies, sampling frames, and time frames (e.g., lifetime prevalence vs. last year). This makes it difficult to compare figures across studies and countries. Taken together, however, data indicate that violence against women by partners is significant and occurs worldwide. Review of a selected number of well-designed, population-based surveys indicates that from 10% to over 50% of women report having been abused physically by a male partner at least once in their lives (WHO 1997f; Heise et al. 1999). Studies on intimate partner violence from diverse countries such as Nicaragua, Zimbabwe, Canada, and United States show substantial overlap among physical, sexual, and emotional violence (Ratner 1993; Ellsberg 1997; Watts et al. 1997).

Data on sexual abuse are even more difficult to come by, yet evidence suggests that forced sex, including rape, is a common occurrence for women. A 1998 Commonwealth Fund Survey on Women's Health in the United States found that one (21%) of five women surveyed reported they had been a victim of rape or assault (Scott-Collins et al. 1999). Here again enormous variations in definitions of rape and sexual abuse make it impossible to compare figures. Rates vary enormously depending on whether the definition of sexual abuse includes physical contact only or also noncontact. For example, in many countries the legal definition of rape only includes penis-vagina penetration and does not count other forms of forced sex.[3] In addition, different forms of coerced sex vary from culture to culture. Keeping these caveats in mind, it was estimated that one in five women worldwide has been forced to have sex against her will (WHO 1997f).

Sexual abuse during childhood also appears to be far more common than previously thought. A study in Barbados of a nationally representative sample of women and men age twenty to forty-five years found that 33% of women and 2% of men reported behavior constituting sexual abuse during childhood or adolescence (Handwerker 1993). A study in Geneva, Switzerland, found that 20% of women and 3% of men age thirteen to seventeen had experienced sexual assault involving physical contact (Halperin et al. 1996).

Several studies also document the extent to which the first sexual experience is unwanted or even forced. For example, in a national HIV-AIDS survey conducted in Central African Republic between September and December 1989, nearly 22% of female respondents reported that their first experience with intercourse was "rape" (Chapko et al. 1999). Thirty percent of teenage mothers attending an antenatal clinic in Cape Town, South Africa (mean age 16.3 years) reported that their first intercourse was forced and 11% said they had been raped (Wood et al. 1998).

The situation may be even more extreme during armed conflict, when mass movements, general insecurity, and the presence of firearms may contribute to increase in violence, including rape and sexual assault, particularly, but not only, of women (Swiss and Giller 1993). This was documented in intranational ethnic wars in Rwanda and the former Yugoslavia, where rape was used systematically as a means of destroying the fabric of society (Human Rights Watch 2000; Degni-Segui 1996). This increased risk of violence is likely to persist after the conflict is over, fueled by the presence of weapons. Accompanying the problem of conflict-related violence is underlying domestic violence, which many of these women also experience. Some suggest that domestic violence may increase during or after a conflict, but this is difficult to document given lack of baseline information about domestic violence in most settings.

There are almost no reliable estimates of other forms of violence against women such as forced prostitution and trafficking for sex. However, anecdotal evidence suggests that this may be growing, particularly in parts of Asia and newly independent states in Eastern and Central Europe (UNICEF 1999b). Trafficking of women and children for sex and

Table 5.1
Prevalence of physical violence against women by an intimate male partner (WHO violence against women database 2000)

Country	Coverage	Year of study	Sample size	% Adult women physically assaulted by an intimate male partner		
				In past 12 months	In current relationship	Ever
Australia (Mazza et al. 1996)	Metro Melbourne	1993–1994	1,494[a]	22.4[b]		
Bangladesh (Schuler et al. 1996)	National (villages)	1992	1,225	19.0		47.0
Canada (Rodgers 1994)	National	1993	12,300	3.0		29.0[f]
Chile (Larrain 1993)	Metro Santiago, Santiago province	1993[c]	1,000		26.0	
Colombia (DHS 1995a)	National	1995	6,097[d]			19.3
Egypt (DHS 1995b)	National	1995–1996	7,121			34.4
India (INCLEN 2000)	National (7 sites in nothern, central, and southern India)	1998–1999	9,938			45.0
Kenya (Raikes 1990)	Kisii district	1985–1986	612		42.0	
Korea, Republic of (Kim & Cho 1992)	National	1989	707	37.5[b]		
Mexico (Ramirez Rodriguez et al. 1996)	Metro Guadalajara	1996	650	15.0		27.0
Netherlands (Römkens 1997)	National	1986	1,016			20.8
Nicaragua (Ellsberg 1997)	Leon	1993	360	27.0[b]		52.2[b]
Papua New Guinea (Bradley 1988)	National, rural (villages)	1982	628			67.0
Paraguay (DHS 1996)	National, except Chaco region	1995–1996	6,465[d]			9.5
Philippines (DHS 1994)	National	1993	8,481			5.1

Puerto Rico (DHS 1998)	National	1995–1996	7,079[d]			12.8[e]
Rwanda (Van der Straten et al. 1994)	Kigali	1990	874[a]	21.0		26.8[b]
South Africa (Jewkes et al. 1999)	Eastern cape	1998	403	10.9		28.4[b]
South Africa (Jewkes et al. 1999)	Mpumalanga	1998	428	11.9		19.1[b]
South Africa (Jewkes et al. 1999)	Northern province	1998	475	4.5		
Switzerland (Gillioz et al. 1997)	National	1994–1996	1,500	6.3		12.6
Thailand (Hoffman et al. 1994)	Bangkok	1994	619		20.0	
Uganda (Blanc et al. 1996)	Lira, Masaka districts	1995–1996	1,660		40.5	
United Kingdom (Mooney 1993)	North London	1993[c]	430[d]	12.0		30.0
United States of America (U.S. Dept. of Justice, 1998a)	National	1998	8,000[d]	1.3		22.1
West Bank, Gaza Strip (Haj-Yahia 1998)	National (Palestinians)	1994	2,410	52.0[b]		
Ukraine (DHS 2000)	National	1999	5,589	21.1		7.9

WHO did not participate directly in collecting any of the data, but compiled it from existing studies. Comparisons must be made with caution because of between-study differences in definitions, sample sizes, data collection approaches, and cultural factors.

[a] Respondents were recruited from women visiting medical practitioners' offices or health care centers.
[b] Definition of physical violence includes throwing and/or breaking objects while arguing.
[c] The year of publication is listed because the paper did not state field work dates.
[d] Sample included women who had never been in a relationship and therefore were not in exposed group.
[e] Statistic was recalculated by WHO from raw data.
[f] Includes physical or sexual contact.

Table 5.2
Prevalence of sexual violence against women by an intimate male partner (WHO violence against women database 2000)

| | | | | % Adult women sexually victimized by an intimate male partner | | | | | |
| | | | | In the past 12 months | | | Ever | | |
Country	Coverage	Year of study	Sample size	Sexual assault	Attempted/ completed forced sex	Completed forced sex	Sexual assault	Attempted/ completed forced sex	Completed forced sex
Canada (Rodgers 1994)	National	1993	12,300				8.0		
Canada (Randall & Haskell 1995)	Toronto	1991–1992	420					15.3[b]	
Chile (Morrison & Orlando 1997)	Santiago	1997	310		9.1				
India (Narayana 1996)	Uttar Pradesh	1996	6,926						28.0[d]
Mexico (Ramirez Rodriguez et al. 1996)	Metro Guadalajara	1996	650	15.0			23.0		
Nicaragua (Ellsberg 1997)	Leon	1993	360					21.7	
Puerto Rico (DHS 1998)	National	1993–1996	7,079						5.7[b]
Rwanda (Van der Straten et al. 1994)	Kigali	1990	874		33.0[a]				

Switzerland (Gillioz 1997)	National	1994–1996	1,500			11.7
United Kingdom (Mooney 1993)	North London	1993[c]	430	6.0[b]		23.0[b]
United States (U.S. Dept. of Justice 1998a)	National	1995	8,000		0.2	7.7[b]
United States of America (McFarlane et al. 1991)	Houston, SE Texas	1991[c]	300			14.7[a,b]
West Bank, Gaza Strip (Haj-Yahia 1998)	National (Palestinians)	1995	2,410	37.6	27.0	
Zimbabwe (Watts et al. 1997)	One province	1996	885			25.0

WHO did not participate directly in collecting any of the data, but compiled it from existing studies. Comparisons must be made with caution because of between-study differences in definitions, sample sizes, data-collection approaches, and cultural factors.

[a] Respondents were recruited from women visiting medical practitioners' offices or health care centers.

[b] Sample included women who had never been in a relationship and therefore were not in exposed group.

[c] Year of publication was used because field work dates were not given in the original study.

[d] Sample was married men reporting on violence against their wives in their current marriage.

the growth of sex tourism is fueled by growing disparities in wealth both within and among countries. In some countries the poorest families may have to sell their daughters to ensure survival of the rest of the family. This is yet another example of the link among violence, poverty, and social inequity.

Health Consequences of Violence Against Women

Health Problem or Risk Factor?

The consequences of violence against women are far reaching. They affect the woman herself and her children, as well as the rest of society. Violence affects all aspects of women's lives, their health, productivity, and ability to care for themselves and their families. It undermines women's sense of self-worth, their sense of autonomy, and their ability to feel and act independently. It also increases their risk for a wide range of negative health outcomes and premature death.

The biomedical model constrains these wide and long-ranging effects by classifying violence as intentional injury. When developing a system for conceptualizing causes and consequences of violence, it is important to understand the similarities and differences in the form, nature, and patterns of violence that are experienced by women, men, boys, and girls.

Men generally experience physical violence from other men (strangers or acquaintances), mainly outside the family context. Physical injury and death are common. In contrast, most violence experienced by women and girls is from men they know, often in the family or home. It may have physical, sexual, and psychological dimensions, may continue for years, and may escalate in severity over time. Physical injury is frequently not the primary outcome, and may not even occur. However, many other important negative health consequences may arise, including sexually transmitted infections (STIs), unwanted pregnancy, depression and other mental health problems, gastrointestinal disorders, and various psychosomatic problems. Furthermore, although there has been little study of co-morbidity in abused women, these problems often coexist (Astbury 1999).

Whereas physical injury may serve as a reasonable, even if limited, proxy for violence among men, it does not provide a broad enough framework to describe and understand many other common forms of violence, such as child abuse, domestic and sexual violence against women, and abuse of the elderly. It is clearly important to recognize violence as a cause of injury, but this focus limits the understanding of the many forms that occur and their many health consequences. The focus on injury may also inadvertently contribute to minimizing the impact of violence on women's health and lives. The profound consequences on women's mental health, for example, are frequently ignored. Yet documentation increasingly shows a strong association between a history of domestic abuse and psychiatric problems, particularly depression, anxiety, and post-traumatic stress disorder (Campbell 1985; Koss 1990).

Furthermore, this focus may distort the response. For example, in some countries, whether or not an act of violence is considered criminal and the victim has legal recourse often depends on the type and severity of physical injury. Research in Nicaragua documented that men learned to modify their behavior to fit the law by, for example, giving blows where they will not show (Ellsberg 1997). The law was subsequently changed and psychological "injury" is now included.

Violence against women is best conceptualized as a risk factor for ill health. This enables better understanding of the many health consequences, interaction and synergies among them, and potential benefits of different forms of prevention and response. It also points to various possible channels in the health system through which to identify women in need of help; not only in accident and emergency departments, but, for example, in psychiatric services, antenatal care services, and clinics for STIs.

Ill Health and Death

Violence against women, particularly domestic violence and sexual abuse, is associated with injuries (ranging from cuts and bruises to permanent disabilities such as loss of hearing), STIs, HIV infection and AIDS, unwanted pregnancy, gynecological problems, chronic pelvic pain and pelvic inflammatory disease, hypertension, depression, anxiety disorders, post-traumatic stress disorder, irritable bowel syndrome, and various psychosomatic manifestations (figure 5.1; Heise 1993; Heise et al. 1994, 1999; Grisso et al. 1996; Drossman et al. 1995; Resnick et al. 1997;

Figure 5.1
Health consequences of violence against women.

Sutherland et al. 1998). Forced sex, whether by a partner or a stranger, can lead directly to an unwanted pregnancy or STI. Violence and fear of violence can indirectly affect sexual and reproductive health, as they affect women's ability to negotiate safe sex, including use of condoms and contraception (Spitz 2000). Data for the United States shows that an estimated 32,101 pregnancies are the result of rape each year, most of them among adolescents. Fifty percent of these women had abortions and 5.9% placed the infant for adoption (Holmes et al. 1996).

Violence during pregnancy has effects on the woman and her fetus. A review of studies from the United States reported a prevalence rate of violence during pregnancy between 4% and 8.3% (Gazmararian et al. 1996). This violence has been associated with miscarriage, stillbirth, preterm labor and birth, fetal injury, and death (McFarlane et al. 1996), as well as low birth-weight (LBW.) For example, rates of LBW increased by 12% among battered women compared with 6% for nonbattered women, even after controlling for variables such as smoking, alcohol consumption, prenatal care, and maternal complications (Bullock and McFarlane 1989). Similar associations with LBW and infant and child mortality were found in Nicaragua (Momeni et al. 1999) and in India (Jeejeebhoy 1998).

A growing body of literature cites the association between violence and mental ill health, particularly depression, anxiety disorders, and posttraumatic stress disorder (Koss and Heslet 1992; Koss 1994; Resnick et al. 1997; Campbell et al. 1996; Astbury 1999; Ellsberg et al. 1999). A history of child sexual abuse is also associated with increased rates of depression and anxiety, as well as with increased rates of victimization later in life (Finkhelor et al. 1990; Mullen et al. 1988). For many women who are chronically beaten or sexually assaulted, the emotional and physical strain can lead to suicide, as shown by research in the United States, Nicaragua, and Sweden (Abbott and Johnson 1995; Bailey et al. 1997; Kaslow and Thompson 1998; Bergman et al. 1991; Rosales and Loaiza 1999). Such deaths are dramatic testimony of the limited options for some women in a violent relationship.

Death from violence is more common among men than women. For example, in the Americas external causes are responsible for 51.7% of male deaths and 24.5% of female deaths. For men, the main external cause of death is homicide, accounting for 39.5%, and for women, murder was the second external cause of death, accounting for 23.2% (PAHO 1998). Worldwide, in 1998, interpersonal violence ranked third as a cause of death in males age 15 to 44, and tenth for females of the same age (WHO 1999g).

Murder of women is associated with a history of partner violence. A high proportion of women are killed by people known to them, particularly partners and expartners (U.S. Dept. of Justice 1988; Crawford 1991; Diniz and d'Oliveira 1998). In the United States during 1992, 5,373 women died as a result of homicide, 6 of every 10 murdered by someone they knew; about half by a spouse or someone with whom they had been intimate (Saltzman and Johnson 1996). Between 1976 and 1996, for persons murdered by intimates, the number of male victims fell an average 5% per year, while the number of female victims went down an average 1% (U.S. Dept. of Justice 1998b).

Use of Health Services

An association between victimization and use of health care services is documented in industrialized countries. One study of a major health maintenance organization in the United States found that a history of rape and/ or assault was a stronger predictor of physician visits and outpatient costs than any other variable, including a woman's age or other health risks such as smoking. Women who had been victimized sought medical attention twice as often as nonvictimized women in the study year, which was not the year the woman was victimized. Medical care costs of women who were raped or assaulted were 2.5 times higher than those of nonvictims after controlling for confounding factors (Koss et al. 1991).

There are few data from developing countries on this. Women in these countries often seek help for the violence from informal sources such as neighbors and family, rather than the formal sector, including health care. However, they may still use health services for a range of violence-related health problems, such as depression, although the root cause of this remains undetected.

The numerous consequences of domestic violence are of relevance to health equity as they increase the need for health care, although women may have difficulty accessing care. According to the 1998 Commonwealth Fund survey on women's health in the United States, women who experienced violence or abuse appeared to have greater difficulty accessing health care than other women (Scott-Collins et al. 1999). More than one-third reported not receiving necessary care at least once. Furthermore, they may not be treated or may receive inappropriate treatment. In Switzerland, abused women were two times more likely to take tranquilizers, antidepressants, and sleeping pills than nonabused women (Gillioz et al. 1997).

Consequences of Domestic Violence Against Women for Children

Violence against women by an intimate partner affects children, whether they only witness the abuse or are themselves abused. Child abuse and partner violence are estimated to overlap in 40% to 60% of cases (Shipman et al. 1999; Edleson 1999). Consequences include child behavioral problems, school problems, including dropping out, and lack of positive peer relations (Jaffe et al. 1990).

Fifty-five percent of a sample of children residing in shelters were characterized as withdrawn and 10% as having made suicidal gestures (Jaffe et al. 1990). Other reports refer to a high degree of anxiety, with children biting fingernails, pulling their hair, and having somatic complaints of headaches and "tight" stomachs. In addition, children who witnessed higher frequencies and severity of abuse against women in the home performed significantly less well on a measure of interpersonal sensitivity (ability to understand social situations and thoughts and feelings of persons involved) than those exposed to less frequent and intense abuse (Jaffe et al. 1990). This in turn is associated with high-risk behaviors such as unsafe sex in later life.

Childhood sexual abuse is associated with low self-esteem, inability to say no to unwanted sexual relations, and other self-destructive behaviors including alcohol and drug abuse (Zierler et al. 1991; Wingwood and DiClemente 1997). It is also strongly associated with depression and anxiety disorders (Finkelhor et al. 1990; Mullen et al. 1988). In Barbados, sexual abuse was the most important determinant of high-risk sexual behavior. After controlling for seventeen possible confounding variables identified in earlier studies, it remained strongly linked to the number of years sexually active before age twenty, number of partners per five-year interval, lack of condom use, and history of STIs (Handwerker 1993). Among 535 pregnant or recently delivered teenage mothers, those abused before their first pregnancy were more likely to have exchanged sex for money, drugs, or a place to stay; were more likely to use alcohol and drugs during pregnancy; and were likely to use contraception and began intercourse one year or earlier on average than other study participants (13.2 vs. 14.5 yrs) and considerably earlier than their nonpregnant peers (16.2 yrs; Boyer and Fine 1992).

The Costs of Violence Against Women

Information on the costs of violence against women is limited, although one may assume that these are likely to be substantial. Violence against women is sustained by and perpetuates inequality, particularly gender inequality. Poverty appears to increase the risk of domestic violence and this in turn can increase poverty by, for example, reducing women's mobility, opportunities for work outside the home, and access to information. It can also have an impact on children's schooling, which is associated with later poverty.

There are direct costs in terms of lives lost prematurely, as well as the cost of services provided (health, legal, protection, others). Indirect costs include days of work lost and reduced productivity. Many other indirect costs (sometimes called "intangible costs") are mostly unaccounted for as they are difficult to measure, such as cost of chronic pain, suffering, fear, depression, attempted suicide, loss of opportunities to pursue one's goals, and loss of self-esteem, among many others. While it is useful to consider the economic consequences of violence against women, the social and human costs are just as important to include when assessing the cost of violence against women to society.

Laurence and Spalter Roth (1996) reviewed data for calculating costs of domestic violence in the United States. They cited estimates between $5 and $10 billion annually to $67 billion in a 1995 study on the cost of crime to victims.[4] They concluded that few studies include indirect costs and that even those limited to direct costs tend to be narrowly focused. Most studies consider only the costs of injury and death. However, there are costs not only to victims, but to families of victims, resources and institutions of communities and societies at large, and programs for perpetrators. Furthermore, violence against women contributes to other problems such as homelessness, foster care, and mental health disorders, which are often not included in the calculations (Laurence and Spalter Roth 1996). More studies are being done, mainly in industrialized countries, to come up with better estimates of these costs (Yodanis Carrie and Godenzi 1999).[5]

Another big knowledge gap is with regard to cost-effectiveness of interventions. To date no attempt has been made to document this (Laurence and Spalter-Roth 1996). Yet this is essential information to guide policy makers, funders, and activists in identifying effective, feasible, and sustainable interventions. This information may help transform the understanding of violence against women into something actionable for decision makers.

Risk and Protective Factors

To prevent and address such a social problem it is necessary to understand its causes. Many theories exist to explain violence against women, but its precise causes remain unclear. It has not been possible to identify specific personal and attitudinal characteristics that make certain women more vulnerable to battering, other than an association with having witnessed parental violence as a child (National Research Council 1996). It appears that the major risk factor is being a woman. In other words, this is a problem that affects women of all countries, social classes, religions, and ethnic groups, even though the rates at which it occurs do vary across these variables.

Research over the last twenty years, mostly from the United States, tended to focus on single causal factors or tried to explain one causal theory (social learning, feminist, family systems, structural), focusing either on the perpetrator or on the victim. Building on earlier work, Heise (1998) proposed "an integrated, ecological framework" for studying and understanding the phenomenon. It looks at factors acting at four levels: individual, family, community, and social and cultural. What is important about this model is that it emphasizes interaction among factors at these levels. These causal factors, as well as protective factors, and their interactions must be better understood in different cultural contexts and settings to help us identify the different starting points and avenues for prevention and other interventions.

Patriarchal Structures and Gender Inequality
Domestic violence against women is supported or reenforced by gender norms and values that put women in a subordinate position to men. Variations in prevalence of violence by race, class, geography, or region have to be explained, but unequal gender relations is a cornerstone. Historically, husbands' domination over wives, including the use of violence, has been sanctioned by cultural beliefs (Dobash and Dobash 1992).

Many factors identified by Heise (1998) in the ecological model are closely related to norms and values around gender and social equity. For example, at the level of the family, male dominance and control of wealth appear important, whereas at the macrosocial level, it is notions of male entitlement and ownership of women, masculinity linked to aggression and dominance, social norms that support rigid gender roles, and acceptance of interpersonal violence as a means of resolving conflict.

The U.S. National Research Council's review claims that several studies support the fact that "men raised in patriarchal family structures in which traditional gender roles are encouraged are more likely to become violent adults, to rape women acquaintances, and to batter their intimate partners than men raised in more egalitarian homes" (Crowell and Burgess 1996). Although most violence by men against women in Bangladesh occurs in the home, it does not originate or persist only there. Rather it is one element in a system that subordinates women through social norms that guide their place and conduct (Schuler at al. 1996). In fact, violence is most frequent when women transgress or challenge the roles traditionally ascribed to them by society.

In an urban poor population in Mexico City, violence against women and disorders related to it are embedded in women's social relations, particularly with their male partners (Finkler 1997). Traditional ideologies reinforce women's economic dependence on men and concepts about their domestic role and social inferiority. Whereas both men and women in lower socioeconomic strata are exposed to many forms of hardship and denigration, the power given to men by the prevailing ideologies and use of physical violence against women generate what Finkler calls "life's lesions" in women. These are associated with sickness and may account for the many subacute nonlife-threatening conditions for which women seek health services and that are not easily amenable to biomedical remedies (Finkler 1997).

Cross-cultural anthropological and ethnographic studies of violence against women (Levinson 1989; Counts et al. 1992) also identify the role of social and cultural mores, including those around gender relations, in the acceptance and promotion of violence against women. The presence and severity of wife beating ranged from very frequent to almost nonexistent, although physical chastisement of wives was tolerated and even considered necessary in most societies (Counts et al. 1992). In many settings violence is considered normal and a prerogative of men and husbands (El-Zanaty et al. 1996; Manh Loi et al. 1999). Cultures with a macho concept of masculinity associated with dominance, toughness, or male honor also have high overall levels of violence against women (Campbell 1985).

Socialization of boys and girls often reflects these cultural norms and values. Males are encouraged to be aggressive and sexually active, and girls are taught to resist sexual activity and be "sugar and spice." Disturbing data from several countries show that girls often experienced their first sexual act as forced and accepted out of fear of violence (Wood and Jewkes 1997). This highlights the need to change social norms and attitudes that promote unequal gender and sexual relationships, starting with children and adolescents.

Witnessing Violence

Exposure to intimate partner violence while growing up was associated with domestic violence against women in studies from Nicaragua (Ellsberg 1997), Cambodia (Nelson and Zimmerman 1996), Canada (Johnson 1996), and the United States (National Research Council 1996), among others. A critical review of fifty-two United States studies (Hotaling and Sugarman 1986) found that the only risk marker for women consistently associated with being the victim of physical abuse was having witnessed parental violence as a child. Sexual assault was generally not predictable (Koss and Dinero 1989), but to the extent it could be, it was accounted for by variables that represent the aftereffects of childhood sexual abuse, including influences on drinking, sexual values and level of sexual activity (National Research Council 1996). This was found as well in Barbados (Handwerker 1993).

A review of U.S.-based research by the National Academy of Science states that "one third of children who have been abused or exposed to parental violence become violent adults" (National Research Council 1996). This is particularly the case for boys, whereas girls witnessing violence are more likely to end up as victims of violent relationships. Thus it becomes difficult to separate causes from consequences, as growing up in a family with partner violence becomes one way in which this violence is perpetuated. Furthermore, it reinforces and perpetuates gender stereotypes and unequal gender relationships, which in turn contribute to violence against women. In witnessing domestic abuse, children learn violence as a way to solve conflict.

In reviewing such studies it is important to note that although witnessing increases the risk of continuing patterns of violence it does not preordain it. "While it is true that the rate of wife beating is much higher for men who have witnessed violence by their own fathers, it is also true that the majority of abusive men were not exposed to violence in childhood. And, over half the men who did have this exposure have not been violent toward their own wives" (Johnson 1996).

Alcohol

Alcohol merits mention since research consistently found heavy drinking patterns related to intimate partner and sexual violence. Data from India show a clear relationship between the two (International Clinical Epidemiology Network 2000); however, the exact relationship remains unclear (National Research Council 1996). Many people drink without engaging in violent behavior and many battering incidents and sexual assaults occur in the absence of alcohol. However, some evidence shows that violent men who abuse alcohol are violent more frequently and inflict more serious injuries on their partners than do men without alcohol problems (Frieze and Browne 1989 cited in Heise 1998). Addressing violence in alcohol-dependence treatment programs can be useful to help reduce the incidence and severity of assaults, but not necessarily to end them.

Protective Factors

Factors that appear to be protective or mitigate violence can provide important leads for the development of interventions. The presence of sanctions against violent behavior and/or sanctuary for women experiencing violence (e.g., family and community intervening in marital disputes or violence) were associated with low levels of violence and vice versa (Counts et al. 1992).

In Nicaragua it was important to have family who could respond or intervene when violence occurred (Ellsberg et al. 1997). In Bangladesh, belonging to a credit program was associated with lower levels of domestic violence by both channeling resources to poor families through women and by organizing women to participate in regular meetings and exposure to outsiders (Schuler et al. 1996). More could be made of this by credit program organizers through, as a minimum, more awareness raising and openness to discussing the issue (Schuler et al. 1996). Globalization and the growing urbanization of developing countries, however, may be contributing to the disappearance of some of these protective factors. They contribute to isolating women from their extended families and also attenuate community sanctions (Finkler 1997). More cross-cultural research is required to document risk and protective factors in different settings.

A Gender Perspective: What about Men?

Although it is becoming more common to talk about intimate partner violence against women, it remains a sensitive issue at many levels. Many feel uncomfortable discussing an issue that at times seems to reflect on men in general, portraying them as aggressive, violent, irresponsible, wife beaters, or sexual predators. Women can be and are violent and many men are not violent. Men are also frequent victims, particularly young men, with homicide a major cause of death among those age fifteen to forty-four years (PAHO 1998; WHO 1999g). However, most violence is perpetrated by men, whatever the age and sex of the victim.

Some studies on intimate partner violence found that men report similar rates of abuse as women. Even so, assaults on women are more frequent and severe, as are their consequences. Women are also many times more likely to fear for their lives and the lives of their children (Statistics Canada 2000; Mirlees-Black and Byron 1999).

Programs for Men Who Batter

The most common interventions for men are batterer intervention programs (BIPs) that aim to change men's behavior. They were begun in the 1970s and tended to focus on group rather than individual treatment. They vary in length, but tend to be relatively short, usually around twenty to thirty weeks. In many cases in the United States they are court mandated in lieu of incarceration.

These programs are not often systematically monitored and evaluated, limiting the potential for improving their effectiveness. Overall, BIPs appear to contribute to cessation of physical domestic violence in around

53% to 85% of men who complete them (Austin and Dankwort 1999). However, these studies have many methodological limitations, including lack of control groups, different outcome measures, small samples, and different post-treatment follow-up periods (National Research Council 1996). Another problem is low compliance rate, except when attendance is mandated by the law. Most studies show a dropout or nonengagement rate of about two-thirds of the rate of completers, and most men do not come back after the first session.

Evaluations that do exist focus on reducing violence rates as reported by batterers themselves (and at times confirmed by their spouses), but not on women's well-being and safety, or whether women are empowered or disempowered by such interventions (Austin and Dankwort 1999). Whereas men may stop physical abuse after participating in a BIP, verbal and psychological abuse may continue or be worse (Edleson 1990). This highlights the need for BIPs to address not only physical but psychological abuse and other forms of control. These programs should have a strong focus on women's safety and on addressing gender roles and power inequalities.

Examining Gender Roles, Values, and Structures

A review of literature on crime and violence (Barker 1999) concludes that the impact of gender socialization on men has largely been ignored in the study of violence (Messerschmidt 1993). Maleness is defined in many cultures in terms of bravado, aggression, and control and dominance of women and others who are considered weaker. Many cultures condone aggression as a means for males to express anger. Some may also have rigid codes around family honor leading to so-called honor killings of women who have been raped, usually by male members of their own family.

In low-income settings, where mainstream sources of masculine identity such as education and stable employment are difficult to access, young men may be more inclined to adopt violence or other behaviors of control as a way to prove their manhood (Baker 1999). Better understanding of how masculinities are shaped in different environments and how this contributes (or not) to violence would be an important contribution to the field of violence against women and violence more broadly.

In terms of primary prevention, addressing gender socialization and use of aggression and violence early on, before behavior patterns are set, is critically important.

Men certainly have an important role to play in challenging violence against women. They have to take some responsibility for changing "the social norms and values that allow this gross violation of human rights to go on unquestioned" (Piot 1999). At the same time it is necessary to assess critically approaches being used, and to ensure that resources channeled to men are allocated in the most effective way and are not diverted from the hard-won efforts of many women's organizations. Since the 1980s these organizations provided basic care and support to women experiencing violence and to their children, and increasingly worked on prevention and programs for batterers. Growing interest in the subject in men's groups is a welcome development. However, it does not always recognize that changing norms and values of relationships from those of control and dominance to those based on mutual respect and equity requires not only individual but also structural change.

Current Policy Responses: Limitations and Proposals

Until recently, most response to violence against women, including the provision of care and support services, has come from the nongovernment, voluntary sector, particularly women's organizations. Shelters for battered women and rape crisis centers are classic examples, and in many developed countries still form the basis of services, albeit with various levels of government funding.

Yet dealing with victims is only the tip of the iceberg. Responding to the needs of individual women is of course necessary. It may also prevent reoccurrence of violence or further health consequences, death, or disability. However, it is also necessary to invest in the search for effective strategies for primary prevention.

A Public Health Approach
A public health approach focuses on prevention and emphasizes opportunities for early intervention. It is based on sound research, includes a social analysis of health, and has an interdisciplinary approach. All of

these are essential to addressing the problem of violence against women. Preventive strategies need to be context specific and address particular risk factors that are relevant to each setting.

Important elements in prevention are interventions to change the social norms and values that discriminate against women and that condone physical chastisement of women by their husbands. Some places started zero tolerance campaigns that use mass media and other information and education channels to promote a culture that does not tolerate violence against women or children. Another approach is to use community sanctions as a deterrent. Examples such as beating pots outside the house of an abuser by women in India, neighborhood watches and whistle blowing in Peru, and strategies to identify and shame an abuser are creative. In many cases these may be more effective than formal sanctions of the police and judiciary, which can often act against women.

Behavior change is never easy and it is a long-term process. Starting early where patterns of aggression are learned and before behaviors are set is crucial. As with women victims, no one profile of men defines who will or will not be a batterer other than having been exposed to violence as a child. Thus, interventions that focus on working with children of women experiencing abuse are important. In addition to benefiting children themselves, they can contribute to decreasing violence and improving the health and well-being of the men and women of the next generation. School programs, starting at an early age, that help to shape and promote more equitable gender relations and nonviolent forms of conflict resolution may help initiate change in prevailing norms. Teaching nonviolent parenting may develop as an intervention (Beaglehole 1999). There are difficulties in measuring the impact of these strategies, and so far, few evaluations exist. It is therefore essential that programs build monitoring and evaluation into their structure and activities.

Training

More and more projects are aimed at developing and improving the response by formal sectors toward women experiencing violence. Interventions traditionally focused on training for the police, the legal and judicial systems and, increasingly, the health sector. Mostly they improve identification of and response to women experiencing violence. This approach has several limitations. First, training is often an isolated intervention, with little follow-up. It becomes the end rather than the means.

Second, training is focused exclusively on technical content and does not address the experiences, attitudes, and values of the providers. For example, a health care provider who is not welcoming and who does not treat women respectfully or listen to them as a matter of course can hardly provide an appropriate environment for addressing violence against them. The experiences and values of health providers are also important to consider. For example, among primary care nurses in South Africa, domestic violence was common for female nurses and most of the male nurses held views that justified that violence (Kim and Motshei 2002).

Third, institutions such as the police and legal and health systems reflect the same gender stereotypes and prevailing norms that underpin violence against women in society. Occasionally training may include looking at the social construction of gender and power relationships, including within the institution, but most often it does not. Training programs rarely address structural barriers that may make it difficult for trainees to put what they learn into practice. For example, many health providers may feel they lack time, support from their superiors, or even facilities such as a private space for interviews to deal with violence, even when they have the information and interest to do so.

Finally, the focus is on the service rather than the woman. Health providers, particularly doctors, often feel that they have "to make things right." This may lead to judgmental attitudes and pressure on a woman to leave the violent relationship or partner. Providers must learn to listen to women as experts, delicately balancing the provision of support and guidance and concern for their safety with respect for their decisions, even if this is to stay with the violent partner. Women may judge that this is the safest option and in many cases they will be right. This fine line is a difficult one, which those working in this area must learn to walk, especially since many deaths from domestic violence may take place around the time that a woman decides to look for help or to leave the abuser (Crawford 1991; Ellis and Dekeseredy 1997).

Whereas the provider usually focuses on the battering, for the woman this is often only one aspect of a complex relationship, and her interpretation of the situation is colored by this. She may be balancing the risks of staying in the relationship with those of extreme poverty or being ostracized by the family and others. Providers must recognize and understand that leaving is a long-term process in which looking for help is an important step (Ellsberg et al. 2001).

Individual women require and should have high-quality care for the consequences of violence. It is also important to keep in mind that the underlying problem is male violence. Providers and institutions that are meant to help her should give a clear message that violent behavior is not acceptable and that no one deserves to be abused. In the health sector, many providers feel that addressing violence is beyond their reach. They may lack basic knowledge, time, or empathy, or simply not know what to do or where to refer women. Some may be experiencing violence themselves. Basic information on domestic violence and sexual assault must be systematically included in all medical and nursing curricula in order to, as a minimum, raise awareness of the problem and provide a basis for in-service training.

In conclusion, training programs in health care settings could be more useful if they addressed violence in the context of broader issues of interaction and communication with patients, gender, and sexuality (Women's Aid 1999). For training to be effective, long-term goals and strategies must ensure that necessary structural changes accompany the training. This requires political and administrative commitment, and development of policies and protocols for different levels of providers and managers within the services.

Limited Knowledge and Lack of Funding for Research

Most published literature on violence against women comes from northern countries, particularly the United States. Whereas a number of prevalence studies were recently conducted in developing countries, data from these countries remain scarce. Overall, data available to estimate the extent of violence in general, and violence against women in particular, are grossly inadequate. There are many reasons for underreporting, and much information obtained from services is incomplete and often unreliable. Furthermore, many studies have methodological design problems or use clinic-based samples that make it difficult to obtain reliable estimates of prevalence.

There is a need for prevalence and incidence data that are comparable across cultures and that start to elucidate determinants as well as protective factors that operate in different settings. This research is essential to improve our understanding of the magnitude and the nature of the problem, to provide guidance to develop interventions, and to allow us to monitor their impact. It will also provide baseline data from which to understand trends and patterns as they appear.

A Multi-Country Study on Women's Health and Domestic Violence coordinated by WHO aims to fill this gap by developing methodologies to measure violence against women and its health consequences cross-culturally (WHO 1999e).[6] In addition, WHO produced ethical and safety recommendations for research on domestic violence (WHO 1999f). Another international initiative is WorldSAFE (studies of abuse in the family environment) supported by the International Clinical Epidemiology Network.

Intervention research is also urgently needed to identify what works and what doesn't in different settings, in particular what is effective, sustainable, and feasible in resource-poor settings. Models come mostly from the developed world and in many cases they are inappropriately copied in settings where conditions for them to be effective are not present. For example, the recommendation for universal screening of women in health centers, while at times useful in settings where services for referral exist and providers have been trained to deal with violence, may not be helpful and can even be damaging in other settings. Furthermore, there is little or no evidence on which to make these recommendations. It is necessary to assess critically evidence for the effectiveness of proposed interventions and to consider their appropriateness and sustainability in different settings, rather than making broad global recommendations.

The role of the health sector in prevention and in responding to the needs of survivors of violence must be better defined. The health sector may not be the most appropriate place to start this work in all settings. Specific contextual analyses and pilot projects must test strategies and identify what works where. A delicate balance exists between encouraging health sector involvement and medicalizing the problem. Gender biases inherent in the health system may act as barriers to an appropriate response and it is necessary to address these in order to respond appropriately to the needs of individual women.

Research funding is biased in favor of biomedical approaches focused on identifying treatments or cures for specific diseases. There is less interest expressed in supporting research to identify effective interventions for more complex social and behavioral issues. This raises questions about how funds are allocated, who sets the agenda, and how much gender equity concerns are genuinely integrated into the agenda. Well-designed and action-oriented research in violence against women can in itself be an intervention by, among other things, raising awareness of the problem and starting public discussion, as well as collaboration across sectors as has been shown by the WHO study. It has to be supported financially and institutionally to ensure the most cost-effective and efficient response to violence, particularly in resource-poor settings.

Multisectoral Approaches

The need for a well-coordinated multisectoral response to violence, including violence against women is obvious. However, it remains the case that the entry point is usually through one sector, and we have few examples of multisector approaches that have been successfully put into practice. It is necessary to pilot models for an integrated response to violence against women, and document their effectiveness as well as the obstacles that they are likely to encounter.

One such model for an integrated response at the community level is being piloted in Latin America by the Pan American Health Organization (PAHO) and the Inter-American Development Bank (IDB). This model aims to create coordinated community networks in which the health system, legal system, police, churches, nongovernment organizations, and other community-based groups meet regularly to design and implement a response to domestic violence. At the national level it seeks to promote adoption of laws and policies to strengthen institutional capacity to respond effectively to domestic violence. It also fosters linkages with mass media to challenge the social attitudes and beliefs that grant men the right to control women and to communicate that violence is unacceptable (WHO 1997f).[7] Such models should be monitored to assess their replicability in other regions.

Forensic Medicine

It is important to address specific issues in which the response of the health sector to women's needs is grossly inadequate, such as the forensic medicine system. In many countries the medical system, particularly forensic doctors, may act as a barrier for women trying to access the legal system (Prasad 1999; Human Rights Watch 1997).[8] In some countries only evidence from forensic doctors is acceptable in court, even though only a handful of these doctors exist. Even where they exist in reasonable numbers, women may face access barriers such as lack of time and money, distance, lack of information, and language.

A woman in a rural area who has been raped and would like to take legal action against the perpetrator stands very little chance of being able to produce the required evidence. Even where any doctor can provide evidence, most are not trained in how to collect evidence properly and in a manner that does not revictimize women. They may also be reluctant to become involved in a court case. Lack of an appropriate quality service to provide care and collect evidence in cases of rape and sexual assault or other forms of assault disproportionately affects women and is therefore another dimension of health care inequity.

Legal and Human Rights Framework

Violence against women is much more than a health issue; it is an infringement of women's human rights, such as the right to bodily integrity. It also impinges on women's ability to exercise other rights, such as the right to the highest attainable standard of health, and sexual and reproductive rights.

Many countries still have to ratify human rights conventions such as the Convention on the Elimination of all Forms of Discrimination Against Women, which provides the framework for revising laws that will begin to support redress of existing inequalities between women and men. A few countries, mostly in the north, have government policies and coordinating mechanisms that provide a framework for action, but in most the responses remain ad hoc.

After the Fourth World Conference on Women in Beijing, a number of developing countries, particularly in Latin America, passed domestic violence laws or revised existing legislation. This is an important step, but much remains to be done before these laws can be put in practice. Furthermore, legal reform is only one of the many changes required to address this problem.

Conclusion

Violence against women is a widespread social, human rights, and public health problem. Its causes are complex and addressing it therefore requires concerted and multisector responses backed by strong political commitment to ending discrimination against women and violence against them. An important focus of this response must be identification of effective primary prevention strategies, including those that serve to challenge gender discrimination by changing attitudes, norms, and behaviors that condone or even promote violence, particularly violence against women by men. The provision of services that respond to those living in violent situations is also important. Much more is needed to ensure these services respond adequately to the needs of women. Any intervention must respect women's autonomy and right to make their own decisions, and have women's safety as its paramount concern.

Notes

1. The views expressed in this chapter are those of the author and do not necessarily reflect the position of the World Health Organization. In preparing this chapter I am grateful for the assistance of Margaret Squadrani and Iris Tetford.

2. Different terminology is used in the literature to describe violence against women by intimate male partners, including domestic violence, intimate partner violence (IPV), spouse abuse, wife battering, and violence against women in families. In this chapter we use domestic violence and (intimate) partner violence.

3. For a detailed discussion on how different definitions affect the measurement of rape, see Koss 1993.

4. The wide variation is due to different methods used to estimate costs of violence and inclusion of different kinds of costs in studies.

5. For other studies on the costs of domestic violence see Greaves (1995), Day (1995), and Kerr (1996) from Canada; Stanko (1998) from Great Britain, and Blumel (1993) from Australia. No published study on this from developing countries is available yet. Attempts to quantify the cost of violence against women in India are under way (D. Jain, IndiaSAFE, personal communication).

6. The WHO multicountry study on women's health and violence is being implemented in Bangladesh, Brazil, Japan, Namibia, Peru, Tanzania, and Thailand, and, with UNFPA funding, in Samoa. Discussions are under way with other countries. For more information on this study, contact Dr. Garcia Moreno (garciamorenocwho.ch). The protocol and questionnaire build on the experience of many researchers who have been particularly concerned with methodological and ethical issues, some of whom came together in the international network of researchers on violence against women (IRNVAW).

7. For more information on this project, contact the Women, Health, and Development Program in PAHO (Velzebom@paho.org).

8. The Women's Human Rights Project of Human Rights Watch commissioned reviews of the forensic legal systems in Pakistan, Peru, Russia, and South Africa. Reports can be obtained directly from Human Rights Watch.

6

Mental Health: Gender Bias, Social Position, and Depression

Jill Astbury

The traditional preoccupation of biomedical research with mortality has distracted attention from evaluating the significant burden of ill health that is associated with mental illness (Murray and Lopez 1996). Growing recognition of its spread and characteristics makes it a matter of urgency that the morbidity caused by poor mental health be addressed, its causes elucidated, and its prevalence reduced. More attention has been paid to health-related quality of life since the 1980s, but a pressing need remains for research into the determinants and mechanisms that promote and protect mental health and foster resilience to stress and adversity. Central to this task is the compelling need to consider the role of gender in mental health.

Nonpsychotic mental disorders are often referred to as common mental disorders (CMDs) because of their high prevalence in the general community. These, including depression, anxiety and somatic complaints, exceed 30% in community samples and up to 50% in some primary care samples in a number of countries (Patel et al. 1999). A primary focus of this chapter is CMDs in general and depression in particular because:

• The most marked gender differences in prevalence are found in these disorders.

• Unipolar or major depression is predicted to become the second leading cause of the global disability burden by 2020 (Murray and Lopez 1996).

• Depression occurs approximately twice as often in women as in men and is the most frequently encountered women's mental health problem (Piccinelli and Homen 1997). It is also more persistent in women (Bracke 2000). Any significant reduction in the overrepresentation of women who are depressed would make a major contribution to reducing the global burden of disability.

• Depression and anxiety are the most common comorbid disorders, and a significant gender difference exists in the rate of comorbidity. Comorbidity contributes significantly to the disability caused by psychological disorders (Kessler et al. 1994; Ustun and Sartorius 1995; WHO and ICPE 2000).

• Depression, anxiety, and comorbidity are significantly related to gender-based violence and the socioecomically disadvantaged situations in which women predominate (Byrne et al. 1999; Patel et al. 1999).

Understanding Mental Health

Definitions

There is no one universally accepted system for classifying mental health and mental disorders. The qualities, behaviors, and experiences that might be used are disputed by health professionals and change over time. Theories vary between and to some extent within various disciplines concerned with the field, including psychiatry, psychology, psychotherapy, social work, and sociology (Pilgrim and Rogers 1993).

Even the idea of normality applied to mental health is problematic. Four approaches to defining normality can be made: it can be conceived as the absence of pathology; it may be equated with ideal functioning or what humanistic theorists called self-actualization; it can be taken as the average or level of functioning enjoyed by most people; or it can be seen as the product of interacting systems that change over time according to the age of the person and the developmental goals appropriate to that age (Offer and Sabshin 1984).

Each approach implies value judgments that can be contested. For instance, the third and fourth approaches could include and endorse gender-stereotypical behavior on the grounds that it is widespread and regarded as normal and appropriate in many cultures. Other notions of normality include the capacity to adjust flexibly or adapt to the external world, form emotionally satisfying relationships, master developmental tasks, learn from experience, take responsibility for one's actions, and deal with conflicting emotions (Kaplan and Sadock 1988).

For convenience, the term psychological disorder is used here because it is employed in systems of classification and research in psychiatric epidemiology. It is critical to remember that diagnostic categories are heterogeneous and the definition of psychiatric caseness is often arbitrary (Piccinelli and Homen 1997). Every culture has some notion of emotional or psychological difference, and laypeople as well as mental health professionals are conscious that mental health problems vary in frequency and cover a broad spectrum of severity.

Poor mental health from a lay perspective tends to be identified with various readily recognizable emotions. These include feeling persistently sad, anxious, or down or suffering from bad nerves together with headaches, aches and pains, or more seriously as having thoughts, feelings, or behaviors that are strange, frightening, frustrating, or antisocial (Pilgrim and Rogers 1993). Mental health professionals argue about diagnostic categories and the precise limits over what should and should not be included. Like laypeople, they distinguish between common neurotic or nonpsychotic disorders that manifest a mixture of depression, anxiety, and somatic symptoms and rare, severe, psychotic disorders such as schizophrenia and bipolar (manic-depressive) disorder in which people lose touch with reality.

Evidence

Evidence is accumulating that mental disorders are more common and more persistent than previously realized. They also appear to be increasing in recent cohorts (WHO and ICPE 2000). They can be episodic, recurrent, or chronic and cover a broad range of conditions. The U.S. National Comorbidity Survey found that lifetime prevalence rates for any kind of psychiatric disorder were high, but that overall they were similar for men (48.7%) and women (47.3%), notwithstanding marked gender differences for specific disorders. The conditions surveyed were affective disorders (major depressive episode, manic episode, dysthymia), anxiety disorders (panic disorder, agoraphobia without panic disorder, social phobia, simple phobia, generalized anxiety disorder), substance use disorders (alcohol abuse with and without dependence, drug abuse with and without dependence), antisocial personality, and nonaffective psychosis (Kessler et al. 1994).

Intercountry variations are wide, suggesting the role of macrosocial factors in mental health. Surveys in seven countries from North America, Latin America, and Europe found lifetime prevalence rates for any psychiatric disorder involving mood, anxiety, or substance use ranging from a high of 48.6% in the United States to a low of 12.2% in Turkey (WHO and ICPE 2000).

Treatment

Despite being common, mental disorders are underdiagnosed. In the WHO collaborative study on psychological problems in primary health care, carried out in fifteen countries, less than half the patients who met diagnostic criteria for depression were identified as depressed by their doctors (Ustun and Sartorius 1995). People also seem reluctant to seek professional help. In Canada and the United States, only 40% of respondents in the WHO–ICPE survey reported seeking professional assistance in the year they first experienced a mood, anxiety, or substance use disorder. Delays of more than ten years were common among those who did not seek help in the year of onset (WHO and ICPE 2000). Even people with severe mental disorders may not receive adequate or, indeed, any treatment. The Australian Human Rights and Equal Opportunity Commissioner (Burdekin 1993) reported that half of all sufferers of serious mental illness received no treatment at all.

In contrast to this general underidentification and undertreatment, physicians are significantly more likely to diagnose depression in women than in men even when they have similar scores on standard measures of depression or have identical symptoms (Callahan et al. 1997; Stoppe et al. 1999). Being female is also a significant predictor of being prescribed mood-altering psychotropic drugs (Simoni-Wastila 2000). What constitutes an appropriate response to treatment is widely disputed and varies according to underlying beliefs about the primary causes of mental illness. It can range from a strict biomedical, psychopharmacological response focused on the individual, counseling, or psychotherapy to broader community-based interventions such as provision of refuges for women affected by domestic violence and experiencing severe emotional distress.

Gender in Mental Health Research

Gender, understood as a social construct and category, has explanatory power regarding differences in men's and women's susceptibility and exposure to specific health risks. Gender influences the power men and women have to control and protect their lives and health, cope with such risks, and influence the direction of the health-development process. The concept permits us to ask questions about how different social categories occupied by women and men affect how they see, experience, and understand the world and themselves.

The role of gender in science, including what is perceived to be a problem worthy of scientific inquiry and the unequal relationship between researcher and research subjects, evaded serious scrutiny until the 1980s, when feminist critiques of science began to appear (Harding 1987). Before this time a mutually reinforcing relationship existed between the scientific construction of gender and the gendered construction of science such that the operation of both processes was obscured.

Gender-blind theories of mental health prompted empirical research that assumed and then sought to prove women's greater biologically based vulnerability or proneness to mental disorder (Astbury 1996). The conflation of sex (a biological given) and gender (a social construct) inevitably led to a systematic bias that conceals interactions between these biological and social determinants. With psychological disorders such as depression, this conflation prompted many researchers to narrow the scope of their investigations to a search for biological causes. Blindness to the effect of gender dictated that these could be found only in women.

Notions of women's greater biologically based vulnerability or proneness to disorder have proved rather resistant to change. They are embedded in the long history of hysteria and the attendant belief that women have an innate tendency to mental disorder. Mental disorder was believed to relate to a corresponding derangement or malfunctioning of women's reproductive organs and hormones (Gitlin and Pasnau 1989).

Research continues to focus on the hypothesized relationship between reproductive-related events, such as menstruation, pregnancy, miscarriage, childbirth, premature delivery, infertility, abortion, and menopause, and women's higher rates of depression. None of these events by itself explains this gender difference, yet some researchers continue to retain a primary interest in the contribution of biological factors and reproductive events to women's higher rates of depression. This interest extends to disorders that have no gender difference in prevalence, such as bipolar disorder (Halbreich and Lumley 1993; Blehar and Oren 1995; Leibenluft 1997). Critical reviews commented unfavorably on the quality of much research in this area and concluded that an interactionist model incorporating individual, psychological, and social factors is necessary (McGrath et al. 1990). However, the search for pathological factors in the minds and reproductive systems of individual women caused long delays in directing research toward social and structural determinants of women's mental health.

The enthusiasm of researchers for biological and reproductive explanations of psychological distress does not necessarily accord with women's own perspectives and health priorities, but these are rarely elicited. One exception, a study in the Volta region of Ghana, did elicit women's predominant concerns and found almost three-fourths of them related to psychosocial health problems such as "thinking too much" and "worrying too much" (Avotri and Walters 1999). Thinking too much is a symptom congruent with the Shona concept of *kufungisisa*, encompassing mental, social, and spiritual distress, and accords closely with the biomedical construct of nonpsychotic mental illness (Patel et al. 1995). Women's own explanations of what ailed them stressed heavy workloads, gender division of labor, financial insecurity, and unrelieved responsibility for children (Avotri and Walters 1999).

Research in the 1990s that adopted an interactionist model clearly reveals that the impact of biological factors on women's mental health is mediated and in many cases disappears once social and psychological factors are taken into account. Emotional well-being in middle-aged women is positively associated with their current health status and psychosocial and lifestyle variables, but not with their menopausal status or hormone levels (Dennerstein et al. 1997). Partner and social support, life events, the experience of motherhood, and infant temperament are critical risk factors for the development of postnatal depression (Small et al. 1994).

Whereas the relationship of women's reproductive functioning to their mental health has received intense scrutiny, the same relationship in men has been virtually ignored. This form of gender bias seems to imply that men either have no reproductive functioning or are not psychologically affected by events and conditions such as infertility, attachment to or loss of the fetus through miscarriage, stillbirth, or extreme prematurity, or the transition to parenthood. The few studies available indicate that men are emotionally responsive to many of the same events as women, not for biological reasons but for psychosocial ones. Men, as well as women, can experience depression after the birth of a child, and a significant correlation was found between parents regarding depressive symptoms (Soliday et al. 1999). This suggests that a "couple in relation" or systems approach should be used in research on postpartum distress. Other reproductive events with psychological importance for men are attachment to the fetus during pregnancy (Condon 1993), miscarriage (Beil 1992), and birth of a preterm infant (Handley 1996).

The research focus on women's reproductive functioning and mental health coexisted with widespread failure to include women in a range of clinical trials for nonreproductive health issues. Women's historical exclusion from research on cardiovascular disease, the leading cause of mortality for women as well as men in developed countries, is well documented (Mastroianni et al. 1994). One obvious and somewhat ironic result of this exclusionary bias and narrowing of research on depression to reproductive and hormonal factors, was to delay the discovery that major depression in women carries an increased risk of cardiovascular morbidity and mortality. A review of all studies on the link between cardiovascular disease and depression carried out between 1966 to 1997, concluded that:

Despite the fact that women are more vulnerable to depression and that cardio vascular disease is the leading cause of death among adult women in the United States, relatively little research has focused on the etiology and pathogenic mechanisms of major depression among women with cardio vascular disease. (Musselman et al. 1998:588)

All diagnostic criteria and assessments of mental health depend on theoretical constructs of human behavior, on what is believed to constitute the normal, and how this can be clearly distinguished from the pathological. Androcentric bias, where men's experiences are taken as the norm or their symptoms and patterns of illness underpin etiological models, produces error in research. For example, men who develop schizophrenia often have earlier onset of symptoms than women. Based on this experience, the American Psychiatric Association's *Diagnostic and Statistical Manual of Mental Disorders,* 3rd edition (DSM-III) stipulated that schizophrenia could be diagnosed only if symptoms were present before forty-five years of age. Application of this criterion to data from the WHO Determinants of Outcome of Severe Mental Disorders (Sartorius et al. 1986) led to the exclusion of 5% of men but 12%, or more than double the percentage, of women (Hambrecht et al. 1993). Implications for the accuracy of prevalence rates are clear.

What is included in or excluded from explanatory models of mental health outcomes changes over time. For example, the contribution that gender-based, intimate violence makes to women's mental health has been investigated consistently only since the 1990s. Before this, even social models of mental health ignored childhood sexual abuse or partner violence in adult life as probable vulnerability factors in the development of depression or other disorders. The role of violent victimization was not recognized as contributing to lower self-esteem in women, and violence was not counted as a critical negative life event or a chronic stressor. This relatively late consideration illustrates how ignorance of gender-specific mental health risks generates problematic research, incomplete data collection, and faulty interpretation of findings.

All levels of scientific enquiry from formulation of research questions, study design, and methodology selected, to interpretation of results must explicitly articulate the contribution of gender. The fact of human gender must be acknowledged in the construction of test instruments and questionnaires if items are to have accuracy. Existing questionnaires assumed to have general validity and, by implication, gender neutrality may have neither. The task of modifying questionnaires to overcome gender bias began in the 1980s (Norbeck 1984) but new instruments are still necessary.

These historical and contemporary biases have retarded our understanding of the relationship between gender and mental health. In conclusion, three main problems persist:

• Evidence on gender is often simply not collected, or if it is, may not be presented in a way that informs researchers, clinicians, and policy makers.

• Evidence is lacking on how the link between gender and mental health is mediated through structural determinants such as income, education, workplace and social position, roles related to family, unpaid and caring work, and the experience of intimate gender-based violence.

• Conceptual remapping is required for all explanatory models of psychological disorders where large gender differences obtain that have not been adequately explained and where gender-based exposure to chronic life stresses, negative life events, and violence has not been assessed.

Gender and Mental Health Outcomes

The WHO (1981) definition of mental health identifies many salient dimensions of functioning required to examine the relationship between gender and mental health.

Mental health is the capacity of the individual, the group and the environment to interact with one another in ways that promote subjective well-being, the optimal development and use of mental abilities (cognitive, affective and relational), the achievement of individual and collective goals consistent with justice and the attainment and preservation of conditions of fundamental equality.

This definition goes beyond biological individualism and the notion that psychological disorder is primarily an expression of brain disease and requires pharmacological treatment. By adopting a positive, multilevel, transactional concept, the definition acknowledges the complex web of interrelationships that extend from the individual to the environment, the critical role of social context, and the importance of justice and equality in determining mental health. Gender is not mentioned, but I maintain that it can and does markedly affect the capacity of the individual, the group, and the environment to attain subjective well-being, justice, and equality.

Common Mental Disorders

The U.S. national comorbidity survey (Kessler et al. 1994), like many other studies (Ustun and Sartorius 1995; Linzer et al. 1996), reported a higher prevalence of most affective disorders and nonaffective psychoses in women and higher rates of substance use disorders and antisocial personality disorder in men. The most common disorders were major

Table 6.1
Prevalence rates of selected disorders, United States, 1994 (Kessler et al. 1994)

Mental disorders	Lifetime prevalence women (%)	Lifetime prevalence men (%)	12-month prevalence women (%)	12-month prevalence men (%)
Major depressive episode	21.3	12.7	12.9	7.7
Alcohol dependence	8.2	20.1	3.7	10.7
Antisocial personality disorder	1.2	5.8		

depression and alcohol dependence. Both showed large gender differences in prevalence (table 6.1).

Gender socialization and stigmatization influence men's and women's help-seeking behavior differently. Men are more likely to admit seeking help for alcohol-related problems and express concern over receiving a psychiatric label. In contrast, women are more likely to request assistance for emotional problems and are concerned over receiving a drinker label (Allen et al. 1998). Unless screening instruments and measures of mental disorder are alert to the possible bias exerted by such gender norms, both underdiagnosis and overdiagnosis of specific disorders could occur.

Nonetheless, the gender difference in depression is a robust finding. A comprehensive review of all general population studies conducted to date in the United States, Puerto Rico, Canada, France, Iceland, Taiwan, Korea, Germany, and Hong Kong reported that women predominated over men in lifetime prevalence rates of major depression (Piccinelli and Homen 1997). This difference is documented in clinical and community samples, across racial groups, and even after statistically controlling for effects of other variables that are strongly related to depression, such as income, education, and occupation (Kessler et al. 1994; WHO and ICPE 2000). Depression may also be more persistent in women (Bracke 2000).

Depression and anxiety are common comorbid diagnoses, and women have higher prevalences than men of both lifetime and twelve-month comorbidity of three of more disorders (Kessler et al. 1994; WHO and ICPE 2000). Almost half of patients with at least one psychiatric disorder have a disorder from at least one other cluster of these illnesses (Ustun and Sartorius 1995). These clusters include most disorders, apart from alcohol dependence, in which women predominate (Russo 1990). They are depressive episode, agoraphobia, panic disorder, and generalized anxiety; and somatization, hypochondriasis and somatoform pain, and alcohol dependence. Psychiatric comorbidity, with depression as a common factor, is a characteristic finding in many studies on women's mental health and on violence (Resnick et al. 1997).

Severe Mental Disorders

Pronounced gender differences in rates of common mental disorders are not found with severe conditions such as schizophrenia and bipolar disorder. Lifetime prevalence rates for those illnesses are much lower, ranging in studies of the general population from 0.1% to 3% for schizophrenia and from 0.2% to 1.6% for bipolar disorder. These disorders also have a strong genetic component (Piccinelli and Homen 1997).

Gender differences do, however, persist in other dimensions of serious mental illness. A comprehensive review of schizophrenia research found frequent reports of differences in age of onset of symptoms, with men typically having earlier onset than women and poorer premorbid psychosocial development and functioning (Piccinelli and Homen 1997). Despite later onset, some studies report that women experience a higher frequency of hallucinations or more positive psychotic symptoms than men (Lindamer et al. 1999). Similarly, whereas the population prevalence of bipolar disorder appears to be similar between men and women, gender differences do occur. Women are more likely to develop the rapid cycling form of illness, have more comorbidity—especially with depression (Leibenluft 2000)—and have a greater likelihood of being hospitalized during the manic phase (Hendrick et al. 2000).

Women with schizophrenia have higher-quality social relationships than men, but a cross-national survey drawn from Canada, Cuba, and the United States (Vandiver 1998) found that this was true only for Canadian women, whereas Cuban men reported higher quality of life than Cuban women. According to a Finnish study on gender differences in independent living skills, involving self-care and shopping, cooking and cleaning for oneself, one-half of men but only one-third of women lacked these skills (Hintikka et al. 1999). Skills inculcated through gender socialization can affect long-term adjustment to and outcome of a severe mental disorder.

Gender-specific exposure to risk also complicates types and ranges of adverse outcomes associated with severe mental disorder. When schizophrenia coexists with homelessness, women experience higher rates of sexual and physical victimization, comorbid anxiety and depression, and more medical illness than men (Brunette and Drake 1998).

Thus gender differences in mental disorder extend far beyond differences in rates of various disorders or indeed their different times of onset or course. They also include a number of factors that can affect risk or susceptibility, diagnosis, treatment, and adjustment to the illness.

Gender, Social Position, and Mental Health

Gender intersects with other critical structural determinants of social position and these typically cluster together. Such differences in material well-being and human development are widely acknowledged. The WHO (1998g) categorically stated:

Women's health is inextricably linked to their status in society. It benefits from equality, and suffers from discrimination. Today, the status and well-being of countless millions of women worldwide remain tragically low. As a result, human well being suffers and the prospects for future generations are dimmer.

The United Nations Development Program (UNDP) attempts to capture the disparity between human and gender development by comparing countries' rankings on the gender development index (GDI) with those on the human development index (HDI).[1] All available data point to the universally inferior position of women. As the 1997 UNDP report put it: "no society treats its women as well as its men."

There are strong, albeit varying, links among gender inequality, human poverty, and socioeconomic differences in all countries. Women constitute more than 70% of the world's poor (UNDP 1995). Even in the developed world, women with children are the largest group of people living in poverty (Najman 1993). Gender must therefore be taken into account in looking at the way income inequality and poverty affect on mental health.

The numbers of people becoming poor are increasing, and inequalities in many countries are widening rather than narrowing (UNDP 1998a). The impact of structural adjustment programs is especially severe in poorest nations and occurs in gender-distinct ways because of roles men and women play and the different constraints they face in responding to policy changes and shifts in relative prices (Kirmani and Munyakho 1996). Conditions attached to structural adjustment loans to developing countries can lead to cutbacks in public sector employment and social welfare spending so that the costs of health care, education, and basic foodstuffs rapidly becomes unaffordable, especially to the poor, most of whom are women (Bandarage 1997).

Economic policies can cause sudden, disruptive, severe changes to income, employment, and living conditions of large numbers of people. It is precisely these negative life events that cannot be controlled or evaded that are most strongly related to the onset of depressive symptoms (Brown 1998). Evidence is beginning to emerge on the gender-specific effect of economic restructuring on mental health. Data obtained from primary care attenders in Goa (India), Harare (Zimbabwe), and Santiago (Chile), and from community samples in Pelotas and Olinda (Brazil) show significant associations between high rates of CMDs and female gender, low education, and poverty (Patel et al. 1999). This study reveals how gender inequality accompanies and is exacerbated by economic inequalities. The result of this interaction is a steep rise in the very mental disorders that already predominate in women.

Significant decreases in social cohesion and increases in inequality engender poor health outcomes. In Russia, significant decreases in life expectancy were reported for both men and women, with premature deaths concentrated in those age thirty to sixty years (Walberg et al. 1998). The most important predictors of decreased life expectancy found were the pace of economic transition, high turnover of the labor force, inequality, and decreased social cohesion together with increased crime and alcoholism. This research did not attempt to measure gender differences in the effect of such changes on mental health. Yet other research on restructuring and erosion of social capital suggests that common mental disorders among women are likely to increase (Patel et al. 1999), especially if women become a greater target for gender-based violence (Byrne et al. 1999).

How gender interrelates with other structural social determinants of mental health has not been adequately investigated, and measurement of women's socioeconomic status is problematic. In many large-scale surveys, significant amounts of income data for women are missing (Macran et al. 1996). The substitution of family income as a proxy variable for the sum of the income of each family member may add another layer of obfuscation, if access to and control over that income are not independently ascertained. Assuming equitable access to and distribution of family income is unwarranted but continues to be widely practiced (WHO and ICPE 2000). Even with crude measures currently in use, adverse physical and mental health outcomes are two to two and a half times higher for those experiencing greatest social disadvantage compared with those experiencing least disadvantage (Stansfield et al. 1998). Similarly, the six-month prevalence of any DSM-III disorder is 2.86 times higher in the lowest socioeconomic status category than in the highest, controlling for age and gender. Over a lifetime, the United States comorbidity survey calculated that those in the lowest income group were 1.56 times more likely to have an affective disorder, 2 times as likely to have an anxiety disorder, 1.27 times more likely to have a substance use disorder, and 2.98 times more likely to have antisocial personality disorder than those in the highest income group (Kessler et al. 1994).

Environmental stressors, including increased numbers of negative life events and chronic difficulties, are particularly significant in accounting for the lower social class predominance of nonpsychotic psychiatric disorders such as depression and anxiety. Less control over decision making, structural determinants of health, and less access to supportive social networks correlate with higher levels of morbidity and mortality (Berkman and Syme 1979; Kessler et al. 1994; Brown 1998; Stansfield et al. 1998; Patel et al. 1999). Single mothers with dependent children living in poverty are at especially high risk for poor physical and mental health (Macran et al. 1996).

Analyses of the social gradient in health outcomes concentrated on material indicators of inequality and social disadvantage. However, the widely observed social gradient in physical and mental health also operates on symbolic and psychologic levels. Social position carries with it knowledge of social rank and clear understanding of where one stands in the scale of things. The pervasive finding that GDI is lower than HDI powerfully indicates where women stand. How these social factors interact with gender is discussed in further detail using the example of depression. Ironically, the same qualities that characterize depression and low social rank are regarded as normal and desirable qualities of femininity and encouraged if not enforced through socialization, tradition, and outright discrimination.

A Gendered, Social Model of Depression

As noted, depression imposes the greatest burden of disability related to mental illness worldwide (Murray and Lopez 1996). Gender differences in rates of depression are strongly age related. The greatest differences occur in adult life, with none in childhood and few in the elderly (Piccinelli and Homen 1997). Depression is not only the most prevalent women's mental health problem but often accompanies other psychological disorders common in women such as somatoform disorders, agoraphobia, and panic disorder.

Wide variations do occur between countries in rates of depression and other disorders such as generalized anxiety (Gater et al. 1998), attesting to the importance of cultural factors and social arrangements in the onset of depressive symptoms. In the WHO multicenter study of psychological problems in primary health care, the lowest rate of depression for women, 2.8%, was in Nagasaki, Japan, and the highest, 36.8%, in Santiago, Chile (Ustun and Sartorius 1995). General population studies in Zimbabwe, London, Bilbao, the Outer Hebrides, rural Spain, and rural Basque country showed that women meeting criteria for the disease varied from a low of 2.4% in the Basque country to a high of 30% in Zimbabwe. Negative, irregular, disruptive life events triggered depression in all six countries (Brown 1998).

Negative life events and difficulties are positively related to psychosocial risk factors such as poverty. The population-attributable risk these factors are estimated to make to depression and anxiety is around 60% to 65% (Brown 1998). Compared with the general population, poor women are exposed to more frequent, more threatening, and more uncontrollable life events, such as illness and death of children and imprisonment or death of husbands. They face more dangerous neighborhoods, hazardous workplaces, job insecurity, violence, and discrimination, especially if they belong to minority groups (Belle 1990; Patel et al. 1999). The net result is to reduce autonomy, control, and decision-making latitude. Other gender-based events such as having two or more abortions, and experiencing sexual abuse or other forms of violence and adversity in childhood or adult life also contribute significantly to poorer mental health (Acierno et al. 1997; Fellitti et al. 1998).

Most research on these risk factors is cross-sectional, a snapshot at one time, and as such is incapable of measuring the true burden that cumulative psychosocial adversity imposes on women's mental health. If persistence in adversity is neither accurately measured nor disentangled from persistence in depressive symptoms, it is impossible to account for its possible role on the latter.

Models of stress and coping informed a great deal of research into depression (Williams and Umberson 2000), as the risk of a depressive episode occurring increases in the presence of continuing anxiety (Brown et al. 1996). One particular line of research concentrated on investigating the social origins of depression in women since the late 1970s (Brown and Harris 1978). It identified three critical interconnecting features of depression:

1. Provoking elements or severe life events

2. Vulnerability factors, which increase risk in the presence of a provoking agent

3. Symptom formation factors, which influence the form but not the risk of a depressive disorder occurring, such as a comorbidity of an anxiety disorder

It was suggested that 85% of women from the community (as opposed to a patient group) who developed "caseness" for depression in a two-year study experienced a severe event in the six months before onset (Brown et al. 1995). Depression occurs when a severe event (or events) is accompanied by vulnerability factors, especially those associated with low self-esteem and inadequate support. Matching the nature of such an event with a pronounced continuing difficulty was critical (Brown 1998).

Severe events that provoked depression almost always concerned a loss or sense of defeat in relation to a core relationship. This lends further support to self-in-relation theorists who hold that women place a high degree of importance on the quality and perceived success of their inter-personal relationships (Jordan et al. 1991). Nevertheless, loss or danger seems to play a much less important etiological role, once humiliation and entrapment aspects of severe events are taken into account. Almost three-fourths of severe events occurring in the six months before onset of depression involved entrapment or humiliation. In contrast, just over one-fifth involved loss alone and only 5% concerned danger alone (Brown et al. 1995).

Humiliation and sense of entrapment could equally be used as indica-tors of a profound sense of inequality and low social position. It is the meaning attached to an event, or its symbolism, not the event per se that must be captured accurately if valid constructs of depression are to be developed:

Probably equally significant to being humiliated and devalued is what is symbol-ised by such atypical events in terms of the woman's life as a whole—in particular, the experience of being confirmed as marginal and unwanted. (Brown et al. 1995:19)

The view that humiliation and devaluation occur only in relation to atypical events is challenged by evidence about the chronic nature of much gender-based violence. The prevalence of such violence is alarm-ingly high (see Garcia Moreno this volume). Compared with men, women are at greatly increased risk of being assaulted by an intimate (Kessler et al. 1995), and violence in the home tends to be repetitive and escalates in severity over time (American Medical Association on Scientific Affairs 1992). Thus it encapsulates all three features identified in social theories of depression: humiliation, enforced inferior ranking and subordination, and blocked escape or entrapment. Violence, physical, sexual, and psy-chological, is linked with high rates of depression and comorbid psycho-pathology, multisomatization, altered health behaviors, changed patterns of health care use, and disorders affecting many body systems (Resnick et al. 1997; Felitti et al. 1998). Being subjected to coercive control leads to diminished self-esteem and coping ability (Ellsberg 1997).

The likely causal role of violence in depression, anxiety, and other con-ditions such as posttraumatic stress disorder is suggested by findings from three separate lines of enquiry.

1. Marked reductions in level of depression and anxiety occur once women stop experiencing violence and feel safe (Campbell et al. 1996), compared with increases in depression and anxiety when violence continues (Sutherland et al. 1998).

2. The severity and duration of violence predict the severity of adverse psychological outcomes even when other potentially significant factors are statistically controlled in data analysis. This was found in studies on the mental health impact of domestic violence (Roberts et al. 1998) and childhood sexual abuse (Mullen et al. 1993).

3. Significantly higher rates of depression and anxiety are seen in large community samples among those exposed to violence compared with those not exposed (Mullen et al. 1988; Saunders and Hamberger 1993).

By contrast, psychosocial resources, the wherewithal to exercise choice, having a confidante, social activities, and a sense of control over one's life form critical bulwarks against depression regardless of a woman's age (Zunzunegui et al. 1998). Autonomy and control are the obverse of entrapment and humiliation. No surprise, they significantly lessen the risk of depression occurring in the context of what might otherwise be considered an important loss. When marital separation was initiated by the woman, only about 10% of such women developed depression (Brown et al. 1995). When separation was almost entirely initiated by her partner, around half the women developed depression. The rate of depression increased again if infidelity was discovered and *not* followed by separation.

Studies conducted in Zimbabwe offer further insight into the relationship between the nature and frequency of severe events and associated rates of depression. The first study reported an annual incidence of depression of 18% (Abas and Broadhead 1997), but it increased to 30.8% in the second study (Broadhead and Abas 1998). According to the researchers, the excess of cases in the second study was due primarily to increased numbers of severe and disruptive events and difficulties occurring in these women's lives. The severe events reflected, "the high levels of physical illness and premature death in family members, the predicaments associated with seasonal migration between rural and urban homes, problems associated with infertility and the large number of marital and other relationship crises" (Broadhead and Abas 1998).

These findings suggest a strong linear relationship between the number and severity of events and the prevalence of depression (Brown 1998). In circumstances of severe psychosocial adversity, interpersonal relationships can function as "conduits of stress" rather than sources of social support (Belle 1990). Clearly, location-specific and time-specific social, occupational, and environmental conditions must be accounted for in determining the true relationship among severe events, life difficulties, and depression.

The link among a sense of loss and defeat, entrapment, and humiliation denoting devaluation and marginalization is strengthened by related research on social rank (Gilbert and Allan 1998). This research reveals that depression is strongly related to perceptions of the self as inferior or in an unwanted subordinate position, low self-confidence, and behaving in submissive or nonassertive ways, having a sense of defeat in relation to important battles, and at the same time, wanting to escape but being trapped. The overlap among these variables, gender stereotypes, and women's inferior social status is striking.

The workplace is another area where rank is predictive of depression. Work characteristics, especially skill discretion and decision-making authority, are closely allied to employment grade and make the largest contribution to explaining differences in well-being and depression. The highest levels of well-being and least depression are found in highest employment grade; the reverse is true for those in lowest grades. Those in lowest employment grades have a higher prevalence of negative life events and chronic stressors and less social support. Women were most likely to occupy lower-status jobs with little decision-making discretion. Their well-being was improved more by contact with friends than relatives, and material problems were more predictive in explaining the gradient in well-being for women than for men (Stansfeld et al. 1998).

Gender socialization and gender roles that stress passivity, submission, and lower rank are reinforced for women by their structural position in paid employment and their larger contribution to unpaid domestic and caring work in the home. Evidence relating to social theories of depression described here, supports Stein's (1997) view that perceptions of equity and equality, the meaning and symbolism attached to particular events and experiences, accurately reflect where one stands in the scale of things and strongly influence mental health.

Research on the subjective correlates of events related to subordinate status or lower rank complements earlier work that documented the relationship between various objective measures of rank and increased likelihood of poor health, depression, and anxiety. Rank-related variables are found in clusters, rarely in isolation, and are strongly related to gender and depression. They include low education status, unemployment or low employment status, single parent status, homelessness and insecure housing tenure, and inadequate income, poor social support, and diminished social capital (Macran et al. 1996; Kawachi et al. 1999; Patel et al. 1999).

A gendered, social determinants view of depression contests traditional biologically based theories of women's increased "proneness" and "vulnerability," by reference to evidence on women's social position and their different susceptibility and exposure to mental health risk factors. Such an approach offers an alternative explanation of gender differences in rates of depression and other common mental disorders by attempting to integrate women's perceptions of themselves and their place in the scale of things with events and experiences that are identified as triggering these perceptions.

Summary and Policy Recommendations

If the global burden of disability associated with poor mental health and especially depression is to be reduced by 2020, available research evidence on the relationship between gender and mental health suggests several developments that are necessary in the areas of policy, research, and clinical practice. Most critical, mental health has to become a priority on the health policy agenda. Its prominence in national health policies should be consistent with evidence relating to the significance of its contribution to the global burden of disease and it must be gender sensitive.

Genderless mental health policy is poor policy, incapable of engaging with the specific risk factors that have to be reduced for mental health to improve. For example, depression has well-identified gender-specific risk factors. Policy that ignores the risks known to initiate and maintain depression in women, while claiming in general terms to be interested in risk factor reduction, is disingenuous, if not nonsensical.

Gendered policy seeks to promote mental health, not merely respond to mental illness. Its overall objective is to assist individuals, groups, and communities increase control over the determinants of mental health, enhance subjective well-being, facilitate optimal development and the use of mental abilities, and work toward achieving goals consistent with justice and gender equality. A gendered view of social capital and a population mental health perspective is necessary to meet this objective. Otherwise long-standing gender inequities and gender-blind policy making will continue systemically to disadvantage women, erode their social capital, and compromise their mental health.

The role of gender requires careful articulation in three broad areas of mental health that require action.

Gender Focus in Mental Health Research

Gender bias in scientific inquiry cannot be overcome or the quality of research evidence improved simply by presenting gender-disaggregated data, while continuing to use the same crude measures of socioeconomic status and other socially structured determinants of health. Existing measures are ill equipped to capture differences in gendered social conditions affecting mental health. They ignore the impact of cumulative psychosocial adversity (Bracke 2000) and are blind to structural economic reforms that pose additional socially based gender-specific risks to mental health (Patel et al. 1999). Measures have to be revised accordingly.

Increased research, with a sharper focus on the mental health impact of gender-specific structural disadvantage that increases vulnerability to the sudden, disruptive changes to income, employment, and living conditions accompanying fast-paced economic reform, structural adjustment, and globalization, is urgently needed to inform policy and programs.

Cross-sectional research has revealed significant factors in the onset of depression but much more longitudinal research is required to understand how changes in social and household conditions mediate the course of depression and its chronicity (Bracke 2000).

Women's overrepresentation among those with psychiatric comorbidity (Kessler et al. 1994) together with the heightened burden of disability associated with comorbidity argues for gender-focused research to identify risk factors for comorbidity. In particular, complex linkages among depression in women, multisomatization, and psychiatric comorbidity in the context of a history of violent victimization have to be clarified.

Better recognition and understanding of mental health aspects of reproductive health for both women and men is necessary. Care must be taken to not focus narrowly on biological causes of mental disorders when researching women's reproductive health. Not only are risks from mental disorders for women's nonreproductive health needs overlooked, but so are men's mental health risks in reproduction.

A reproductive rights framework should be adopted in research to improve the ethical and interpretive dimensions of research into reproductive psychology. The impact on mental health of reproductive rights violations such as failure to gain informed consent, denial of patient privacy, and use of interventionist practices that have no scientific justification scarcely figures in the voluminous body of research on the psychological aspects of infertility, pregnancy, childbirth, and parenting. Improving reproductive health outcomes of women in developing countries is unlikely to be achieved unless women's own mental health concerns and life priorities are taken into account in program design and implementation (Avotri and Walters 1999).

The link among gender, depression, and cardiovascular disease (Musselman et al. 1998) illustrates why gender must be mainstreamed into the broader research agenda. Unless this occurs, significant associations between gender and physical and mental health will continue to be overlooked.

Gender Considerations in Health Promotion and Health Care

Mental health-promotion strategies cannot expect to reduce single risk behaviors, such as smoking, while ignoring concurrent behavioral, social, and psychologic conditions within which the targeted behavior is embedded. The many reciprocal levels of functioning among the individual, the group, and the broader social environment have to inform a broader concept of mental health promotion.

Gender equity and access considerations must be recognized in promoting mental health and providing health services if realistic assessments are to be made regarding the controllability and modifiability of risk factors. Programs that focus solely on individual lifestyle factors are in danger of ignoring the structural disadvantage in which behavioral risk factors such as smoking are embedded.

The concept of meaningful assistance in health care must be promoted. It implies a patient-centered approach. Underdiagnosed and poorly treated conditions, especially the combination of depression, violence-related health conditions, and significant psychosocial problems, urgently require meaningful assistance.

Zero tolerance health education and promotion campaigns around violence against women should be designed using culturally appropriate formats to counter cultural beliefs and attitudes that condone and perpetuate violence, and to reduce the prevalence and adverse mental health effects of gender-based violence.

The high rates of depression in women and alcohol dependence in men strongly indicate a large unmet need for improved access to low-cost or preferably no-cost gender-sensitive counseling services.

Gender Determinants of Mental Health

Intersectoral collaboration and across-government gender-sensitive policy making must be carried out in relation to education, social security, housing, workplace relations, transport and employment as well as health. These areas reflect the many structural determinants of mental health and it is imperative, at a policy level, that they be facilitated to work in positive synergy with one another, maintain social capital, and support social networks (Kawachi et al. 1999). Social safety nets are particularly important for women given their overrepresentation among those living in poverty and dependence on Social Security benefits.

Without gender equity in the distribution of the profits associated with economic growth, an unacceptable rise will occur in the severe events and life difficulties that trigger common mental disorders. These will be concentrated among women who already bear the brunt of socioeconomic disadvantage (Broadhead and Abas 1998; Patel et al. 1999).

Finally, women's status and life opportunities remain "tragically low" worldwide (WHO 1998g), and research shows that low status is a potent mental health risk. For too many women, experiences of self-worth, competence, autonomy, economic independence, and physical, sexual, and emotional safety and security, so essential to good mental health, are systematically denied because they are women. This gross violation of women's human rights directly contributes to the growing burden of disability caused by poor mental health.

Note

1. The same three indicators are used in both composite indexes, namely, life expectancy, education attainment, and income.

7

Reorienting Public Health: Exploring Differentials in Hip Fracture[1]

Rachel Snow

At the beginning of the twenty-first century the search for genetic knowledge dominates health research and informs our paradigms of causality and prevention. Developments in molecular epidemiology permeate every aspect of biological science and a large measure of behavioral science as well. Our understanding of the major causes of human death and disability, however, suggests that genetic and social determinants of health rarely operate independently, but undergo myriad complex interactions from fetal life on.

The objective of public health is to reduce health inequalities and raise overall health standards. To this end, we investigate the causes of differences in health status and outcomes to identify whether such differences are a consequence of social inequalities (which can be modified) or inherent biologic (genetic) factors. Sorting out the relative contributions of experiential versus genetic determinants of human health is no simple task.

Hip fracture is one of the most important causes of morbidity and mortality among older people, and among older women in particular. Although overall population burden is currently highest in Europe and the United States, rapid increases in age-specific incidence rates in Asia combined with demographic aging, warn of an emerging epidemic in developing countries.

Focus on bone mineral density (BMD) as a determinant of hip fracture mirrors a more general, exaggerated enthusiasm for genetic models of disability that emphasize one's sex and racial biological characteristics. Epidemiological evidence, however, points to more social and environmental determinants, some of which are gendered, but each of which warrants further exploration.

Locating Genetics in a Gender and Equity Analysis of Health

Differences in health between males and females have come under in-creased scrutiny in recent years. In particular, interest is growing in the extent to which they are attributable to sex-linked genetic differences or to social roles.[2]

Developmental differences due to sex (e.g., whether the fetus develops testis vs ovaries, or produces more testosterone than estrogen) affect a person's vulnerability to specific diseases or disabilities and their severity and prognosis (Garenne and Lafon 1998). Gender analysis attempts to distinguish health conditions attributed to the genotype versus the sex phenotype. In biologic shorthand, gender differences in health are caused by society's response to secondary sex characteristics that distinguish males from females. Because a child appears to be male, society provides opportunities and constraints that affect his health. If he were male, yet appeared female to society (and himself), he would presumably experi-ence the gendered health risks common to females.

Whereas distinctions between sex and gender are the backbone of a gender analysis of health, locating genetic determinants in a gender and equity analysis of health is more complex. In addition to asking to what extent genetic sex accounts for health differences between males and fe-males, we are challenged to ask to what extent other genetic factors also contribute to differences in health outcomes? Of social and environmen-tal determinants, to what extent are these nongenetic factors a conse-quence of gender or of other forms of discrimination?

Gender and equity analysis can be approached as a four-step game of elimination. First, identify to what extent genetic sex contributes to observed male-female differences. Second, identify to what extent other genetic factors contribute to the disparities. Of the remaining differences for which there are no known genetic determinants, how much of the experiential (social and environmental) component is gendered? Finally, how much is due to other social inequalities?

Whereas this model represents the minimum analytic steps necessary to undertake a gender and equity analysis of a given disease or disability, few studies have carried out such an analysis. Instead, a growing tendency has been to emphasize either a genetic approach or a social discrimination approach to explain male-female differences, as well as differences among women (or among men).

The combination by which sex traits, genetic traits other than sex, gender inequalities, and other social inequalities contribute to ill health is probably specific to a given disease or disability. One can find diseases or disabilities for which each of these is dominant to varying degrees. For example, in the case of maternal mortality, the male-female disparity is due to sex. However, disparities between women are rarely attributable to genetic traits other than sex, but overwhelmingly attributable to social inequalities among women and among regions. Some social inequalities are gendered, but these are eclipsed by the greater role of poverty.

A contrasting example is death and disability due to traffic accidents, where the risk is partly attributable to sex (Resnick et al. 1993), but has no associations with other genetic factors. It is significantly gender based, as men own more cars, drive more often and faster, wear seatbelts less often, and drink and drive more. But is also a consequence of social inequalities other than gender. More accidents and more fatal accidents per driver occur in poorer countries for a range of economic and structural reasons.

In cases where sex differences in health are largely due to gender (traffic accidents, lung cancer, interpersonal violence), differences *within a given sex* are also largely a consequence of social inequalities, albeit inequalities other than gender inequality. Indeed, it is difficult to identify a health condition for which significant disparities between the sexes are attributable to gender, and for which disparities in that same condition between women, or between men, are not also largely attributable to social inequalities. Simply put, where social bias determines the health risks between the sexes, it is a forewarning that this particular health condition is subject to social configurations overall, to employment opportunities, education levels, economic security, or social prejudice.

Case Study: Determinants of Hip Fracture

The Burden of Hip Fractures
Hip fractures are one of the most disabling health problems among the elderly, and their incidence among women is almost three times that of

Table 7.1
Regional and ethnic differences in the incidence of hip fracture

Country (year)	Women	Men
Singapore (1955–62)[a]	80	100
Beijing, China (1990)[a]	87	97
Hong Kong (1965–67)[a]	150	100
Hong Kong (1985)	353	181
Kuwait (1985)[a]	295	200
California Hispanics (1983–84)[a]	200	90
California blacks (1983–84)[a]	220	140
California Asians (1983–84)[a]	340	100
California whites (1983–84)[a]	560	210
USA Caucasians (1985)	510–559	174–202
Sweden (1992–95)	850	360
Norway (1983–84)	1290	550

[a] All rates are age-standardized to the United States population.
Adapted from Lau 1996; Memon et al. 1998; Xu et al. 1996; Rogmark et al. 1999.

men. Overall risk and the sex ratio increase after age sixty-five, as women make up an ever-increasing segment of the population. In 1990, women experienced 73% of the global total of 1.7 million hip fractures (Gullberg et al. 1997). A sex ratio of 3:1 female:male is common in high-incidence countries (North America, northern Europe) and ranges as high as 4:1 in Iceland (Lips 1997). Where overall incidence rates are low, the sex ratio is closer to unity.

Historical data suggest that when overall incidence begins to increase, excess female vulnerability emerges (table 7.1; Lau 1996). However, in several high-incidence countries the extreme ratio may be declining slightly. As age-specific fracture rates leveled off in the last decade among women age sixty to eighty-nine years (Denmark, United Kingdom, United States), rates among men continued to increase (Kannus et al. 1996; Cumming et al. 1997a).

Hip fracture is associated with up to 35% mortality after fracture (Jacobsen et al. 1992), with most of that excess risk occurring in the first six to twelve months. Excess mortality is higher for hip fractures than other fractures (Center et al. 1999) and in people with comorbidities (Marottoli et al. 1994). Mortality and disability after hip fracture are a consequence of overall health, good clinical care, and social support. Hence, the rise in fracture rates in poorer regions will likely be linked to worsening trends in prognosis, but sound data are hard to find. A more common consequence is loss of functional independence. In Switzerland, at least 10% of patients lose functional independence after hip fracture accidents and a further 10% are placed in home care (Bonjour et al. 1997).

Changing Epidemiologic Patterns Worldwide

Whereas hip fracture is a disability found among the affluent countries, rapid increases in developing Asian countries foreshadow an epidemic in poorer regions.[3] Gains in life expectancy in much of the developing world in the coming decades will lead to a sharp increase in the global burden of these events. An estimated 1.7 million hip fractures occurred world wide in 1990. Without changes in age-specific rates, total annual numbers will reach 2.6 million by the year 2025 and 4.5 million by 2050 (Gullberg et al. 1997).

To worsen projections, there is an unexplained rapid rise in age-specific rates in many regions, particularly in urban areas (Larsson et al. 1989). Age-standardized rates among persons over age fifty in Finland increased by 51% among women and 80% among men between 1970 and 1991 (Pakkari et al. 1994). Similar trends were seen in other European countries; age-standardized rates in Greece increased by 80% from 1977 to 1992 (Paspati et al. 1998). Particularly notable are the rapid increases in Asia, given that starting rates in the mid-twentieth century were well below those in Europe or the United States. In Singapore, age-specific hip fracture rates among women over sixty more than doubled between 1957 and 1985 and in Hong Kong they nearly doubled from 1966 to 1985 (Lau 1996; Lau and Cooper 1996). Most recently (1988–1992), rates in Beijing increased by approximately 33% (Xu et al. 1996).

Reasons for these increasing rates are poorly understood. Evidence implicates changes in physical work (specifically increases in desk work and car ownership), possibly accompanied by changes in diet. Whereas regional determinants of the trends may differ, Singapore and Beijing may simply be initiating a delayed epidemiological transition that will see hip fracture incidence rise to Western levels. Trends in developing regions such as Africa and south Asia should be closely monitored.

Regardless of cause, if upward trends in age-specific rates continue, the total global number of hip fractures by the year 2050 could range from 13.3 to 21.3 million (Gullberg 1997), three to five times the rates projected by increases in life expectancy alone. The combination of increased population aging in East and south Asia and the increase in age-specific rates will cause a dramatic shift in the global burden of fracture to Asia in the coming two to three decades. In 1990 only 26% of all hip fractures occurred in Asia, but the region will have close to 50% by 2025 (Cooper et al. 1992).

The Determinants of Hip Fracture from a Gender and Health Equity Analysis

Hip fracture provides an illustrative case for a gender and health equity analysis, because the risk is a complex mixture of both biologic sex and social factors, some of which are gendered. I believe undue emphasis is placed on bone density and genetic (sex and race) determinants. A research agenda that would more fully explore the social and interactive determinants of the disability may offer more practical and affordable public health prevention strategies.

Sex and the Risk of Hip Fracture

The risk of hip fracture increases with age and therefore women's greater life expectancy relative to men's leads to an overall greater lifetime risk. Among persons age sixty-five years and older in the United States in 1996, almost 60% were female; among those eighty-five and older, more than 70% were female. In addition, age-adjusted incidence rates for hip fracture show women at greater risk than men in almost all studies, but the ratio varies across population groups (see table 7.1). In Netherlands in 1993, one-fourth of all hip fractures occurred in males. In each age group, the incidence in men was approximately half that of women and equivalent to the rate in women approximately five years younger (De Laet et al. 1997).

Age-adjusted male-female differences are largely attributed to hormonally dependent sex differences in BMD. Indeed, the BMD of male infants

(1–18 mo adjusted for weight, age, and height) is significantly, albeit slightly, greater than that of female infants (Rupich et al. 1996), but this difference is more pronounced after puberty. The pubertal growth spurt is longer in boys, leading to greater peak bone mass at skeletal maturity, and BMD at the femoral neck (hip) is higher for males than females at all ages (Diaz et al. 1997). After menopause (after 49 yrs of age) BMD drops precipitously in women (Tsouderos et al. 1994; Soda et al. 1993), whereas loss in men is minimal until almost 70 years (Diaz et al. 1997).

Whereas the postmenopausal (estrogen-dependent) decline in BMD coincides with the age-related rise in the risk of hip fracture, the overall predictive value of bone density on hip fracture is weak (Seeman 1997; De Laet et al. 1997; Aspray et al. 1996; Marshall et al. 1996; Cummings 1985). A review of fifteen case-control studies (Cummings 1985) concluded that patients with hip fracture were not significantly more osteoporotic than age-matched controls.

A more recent meta-analysis reported that a BMD below 1 standard deviation of the age-adjusted mean was associated with a relative risk for hip fracture of approximately 2.6 (Marshall et al. 1996), but nonetheless concluded that they could not recommend a screening program measuring bone density: "There is a wide overlap in the bone densities of patients who develop a fracture and those who do not. Thus BMD can identify people who are at increased risk of developing a fracture, but it cannot with any certainty identify individuals who will develop a future fracture." The distribution of bone density (standard deviations from the population average) from British Columbia among women with hip fracture and age-matched controls illustrate this extensive overlap (figure 7.1; Law et al. 1991 cited in Green et al. 2000).

Among the oldest cohorts, who are at the highest risk of hip fracture, the contribution of the decline in bone density to the exponential increase in risk with age is relatively small (De Laet et al. 1997). A summary assessment from Germany concluded that the relative contribution of the reduction in bone density to fracture actually declines with age, whereas the relative contribution of nonskeletal risk factors, especially the risk of falling, increases (Luehmann et al. 2000).

Hormone differences between sexes may affect the risk through other mechanisms. Overall muscle mass appears to be protective, and this may

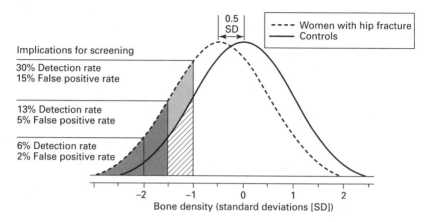

Figure 7.1
Distribution of bone mineral density in women with hip fracture and age-matched controls. Implied vertical axis is proportion of cases and controls within a marginal unit of bone density. Expected screening performance of measurement is shown by three examples, 1991. (Law et al. 1991, cited in Green et al. 2000).

contribute to a biological advantage for males. Males develop more lean (muscle) mass than females during puberty and sustain greater muscle mass through adulthood. Hip fracture is associated with lower quadricep (thigh) muscle strength (Nguyen et al. 1996), greater age-related loss of muscle fiber size in the quadriceps (Aniansson et al. 1984), arm muscle area (Huang et al. 1996), and lower lean mass overall.

Within a given ethnic group, males also have on average greater overall body mass than females. This is associated with fewer fractures. Again the association holds within, but not necessarily across, different ethnic groups. Male-female differences in falling might conceivably reflect sex differences in lateral stability due to greater muscle mass in men.

Sex hormone profiles also vary among women (and among men), and clinical conditions associated with certain hormone profiles show some associations with hip fracture. For example, endometrial cancer is a consequence of prolonged exposure to excess estrogens (due to excess production and/or decreased binding) and hip fracture is lower among women with the disease (Persson et al. 1992). Excess estrogen production may also account for evidence of a low risk of hip fracture among women of high parity (Wyshak 1981), but contradictory associations with parity were observed in Japan (higher hip fracture with higher parity) (Fujiwara et al. 1997).

Genetic Factors other than Sex

There is almost no available documentation on the inheritability of hip fracture risk. Hip fracture is just rare enough and occurs late enough in life that adequate family studies would have to be extremely large and take place over many years. However, dramatic differences in hip fracture incidence by region and ethnic group have led to speculation that hip fracture may be associated with inherited differences in bone density. Data to support such speculation are weak. Differences in hip fracture rates across regions and population groups are considerable and they eclipse sex differences within a population; that is, differences between women of different ethnic, regional, or social groups are often greater than differences between males and females within a given population. There is consistent evidence that African-Americans have lower hip fracture rates (figure 7.2; Gilsanz et al. 1998) and greater BMD than Caucasian Americans, and the difference in bone density remains significant after adjustment for body size (Kleerkoper 1994). Multiracial studies

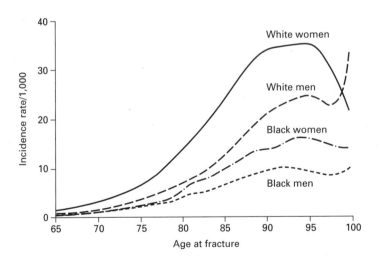

Figure 7.2
Age- and sex-specific annual incidence of hip fracture, United States, 1990. (Jacobsen et al. 1990, cited in Cumming et al. 1997a).

from South Africa also concluded that persons of African descent have higher BMD than whites or people of color (Patel et al. 1993).

Notable as the American and South African data may be, generalizations that populations of African descent have genetically higher BMD and therefore are at low risk of hip fracture (leading to low projections for hip fracture in continental Africa) should be regarded with caution. In the Gambia and the United Kingdom, BMD measured at the lumbar spine in Gambian women was about half that in United Kingdom women and declined at younger ages (Asprey et al. 1996; figure 7.3). In light of

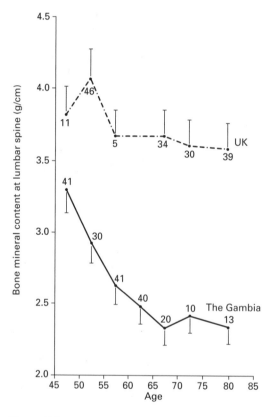

Figure 7.3
Changes in bone mineral content between the ages of 45 and 85 years in Gambian and British women at the lumbar spine between L2 and L4. Data presented are mean ± SE, and the number of subjects scanned is stated for each half-decade group, 1996. (Aspray et al. 1996.)

the low fracture rates among Gambian women, it is necessary to reevaluate the hypothesis that differences in BMD account for population differences in hip or vertebral fracture. The findings also challenge the presumption that with regard to bone density, African-Americans are representative of populations in Africa.

East Asian data also consistently challenge the hypothesis that racial differences in BMD explain population differences in fracture rates. The BMD among Asian-American or Japanese populations is similar to that of Caucasian Americans (Cundy et al. 1995; Russell-Aulet et al. 1993)[4] and based on standard measures, the proportion of women in Japan estimated to have low BMD is approximately the same as in the United States. Furthermore, a study comparing native Japanese, Japanese-born Americans, and American-born women of Japanese ancestry found progressively higher BMD among the latter two groups (Ross et al. 1989; table 7.2). Such migration data not only underscore that BMD is adaptable to social and environmental conditions, but further weaken the hypothesis that it plays a prominent role in hip fracture, because it is in Japan that hip fracture rates are lowest.

Fracture rates among Asians are significantly below those of Caucasians in the United States or Europe. The overall incidence in Japan is approximately 1 in 2,500 (50,000/125,000,000), compared with about

Table 7.2
Adjusted bone mineral density (g/cm^2) comparison among Japanese Americans born in the United States (JA), Japanese Americans born in Japan (JB), and native Japanese (NJ), 1993

Location	Age-, height-, and weight-adjusted BMD[a]		
	JA	JB	NJ[b]
L2–4 spine	1.075[b]	1.059[b]	1.029[c]
Femur neck	0.851[b]	0.830	0.813
Ward's triangle	0.744[b]	0.722	0.716
Trochanter	0.736[b]	0.729	0.714

[a] Analysis of covariance with age, age squared, age cubed, height, and weight as covariates.
[b] Significantly different from the MJ group at 0.05.
[c] Significantly different from the JB group at 0.05.
Adapted from Kin et al. 1993.

1 per 1,000 in the United States (Fujita and Fukase 1992). Age-standardized rates among women and men in Beijing are one-sixth and one-half those of Caucasian American women and men, respectively (Xu et al. 1996). Lower rates are also seen among Asian ethnic groups living in the United States, where Korean, Chinese, and Japanese groups all have lower age-adjusted rates than American Caucasians (Lauderdale et al. 1997).

The extent to which BMD is associated with fracture appears to be modified by other factors that are not well understood. Within populations at high risk, women with bone densities in the lowest percentiles (5th) are significantly more vulnerable than those in the highest percentiles (75th; Huang and Himes 1997). A relative risk of 2.6 was suggested when BMD dips below 1 SD of the age-adjusted mean (Marshall et al. 1996). Even in this setting, clinical benefits of screening are not apparent, as the predictive value is too low (Luehmann et al. 2000; Marshall et al. 1996). In populations that have an overall low incidence of fracture (Japan, rural Gambia), even a low BMD appears to bear no increased risk for fracture (Fujita and Fukase 1992; Aspray et al. 1996, 1997). Hence, other risk factors must be investigated and a focus on BMD would be misleading.

Despite the ambivalence of these data, research efforts are under way to explore the genetic basis of BMD. Gene polymorphisms of interest include vitamin D-receptor (VDR)-3, VDR-5, collagen type 1-Sp1-binding site, estrogen receptor, transforming growth factor-β, interleukin-6, and a gene or genes at chromosome 11q12–13 (Ferrari et al. 1998).

Most authors acknowledge that BMD is a complex trait, and that gene(s) are likely only to contribute to differences found in human populations. Nonetheless, several studies (Koller et al. 1998; Ferrari et al. 1998; Kiel et al. 1997) support possible ethnic genetic differences in the nutritional regulation of bone density. Given that the overall explanatory power of bone density to predict fracture risk is weak, it is hard to sustain intellectual enthusiasm for these studies. A likely outcome of the research is the development of targeted drugs for enhancing BMD, but the question remains whether such therapies are the most cost effective for reducing hip fractures (Seeman 1997).

Discounting BMD as a means of explaining ethnic variations in hip fracture, is there evidence for other structural genetic distinctions that may account for ethnic differences? Hip geometry among some Asian populations differs from that of Caucasians (Chin et al. 1997), but its association with risk of falling or hip fracture remains speculative. Both Indians and Chinese are distinguished by shorter femoral neck length and shorter hip axis (after adjusting for height) relative to European Caucasians. Further research on possible associations between hip geometry and the risk of falling, or hip fracture, would be helpful.

Social and Environmental Determinants: Gendered and Nongendered Factors

While studies explore the genetic basis of BMD, rapid increases in hip fracture incidence suggest a more prominent role for social and environmental determinants. The most blatant socioeconomic difference is that risk is higher in rich than in poor countries. Within given regions, hip fractures are also more common in urban than rural populations (Kaastad et al. 1998). Higher rates among urban dwellers are hypothesized to result from a combination of reduced physical activity, sedentary jobs, higher rates of smoking, reduced exposure to sunlight, and poorer nutrition. But the interaction of such risk factors in large controlled studies has not been adequately explored, and roles of gender, social class, and changing lifestyles among the elderly remain unexamined.

Isolation at Older Ages   Sex differences in life expectancy contribute directly to the greater burden of hip fracture among women through higher percentages of women living among older groups. Such differences are not static, but were closer to unity in mid nineteenth-century Europe and appear to be contracting again (Arber and Thomas 2000). Therefore, they appear to reflect dynamic social factors and can therefore be attributed to gender as easily as to genetic attributes.

Differences in life expectancy between sexes contribute to the greater probability that older women live alone, without spousal support. Gendered social norms for marriage encourage husbands to be older than wives in most cultures, increasing the probability that women will outlive their spouses and be left without a domestic partner beyond that which would have occurred if they married partners of the same age. Furthermore, older widowed or divorced men are more likely to remarry than women in similar circumstances. The British general household survey (1992–1994) found 61% of men over sixty-five live with a spouse, versus 35% of women (Arber and Cooper 1999). Being unmarried (or more likely, living alone) enhances the risk of hip fracture and one might argue that gendered social norms for spousal ages are in this case detrimental to women's old-age care.

The domestic independence of older women is not solely a function of greater survival time or even of age differences among spouses. Looking only at older persons without a spouse, women in the United Kingdom are still more than twice as likely as men to live alone rather than with others. Such social and domestic arrangements vary significantly across culture and region. United Nations data (figure 7.4) indicate that only 30% to 35% of men age over eighty-five live alone in France or Netherlands and 8% to 12% live alone in Hong Kong or Japan. But for women, a stark regional contrast is apparent. Whereas only 10% to 15% of women over eighty-five live alone in Hong Kong or Japan, close to 60% in France and Netherlands do (UN 1993).

It may be fruitful to examine more fully the extent to which international social differences in elderly women's independence (or isolation) contribute to regional and ethnic differences in hip fracture. Widowhood or being single in the West is associated with a high probability of being alone, but the same does not hold in east Asia or possibly in other settings. Hence while being unmarried and elderly is a risk factor for hip fracture in the West, it may not be the case in other settings.

Living with a partner, being married, and the presence of social support more broadly are positive predictors of recovery after hip fracture (Cummings et al. 1988; Schurch et al. 1996; Steiner et al. 1997) and they are also gendered. A range of studies from the United Kingdom indicates that the likelihood that a spouse will care for a disabled partner is similar, regardless of sex (Arber 2000). However, men who provide care for their wives relinquish the responsibility more quickly, are more likely to have supplementary help in caring for wives, and receive more social reward for their caretaking.

Falling   Elderly men appear to fall less often than elderly women. Studies in Jerusalem and Hawaii report female:male ratios of 2:1 for falls (Dresner-Pollack et al. 1996; Davis et al. 1997). These differences may

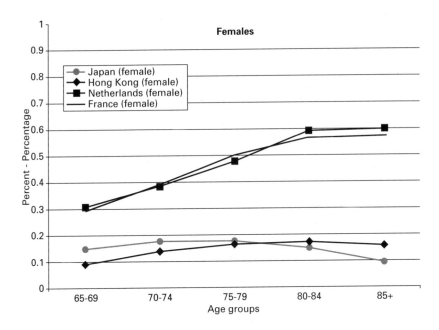

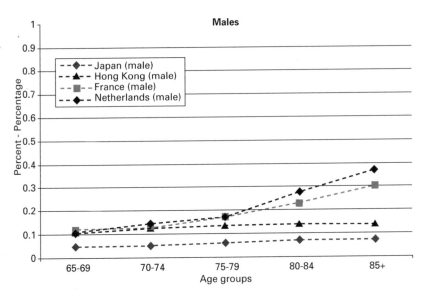

Figure 7.4
The percentage of elderly males and females living alone at different ages, Netherlands (1990), France (1990), Japan (1990), Hong Kong (1986). (United Nations Demographic Yearbook, Special Issue on Population Aging 1993.)

reflect genetic sex differences in muscle strength (enhanced by gender differences in physical work) or gender differences in old age social support or isolation. It would be worth while to examine the universality of the male-female difference in falling and the extent to which it reflects muscle or social risks.

Significant nongender social disparities seem to exist in the occurrence of falls among elderly people in different populations. Japanese women living in Hawaii have age-adjusted rates that are approximately half those of predominately white populations in New Zealand, Finland, or Canada (rate ratios 1.8–2.6). Japanese men in Hawaii fall at rates that are even lower than those of men in these three countries (rate ratios 2.6–4.7; Davis et al. 1997).

The reasons for this Japanese advantage are not clear and speculation touches on a wide range of possibilities: balance, strength in specific muscle groups, hip structure, overall health, vision acuity, and risk taking. In addition, Hawaii has a temperate climate without an icy season, whereas seasonal variations in other countries indicate greatest risk during winter months. Researchers also speculated that the traditional Japanese practice of sitting on tatami mats or on low seats with flexed knees may develop protective hip musculature (Fujita and Fukase 1992). Clearly, the lower probability of living alone at older ages should be included. Identifying the extent to which cultural differences in falling contribute to differences in hip fracture is an important goal for future research.

Trials show a direct impact of physical exercise on reducing rates of falling, but the changes were in the range of 10% (Province et al. 1995; Wolf et al. 1996). If further research shows such effects to be more substantial, targeted physical training is an obvious area for intervention. However, public health strategies need not only focus solely on individual behavior change. The most successful strategies to decrease the occurrence of fractures in the populations are those that prevent people from falling down by keeping roads and sidewalks free from snow and ice and making homes, hospitals, and specific rooms (bathrooms) for the elderly safe.

Physical Work   A particularly gendered dimension of overall health and risk of hip fracture is occupational history. One of the strongest protections against hip fracture is a long history of physical activity, most obvious in a strong protective effect of working at least twenty years in a job with moderate physical labor (Jaglal et al. 1995). A hallmark of urbanization and social development is the reduction of physical work for both sexes, but gender differences persist in trade work (construction, engineering, etc.) in many countries. The continuing physical labor of women in rural areas and in most developing countries may explain in part the low sex ratio in hip fracture in these countries.

Although males have a genetic advantage over females with regard to sheer number and size of muscle fibers, both sexes can increase muscle mass through exercise or physically demanding occupations. People with hip fracture have small quadricep muscles (Aniansson et al. 1984) and little arm muscle (Huang et al. 1996). In both sexes more physical exercise (whether as a youth, an adult, or as an elderly person) is consistently associated with a reduced risk (Cline et al. 1998; Jaglal et al. 1993). Fractures are probably reduced through increased muscle mass, improved hip flexion, greater bone density (a consequence of weight-bearing exercise), and improved lateral stability (i.e. balance), thereby reducing the risk of falls (Shaw and Snow 1998). Physical activity need not be vigorous to have a positive impact: daily walking outdoors, upstairs, uphill, or with a load can be protective (Lau et al. 1988).

Nutrition   Overall poor nutrition status, low total energy intake, protein-calorie malnutrition, weight loss, and low food intake are risk factors (Bonjour et al. 1997; Huang et al. 1996; Meyer et al. 1996). Deficiencies in several nutrients are also important, including vitamin D (LeBoff et al. 1999), zinc (Elmstahl et al. 1998), vitamin K (found in lettuce; Feskanich et al. 1999), and total protein intake (Munger et al. 1999). Evidence shows that higher intakes of vitamin A are associated with an increase in hip fractures. Retinol intakes greater than 1.5 mg a day versus 0.5 mg a day were associated with a doubled risk (Melhus et al. 1998). Of note, vitamin A intake is deficient in many developing countries.

Despite widespread public perceptions that dairy consumption leads to strong bones and reduced hip fracture, this is not the case. Rather, the associations are consistently insignificant, whether looking at total calcium, total dietary calcium, total dairy calcium, or intakes of either milk or cheese (Munger et al. 1999; Owusu et al. 1997; Cumming et al. 1997b; Feskanich et al. 1997; Tavani et al. 1995). It is notable that hip

Table 7.3
Bone mineral content and body size of 5-year-old Hong Kong and Jiangmen children by sex, 1993

	Weight (kg)		Height (cm)		BMC (g/cm)		BMC/BW (g/cm^2)	
Boys								
Hong Kong (n = 67)	17.68[a]	(2.5)	108.28[a]	(4.1)	0.324[a]	(0.039)	0.418[a]	(0.041)
Jiangmen (n = 63)	15.85	(1.6)	103.75	(3.7)	0.278	(0.040)	0.369	(0.04)
Girls								
Hong Kong (n = 61)	17.11[b]	(2.7)	107.9[b]	(4.3)	0.310[b]	(0.046)	0.422[a]	(0.041)
Jiangmen (n = 52)	15.39	(1.7)	103.39	(4.4)	0.269	(0.034)	0.365	(0.037)

BMC, bone mineral content; BW, bone width.
Values are mean (S.D.).
[a] $p < 0.001$.
[b] $p < 0.01$.
Adapted from Lee et al. 1993.

fracture rates are highest in countries with the highest overall intakes of dietary calcium worldwide (Scandinavia, North America).

The confusion reflects the fact that calcium intake is positively associated with bone density. For example, a comparative study of Chinese children living in Jiangmen province and Hong Kong found that, despite being racially identical, the two groups differed dramatically in bone density (Lee et al. 1993). Bone density among mainland Chinese children was approximately half that of Hong Kong children (table 7.3). The authors attributed the difference to significantly lower calcium consumption in Jiangmen. However, the association between dietary calcium and hip fracture is not significant and that between bone density and hip fracture is weak. In China, lower calcium intake does not appear to be a strong risk factor for hip fracture. Rates there are among the lowest in the world, whereas those in Hong Kong are starting to approach figures in the West.

A detrimental impact of high consumption of carbonated cola beverages on bone fractures was suggested (Wyshak and Frisch 1994; Wyshak et al. 1989) and warrants further systematic attention in larger studies. Is this but one component of the urban diet that is detrimental to fracture risk? Are other aspects of traditional diets protective (slow-cooked foods, use of bone, fresh foods, etc.) that are uniformly abandoned with the shift to urban lifestyles?

Overall Health Status and Poverty   Overall ill health is a strong predictor of hip fracture (Proctor et al. 1997; Schurch et al. 1996). Persons with one or more chronic health conditions are at increased risk (Mussolino et al. 1998), as are those with frequent admissions to hospital, poor self-perceived health, and symptoms of poor health such as dizziness and difficulties in daily living (Meyer et al. 1996; Ho et al. 1996). Greater risk is also associated with lower serum albumin, lower overall lymphocytes, smoking, and heavy drinking (Davis et al. 1997; Huang et al. 1996; la Vecchia et al. 1991).[5]

The impact of hip fracture on morbidity and mortality is greatest among individuals with poorest health. Hip fracture patients admitted with a higher total number of diagnoses, lower hemoglobins, or greater cognitive impairment have longer hospitalizations and are less ambulatory at discharge (Furstenberg and Mezey 1987). Those discharged after hip fracture with poorer overall health, poorer cognitive status, or less evidence of social support show lower rates of overall recovery (Schurch et al. 1996; Cummings et al. 1988).

The added risk of hip fracture among those with comorbidities and poor nutrition status increases risk for the poor. In general, persons with low socioeconomic status are most likely to suffer overall poor health and disability, with greater health problems with increasing economic disadvantage. Persons in the United States with family incomes below $14,000 are five times more likely to report only fair or poor health compared with those earning above $50,000. Other correlates of poverty, such as education status, poor nutrition status, and poor health care, also affect the risk of hip fracture. High education is associated with two to four extra years of life free from general disability (National Center for Health Statistics 1997), reducing the risk of comorbidities during hip fracture and the associated poor prognosis.

Gender and income combine to put elderly women at great risk. Older women in the United Kingdom are far more likely to be poor than men of similar age (Arber and Ginn 1991) and more likely to suffer overall poor health and disability (Arber and Cooper 1999). Data from the United States show a similar pattern for disability, with only 37% of men over age eighty-five requiring help with activities of daily living or living in an institution, while 55% of women need help (Guralnick et al. 1997).

Public Health Response: Screening, Therapy and Prevention

International public health discourse on the prevention of hip fracture has been dominated by promotion of diagnostic and screening programs for bone density and of therapies to enhance BMD. Unfortunately, far less attention has been given to identifying and encouraging preventive lifestyles or identifying and eliminating risk factors at the broader societal level.

Diagnostic Standards

The WHO Task Force for Osteoporosis recommends diagnostic standards for screening and preventing hip fracture (WHO 1999b, 1994b). Given that the group is organized by a common interest in osteoporosis (as opposed to fracture prevention), it follows that the scientific and clinical emphases of their recommendations focus on the association between bone density and fracture. Diagnostic criteria for osteoporosis is 2.5 standard deviations (SD) below the young mean adult BMD (WHO 1994b). "Women with BMD below these values should be offered appropriate treatment, but intervention can also be directed at menopausal women with BMD between -1 and -2.5 SD because of their increased future fracture risk." Acknowledging that universal BMD screening is not cost effective, they suggest that "it should be applied to those with one or more strong risk factors; it could be argued that menopause is one such risk factor."

The WHO criteria would diagnose at least 30% of women over age fifty years as having osteoporosis and thereby be candidates for therapeutic intervention (Seeman 1997). Sixty-six percent of women in British Columbia would be at risk by these standards (Green et al. 2000). Bone density among Gambian women drops at younger ages than in the United Kingdom, which suggests that this percentage could be even higher in other populations (Aspray et al. 1995). In either case, treatment implications are overwhelming.

Measuring BMD is not simple and requires expensive equipment. The method of choice is dual-photon absorptiometry. Reference data and algorithms provided with such instruments must be adjusted for different populations. Data from the United Kingdom showed disparities close to

300% between direct and estimated measures of bone density when estimates were based on the manufacturer's reference population (Petley et al. 1996), even though that reference population was in the same country.

Increasing hip fracture rates in poor countries may create demand for such equipment but benefits at the population level are too low to justify routine screening. An international collaborative review stated that there is "fair evidence" that screening can assess the risk of future fracture over the short term, "but not with a high degree of accuracy" (Hailey et al. 1998). Given the extensive overlap between the distribution of BMD of individuals who have and do not have fractures, screening cannot reliably distinguish those who will have a hip fracture from those who will not (Green et al. 2000; Luehmann et al. 2000; Hailey et al. 1998; Marshall et al. 1996).

Preventive and Therapeutic Drugs

Given the prominence of drug therapies promoted to prevent hip fracture, there is a surprising lack of randomized, controlled trials for most agents. Many clinical trials suffer from small samples, are too short in duration, or fail to differentiate between multiple fractures in one patient or many patients (Seeman 1997).

Among a range of new drugs, bisphosphonate alendronate is the most promising and was approved by the U.S. Food and Drug Administration. Clinical trials were well designed, and two multicenter, double-blind, placebo-controlled trials found measurable reductions in hip fracture. A 29% reduction was seen in the number of women sustaining nonvertebral (including hip) fractures after three years of treatment (Liberman et al. 1995) and in the United States the incidence of hip fractures was significantly reduced with treatment (relative risk 0.49, 95% confidence interval 0.23–0.99; Black et al. 1996).

A compelling argument in favor of hormone replacement therapy (HRT) for postmenopausal women is that HRT sustains bone mineral density and thereby reduces the risk of fracture. However, data showing a protective effect is neither consistent nor strong. Available studies generally show more positive effects of HRT on vertebral than on hip fracture. The one placebo-controlled trial of transdermal estrogen replacement found significant positive changes in BMD in the spine, but not the femoral neck (Lufkin et al. 1992). A positive long-term prospective study that followed estrogen users and controls for seventeen years reported a relative risk of 0.85 for hip fracture (95% confidence interval 0.41–0.92). An observational study reported a reduction of 40% in hip fracture risk among current users of HRT, but the confidence interval included 1.0 (relative risk 0.60, 95% confidence interval 0.36–1.02; Cauley et al. 1995). However, when the analysis was limited to women who started HRT within five years of menopause, the relative risk at 0.29 was more impressive, with a 95% confidence interval of 0.09–0.92.

Nonetheless, when measures of current bone density were included in the above analysis, they showed no evidence that the reduced incidence of hip fracture among those taking HRT was mediated by bone density (Cummings 1985). This is an important finding, because if HRT was having its effect on fracture by changes in bone density, statistical adjustment for BMD in the models would indicate this. The finding further weakens hypotheses that bone density is a substantial determinant of hip fracture risk (Cauley and Danielson 2000).

There are negative trade-offs to taking HRT to prevent hip fracture, including the need to sustain therapy indefinitely to maximize effects (Cauley et al. 1995). An international review group identified "fair evidence, from low quality randomized control trials and observational studies" of the effectiveness of HRT in preventing fractures "while therapy is continued" (Hailey et al. 1998). Long-term therapy (20–30 years if it is sustained from menopause until death) raises concerns about both affordability and the threshold of side effects that are tolerable. The prospect of long-term therapy (if use is sustained from menopause until death) also raises concerns about the unresolved findings concerning HRT and the risk of breast cancer, and realistic affordability in poor countries.

The potential market for fracture-reducing agents is substantial enough to spur research and development for better drugs, and bisphosphonate is promising. But drugs have numerous drawbacks, including the need for long-term treatment, with ensuing demand for long-term access, compliance, expense, and possible side effects (Rosenberg 1993). Access and expense are of particular concern for developing countries. The public health policy challenge is whether we shift to therapeutic solutions at the expense of pursuing preventive lifestyle and environmental public health strategies that may be affordable and accessible to more people.

A Gender and Equity Analysis Revisited

Conclusions from an epidemiological review of hip fracture are at odds with the prevailing public health response. Like cardiovascular disease and diabetes, hip fracture appears to be a consequence of affluence and social development, particularly urbanization. Although it is less common in rural, laboring (and usually poorer) populations, rising age-specific rates in several developing countries underscore the need to identify preventable risk factors and direct interventions accordingly.

The importance of genetic (sex or racial) determinants appears to have been overestimated. Whereas these differences are frequently attributed to genetic differences in BMD, comparison of cross-national studies offers limited support for this hypothesis. Bone mineral density does not appear to account for racial differences in hip fracture and at best it may contribute partially to sex differences. Whereas sex differences may be associated with underlying hormone and structural differences that are genetically determined, changes in the sex ratio of fracture over time and across different regions suggest that genetic vulnerabilities due to sex are strongly modified by social risk factors.

Which social and cultural risk factors are most promising for further research and how many of these appear to be gendered? Understanding risk factors for falling is critical and exploring how sex, gender, and social equity factors contribute to that risk is an obvious point for cross-population research. In turn, the importance of domestic isolation among elderly women in European countries, women's lower muscular strength than men's, and poorer overall health at older ages, reduced economic security, and low occupational and physical work history warrant further investigation. Identifying the extent to which hip fracture is attributable to such factors is important not only for a gender analysis, but for exploring social and class differences. Indeed, available data suggest that domestic isolation (or independence) among the elderly is a highly cultural phenomenon, with distinct social patterns for men and women. How these are further modified by social class and economic security remains largely unexamined.

Given the hypotheses that emerge from an even superficial review of international incidence rates, why is public health discourse focused on bone density screening, genetic determinants of bone density, and drug therapies? In part this may reflect widespread enthusiasm for genetic epidemiology made possible by advances in molecular research. Certainly development of probes for the diagnosis of a range of important human diseases (muscular dystrophy, cystic fibrosis, Huntington's disease) prompts hope of locating genetic determinants of other diseases and disabilities. But for many conditions, known genetic mutations appear to account for only a small proportion of the overall risk (breast or ovarian cancer). Where a mutation confers an elevated risk, the magnitude of that extra risk is often difficult to pin down and the interaction of the genetic factor with other social or environmental risks is often poorly understood.

Appreciation of such a partially deterministic genetic model is critical for a balanced assessment of public health research priorities. Detailed mapping of the human genetic code will uncover important genetic linkages with disease, but its greatest contribution may be the opportunity it provides to understand how social or environmental circumstances draw out or mitigate genetic vulnerabilities. Even then the contributions may be limited, and in the case of hip fracture the more fundamental gap appears to lie in our poor understanding of social risk factors. A danger posed by molecular research is that by offering the promise of direct causal linkages and ensuing therapeutics and saleable interventions, it receives greater investment at the expense of research on preventable social determinants.

Green and colleagues (2000) offer an alternative and more radical analysis of why BMD screening is so prominent in the international discourse, given its limitations. They maintain that the marketing of BMD screening technology reflects a redefinition of the aging female body as a diseased "abnormal" body and aging itself as something that we can pay to avoid. Defining fracture risk on the basis of bone density transforms a natural condition of aging (and a weak risk factor) into a disease entity of its own. Expensive screening procedures define most elderly women as candidates for long-term drug therapy and the principal beneficiary is the private sector. "The area of the continuum that characterizes normal is shrinking, while that defining abnormal is increasing. The power relations and private interests served by this altered continuum remain largely unexplored" (Green et al. 2000).

Research Agenda

Hip fracture appears to be a consequence of development and urbanization and, like other diseases of affluence, is most likely attributable to preventable social determinants. Rapid changes in incidence rates, including sex ratios, suggest a dominant role for lifestyle and structural risks. Such risk factors, however, are not well understood and the following research questions might, if answered, inform health-promotion strategies.

What Are Risk Factors for Falls?

To what extent do differences in fracture rates between men and women and among ethnic groups reflect differences in rates of falling? If gender and population differences indeed account for a significant component of the variation fracture incidence, it would be worth while to explore further what factors explain differences in falling. Is falling a consequence of differences in risk taking, domestic isolation, hip muscles, visual capacity, quality of shoes, or height of beds? Do differences in hip flexion strength mitigate other risks? Can falls be substantially reduced through social interventions?

What Is the Effect of Physical Work?

Prospective studies on the long-term impact of different physical regimens at different ages would be worth while. What impact do various forms of hip flexion work (squatting, kneeling, climbing) have on long-term risks? How important is load-bearing work (hill or stair climbing, especially while carrying loads)? Are there optimal ages at which selective interventions are most beneficial?

How Important Is Old-Age Support?

How much of the regional and ethnic variations in hip fracture are a consequence of different domestic arrangements that provide for or isolate older women? To what extent do increasing rates of hip fracture reflect the greater independence of the elderly, whether due to smaller families, greater difficulties accommodating aged parents at home, or changing cultural expectations about independence among elderly women?

How Does Nutrition Contribute?

Most pressing would appear to be the need for greater attention to components of the diet that change with urbanization (most recently in Asia). This includes looking at traditional foodstuffs consumed less often in the urban setting (slow-cooked foods, bone soups, fish bones, leafy greens), as well as modern foods consumed more often (carbonated soft drinks, white breads, fast foods, etc.). The detrimental effect of high consumption of carbonated cola on fracture risk is suggestive and warrants further attention. A range of nutrition trends with urbanization should be considered.

Where Do Socioeconomic Factors Fit In?

In light of evidence that poor diets and poor overall health are important risk factors, the role of economic status deserves closer attention. It is possible that higher physical work among lower socioeconomic classes offers compensatory protection. However, given high overall rates of other disabilities among the poor and high rates of known risk factors such as smoking and low food intake, systematic research into the role of poverty, while accounting for physical work, is badly needed.

Summary

Hip fracture is a complex disability, but genetic differences between the sexes and among ethnic and racial groups do not appear to account for global variations in incidence. To the extent that genetic factors are operative, they appear to be modified or eclipsed by other nongenetic determinants that are undergoing rapid change.

Current public health response to hip fracture, emphasizing promotion of BMD screening and therapeutic drugs, is unlikely to have a substantial impact, and further investment in social risk factors is called for. Determinants that warrant further research include isolation among the elderly (especially women), physical attributes and exercise, public and private infrastructures that reduce the risk of falling, and possibly some features of traditional diets. Hypothesis-generating research that draws on an international, cross-cultural perspective is likely to be particularly fruitful, but such efforts should be followed by controlled interventions.

The excess of hip fractures among Caucasians in the developed world foreshadows a worsening trend for other groups, as populations age and urbanization progresses worldwide. Given that affluence, through its associations with better overall health, better nutrition, and the possibility to afford extrafamilial support and better structural facilities and institutional care, buffers the risk of mortality and disability after hip fracture, emerging rates in developing economies suggest worsening trends in morbidity and mortality from this event and call for increased exploration of low-cost, preventive interventions.

Notes

1. In preparing this chapter I'm grateful for the assistance of Tracy Slanger.

2. Hereafter, I use the term gender to indicate differences in social opportunity between males and females, consistent with WHO definitions (1998b).

3. There is a substantial and growing body of data on hip fracture in Japan, Hong Kong, Singapore, and China, whereas data from the subcontinent (India, Bangladesh, Nepal, Pakistan) are comparatively scarce in the international literature.

4. Unadjusted bone mineral density among east Asians is frequently lower than that in Caucasians, but the difference is no longer apparent after adjusting for differences in skeletal size.

5. Part of the increased risk of hip fracture among smokers is accounted for by their lower body weight (la Vecchia et al. 1991), but an added risk persists.

8

Health and Environment: Moving Beyond Conventional Paradigms[1]

Jacqueline Sims and Maureen Butter

The Need for a Broader Approach to Environmental Health

Attention to securing human health and a healthy environment has grown, as governments and people struggle with problems of differential access to diminishing resources. Whereas the environmental movement highlighted aspects of environmental sustainability, changes in the health field emphasized issues of social justice, equity, and human development (WHO 1997d). In this spirit, significant policy commitments were made to gender, health, and environment issues at global meetings since the Earth Summit in 1992.

Before these changes, environmental health was for many decades associated with a narrow, sanitary engineering approach. Characterized by pipes and pumps, sewage and garbage, norms and standards, environmental health research and policy did not lend itself well to either gender or social development perspectives. Only recently have processes of urbanization, industrialization, and globalization given priority to the need to understand health-and-environment issues in the broader context of sustainability. At the same time research and advocacy on women's roles and the gender division of labor led to the recognition that women, particularly poor women in developing countries, are vulnerable to effects of environmental degradation in ways that differ from men. Together these pressures broadened definitions of environment to value health, social, and technical dimensions equally.

Nonetheless, the health sector in general has not been quick to grasp that many health and environment problems have different impacts on men and women. Issues long debated in other disciplines are only now being "discovered" by the mainstream health sector, as the need to look beyond the curative medical approach and along the axis of preventive public health is accepted.

Another obstacle to accepting this broader paradigm is that it is notoriously difficult to arrive at an accurate estimate of the disease burden of health and environment concerns. Absence of data is most stark for developing countries and for poor women. Although estimates and projections abound, there is relatively little systematic, rigorous, and clearly articulated research in this field (WHO 1998f). Reasons for this include the multiple and interconnected nature of many risks. In addition, general data in developing countries are lacking, and data in developed countries are fragmented and discipline oriented. Finally, environmental causes, except for infectious diseases and acute poisonings, are often masked in health statistics. Despite these problems, it is agreed that environmentally related ill health is broadly underestimated (WHO 1996b, 1997a).

In addition to lack of data, research is constrained by methodologies that tend to privilege pathogens and pollutants while neglecting social determinants linked to poverty and gender discrimination. It is difficult to provide scientifically acceptable causal connections in the areas of environment, poverty, and health. As a result, linkages among gender, health, and environmental factors remain hidden and elusive. Acquisition of meaningful data in this area is only just beginning (Sims 1994).

Yet it is essential for reasons of equity that we do address the multifactorial causes of these issues in research and policy terms. Between one-fifth and one-fourth of the world's population live in absolute poverty, more than 90% of whom live in developing world (UNCHS 1996). These poor people are found predominantly in remote, ecologically fragile areas and at the margins of expanding urban areas (Leonard 1989). Despite aggregate global indications of overall improvements in health and welfare, absolute numbers of poor people are growing and they are living and working in increasingly unhealthy and unproductive conditions. Environmental health risks and hazards facing poor communities low-income countries, is where the effects of the environment on human health and of people on the environment are greatest (WHO 1997d).

Although health risks are great for these poor people, those most disadvantaged and resource deprived are still predominantly women, especially poor rural women (Jazairy et al. 1992). Unsustainability threatens the whole global system, but women feel the first and worst effects. They are particularly at risk because their options are doubly restricted, not only through poverty but also through their nonnegotiable responsibilities. Any meaningful strategy to address environment and health issues must therefore take a broader perspective that includes gender-sensitive poverty alleviation, in both rural and urban settings, as a central component.

Linking Health and Environment with Poverty, Development, and Equity

Many definitions of environment in relation to health exist. Some follow a physiological perspective that distinguishes between internal and external environments, and others focus on chemical, biological, and physical agents. In its broadest sense environmental health is concerned with assessing, understanding, and controlling the impacts of people on their environment and the impacts of the environment on them (Moeller 1997). Other definitions are more restrictive and focus on physical and chemical stressors that occur primarily in the nonoccupational environment (Silbergeld 2000). We focus on health effects of chemical, physical, and biological agents in ambient and work spaces, but from a broader perspective of resource availability and quality in relation to gender and development.

In this context it is also important to differentiate between environmental *hazards* (chemical, air and water pollution) and environmental *factors* (urban or rural residence, quality of natural resource base, agricultural or other lifestyle). Both have an impact on health, but direct and measurable health outcomes are more easily linked to environmental hazards. However, environmental factors, in conjunction with social determinants of health, contribute to gender differences that are hard to capture with conventional measurement methods.

By defining it as the geographic space that sustains but also limits human life and health, the environment becomes a source of both hazards and resources. Throughout history, human settlement, organization, and technology served to overcome environmental constraints. Economic development in general focused on yielding better exploitation methods. However, rapid industrialization and scaling up can also disrupt existing social arrangements and patterns of resource exploitation. If not carefully checked and accompanied by new institutional and social arrangements, they may introduce new or increase existing inequalities and hazards. For example, dams may increase water supplies to distant urban centers or for large-scale agriculture, but they also may increase prevalence of waterborne and vector-borne diseases and exposure to pesticides, as well as result in uprooting or loss of livelihoods of entire communities (Kettel 1996).

In the glare of publicity surrounding modern environmental hazards, such as oil spills, radiation, urban air pollution, pesticide intoxication, and climate change, it is easy to overlook the reality of the poor who continue to struggle with basic issues, such as access to adequate water and sanitation, safe food, and protection from infectious diseases. These traditional hazards often associated with lack of development are sometimes contrasted with modern hazards associated with uncontrolled development (box 8.1). The changing pattern of exposures and health risks

Box 8.1
Hazards connected with poverty and lack of development (WHO 1997d)

Traditional hazards
- Lack of access to drinking water
- Inadequate basic sanitation
- Microbiologically contaminated food
- Indoor air pollution from biomass fuel or coal
- Inadequate solid-waste disposal
- Injuries from agricultural work and cottage industries
- Natural disasters
- Disease vectors (insects and rodents)

Modern hazards related to rapid and unsustainable development include
- Food and water pollution from densely settled areas, industry, and intensive agriculture
- Chronic water shortage
- Ambient air pollution
- Accumulation of waste
- Chemical and radiation hazards
- New and reemerging infectious diseases
- Deforestation, land degradation, and major ecological changes
- Climate change, ozone depletion, and transboundary pollution

that change over time with economic growth is known as risk transition. For millions confined to the poverty trap, the impact of unregulated industrialization and globalization may well be simultaneous exposure to both traditional and modern hazards. This phenomenon is termed risk overlap (Caldwell et al. 1990; Smith 1990) and it demonstrates that issues of concern in high-income countries are also relevant to poor countries.

As virtually no systematic data are available on industrial sources of persistent toxic substances in most poor countries, and given paucity of data on pesticide use (UNEP 1999b), some examples roughly sketch the nature of existing problems. Large industrialized sectors often operate with few environmental safeguards. For example, Greenpeace carried out a sampling and analysis program in the heavily industrialized Indian province of Gujarat and found extensive surface water and groundwater pollution (Labunska et al. 1999). Industrial pollution is also found in ship-breaking. Young men in Bombay and Alang strip asbestos coating from ships using electric drills without protection, exposing themselves and others in the vicinity to dangerous levels of asbestos, apart from other hazardous waste (Kanthak et al. 1999).

Workers in small enterprises face a similar range of occupational hazards as those in larger sectors, but are further at risk because of poorer access to clean workplaces, toilets, and water, as well as lack of occupational health legislation and services. Their working and living quarters are close to each other, increasing the risks of exposures and accidents. Textile dyeing, car painting and repair, small metalry, pottery, shoe making, and carpentry are examples of small industries that generate physical and chemical hazards and that are often located within or very close to home.

An important source of occupational and nonoccupational exposure to toxic pollution is small-scale agriculture. This is the major sector for employment for many of the poor and also the major producer of basic commodities for survival. Small-scale farmers with limited land have to maintain constant levels of production and so tend to use large quantities of pesticides and fertilizer. They apply pesticides manually using old and poorly maintained equipment. The agents are transported and stored together with food products, and containers are frequently reused to pack food products for the market (Maroni et al. 1999; Ndoye 1998; Sow 1994).

Consumption of small-scale food products can create health risks as they may contain pesticide residues or mycotoxins (Loewenson 1995). Mycotoxins are suspected or proved carcinogens produced by molds that commonly occur in nonoptimally stored dried food items, such as grains, copra, and peanuts. They have been associated with esophageal, urinary tract, and liver cancers. They are a thousand times more potent than most synthetic carcinogens found in food, but constitute just one of the many threats to food safety in the developing world (Miller 1996).

Whereas chemical pollution is a prominent issue in environmental health, it should not be understood that it is a greater health hazard than microbiologic pollution of food and water, which continues to be a major public health risk for millions. For example, diarrheal diseases account for 1.5 billion episodes of illness a year among children under age five, with some 2 million resulting in death (WHO 1999c). The bulk of morbidity, mortality, and lost productivity from microbiological contamination occurs in poor countries.

Development should imply the creation of infrastructure such as roads, water, electricity, and sanitation, as well as public services such as transport, immunization, and environmental surveillance. One aspect of poverty is inability to overcome environmental constraints and to be shielded from environmental hazards. Although the poor in high-income countries may be materially better off than the poor in low-income countries, both tend to lack access to public resources that should shield them from modern and traditional environmental hazards. This is particularly the case of high-income countries with generally weak support for social policies, such as the United States, but perhaps less the case in those with stronger public infrastructure and safety nets, as in Europe.

For example, indigenous peoples in both high- and low-income countries face high levels of pollution and poor public infrastructure and services, while remaining highly dependent on ever diminishing natural resources (Alderete 1999; Indigenous Environmental Network 1999). A rural Yaqui population in Mexico have alarming rates of impaired neuromuscular and intellectual development, in contrast to a similar community in a less contaminated area (Guillette et al. 1998). Poor people living in urban areas face similar problems.

This predicament led to accusations of environmental racism, demonstrated by empirical findings documenting that the marginalized suffer disproportionately from environmental risks due to industrial pollution, waste dumps, and occupational exposure (Bullard 1999; Salmond et al. 1999; Clarke and Gerlak 1998). The resulting controversy and debate about environmental racism and injustice spread from the United States to other industrialized and developing countries (McDonald 1998; Costi 1998), with participation of feminists and indigenous peoples (Prindeville and Bretting 1998; Schneiderman 1997).

Decisions of those who control resources and policies may affect resource accessibility and hazard characteristics of those who do not. Unsustainable consumption, largely a problem caused by the rich, is a major equity issue and a threat to environmental sustainability. A 90% reduction in resource consumption in rich countries is necessary and achievable if poor countries are to have a chance to emerge from poverty (UNEP 1999b).

In summary, health and environment issues are linked to and exacerbated by income poverty, but also by the lack of infrastructural resources and public services. More fundamental, they are related to lack of political influence of those most marginalized in society. They cannot be understood in isolation from this larger, multifaceted development context in both high- and low-income countries.

How Gender Matters

Within this development context, gender differences in mobility, roles, and responsibilities create differences in women's and men's personal environments, leading to different hazards and exposures. These differences tend to reflect women's lesser status, power, and control over resources. As a result, women's economic opportunities are often constrained, leading to a higher degree of dependence on locally available resources despite their sometimes poorer quality (Butter 1999a; WEDO 1999). For example, deforestation and unsustainable use of water and marginal land exacerbate rural women's heavy workloads and time constraints, as they have to walk long distances for fuel and water (Kettel 1996; Sims 1994; Douma and Van den Hombergh 1993).

Even when infrastructure and services exist, they frequently do not meet women's needs. Although large amounts of money are invested in energy production, poor women continue to toil in smoke-filled kitchens. Hence among the poor, women and their health are often most affected by the lack of quality environmental resources and appropriate public infrastructure.

In South Africa, public transport subsidies are targeted at formal sector workers and operate only during peak hours. This is unlikely to meet to the needs of many women working in the informal sector (UNDP 1998b). Women struggle to coordinate domestic and productive roles and responsibilities and often have no alternative to using public transport. Frequently, the design of public spaces and transport services lacks attention to their safety and sanitation needs (Peterson 1997).

Occupational risks and exposures form a key part of poor women's health and environment. That this is not recognized is a function of the undervaluation of women's productive roles and their high input to often unpaid domestic or agricultural labor. United States farm-work studies often excluded women because they are categorized as unpaid labor, despite their exposure to the same risks as men (workers) (Engberg 1993).

The overlapping of risks from both inside and outside the formal sector is still underresearched, and is a disadvantage for women who face many and often synergistic exposures that can negatively affect their health. A marginal farming area in Kenya shows disability levels in women age twenty to sixty years that are approximately double those of men. Disability was greater only for men age fifteen to nineteen years and over sixty years (Ferguson 1986).

Physical strain, regardless of its source, is included in most medical definitions of environmental health (Moeller 1997). There is a strong case also to include it in stricter, more environmentalist definitions if it is caused by effects of working on marginal land coupled with lack of equipment and infrastructure. Physiological stress caused by high workloads, along with nutritional deficiencies, increases the body's vulnerability to other environmental hazards.

As women predominate among the poor, it can be argued that poverty as such is a gender issue. However, there are many more justifications for a gendered approach to health and environment issues. The health risks of poverty tend to be greater for women than for men because poverty is compounded by gender inequality. Gender inequality underlies women's lack of decision-making power, invisibility or suppression of their concerns and priorities due to biased social norms, low levels of education, and reduced access to health services.

Although most gender issues in health and environment are complex, they can be grouped under three main categories: biological differences, division of labor, and differences in power and status. For example, differences in biology have to be considered when developing safety standards and preventive measures. Risks derived from the gender division of labor demand more cautious interventions to prevent locking women into socially constraining roles. Lack of power usually translates into women's invisibility and neglect of their needs and concerns. In practice, all three factors may be present.

Biological Differences in Responding to Chemical Pollution

Even though physiological stress, such as pregnancy and lactation, can affect women's capacity to deal with environmental exposure, general toxicological research predominantly uses male subjects to avoid variation caused by the female hormone cycle. In contrast, within reproductive health, toxicity is better researched in women than in men, although the latter also run considerable occupational risks to fertility and reproductive health cancers (Stijkel 1995; Colborn et al. 1996; Butter 1999a). Consequently little is known about biological differences in environmental health between men and women in areas not linked to reproductive health.

Apart from differences in hormone status, which have scarcely been researched, sex-related differences in sensitivity to toxic substances might be due to differences in detoxifying activity. Animal research indicates that males have five times greater detoxifying capacity than females (Hughes 1996). The challenge in researching chemical effects on health is daunting due to different degrees and dimensions of exposure that can occur throughout life. Variations also may exist in ability to absorb chemicals (children absorb lead twice as fast as adults) and in susceptibility to damage (greater vulnerability of the fetus to many toxic and mutagenic compounds) (Institute of Medicine 1998). Science and medicine are still at the threshold of understanding the complex mechanisms and pathways through which exposure to and illness from chemical pollution occur.

Of many hundreds of chemical compounds being manufactured and used for industrial, agricultural, and domestic purposes, some are of particular concern as they persist in the environment, resistant to photolytic, chemical, and biological degradation. They tend to accumulate in fatty tissues of living organisms and thus are easily absorbed through the food chain and through water. Persistent organic pollutants (POPs) are highly toxic, with potential to injure human health and the environment at very low concentrations. International action is under way to ensure that twelve of the most frequently occurring POPs are phased out. These include several insecticides such as DDT, chlordane, heptachlor, mirex, toxaphene, aldrin-dieldrin-endrin; the fungicide and industrial by-product, hexachlorobenzene; and other unintentional chemical by-products such as dioxins and furans (Commonweal et al. 1999). Many POPs function as endocrine disruptors.

Endocrine disruptors are exogenous chemicals that either mimic or antagonize the action of endogenous hormones in the human body. Research focuses particularly on processes or tissues affected by estrogens, androgen blockers, and thyroid hormones. Sex steroids specifically affect the central nervous, immune, and reproductive systems, whereas thyroid hormones affect most tissues in the human body (Bigsby et al. 1999).

A finding of interest in connection with environmental estrogens is that women are more susceptible than men to autoimmune conditions. Women's heightened immune response to both foreign and self-antigens appears to account for this. Diseases such as thyroid disorders, rheumatoid arthritis, insulin-dependent diabetes mellitus, and pernicious anemia predominantly afflict women. It is not clear if this higher incidence is due to higher exposure to environmental estrogens or to improved recognition and reporting, and increasingly sensitive diagnostic procedures. What is clear is that estrogens induce imbalances in critical cell function, which is thought to promote immune disorders (Ansar Ahmed et al. 1999).

Much less is known about the effect of environmental androgens on human health. A common contaminant is the organotin compound tributyltin, which is an antifouling agent in ship's paint. It induces masculinization in marine animals and there is every reason to expect similar effects on humans.[2] Exposed groups to organotin compounds include harbor workers, but also farmers and their families as the compounds are common ingredients in fungicides.

Much attention has focused on prenatal exposure to endocrine disruptors, as many of these substances pass freely through the placenta, exposing and adversely affecting fetal development. It is estimated that background concentrations of dioxins and polychlorinated biphenyls (PCBs) in industrialized areas in North America and western Europe account for subtle congenital disorders such as hyperactivity and low IQ in 10% of newborns (Koppe 1995; Patandin 1999). Other effects include low birthweight, vitamin K deficiency, hypospadia (congenital malformations of the penis), spina bifida, and neurological disorders due to exposure in utero (Koppe et al. 1999).

Breast milk analysis is an increasingly common method to monitor body burdens of persistent contaminants. Since many of these substances enter the body through the food chain, it is taken to reflect background levels of contamination. However, specific mechanisms of contamination may be unclear, as DDT contamination, for example, can occur through both the food chain and from direct exposure. In fact, DDT was found in breast milk of women from an isolated community in Papua New Guinea, where it has never been sprayed (Spicer and Kereu 1993). Similarly, due to atmospheric transport, high levels of POPs settled in the Arctic where they have never been used. Inuit women report increased incidence of cancers from eating fish and game from the region (Indigenous Environmental Network and Greenpeace 1999). In Uganda, urban women had significantly higher breast milk contamination levels than rural women, but DDT levels did not relate to vegetarian or nonvegetarian diet, indicating that in this case the food chain was not the primary route of exposure (Ejobi et al. 1998).

Both DDT and PCBs in breast milk are reported to be associated with short lactation periods and less ability and willingness to breastfeed

(Gladen and Rogan 1995; Lanting 1999). Lack of breastfeeding is of concern, particularly in poor populations, as it can lead to increased birth rates and infant mortality. It is still unclear at what levels of contamination the advantages of breastfeeding are outweighed by its risks. Any such evaluation would have to compare hygienic conditions affecting the risks of infant formula feeding. In general, breastfeeding is still considered best (Patandin 1999; Lanting 1999; Hooper et al. 1999).

Fears about breastfeeding and safety of the food chain greatly added to the trauma of affected populations in eastern Europe after the Chernobyl nuclear disaster of 1986. Estimations calculate that the psychosocial dimensions far outweighed physical disease manifestations for many years afterward (WHO 1990; UNESCO 1996). Women are also disproportionately physically affected in such a situation due to their higher susceptibility than men's to iodine deficiencies and goiter, which can lead to increased uptake of radioactive isotopes (Institute of Medicine 1998).

A less publicized but no less extensive environmental catastrophe has been taking place for over twenty years around the Aral Sea, which has shrunk to almost half its original size. Intensive cotton cultivation involving aerial spraying, diversion of feeder rivers for massive irrigation schemes, soil salinization, mineralization, and heavy erosion created a series of environmental, health, and social problems from which the region, which includes five central Asian countries, is unlikely to recover. Significant destruction of livelihoods occurred, followed by massive impoverishment and outmigration, and weakening of family and social networks (Kiessling 1999).

Breast milk monitoring in southern Kazakhstan revealed levels of dioxin-like compounds ten times higher than those in the United States. Concentrations of tetrachlorodibenzo-p-dioxin in Kazakh women's breast milk resembled those in populations exposed to industrial accidents. The data suggest that exposure is constant, environmental, and long-term. Cotton defoliants are a probable origin of exposure, with the most likely pathway being contaminated foodstuffs (Hooper et al. 1999). Similar findings were reported from the state of Karakalpakstan in Uzbekistan (WECF 1999). Tetrachlorodibenzo-p-dioxin is designated by WHO as a known human carcinogen, and several less potent dioxins as probable human carcinogens, although the precise causal mechanisms remain poorly understood (Colborn et al. 1996).

Gender Inequalities Related to Societal Inequalities

Differences in the Division of Labor: Indoor Air Pollution

Indoor air pollution is described as the last major unaddressed public health problem and cooking with biomass fuel as "possibly the greatest occupational hazard faced by poor women" (WHO 1984). Significant questions linked to exposure to biomass or coal smoke, nutrition, and pregnancy remain to be researched. Depending on the type of housing, fuel, stove, ventilation, and cooking patterns, exposure to particulates and gases in biomass and coal smoke can be very high. The issue can be further compounded through exposure to environmental tobacco smoke. Research in China established that the risk ratio for respiratory symptoms linked to use of coal as a cooking fuel increased in the presence of environmental tobacco smoke (Pope and Xu 1993).

High prevalence of chronic bronchitis in women in developing countries is associated with exposure to indoor smoke from cooking. A complication of chronic bronchitis is cor pulmonale, or hypertrophy of the right ventricle. This can lead to pulmonary embolism and failure of the right side of the heart, which is associated at an uncommonly early age in women with long-term exposure to domestic smoke, particularly in high, cold regions. As women with these conditions are often not treated or hospitalized, official statistics still report those mainly affected by chronic lung diseases to be male (Sims 1997). Pioneering research in India strongly suggests that use of biomass fuels for cooking substantially increases the risk of active tuberculosis, particularly in rural areas (Mishra et al. 1997). It is suggested that exposure to air pollutants hinders uptake of essential nutrients (Kamat and Deshi 1987).

Where biomass fuel is scarce, other hazardous energy sources may be employed. Due to prolonged energy scarcity, many Armenian urban women burn municipal waste for cooking and house heating. Burning plastic, bleached paper, preserved wood, and many other modern types of household wastes exposes them to heavy loads of dioxin-like substances, polyaromatic hydrocarbons, and heavy metals (WECF 2000).

Cooking with biomass fuel or coal, not to speak of modern waste, generates multiple risks and exposures that form an intergenerational vicious circle. Health risks to women and infants who depend on low-grade fuel for cooking and heating can be characterized as follows (Smith 1987; WHO 1992):

• Gathering and transporting fuel (time and energy costs, musculoskeletal disorders, falls and fractures, increased risk of prolapsed uterus)
• Smoke from biomass and coal burning (respiratory disease, eventually heart disease)
• Eye infections and disorders (conjunctivitis, cataract)
• Depressed immune response from smoke exposure
• Exposure of fetus to carbon monoxide, which can affect fetal development and birthweight
• Low birthweight and infant vulnerability to infectious disease
• Risk of stunting

Differences in Access to and Control over Resources: Water
Access to and control over environmental resources is of vital importance to those dependent on them. Water scarcity for a large part is human made, as many irrigation projects have specifically targeted the larger landholders, assuming trickle-down effects to the poor that do not occur. Typically, women are not acknowledged as stakeholders in irrigation, despite lifelong user rights to land and willingness to invest in land improvement. Falling groundwater tables in India allow those in possession of more expensive equipment or deep tube wells to keep on extracting water. Meanwhile those with shallow wells and hand pumps, who are most likely to be women, face water shortages with adverse effects on nutritional status, income, and workloads (World Water Council 2000). Those who lack good public infrastructure, like many poor urban women, have to pay exorbitant prices to water sellers.

More than a billion people are deprived of water of sufficient quantity and quality to meet even minimal levels of health and well-being. Absolute water scarcity is increasing in many parts of the world, making equitable access a pressing issue (World Water Council 2000). Severe shortage is predicted for 2.7 billion people, one-third of the world population, in the first quarter of this century. In sub-Saharan Africa, this has been caused mainly by ecologically or socially mismatched infrastructural investments, and in Asia overpumping with cheap equipment has led to a dire trade-off between food security and water security. In both cases the poor, and especially poor women, are most heavily affected (IWMI 1999).

Female Invisibility: Ergonomics

Together with chemical and microbiologic exposure in domestic, agricultural, and occupational settings, ergonomic problems are environmental health hazards for both men and women. Traditionally linked exclusively with occupational health in the formal sector, understanding that ergonomic problems pose health risks in a broader range of settings is growing. Much of this increased awareness is derived from gender debates as well as from more comprehensive definitions of the nature of work.

In the traditional view, men were seen as the main victims of occupational hazards and serious injury. Now it is recognized that women suffer many chronic, often undiagnosed and untreated occupational health problems. These include cumulative trauma disorders and specific musculoskeletal disorders in the supposedly safe jobs ascribed to them in both formal and informal sectors. Women's work on conveyer belts, in electronics plants, garment and textile factories, hospitals, and piecework at home involve speed, repetitive motions, and restricted positions. All of these conditions tend to produce disease patterns that are rarely recognized or compensated in equal proportions to male disability (Bru et al. 1994; Brabant 1992; Brisson et al. 1989; Punnett and Keyserling 1987).

In recent years, research called attention to the design and use of equipment, tools, workstations, and protective clothing that are inadequate or unsuitable for users' size and strength. Men are affected mainly when equipment, tools, or clothing are imported by foreign-owned enterprises, but women are further disadvantaged as most equipment remains designed around male physical norms. Failure to take these issues into account results in work inefficiency, accidents, additional energy expenditure, and cumulative trauma in working women (Morse and

Hinds 1993; Chavalitsakulchai and Shahnavaz 1993; Abeyesekera and Shahnavaz 1988).

Rural women's domestic or agricultural tasks often require prolonged work in stooping or squatting positions, or regular weight bearing. Little research has been done on musculoskeletal disorders from these causes, although work in awkward positions reduces lifting power and requires greater energy expenditure (Gallagher 1991). Kitchen work is also responsible for extended periods of time spent in stooped and uncomfortable postures (Nystrom 1995), which in conjunction with agricultural tasks may result in several hours daily spent in ergonomically unhealthy positions.

The need for attention to multiple exposures is underlined through a Swedish study on the impact of heavy lifting on birthweight. Lifting alone had no negative effect, but in conjunction with other risk factors, for example, chemical exposure, it could influence pregnancy outcomes (Ahlborg et al. 1990). A study on fractures in Indian women found that most were the result of work-related accidents and could be traced to a combination of prolonged unnatural work postures, nutritional deprivation, and repeated childbearing (World Bank 1995b). In the Gambia and Ethiopia, studies found that only half the amount of weight gain during pregnancy took place in peak agricultural season compared with the low season. It was established that birthweight could be affected by changes in work conditions right up to delivery, and high work intensity was involved in premature delivery. Lower survival rates were detected among infants whose mothers operated heavy farm tools while pregnant (Holmboe-Ottesen and Wandel 1988).

Female Invisibility: Pesticides
Severe underreporting and lack of research of women's health and environment problems are also found in the case of pesticides. Pesticide Action Network Asia and Pacific carried out case studies in eight countries and found that more than 90% of women involved regularly sprayed pesticides without adequate protection and know-how. All of them were exposed during weeding, while cleaning equipment and clothing, and when disposing of chemical leftovers. In Africa, women often use pesticides while carrying a baby on their back. Many cannot read labels or

do not follow instructions (Sow 1994). Most women reported symptoms of intoxication, which as a rule go untreated (Rengam 1994). Highly toxic pesticides such as parathion, endosulfan, phorate, monocrotophos and phosphamidon were used frequently (Partanen et al. 1999; Rengam 1994; Sow 1994). In Sudan, a consistent and significant association was seen between pesticide exposure and perinatal mortality, with 50% higher risk in rural women (Taha and Gray 1999).

Lack of adequate legislation, ignorance of standards, poor labeling, illiteracy, and lack of protective clothing increase the hazards to agricultural workers and the environment (Maroni et al. 1999; Yousefi 1999; Partanen et al. 1999). As in many developing countries, agricultural training is traditionally targeted to men, so women are less likely to receive instructions on safe handling of pesticides (Rengam 1994; Sow 1994). Women buy pesticides at markets that have been repackaged from large containers into smaller ones, frequently lacking labels or instructions for use (Sow 1994; Ndoye 1998; Ton et al. 2000).

Worldwide prevalence of acute pesticide poisoning is estimated at 1 to 3 million, resulting in 220,000 deaths per year, most of which occur in the developing world. These figures are probably inaccurate, as underreporting is a major problem (Maroni et al. 1999). Intensification of monitoring pesticide poisoning in South Africa resulted in a tenfold increase in the cases reported and a completely inverted picture of the gender profile of poisonings. Routine surveillance suggested that 66% of poisonings involved men, but intensified surveillance found 66% in women (London and Bailie 1998).

A crucial environmental health problem in developing countries is the use of highly toxic substances that are restricted or banned in industrial countries. Although DDT has been phased out in most countries, it is still used for pest control in some low-income countries, to an unknown extent. Related compounds such as chlordane are widely used to control termites (UNEP 1999b). Products are used continuously throughout the year, instead of only four to six months as is usual in temperate climates where winters kill many crop pests, leading to lower disease pressure. Obsolete pesticide stocks are problematic in most regions, but especially in poor countries that lack appropriate disposal methods (UNEP 1999b). The costs of safe disposal amount to $1,000 to $2,000 per ton excluding transport, hardly affordable for most developing countries (PANAP 1998).

Challenges for Research

Environmental epidemiology is notoriously difficult. Biological responses to hazardous substances are often nonspecific and long delays may occur between exposure and effect. In addition, many pollutants are so widespread that it is hard to find a control group. Consequently, epidemiology has yet to show clear and consistent associations between hazardous substances and health damage (Moeller 1997). By default the method of choice is risk assessment, which relies on toxicological data, exposure assessment, and dose-response extrapolations (Zakrzewski 1997). Yet both environmental epidemiology and risk assessment are criticized by community groups; the former for its inability to produce results and the latter for its heavy reliance on assumptions and fragmented, hazard-by-hazard approach (Butter 1999b).

Health and environment issues are so vast and the problems encountered so complex, that research must be carefully targeted and focused to respond to the gender and poverty needs of those affected. This is far from easy, as the current dearth of data, methods, and linkages shows.

To begin with, a more integrated research approach is necessary. At a minimum, exposure measures should take into account the following: chemicals; pathogens; physical agents (noise, temperature, vibration, radiation, pressure); nutrition (calorie intake, vitamin intake, fat ratio); biomechanical risks (sustained awkward positions, frequent repetitive movements, force, lifting); psychosocial factors (stress, levels of control, social support); and behavioral factors (substance abuse, smoking, weight fluctuation (Institute of Medicine 1998).

The literature presents fragmented and decontextualized information. A review of eighty articles on back disorders showed that no data on exposure were given in over half of them, whereas in others such data were incomplete (Burdorf 1992). A study of garment workers in Quebec found that only part of the substantial force exerted during an average working day was possible to measure with current technology (Vezina et al. 1992). Measurement methods must take all aspects of exposure into account and they must fully describe exposure settings if interventions are to be appropriate (Institute of Medicine 1998).

More fundamental, a different kind of research is necessary to establish the knowledge required to take gender, health, and environment issues further. Limitations of epidemiology in capturing all the required determinants of health should be underlined. Creation of more gender-sensitive, participatory, and pro-poor approaches to research should be encouraged. Multidisciplinary and applied research must give necessary attention to social factors, exposure settings, and general context.

The integration of qualitative and quantitative methods is critical to effective macro-micro linkages. These linkages are essential to overcome limitations of small project approaches on the one hand and research that is devoid of local context and realities on the other hand. Contextual research should be reviewed continuously in relation to findings from basic research to establish more comprehensive understanding of risks that are synergistic and/or cumulative. Only with such understanding can appropriate preventive and health-promotion strategies be devised and implemented.

Rapid, preferably low-cost, environmental health-assessment tools at community levels are urgently needed. One alternative research approach is community health diagnoses, which involve testing blood and urine of community members in heavily contaminated areas. This reveals possible biological markers, showing the degree to which people's bodies have taken up contaminants (Bertell 1999). Community health surveys by health professionals or community members are cheap alternatives to physical examinations.

Self-assessment, as practiced in The Netherlands, is another tool designed to provide early warning to public authorities. It involves scrupulous and consistent registration by volunteers of health complaints and environmental circumstances using a carefully designed questionnaire. Registrations are maintained in a national database that can reveal previously unnoticed patterns of morbidity related to specific environmental sources (Butter 1999b). Environmental nongovernment organizations (NGOs) from southeast Asia as well as Africa have shown interest in this tool.

Incorporating gender dimensions into tools such as health impact assessment (HIA) and environmental health impact assessment (EHIA) would be a promising step forward. At present, such tools are not regularly used as part of decisionmaking, although a number of European countries are paying more attention to institutionally relevant HIA systems (Lehto and Ritsatakis 1999). If HIA and EHIA were conducted from a gender perspective and their use widely promoted, it would facilitate establishment of gender-sensitive health and social indicators.

Obstacles to Policy Implementation

Integrating health and gender as dimensions of environment issues is a major challenge. Currently, mainstream environmental decisionmaking is rather gender blind, despite persistent effort from women's environmental NGOs. A case in point is the last UNEP conference intergovernmental negotiating committee on phasing out POPs. Gender issues were not addressed by the draft document under negotiation (UNEP 1999a), even though women's NGOs were campaigning for recognition of hazards posed by POPs to reproductive health (Guillette 1994; WECF 1999; WEDO 1999). At the same time, environmental threats to public health hardly figure on the population and health agenda. Despite commitment in the Cairo ICPD Platform of Action to address broader determinants of population health, including environmental constraints, the ICPD+5 was not able to address this larger agenda (De la Rosa 1999; UNGASS 1999).

Yet given the strength and ubiquity of gender and environment linkages globally, a strong case can be made for institutional recognition of the need to link gender equality with broad health and environment issues. This was underlined in the OECD-DAC's work on gender equality and environment (OECD 1999). In general, this review found the formal integration of gender equality issues into environment, environmental health, or environmentally sustainable development policies to be weak, or to take a largely instrumental view of women's input. No participating donor agency had a policy that explicitly linked gender and environment issues as essential and complementary goals for development cooperation.

A policy document outlining clear linkages between gender equality and other sectoral issues can be crucial for work at the national planning level, and can support other national gender commitments that often prove difficult to implement in isolation. Understanding the linkages is critical if gaps between international instruments and national action are to be bridged. This will be an important step to assist countries in overcoming difficulties in implementing the commitments they made at major summits of the last decade.

The OECD-DAC review (1999) also stressed the importance of donor agency commitment to gender equality as a cross-cutting theme. Unless gender equality is given greater priority, resources for implementation are unlikely to become available. This is important, as the consistent tendency is for gender equality policies and programs to be underresourced. This is hardly surprising when donor countries' domestic environmental policies also typically lack a gender perspective (WECF 2000).

Among the numerous obstacles to meaningful integration of gender perspectives into environmental health policy, the following are perhaps the most significant.

Fragmentation

Many policies originate in many ministries and government departments spanning a range of environmental health issues. Ministries of environment, natural resources, agriculture, mines and energy, construction, labor, and planning will all be involved in different ways in health and environment issues. Typical examples are water and forestry, where responsibilities may be fragmented among a number of branches that do not necessarily interact or take common decisions. This pattern is mirrored in universities and research institutions that similarly fragment environmental health issues among different faculties and departments, hindering acquisition of an integrated and synergistic understanding of the problems.

Vacuums

A major shortcoming of national policy is that it frequently fails to reach out or down to those most in need. In developing countries, most rural and many urban slum and peripheral dwellers live beyond the scope of official policy and services. Examples are energy, transport, and health. Economic and opportunity costs to poor families of making good these shortfalls through private or illegal services, or personal energy output, are high. Macroeconomic policy reinforces this trend through structural adjustment programs in developing countries by severely reducing social spending. Biased household coping strategies can further discriminate against women who are responsible for providing household needs even in the absence of basic services.

Conflict

When gender policy is officially adopted at the national level it may not always be compatible with existing policies in other sectors. This significantly reduces the chance that it will be successfully implemented.

An example of this might be alterations in trading patterns for coal. If a country promotes internal use of coal supplies for household use instead of exporting it, this can conflict with health sector recommendations to promote cleaner fuels. Similarly, gender policy may actively promote equal employment opportunities for women by removing legal barriers and promoting macroeconomic growth. But labor rules that prevent women from working night shifts, limited transport facilities, or inaccessible skills training may constrain women's ability to take advantage of these new opportunities.

Enforcement

Although environmental standards and regulations pertaining to air, water, food, vehicle emissions, labor, and related matters can be better enforced in developed countries, it is more difficult in the developing world where such standards often do not exist, and if they do, enforcement mechanisms are lacking. Whereas women and men alike are at risk from lack of regulation, women may be further disadvantaged as gender-sensitive methods are not yet used to establish standards, which are therefore set at male dose-response levels. For example, air pollution standards fail to reflect the additional indoor pollution to which most populations in developing countries, and particularly women and infants, are exposed.

Capacity

To carry out appropriate policy making and research that underpins it, adequate capacity in environmental health management, planning, and epidemiology is necessary. The developing world is again at a disadvantage, as capacity in the area is still dominated by sanitarians and engineers, most of whom are men. In addition, gender issues are conceptually remote from areas of work traditionally covered by environmental health practitioners. The human resource capacity to draw together gender, health, and environment issues at policy and planning levels is largely deficient.

The Way Forward

Given the tendency for environmental issues to be set against economic growth and progress, it is critical for health and environment planning to work in coordination with macroeconomic policy. Integrating these areas may in some cases assist in maintaining state control of industrial and economic policy that can be weakened by globalization. International initiatives aimed at including gender issues in macroeconomic policy will facilitate this task (UNRISD 1997).

Harmonization and joint planning should be obligatory features of national planning in recognition that health and environment problems are neither caused nor solved by any single sector or approach. Effective harmonization of policy must include gender mainstreaming. Consideration of gender issues should not be left until a late stage in planning when their inclusion may prove problematic. Evidence shows that some countries are making this effort to move toward more integrated policy and planning approaches (von Schirnding 1999). Much of this progress is due to national and local commitment to Agenda 21 plans, which involve improved transparency and public participation in decision making (box 8.2).

An interesting initiative was taken by fifty-two countries in the European Community region. Ministerial conferences on environment and health were held in Frankfurt (1989), Helsinki (1994), and London (1999). This led to the adoption of a European Health and Environment

Box 8.2
Possible outcomes of gender, health, and environment work

- Broad (including social) determinants of health integrated into environmental health research
- Greater understanding and recognition of women's roles in and contributions to sustainable development in general and environmental health, in particular at all levels of decision making
- Gender criteria included in assessment tools such as health impact assessment and environmental health impact assessment, and strengthening of linkages with social impact assessment
- More gender-aware macroeconomic and urban planning
- Closer links between occupational and environmental health research, particularly in the informal sector
- Efforts to establish and monitor environmental and occupational standards and regulations that respect biological differences between women and men without socially discriminating against women
- Participatory procedures to empower community members to improve environmental health and achieve environmental justice

---

Action Plan, the development of national health and environment action plans (NEHAPs), and finally to the intention to develop local environment and health action plans (LEHAPs; Butter 1999b). Both NEHAPS and LEHAPS also were established in a number of developing countries (WHO 1997e).

A related regional initiative is the Aårhus Convention, granting public participation and access to information in environmental decision making (UNECE 1998). To date, only two states have ratified this convention. Civil society organizations hope that these mechanisms will provide an opportunity for fuller participation in addressing environmental health issues (EcoForum 1999).

Another example of integration, civil participation, and gender sensitivity is the National Water Act of 1998 in South Africa. It aims to ensure sustainable management of water resources, promote equitable access, and redress past racial and gender discrimination. To this end, decentralized, multistakeholder, public management agencies were set up with far-reaching powers for water allocation and licensing. Despite its intentions, the program has not sufficiently included women's participation, for reasons that include their lack of organization and power. Capacity building is being encouraged by a new round of consultations among smallholders, building on informal networks and NGOs (World Water Council 2000).

NGOs have often been at the forefront of creating integrated projects. The Self Employed Women's Association (SEWA) in India involved women in water management, first by consultations at the community level and then through various interventions. These included providing training for pump repair, which yielded additional income-generating activities, and constructing roof water tanks or caves for water storage, depending on the local situation.[3]

An integrated framework used by both high- and low-income countries to promote better health at all socioeconomic levels, and to integrate environment, health and development concerns, is the healthy settings approach. With appropriate care to avoid an instrumentalist approach to women, this can be used easily to incorporate gender perspectives into health and environment work. Better defined as social movements or processes rather than specific projects, the activities undertaken are selected by a wide range of stakeholders from public and private sectors. The best known is the Healthy Cities movement (Ashton 1992).

Since the 1990s numerous other settings approaches have been built up, such as Healthy Schools, Markets, Hospitals, Homes, and Workplaces. Some developing countries and small island states have started Healthy Villages and Healthy Islands approaches. All are useful platforms for advancing gender, health, and environment concerns. The approach, applied with appropriate gender criteria, could fill many current data and contextual gaps, helping to bridge the persistent gap between requirements of international instruments and effective policy and strategy at country level.

Whatever the origin of environmental risks and constraints, the impact is most keenly felt at individual and household levels, where no artificial separation of sectors and policies exists, but where end results of policy vacuums, conflicts, and problem are most evident. It is in local environments that exposure to environmental, lifestyle, and social hazards combine to determine health. Given the high dependence on local resources by the world's poor, a strong focus on the local level and a participatory approach to health, development, and policy making is indispensable.

Notes

1. We thank Gita Sen, Piroska Östlin, Yasmin von Schirnding, and Jing de la Rosa for their useful suggestions and comments. Most of all we acknowledge Asha George for her splendid technical editing work, without which this chapter could not have been completed, and for her unrelenting support to both of us. The views expressed in this paper are those of the authors and do not necessarily reflect the position of the World Health Organization.

2. Cato ten Hallers-Tjabbes, personal communication. A marine biologist and senior researcher at Netherlands Institute of Sea Research, she was one of the first to draw attention to the effects of TBT on sexual development of marine mollusks.

3. SEWA. 2000. Workshop March 17–22 at World Water Forum, The Hague. M. Dave, personal communication.

II

Research and Policy

9

Social Discrimination and Health: Gender, Race, and Class in the United States[1]

Nancy Breen

The United States is the largest economy in the world, has high per capita income, and spends more per person on health care than any other country in the world. At the same time, it also has greater income inequality than other high-income countries and worse health outcomes, including shorter life expectancy and higher infant mortality. Findings from economics and social epidemiology clarify how the United States economy maintains social hierarchies that systematically shape health and use of health care. Specifically, they show how the distribution of wealth, jobs, and income shapes the use of health services and self-reported health status. This analysis assumes that gender, race-ethnicity, and class are socially constructed, historical categories.

Social Class and Health

The most general finding from research on social class and population health over several decades is that higher social status, however measured, is consistently associated with better health, however measured. Although specific diseases may be exceptions (breast cancer incidence is associated with higher social class in women, lung cancer is associated with higher social classes in countries where smoking is more prevalent among higher social classes), these can be explained by particular causes. There are virtually no examples of societies in which overall health status is inversely related to wealth, income, or social status (Evans et al. 1994a; Townsend et al. 1992).

This powerful relationship of the social environment to health is validated by studies in high-income countries and reveals a deep structural connection between them. For example,

• Poverty, low educational attainment, and social deprivation are associated with poor health status, high illness rates, and death at early ages (Kitagawa and Hauser 1973; Pamuk et al. 1998; Syme & Berkman 1976).

• Associations between resources and health form a gradient with increasingly worse outcomes as one moves down the income ladder and better outcomes as one moves up it (Marmot et al. 1987; Adler et al. 1994; Menchik 1993).

• Returns to investments in health are greatest at the bottom rungs of the ladder and diminish in the highest-income groups (Backlund et al. 1996; Sorlie et al. 1995; Chapman and Hariharan 1996).

• Income equality within populations is directly associated with median longevity, regardless of median per capita income (Wilkinson 1992; Kaplan et al. 1996; Kennedy et al. 1998; Lynch and Kaplan 1997) and worsening income distribution is associated with worsening health over time (Pappas et al. 1993).

• The consistent gradient between inequality and health has been shown for all-cause mortality as well as specific disease mortality and incidence (Townsend et al. 1992).

• Racial differences in health are not entirely explained by income or other social class indicators; discrimination and stress also play a contributing role (Sorlie et al. 1992; Dressler 1990; James et al. 1983).

• Gender differences in morbidity and mortality are more complex than income gradient associations would predict. For example, women live longer than men but they experience more morbidity than men (Nathanson 1975; Verbrugge 1976b; Lillie-Blanton et al. 1993; Krieger et al. 1993; Nathanson & Lopez 1987).

Two long-term cohort studies stand out as particularly useful for studying social class and health. These are the Whitehall study in England (Marmot et al. 1984), now in its second generation (Marmot 1991), and the Alameda County study (Berkman and Breslow 1983) begun in the

United States in 1965. Their findings broadened the purview of epidemiology by suggesting that restricting studies of causality to the effect of one social factor on one disease may miss its more pervasive influences on health (McMichael 1995) and may underestimate its impact on a range of diseases (Amick et al. 1995).

The Whitehall study of British civil service workers found a clear and consistent gradient whereby workers in each occupational grade had worse health and higher mortality than the grade above it. Previous studies focused on absolute poverty, not relative inequality. This work was the first to suggest that social factors work across the whole of society (Gottschalk and Wolfe 1993). Explanations for the socioeconomic differentials in the 1990s must be broader than the simple threshold effect of poverty (Kogevinas et al. 1999).

Risk factors for disease also show a social class gradient. Obesity (Flegal et al. 1998), physical activity, smoking, and healthy eating (Kumanyika and Krebs-Smith 2000), all of which are associated with overall health and with particular diseases, vary by social class, race, and gender. The Alameda County study controlled for seven health-related risk factors and still found that income remained closely related to health (Syme 1998). Nor did adjustment for known risk factors, including smoking, drinking, and diet, eliminate the social class gradient in the Whitehall study (Smith and Shipley 1991). These authors concluded that because unhealthy environments and unhealthy individual behaviors are highly correlated, risk behaviors can seem more important than they really are unless analyses also include social class variables.

The overwhelming evidence is that differences in lifestyles cannot be explained simply as a matter of choice. Individual choice is limited by resources and position in the social hierarchy, and shaped by advertising and peer influence. Some people cannot avoid being exposed to certain health hazards because of their location in the social distribution (Townsend et al. 1992; Evans et al. 1994a). Consequently, social structures and discrimination play at least as important a role as personal decisions in the association between social class and health (Stronks et al. 1996).

Nonetheless, how lived experience directly affects the ability of individuals to thrive is not well described. Generally it can be said that people in lower social positions are continually faced with a wider array of external stresses, but have fewer resources to cope with them (Evans et al. 1994b; Wilkinson 1996; Stack 1974). Low income affects health directly through relative deprivation, and psychological or behavioral factors are indirectly linked to health (Stronks et al. 1998). Stress; power, control, and authority; social networks, and social cohesion are hypothesized as pathways bridging social class and health in rich societies.

Health results from a sense of coherence, which is achieved by finding one's life situation meaningful, comprehensible, and manageable. The ability to solve problems effectively and to give up when appropriate, or coping skills, are acquired over a lifetime and especially in childhood when one learns to master feelings of helplessness and hopelessness. Greater access to material resources is associated with greater likelihood of developing better coping resources and a stronger sense of coherence (Antonovsky 1967).

Identifying direct pathways and risk factors caused by social discrimination is further complicated because different determinants may underlie similar health outcomes among different groups, which have access to different types and amounts of resources. For example, according to a study of prenatal weight gain among black and white working women, working more than forty hours was a predictor of low weight gain for white women. Predictors for black women included having a mistimed or unwanted pregnancy, caring for more than one preschool child at home, and not using their own car for errands (Hickey et al. 1997).

These associations also change over time. In 2001, heart disease fits the pattern of higher rates among lower social-class men; however, as recently as the 1950s heart disease mortality rates were greater among men of higher social class men (Marmot 1991). Leading causes of death for women also varied with changes in marriage, rising labor force participation, and unemployment (Waldron 1976). Causes of death and disease prevalence ratios vary over time by social class, gender, race, and even age, indicating that social factors shape health in important ways. This remains true even if the explicit pathways are not articulated and the relative importance of the various factors is not determined.

Social Discrimination in the Contemporary United States

We know that gender, race-ethnicity, and class change over time and vary across societies. Yet little attention has been given to understanding how race and gender cross-cut and lend new meanings to social class. Systematic attention to race, class, and gender is necessary to understand how the United States economy shapes social hierarchy and health disparities. Because economic inequality has reached an historic extreme in the country, the history of the last three decades provides an excellent opportunity for studying these relationships.

Distribution of Wealth and Citizenship

Modern social class hierarchies in the United States can be traced to the processes of colonialization and citizenship. Citizenship was originally limited to white male property owners. It was not until the 1840s that propertyless white men were granted citizenship rights. The formal process of granting citizenship to all adults was completed only in the mid-1960s. Because this step-wise integration took nearly 200 years, it created a hierarchy of citizenship based on race, gender, language, and culture that paralleled and reinforced hierarchies of property ownership, income, and wages (Glenn 1999).

Unequal wealth has characterized the country since its beginning. In 1774, the richest 10% of households in the North American colonies held half the wealth. At about the same time, the richest 10% in the southern colonies, which depended on slave labor, held about 80% of the wealth (Jones 1980). Almost 200 years later, in 1983, only 5% of wealth holders controlled 51% (Wolff 1995).

Given the importance of wealth to security, well-being, and political and social influence, it is important to know that it is concentrated almost exclusively in white families. The federal Survey of Income and Program Participation (SIPP) reports wealth data for households. It understates median net worth by capping wealth during data collection. Nevertheless,

SIPP data show that median net worth in 1993 was approximately $46,000 for white householders and less than $5,000 for black and Hispanic householders (Eller and Fraser 1993).

Since World War II, family income was the most equal in 1968. Inequality grew slowly in the 1970s and rapidly during the early 1980s (Weinberg 1996). During the 1980s, a greater share of total income was generated in the form of capital (rent, dividends, interest payments, capital gains) and a smaller share in earned incomes, such as wages and salaries (Mishel and Bernstein 1994). As a result, in the 1990s the income gap was wider than at any time since the 1920s (Glenn 1985; Amott and Matthaei 1991; Levy 1995). In 1996, the richest one-fifth of American households held 46.8 % of national income.

Employment Hierarchies

Economist David Gordon grouped Americans between those employed as managers or supervisors and those working in nonsupervisory capacities. For those who were not supervisors, the average hourly wage declined between 1972 and 1994 from $13.11 to $11.13 (adjusted to 1994 dollars). This translated into a median family income (excluding households with only one individual) of $27,730 before taxes in 1993. On average, these families spent about $2000 more per year than they earned before paying their taxes. Meager livelihoods are typical in the United States and not a rare condition (Gordon 1996; Mishel and Bernstein 1994).

The situation was better for the 20% employed as managers or supervisors. Although total employee compensation as a percentage of national income stayed about the same between 1973 and 1993, the percentage paid to supervisory employees increased from 16% to 24% of national income (Gordon 1996). This shift in income from workers to managers and supervisors was attributed to corporate bloat and falling wages. This management approach deploys a pyramid of well-paid supervisors to monitor closely and punish workers. Implemented in the 1970s, it led to income redistribution that favored managers and supervisors to the detriment of those working in nonsupervisory capacities.

Workforce segregation by race and gender is critical to understanding social inequality in most United States households. With more than 60%

of women employed, it might be expected that women would depend on their own earnings rather than unpaid work or men's earnings. However, except for well-educated women, this is not the case. Despite increases in women's earnings, women's average pay remains lower than men's (Albelda 1985; Anker 1998). Men and women work in different occupations (Blau et al. 1998) and women's jobs are associated with fewer fringe benefits and lower rates of unionization (associated with better benefits and higher wages).

In addition to being remunerated at lower rates than men, women are paid only for their participation in the labor force. Yet, almost invariably they perform more household work than men (Shelton 1992). Since wage differences by gender usually count only pay for hours of waged work, women's remuneration for total hours worked is considerably less than men's (Fuchs 1988; Schor 1991). Moreover, since most jobs allow little control over the timing or location of work, and since women have more roles and obligations than men for child care, elder care, and homemaking, women may experience exceptional difficulties in reconciling the competing demands of home and work (Hall 1989).

A review of the empirical literature on housework concluded that, employed or not, women do the bulk of housework; estimates for men's share ranges from 20% to 30% (Shelton 1992). Better-educated women did less housework, and better-educated men did more. This tendency could increase population health disparities between educated and non-educated women over time.

Deployment of women's labor in the United States economy varies by race and ethnicity. Although most women were not in the United States labor force in 1955, more nonwhite[2] (46%) than white women (35%) were (Blau and Ferber 1986). The steady increase in white women's labor force participation, especially among married women with children, equalized rates between races until 1990, when 58% of white and 61% of black women were in the labor force. In 1999, respective figures were 60% and 66% (Bureau of Labor Statistics 1999).

During the 1970s, black women shifted out of domestic service into sales, clerical, service, and manufacturing occupations where white women were concentrated. This convergence tended to equalize black and white women's wages. Growth in sectors employing women, especially clerical, and concurrent slowdown in growth in manufacturing, which largely employed men, led to a decline in the gender gap. This occurred not only because women's wages were rising, but also because men's wages were falling (Albelda 1985).

Labor force participation and occupational desegregation increased among women of other racial-ethnic groups too, but less dramatically than entry into the labor force for white women or higher wages for black women. Estimates from the Bureau of Labor Statistics included only white and black women, not Hispanic, Asian, or Native American women.

In conclusion, occupational desegregation led to labor force hierarchies within racial-ethnic groups as well as among women. Privileged women or persons of color can now make it to the top tier of the labor market, although they may experience limits on their achievements relative to white men. However, most women and people of color are still concentrated in lower positions in the hierarchy (Amott and Matthaei 1991).

Household Earnings

The only families that experienced income growth since the 1980s were married couples with both partners in the paid labor force. The distribution of household and family incomes for 1989[3] by race, ethnicity, and family structure is shown in table 9.1. Both husband and wife were employed in about 50% of married-couple families for all five racial-ethnic groups. These dual-income households were the best-off households in each racial-ethnic group. However, among racial groups, white households fared best. Less than 10% of white married-couple households were poor (defined as less than $15,000), and more than one-third (36.1%) were at least comfortably well-off (with at least $50,000). Among racial-ethnic groups, the ranking is white and Asian, followed by black, Hispanic and Native American.

Asians were less than 4% of the United States population in 1990, and include Asians and Pacific Islanders in all post-World War II data unless otherwise indicated. Many nationalities with different migration patterns constitute this group, including some of the worst-off as well as some of the best-off households in the country. Starting in 2000, Asians and Pacific Islanders are reported separately.

Households with married couples reported median incomes two to three times higher than female-headed households in each racial-ethnic group. Black, Hispanic, and Native American households are more likely than white households to be female headed and living in poverty, and so are their children. The main reasons for the poverty of female-headed households with children are little or no child support from fathers, women's child care responsibilities, women's low-wage jobs, and lack of health insurance[4] (Montgomery and Carter-Pokras 1993). Despite the difficulty of managing housework, children, and waged work alone, only 55% of black and Latino single mothers received Aid to Families with Dependent Children (AFDC; social welfare transfer payments) in 1990 (Hacker 1992).

Compared with white women, nonwhite women married to a nonwhite man are more likely to earn at least as much as their husband. This might be expected to give women of color a gender advantage within the household because they contribute more income (although this has not been shown empirically). However, when two spouses are earning two low incomes, the main effect will be lower total household income (Jones 1983).

Unemployment and Marginalization

Like wealth distribution, segregation in the labor force, and differential wages, people outside the labor force form an integral part of the American economy and they are also characterized by race-ethnicity and gender. Unemployment could be hypothesized to maintain hierarchy in the economy in three critical ways. First, it could make the employed population more vulnerable, encouraging wage workers to accept lower rates or overtime and those with salaries to work excessive hours to maintain their jobs. Second, joblessness makes family formation, credit, bank accounts, housing, health insurance, a regular doctor, and planning for the future difficult or impossible. Third, marginal participants in the economy may be unlikely to participate in politics and community activities, which undermines social cohesion.

Large percentages of blacks, Hispanics, and Native Americans, especially men, are unemployed. Unemployment rates are understated because only those who are currently seeking employment are counted. Men

Table 9.1
Measures of social discrimination in the U.S. by five major racial ethnic groups (1990)

Measure	White			Black			Native American, Alaska native			Asian, Pacific Islander			Hispanic[a]		
	All	F HH	Married	All	F HH	Married	All	F HH	Married	All	F HH	Married	All	F HH	Married
% Families[b] in poverty 1989	7.0	23.2	4.5	26.3	44.5	11.0	27.0	50.4	17.0	11.6	25.7	9.3	22.3	45.7	15.3
% Children in poverty 1989	12.1			39.5			38.3			16.7			31.8		
% Persons[c] age 65+ in poverty 1989	10.8			31.9			29.4			12.0			24.0		
Median household[d] income 1989 ($)	37,153	20,340	40,396	22,429	12,522	33,538	21,750	10,742	28,287	41,251	22,983	44,965	25,064	12,406	29,930
% Household[d] w/income <$15,000 1989	13.6	36.8	9.9	35.1	55.9	17.1	35.4	62.8	23.2	15.5	34.7	12.3	29.0	56.6	19.9
% Households[d] w/income ≥$50,000 1989	32.3	9.6	36.1	16.1	4.8	26.6	14.2	3.1	19.5	39.8	17.6	44.0	16.9	4.9	21.4

	Male	Female	Male	Female	Male	Female	Male	Female	Male	Female
% Unemployed 1990	7.0	5.0	17.2	12.2	18.0	13.1	7.4	5.5	13.7	11.2
	All		All		All		All		All	
% Persons[c] who remained poor during 24 months 1991–1992	3.4		16.1		NA		NA		12.2	
% Married-couple families[b] w/husband & wife both employed (incl. Armed Forces)	49.7		53.2		44.5		55.2		45.1	
% Female-headed families[d] with woman employed (incl. Armed Forces)	61.3		53.1		48.3		62.8		49.9	
	Male	Female	Male	Female	Male	Female	Male	Female	Male	Female
% Persons 25+ years who graduated high school	78.4	77.4	62.2	63.8	65.2	65.3	81.5	74.0	49.8	49.9
% Persons 25+ years old w/ bachelor's degree	25.0	18.4	11.0	11.7	10.1	8.6	41.9	31.8	10.0	8.3

FHH, female-headed households.

[a] NA, not available.

[b] There were 65,049,428 families counted in the 1990 U.S. Census.

[c] Percent persons who remained poor are from the Survey of Income and Program Participation (SIPP).

[d] There were 91,993,582 households counted in the 1990 U.S. Census.

in prison are not counted as unemployed and they are disproportionately black, Hispanic, and Native American. If the 8% of black adult males incarcerated in 1999 were counted as unemployed, black men's unemployment rate would rise from 6.7% to 16.5% for that year (Henwood 1999).

Layoffs in manufacturing in the 1970s primarily affected men and women with a high school education or less. In contrast, layoffs during the 1980s largely affected managers and were accompanied by job growth in the finance, real estate, and investment sectors, as well as the computer industry they depend on. A college education, youth, and willingness to work long hours, often without benefits, were the main qualifications for entry into the computer industry. For those seeking jobs for the first time, race and gender seemed less important than youth and education. However, more whites and Asians had higher educational attainment than blacks, Hispanics, or Native Americans, and larger proportions of men than women held college degrees.

Women from minority backgrounds are not always relatively worse off than their male counterparts in terms of social class because of the complex interaction between gender discrimination and race discrimination (Amott and Matthaei 1991; Glenn 1985). An example from the worst-off, most isolated population in the country, Native Americans living on reservations, illustrates this. In many tribal traditions, women are a force for balance and harmony. Not only do they use welfare benefits to provision their extended households, but some tribes have hiring practices that offer equal or better opportunities to women. The 1980 Census data for some of these tribes showed women's average annual incomes were at least on a par with men's and at least as stable as men's (Albers and Breen 1996). As the examples above make clear, both native women and educated women have used or changed tradition to ameliorate their situation.

Nonetheless, social welfare is not available to able-bodied work-age (18–64 years) men or even to families with dependent children with such a man in residence. Only women with dependent children were eligible for AFDC payments. This policy discourages family formation and stigmatizes women welfare recipients and their children. Parents with a connection to the Temporary Assistance for Needy Families (TANF) program, which replaced AFDC in 1996, were more likely to report poor health than parents in the general population (Sweeney 2000).

Historical differences in how each group was integrated into the United States labor market created complex hierarchies in which economic class, race, and gender cross-cut and often reinforce each other. Economic data presented in table 9.1 suggest that married white men are the most privileged and Native women heads of household are least privileged of all groups shown. Opportunities improved in the last few decades for women, especially white women. At the same time, social class hierarchies within each racial-ethnic group emerged to exacerbate the class and race disparities among women. Finally, despite some leveling of the playing field by gender and race, class inequalities grew wider during recent decades.

Social Discrimination and Health

How Economic Disparities Affect Access to Health Care

Health improvements for all social groups in the United States were documented throughout the twentieth century until around 1970 (Haan et al. 1989; Adler et al. 1994). During the 1980s, income differences widened, improvement in life expectancy slowed, and among the black population life expectancy declined (Kochanek et al. 1994). The yawning income gap was reflected in a steeper mortality gradient in 1986 than in 1960 (Pappas et al. 1993). No surprise, poor Americans use fewer health services (Hofer and Katz 1996; Katz and Hofer 1994; Katz et al. 1996), report less access to and satisfaction with care (Blendon et al. 1989), worse health, and more health limitations compared with richer Americans (Rogers 1992). They also spend more of their income on medical services (Gottschalk and Wolfe 1993), even though fewer services are available to persons living in poor neighborhoods (Wolfe 1994).

Social services provide important resources that protect health and promote general well-being. In contrast, medical services largely affect people when they are already ill. Poor communities have fewer of both kinds of services available than richer ones (O'Campo et al. 1997; Macintyre et al. 1993) as well as worse disease outcomes (Breen and Figueroa 1996). Finally, medical services delivered at home is another area where social discrimination is evident. An analysis of persons age seventy and older in the United States in 1995 found women were more likely than men to require help in activities of daily living. For each sex, there was a gradient whereby poorer men and women were more likely to need help and less likely to receive it than those with higher incomes (Pamuk et al. 1998).

Although most people in the United States eventually obtain necessary medical treatment, they may not receive it in a timely manner (Institute of Medicine 1993; Breen et al. 1999; Weissman and Epstein 1994). Late diagnosis and delayed treatment can exacerbate problems related to disease, illness, or injury. When disease is diagnosed, people are faced with a series of medical choices. Those in lower social classes are less likely to have the resources to make decisions and carry out the range of treatments required. For complicated or chronic illness, optimal service delivery includes making informed decisions and carrying them out. This requires not only the ability and fortitude to query medical professionals, but the wherewithal to implement expensive, time-consuming decisions.

These problems can be illustrated by comparing two types of breast cancer screening: mammography and clinical breast examination. Clinical breast examination exams is performed as part of a regular check-up. Mammography requires a referral, a second appointment, and a second payment. So it is not surprising that more women report having clinical breast examination than mammograms and that they are likely to be of low socioeconomic status and to be cared for by a nonspecialist physician (Breen et al. 1996).

What is critical to understand about medical care in the United States is that no system of coverage is routinely accessible. Coordinated, integrated care is variable and depends on type of insurance coverage and the particular health care delivery system. As a result, each step in obtaining health care must be separately discovered, located, discussed, decided, and often negotiated with a new provider at a separate location. Each appointment and procedure requires separate payment.

A wide range of tests and procedures are available to American physicians who, wary of malpractice lawsuits, usually order them to rule out alternative diagnoses before making a definitive diagnosis. Tests are costly and time consuming, and increasingly, as medical care moves outside hospitals into specialized facilities, require separate appointments with different specialists and trips to different locations.

Cheaper medical care requires more waiting, increasing patients' indirect costs. Less costly or free care is available in clinics and hospital emergency rooms, which the uninsured or persons with Medicaid are likely to use. Not only are persons of low socioeconomic status limited by lack of money, health insurance, and a trusted regular provider, they are also likely not to have ready transportation, reliable child care, job flexibility, and ability to leave work to keep appointments. Consequently, they might not obtain care, or not obtain it in a timely manner. In addition, they may not be offered a service, may reject it because they cannot afford it, or may simply not make an appointment for it, all at higher rates than persons from higher social classes. This would be expected to worsen morbidity and mortality in these groups (Hofer and Katz 1996).

Sociodemographics of Medical Insurance Coverage

Stable full-time employment subsidizes medical insurance coverage for most Americans, which is primarily private. However, by removing public sector employees, whose share of employer insurance premiums is paid for by taxes, the estimated percentage of insurance paid for by private sector employers fell from the official government estimate in 1996 from 61% to 43% (Carrasquillo et al. 1999a).

After private health insurance, the second most common type is Medicare, the program designed for retired persons age 65 and older, although it covers some other high-user populations as well (e.g., those with end-stage renal disease). The third major type of insurance, Medicaid, covers eligible women with children who are low income, the unemployed, and disabled persons. Medicaid is less generous than Medicare, although it provides better access to health care than no health insurance, the situation for about 42 million Americans (20%) in 1996 (U.S. Bureau of the Census 1998).

As noted earlier, income and employment are not directly correlated with health insurance. Persons working in poorly paid jobs without benefits (the working poor) are not usually eligible for Medicaid. Fifty-four percent of uninsured nonelderly persons were employed in 1990 (Foley 1991). Unemployed men have little access to health services because Medicaid, like welfare, is not available to able-bodied work-age men. Thus, insurance coverage and use of health services, shown in tables 9.2–9.4, do not reflect the same race, class, and gender hierarchies shown in table 9.1.

Table 9.2
Measures of health insurance coverage in the U.S. by the five major racial ethnic groups (National Health Interview Survey, 1993–1994)

Measure	White				Black				Native American, Alaskan native					Asian, Pacific Islander				Hispanic			
	Private	Public	Other	None	Private	Public	Other	None	Private	Public	I H S	Other	None	Private	Public	Other	None	Private	Public	Other[a]	None
Women age 18–64																					
Households w/income <$15,000	35.7	26.3	2.6	35.5	20.7	47.2	2.3	29.8	7.6[b]	25.1	43.2	1.3[b]	22.8	44.7	29.1	1.5[b]	24.7	14.7	36.4	1.6	47.3
Households w/income ≥$50,000	94.3	0.4	1.0	4.3	90.4	1.1[b]	1.6[b]	7.0	71.0	0.0	20.4[b]	1.9[b]	6.7[b]	91.3	0.1[b]	1.3[b]	7.3[b]	90.0	1.3[b]	0.7[b]	8.0
Unemployed	59.1	9.9	3.0	28.0	31.4	33.9	1.9[b]	32.8	5.4[b]	22.0[b]	52.5	3.9[b]	16.3[b]	56.6	6.1[b]	6.3[b]	31.1[b]	29.8	14.8	1.7[b]	53.7
Persons 25+ w/less than H.S.	51.5	16.0	2.8	29.8	31.5	36.3	2.6	29.6	13.2	25.3	34.9	2.3[b]	24.3	40.9	29.9	7.2	22.0	33.4	21.3	1.5	43.8
Persons 25+ who graduated H.S.	83.6	3.0	1.7	11.7	65.9	14.5	2.7	17.0	38.9	7.5	38.8	1.5[b]	13.3	77.5	2.6	3.0	16.9	66.7	7.1	1.8	24.2
Persons 25+ w/bachelor's degree	92.3	0.5	1.2	6.0	88.3	2.0	2.0[b]	7.7	49.8	8.7[b]	21.3[b]	0.0	20.1[b]	85.0	0.8[b]	1.2[b]	13.0	79.3	0.7[b]	2.3[b]	17.7
Men age 18–64																					
Households w/income <$15,000	35.3	13.0	5.6	46.1	24.6	19.3	7.5	48.6	12.1	13.1	24.5	8.2[b]	42.1	40.3	21.1	1.8[b]	36.7	18.2	14.5	2.8	64.5
Households w/income ≥$50,000	93.3	0.1[b]	0.6	5.9	88.8	0.2[b]	1.6[b]	9.4	55.0	0.0	39.3[b]	1.3[b]	4.5[b]	91.0	0.0	0.3[b]	8.6	88.7	0.9[b]	0.5[b]	9.9
Unemployed	43.7	7.2	3.2	45.9	31.5	10.1	4.8[b]	53.6	17.7[b]	2.5[b]	52.7	0.0	27.1[b]	41.8	8.4[b]	0.0	49.8	26.9	11.6	2.2[b]	58.6
Persons 25+ w/less than H.S.	54.0	8.0	4.4	33.6	40.8	14.7	7.8	36.7	27.9	5.1[b]	38.5	7.0[b]	21.6[b]	38.1	26.1	1.0[b]	34.8	35.4	8.3	2.7[b]	53.6
Persons 25+ who graduated H.S.	83.2	1.4	2.1	13.4	68.8	4.6	5.2	21.4	42.3	4.2[b]	29.8	4.4[b]	19.2	77.1	2.7	0.4[b]	19.8	68.5	3.4	2.2	25.8
Persons 25+ w/bachelor's degree	91.4	0.5	1.1	7.0	81.1	1.0[b]	4.4[b]	13.5	46.1	2.0[b]	31.8[b]	7.9[b]	12.2[b]	82.4	1.5[b]	0.0	16.2	81.0	1.3[b]	1.3[b]	16.3

	Priv. + Medicare	Medicaid +care	Other (incl Milt.)	Medicare only	Priv. + Medicare	Medicaid +care	Other (incl Milt.)	Medicare only	Priv. + Medicare	Medicaid +care	Medicare +IHS	Other (incl Milt.)	Medicare only	Priv. + Medicare	Medicaid +care	Other (incl Milt.)	Medicare only	Priv. + Medicare	Medicaid +care	Other (incl Milt.)	Medicare only
Women age 65+																					
Households w/income <$15,000	68.8	12.3	1.8	17.2	35.9	19.4	5.6	39.1	49.0	27.3[b]	18.7[b]	2.0[b]	3.0[b]	38.5[b]	16.0[b]	32.3[b]	13.2[b]	24.0	40.1	2.8[b]	33.1
Households w/income ≥$50,000	87.0	1.8[b]	1.6	9.6	60.2	1.8[b]	8.4[b]	29.6[b]	0.0	0.0	100.0	0.0	0.0	53.6	21.0	19.0[b]	6.3[b]	38.1	21.1[b]	8.2[b]	32.5[b]
Unemployed	72.1	0.0	7.2[b]	20.7[b]	71.8	24.3[b]	0.0	3.9[b]	NA	NA	NA	NA	NA	NA	NA	NA	NA	0.0	0.0	0.0	100.0
Persons 65+ w/less than H.S.	66.9	12.1	2.3	18.7	34.1	20.6	7.0	38.3	31.6[b]	26.1[b]	31.6[b]	0.0	10.7[b]	25.8[b]	22.4[b]	30.3	21.6[b]	27.1	36.0	5.7	31.3
Persons 65+ who graduated H.S.	87.2	1.6	1.3	10.0	60.9	7.9	3.3[b]	27.9	34.0[b]	0.0	51.0[b]	1.3[b]	13.7[b]	71.6	7.8[b]	13.8[b]	6.8[b]	69.8	4.7[b]	4.0[b]	21.5
Persons 65+ w/bachelor's degree	90.3	1.0[b]	1.1[b]	7.6	78.6	7.4[b]	0.6[b]	13.4	54.5	0.0	0.0	0.0	45.5	78.0	2.2[b]	8.2[b]	11.6[b]	75.7	5.0[b]	1.1[b]	18.3[b]
Men age 65+																					
Households w/income <$15,000	62.0	8.3	7.9	21.8	31.4	13.6	19.0	36.0	4.3[b]	20.6[b]	39.6[b]	4.0[b]	31.4[b]	23.5[b]	15.5[b]	21.5[b]	39.5[b]	35.0	20.3	12.3[b]	32.4
Households w/income ≥$50,000	93.7	0.4[b]	1.4[b]	4.5	74.9	6.5[b]	3.1[b]	15.5[b]	0.0	0.0	89.8	10.2[b]	0.0	55.8	10.2	10.6[b]	23.4	72.3	7.0[b]	3.4[b]	17.3[b]
Unemployed	92.6	0.0	0.0	7.4[b]	46.7[b]	0.0	9.3[b]	44.1[b]	NA	NA	NA	NA	NA	NA	NA	NA	NA	51.1[b]	0.0	0.0	48.9[b]
Persons 65+ w/less than H.S.	73.1	4.3	5.1	17.5	41.1	10.7	13.6	34.6	13.2[b]	22.4[b]	46.8[b]	3.6[b]	14.0[b]	38.8[b]	18.3[b]	28.4[b]	14.4[b]	36.0	14.7	16.7	32.6
Persons 65+ who graduated H.S.	87.7	1.0	2.6	8.7	64.5	2.3[b]	14.3	18.9	41.9[b]	0.0	22.0[b]	19.3[b]	16.9[b]	74.6	5.1[b]	4.8[b]	15.6	73.7	5.2	8.6[b]	12.4[b]
Persons 65+ w/bachelor's degree	91.8	0.7[b]	1.4	6.1	72.8	10.4[b]	4.8[b]	12.0[b]	28.5[b]	0.0	71.5[b]	0.0	0.0	80.9	1.6[b]	6.5[b]	11.1[b]	81.4	4.4[b]	5.3[b]	8.9[b]

NA, not available; H.S., high school; IHS, Indian Health Service.

[a] Noninstitutionalized population only.

[b] Hispanics may be of any race.

[c] Relative standard error is greater than 30% of the estimates.

[d] Medicare is a nationwide program providing health insurance to people 65 years of age and older, people entitled to social security disability payments for 2 years or more, and people with end-stage renal disease, regardless of income.

[e] Medicaid is a jointly funded cooperative venture between the federal and state governments to assist states in the provision of adequate medical care to eligible needy persons.

[f] Special insurance programs are available to military personnel, base staff, and their dependents.

Private health insurance (with or without Medicare) is generally considered the best type of insurance. As table 9.2 shows, it is strongly associated with high household income and college education in all racial-ethnic, gender, and age groups. For both age groups and within each racial-ethnic and gender group, persons in low-income households, unemployed, or with low education are less likely to be insured. For all the racial-ethnic groups, women more often have public coverage than men and men are more likely than women to have no insurance at all.

A decline in insurance coverage occurred simultaneously with the decline in earnings for most Americans during the 1980s. Under age 65, 12% of whites, 18% of blacks, and 20% of Hispanics in 1977 reported no insurance; this increased to 15%, 25%, and 35%, respectively, in 1987 thanks to a declining proportion with private insurance. Public coverage remained about the same (AHCPR 1992).

An analysis of trends between 1989 and 1997 shows a continuing increase in the percentage of uninsured from 13.6% to 16.1% (from about 33.3 million to about 43.4 million persons), although the trend may be slowing. The most rapid rise was in blacks (from 19.2%–21.2%). Hispanics remained the highest (33.5%–34.2%). Rates by gender show that in 1989, 14.8% of men and 12.4% of women were uninsured; this rose to 17.6% and 14.8%, respectively, in 1997. After being Hispanic, the most dramatic association with no insurance was family income. In 1989, 23% of families with income less than $25,000 reported no health insurance, and that rose to 25% in 1997 (Carrasquillo et al. 1999b).

Effects of Medical Insurance on Access to Health Services
Persons without health insurance are less likely to have a usual source of primary care. They are also less likely to obtain preventive services and immunizations, and because they are less familiar with it, less likely to be able to negotiate the complexities of obtaining medical care. A study of the effect of insurance on mortality using a large national examination and interview survey, controlling for sociodemographics, risk factors, morbidity, and self-rated health at the time of the examination, suggested

that lack of health insurance may even be linked to higher mortality (Franks et al. 1993).

Patients of lower social class enrolled in a health-maintenance organization (HMO) were more likely to obtain services than those in a fee-for-service setting (Makuc et al. 1994) and were also more likely to enjoy continuity of care (Schulman et al. 1999). These and other studies suggest that staff or group model HMOs, in which all services are prepaid on the premises, and doctors develop patient protocols using consensus, constitute a system of health care delivery in which services are equally accessible to patients of high and low socioeconomic status. Recent studies that do not distinguish between HMOs and managed care facilities suggest that the positive affects of the HMO delivery system for low-socioeconomic patients were diluted when other kinds of capitated services entered the market (Phillips et al. 2000).

Table 9.3 shows rates of use of some common health services. Most Americans report having a regular source of medical care. However, men less than women, and persons with low household income, no employment, and low education are less likely to report a regular source. Despite lower incomes, black and Native American women report a regular source of care at higher rates than white women. Black women are more likely than white women to have had a routine check-up in the previous three years. A comparison of insurance coverage with use of services reveals that service use is more closely associated with health insurance coverage than with socioeconomic status.

Dental care shows the strongest variation in use of services by social class. Most dental care requires out-of-pocket expenditures because few medical insurance policies in the United States cover it. A social class gradient is also apparent for mammography, even though most states require private insurance companies to cover the test (McKinney and Marconi 1992). Both dental and cancer screening are preventive services, which, as noted earlier, are especially sensitive to social class.

In short, health service use in the United States is closely associated with insurance coverage. This results in women having more access to medical coverage and services than men within their social class and racial-ethnic group. Another result is that black and native women, who

Table 9.3
Use of selected health care services in the U.S. by the five major racial ethnic groups[a]

Measure	White				Black				Native American, Alaska native				Asian, Pacific Islander				Hispanic[b]			
	Regular source of care[c]	Routine check-up[d]	Dental care in last year[e]	Mam in past 2 years[f]	Regular source of care[c]	Routine check-up[d]	Dental care in last year[e]	Mam in past 2 years[f]	Regular source of care[c]	Routine check-up[d]	Dental care in last year[e]	Mam in past 2 years[f]	Regular source of care[c]	Routine check-up[d]	Dental care in last year[e]	Mam in past 2 years[f]	Regular source of care[c]	Routine check-up[d]	Dental care in last year[e]	Mam in past 2 years[f]
Women																				
Persons 18+ households w/income <$15,000	82.9	80.8	45.1	45.2	87.3	88.5	41.8	62.8	88.3	78.2	45.8	47.1	72.7	75.0	55.9	49.0	71.2	81.9	39.9	44.0
Persons 18+ households w/income ≥$50,000	93.8	87.2	82.4	78.3	95.9	97.4	72.7	77.0	100.0	100.0	64.3	60.3[g]	90.1	90.3	65.4	58.9	92.0	91.9	76.2	69.7
Persons 18+ unemployed	80.7	81.1	64.4	74.9	84.8	89.6	49.4	62.6[e]	91.1	88.4	71.4	NA	80.3	57.1	54.5	100.0	73.2	85.8	56.4	18.5[g]
Persons 25+ w/less than H.S.	87.9	79.8	38.1	45.4	89.9	85.4	34.5	57.4	89.1	68.2	29.4	43.9	81.1	66.9	45.6	55.8	79.3	80.6	39.2	46.3
Persons 25+ who graduated H.S.	90.7	83.8	71.6	66.0	91.2	92.5	59.6	66.2	90.3	87.1	62.6	63.1	85.2	82.3	65.2	59.2	84.5	85.4	67.0	63.7
Persons 25+ w/bachelor's degree	90.9	87.0	83.6	76.3	94.0	95.9	71.7	74.3	91.2	64.3	83.1	100.0	85.4	81.5	72.2	54.5	86.3	90.2	75.9	65.5
Men																				
Persons 18+ households w/income <$15,000	68.1	68.5	38.9	NA	73.4	75.2	35.2	NA	69.9	67.5	29.3	NA	66.2	69.5	45.3	NA	51.5	63.2	29.0	NA
Persons 18+ households w/income ≥$50,000	88.1	77.2	74.7	NA	89.3	91.0	59.7	NA	87.7	73.5	72.4	NA	84.8	77.6	62.0	NA	85.9	77.8	63.7	NA
Persons 18+ unemployed	65.0	72.0	46.1	NA	69.2	80.5	39.3	NA	76.4	35.8[g]	37.7[g]	NA	62.1	83.0	37.7[g]	NA	52.0	76.6	32.0	NA
Persons 25+ w/less than H.S.	79.9	69.2	35.3	NA	83.6	78.9	30.7	NA	83.2	68.7	29.7	NA	70.2	87.5	47.5	NA	65.1	59.7	32.6	NA
Persons 25+ who graduated H.S.	83.2	72.9	64.4	NA	80.7	81.6	49.9	NA	81.1	69.8	53.1	NA	76.4	69.8	58.1	NA	71.9	72.9	51.4	NA
Persons 25+ w/bachelor's degree	85.1	75.6	76.2	NA	83.0	83.4	62.3	NA	89.3	58.0	62.5	NA	76.2	72.9	58.4	NA	75.2	74.1	64.1	NA

NA, not available; H.S., high school.

[a] Noninstitutionalized population only.

[b] Hispanics may be of any race.

[c] Regular source of care pooled 1993–1994 National Health Interview Survey data.

[d] Routine check-up pooled 1993–1994 National Health Interview Survey data.

[e] Dental visit in last year pooled 1989–1991 National Health Interview Survey data.

[f] Mammogram in past 2 years pooled 1993–1994 National Health Interview Survey data—women ages 50+ except for unemployed, which is 50–64.

[g] Relative standard error is greater than 30% of the estimate.

disproportionately use public programs (Medicaid and the Indian Health Service, respectively), report having a usual source of care and use some preventive medical services at higher rates than white women for their social class group. Even black and native men use medical services at rates similar to white men. These data suggest that public insurance programs may be less stigmatized in nonwhite populations, which depend more on them. Also, they suggest that medical services are being used to offset some of the effects of hierarchy established by the economy.

Social Hierarchies and Health Outcomes

Table 9.4 shows current smoking and hypertension prevalence for the groups shown in previous tables. Except for Native Americans, smoking prevalence is higher among men than women in every racial-ethnic group. This differential is especially large among Asian and Pacific Islanders. Women in this group report lower smoking rates than other women. Smoking is most concentrated among blue-collar male workers (Nathanson and Lopez 1987). Although the cross-sectional data cannot show it, other data show that rates of smoking fell for men and rose for women before 1990 (National Cancer Institute 1991).

The most striking finding concerning hypertension is the strong social class gradients associated with hypertension for whites, Asians, and Hispanics. Conversely, black persons with a college degree report higher rates than those with only high school graduation. Native Americans' rates are high even with high educational level or income. It is unclear whether higher rates reflect more use of services and consequently more diagnosis or more actual prevalence (Verbrugge 1989; Nathanson 1975).

Table 9.5 shows that perceived health status is consistent with the social gradients presented in table 9.1. This is striking because findings in tables 9.2 and 9.3, showing health insurance coverage and use of services, did not conform to the economic hierarchies in table 9.1. High socioeconomic status is positively associated with excellent or very good health and negatively associated with fair or poor health. Gender reflected the expected hierarchy: fewer women than men in each racial-ethnic group reported excellent or very good health, except for Native women in high-income households.

Table 9.4
Measures of risk and illness in the U.S. by the five major racial ethnic groups[a]

Measure	White		Black		Native American, Alaskan native		Asian, Pacific Islander		Hispanic[b]	
	Current smoker[c]	Hypertension[d]	Current smoker[c]	Hypertension[d]	Current smoker[c]	Hypertension[d]	Current smoker[c]	Hypertension[d]	Current smoker[c]	Hypertension[d]
Women										
Persons 25+ households w/ income <$15,000	27.6	31.8	30.3	34.3	35.5	28.6	6.8[e]	8.1	18.6	20.2
Persons 25+ households w/ income ≥$50,000	18.5	9.3	19.7	22.0	47.8	0	5.5[e]	6.6	17.2	10.3
Persons 25+ unemployed	34.2	12.2	39.0	18.5	60.8[e]	0	3.1[e]	10.6[e]	21.3	9.8
Persons 25+ w/less than H.S.	27.0	29.2	25.5	38.2	33.2	30.0	10.6	20.2	15.6	19.3
Persons 25+ who graduated H.S.	22.7	15.0	25.2	22.2	41.7	9.7	7.9	5.4	19.0	9.2
Persons 25+ w/bachelor's degree	13.1	10.0	16.6	21.8	11.0[e]	28.2	4.5[e]	3.8	16.3	4.8
Men										
Persons 25+ households w/ income <$15,000	38.2	19.9	44.4	24.7	38.3	9.6	34.8	11.5	33.8	6.4
Persons 25+ households w/ income ≥$50,000	21.1	11.9	27.4	15.7	24.9[e]	22.1	19.8	9.3	19.6	6.6
Persons 25+ unemployed	48.3	12.1	59.2	2.1[e]	34.6[e]	33.9	47.1[e]	11.2[e]	41.0	2.8[e]
Persons 25+ w/less than H.S.	36.2	19.3	42.1	27.1	35.6	3.7[e]	40.3	17.4	32.8	8.7
Persons 25+ who graduated H.S.	26.3	14.3	35.2	17.2	32.3	18.5	23.7	8.2	28.5	7.4
Persons 25+ w/bachelor's degree	15.0	12.1	19.1	19.2	10.1[a]	19.7	14.6	9.5	16.9	6.1

H.S., high school.
[a] Noninstitutionalized population only.
[b] Hispanics may be of any race.
[c] Current smoker—pooled 1990–1991 National Health Interview Survey data.
[d] Hypertension—pooled 1989–1991 National Health Interview Survey data.
[e] Relative standard error is greater than 30% of the estimate.

Table 9.5
Measures of health status in the U.S. by the five major racial ethnic groups[a]

Measure	White			Black			Native American, Alaskan native			Asian, Pacific Islander			Hispanic[b]		
	Excellent, very good	Good	Fair, poor	Excellent, very good	Good	Fair, poor	Excellent, very good	Good	Fair, poor	Excellent, very good	Good	Fair, poor	Excellent, very good	Good	Fair, poor
Women															
Persons 18+ households w/ income <$15,000	44.8	31.2	24.1	41.0	30.6	28.4	37.9	40.2	21.9	55.2	26.0	18.9	42.9	33.9	23.2
Persons 18+ households w/ income ≥$50,000	77.3	18.4	4.3	56.3	35.2	8.5	81.4	18.4[c]	0.2[c]	64.8	26.3	9.0[c]	69.8	20.4	9.8
Persons 18+ unemployed	61.6	28.8	9.5	50.0	32.6	17.4	66.9	32.8[c]	0.3[c]	60.4	36.4[c]	3.2[c]	52.7	34.9	12.4[c]
Persons 25+ w/less than H.S.	35.3	35.2	29.5	33.0	29.9	37.1	25.3	40.3	34.4	38.1	29.1	32.8	38.5	35.1	26.4
Persons 25+ who graduated H.S.	66.6	24.9	8.5	52.8	32.6	14.6	58.0	33.3	8.7	63.7	28.7	7.6	61.8	28.2	10.1
Persons 25+ w/bachelor's degree	78.7	16.8	4.5	63.3	30.1	6.7	67.2	29.7[c]	3.1[c]	68.0	26.2	5.8[c]	68.7	24.5	6.8
Men															
Persons 18+ households w/ income <$15,000	49.5	26.5	24.0	45.0	27.2	27.8	51.5	28.0	20.4	58.9	31.0	10.0	54.7	27.3	17.9
Persons 18+ households w/ income ≥$50,000	80.7	16.1	3.1	71.1	22.9	6.1	71.7	19.5[c]	8.8[c]	72.2	22.2	5.6	74.5	20.1	5.4[c]
Persons 18+ unemployed	65.4	24.3	10.3	53.7	34.8	11.5	37.8[c]	47.6[c]	14.6[c]	60.1	39.7[c]	0.1[c]	62.8	26.3	11.0
Persons 25+ w/less than H.S.	41.3	31.6	27.1	37.0	28.5	34.5	51.6	31.4	17.0	41.0	36.7	22.2	51.7	29.9	18.4
Persons 25+ who graduated H.S.	72.0	20.5	7.5	61.6	27.8	10.5	63.0	26.4	10.6	71.7	23.4	5.0	67.8	23.4	8.9
Persons 25+ w/bachelor's degree	81.1	15.2	3.7	72.9	20.5	6.6	76.3	17.6[c]	6.1[c]	74.5	21.3	4.2[c]	73.8	19.8	6.5[c]

H.S., high school.
[a] Pooled NHIS data for 1989–1991; noninstitutionalized population only.
[b] Hispanics may be of any race.
[c] Relative standard error is greater than 30% of the estimate.

Examples of Social Discrimination in Cancer

Cancer is the second leading cause of mortality in the United States, after heart disease. Between 1973 and 1996, death from cancer in the country increased from 17.7% to 23.3% (Ries et al. 1999). Only a small percentage (estimated at less than 5%) of fatal cancers are hereditary (Trichopoulos et al. 1996). The main risk association is age, and it appears that most cancers are caused by genetic alterations due to environmental or behavioral agents. Tobacco and diet, for example, may account for up to two-thirds of all cancer deaths (Trichopoulos et al. 1996).

Most studies of socioeconomic status and cancer grouped all cancers together for analysis, which may explain why one conclusion is that social differences are more strongly associated with cardiovascular and mental illness than with cancer (Marmot and Feeney 1997). However, focusing on specific sites is more fruitful than studying all sites combined because different sites have different relations to the social gradient.

Epidemiological studies associated poverty with cancers of the mouth, stomach, lung, cervix, and liver, and squamous cell esophageal cancer. A longitudinal survey using a 1% sample of the 1971 British census showed that social class differences in cancer mortality largely result from differences in cancer incidence and that survival differences make only a minor contribution (Kogevinas and Porta 1997). This is equivalent to saying that social discrimination is more important to cancer mortality than access to medical care. Lung cancer conforms closely to this model because most persons diagnosed with lung cancer die within one year of diagnosis. Moreover, smoking is the leading cause of lung cancer, which in turn drives overall cancer mortality (Miller et al. 1993), and is closely related to social class.

Although screening is not available for all cancers, where it does make early diagnosis possible, medical care may make a difference in outcomes. Screening and early detection followed by timely treatment increase survival for cervical, breast, colorectal, and possibly prostate cancers. Breast cancer is a good case to evaluate because it is associated with high social class, so most women diagnosed have the means to be screened and treated.

Lung, breast, and prostate cancers are used in the following sections to highlight how disparities in access to resources, including medical care, social networks, and political power, may promote disparities in outcomes. Lung cancer is the leading cause of cancer death in the United States for men and women. Breast cancer is the next leading cause of cancer death in women. Prostate cancer is the second leading cancer in men. Although breast and prostate cancers are not directly comparable, both are cancers of hormone-dependent organs with controversial screening and treatment modalities.

Lung Cancer

Between 1930 and 1990, deaths from lung cancer increased more than tenfold. This is the only cancer with evidence directly linking it to a predominant single cause; cigarette smoking is estimated to be responsible for more than 90% of cases. The U.S. Surgeon General officially reported results of prospective studies conducted in 1954 establishing this link ten years after their publication (U.S. Surgeon General 1964). The delay is not surprising in light of conflicting tendencies in the federal government, which subsidizes the tobacco industry (albeit at a steady decline), reimburses treatment for lung cancer by Medicare and Medicaid, and also funds demonstrations and behavioral interventions to promote smoking cessation. The success of smoking-cessation campaigns are impressive given the enormous amount of money the tobacco industry has spent on advertising and lobbying.

In 1964–1965, 51% of men and 34% of women reported they were current smokers (Gritz 1987). Blue-collar men are most likely to smoke (Nathanson and Lopez 1987). There have been declines in smoking by both sexes, but the pace has been slower for women than men (Blake et al. 1989). As its hazards were widely publicized, smoking became concentrated in disadvantaged social groups (Neuhauser 1999). This change paralleled marketing of tobacco products, which shifted its focus toward women and ethnic minorities (Davis 1987).

Young girls with limited horizons were especially vulnerable to smoking ads (Blake et al. 1989). Similarly, analyses of the Alameda study showed that socially isolated women were at significantly higher risk of smoking-related cancers. Social connections were not associated with cancer deaths among men (Reynolds and Kaplan 1990). Smoking is a rare but affordable luxury for poor British women, and the author concluded that poor families in high-income countries should not be the target of smoking-cessation activities unless programs are put in place to improve their life situations (Townsend 1996). This research underscores the limitations of the medical approach and its focus on individuals outside their social context. Race, gender and class disparities in population health are inherently about relative position in a social hierarchy.

Improvement in Treatment for Breast and Prostate Cancers

Breast cancer is the most commonly diagnosed cancer in women. The current view is that the disease is systemic and that tumor cells access the body through lymph nodes and blood circulation. As a result, the medical focus is on early detection and timely treatment. This thinking is in sharp contrast to how the disease was conceptualized and treated during the first three-fourths of the twentieth century.

Initially, it was thought that breast cancer was spread by direct contact of the tumor with surrounding tissue. Treatment, radical mastectomy, entailed opening the chest cavity and resecting large portions of the sternum, ribs, and internal mammary vessels. In addition, the entire breast and the muscles under it were removed. This radical and debilitating treatment left survival rates unchanged until the 1970s (Kaluzny and Warnecke 1996), when women's health and consumer health organizations began to challenge this medical practice (Kaufert 1998).

As a result, clinical trials investigated the possibility of a mortality benefit from early detection with mammography (Shapiro et al. 1982) and the equivalence of mastectomy versus lump removal followed by radiation (Fisher et al. 1985), both less debilitating than radical mastectomy. A 30% mortality benefit was seen with mammography screening (followed by timely treatment) for women age fifty to sixty-four, and survival with less debilitating treatments were shown to be equivalent to that for radical mastectomy.

Incorporation of these findings into routine medical practice considerably improved quality of life for women with breast cancer. In 1994, almost 61% of women in the United States aged fifty and older had had a mammogram in the previous two years (Pamuk et al. 1998). The proportion of breast cancers detected early increased and five-year survival rate improved from 75% in 1974–1976 to 85% in 1989–1995 (Ries et al. 1999).

Armed with these scientific findings, women organized to demand funding to speed the process of scientific discovery to prevent, detect, treat, and cure the disease (Kaufert 1998). Because expected survival is more than ten years, women have been able to initiate and sustain this movement and enjoyed considerable success in mobilizing additional funding. Consequently, after lung cancer, breast cancer is one of the best funded and most thoroughly studied of all malignancies. This is a considerable achievement since the disease largely affects women and doubtless, this success is due in no small part to the fact that women from higher social classes with substantial resources at their disposal are most frequently afflicted.

Before examining issues of race, class, and age discrimination related to breast cancer treatment, it may be useful briefly to contrast historic progress in its detection and treatment with that of prostate cancer. Surgery is the most common treatment for prostate cancer; however, it can result in incontinence or impotence. Although first described by Millen in 1945, medical prostatectomy became accepted only after nerve-sparing surgery was developed in the 1980s to reduce the risks (Lassen and Thompson 1994). Radiation treatment and watchful waiting (frequent observation and evaluation) were widely publicized, despite lack of evidence, so men had alternatives to surgery.

The unwillingness of physicians to perform debilitating treatment on men for prostate cancer is in sharp contrast to the seventy or more years during which debilitating treatment was routinely done to treat breast cancer in women. Sea-changes occurred in attitudes about health and the role of patients in obtaining medical care in the United States (Rodwin 1994), so that today consumers who have knowledge, resources, and desire routinely participate in decisions about their medical care.

It is nonetheless striking to note that prostatectomy was not done until its debilitating aspects were addressed, whereas radical mastectomy was routinely performed despite its debilitating aspects. Various factors such as speciality-physician culture and scientific understanding of cancer among others, may have played a role in early differences in breast and prostate cancer treatment. However, it seems important to ask whether sexism played some role and whether men's quality of life is more vigilantly protected than women's in American society. This is particularly true since higher social class did not protect women from gender-discriminatory medical practice until women were politically mobilized around the issue. The example of consumer mobilization to improve scientific understanding and change in treatment for breast cancer provides a model for improved patient care for other diseases.

The relative value of men's and women's lives is further called into question by the current emphasis on prostate cancer. The rapid increase in incidence resulted from changes in diagnostic practice and, more recently, from widespread use of the prostate-specific antigen (PSA) test (Potosky et al. 1990). However, autopsy studies show that virtually all American men die with the disease; no mortality benefit for screening has been shown in a clinical trial; and researchers question whether it is useful or cost effective to diagnose a disease that most men are thought to die with rather than from (Kramer et al. 1993). The median age of prostate cancer diagnosis is seventy-one years for white men and sixty-nine for black men, three years less than the average life expectancy for men in 1997. Nevertheless, some evidence indicates that PSA testing is widely recommended by American physicians (Legler et al. 1998), and research suggests that greater use of the test was accompanied by a reduction in prostate cancer mortality (Etzioni et al. 1999).

The disease occurs more frequently and at younger ages in black men than in white men. Whereas the relative benefits of the three treatment modalities (surgery, radiation, watchful waiting) have not been compared formally, observational studies using cancer registry data showed that black men are more likely to be treated with watchful waiting than white men (Klabunde et al. 1998). Whether this results from personal choice, physician recommendation, or medical care access is not known. Nor are the reasons known for excess prostate cancer incidence and mortality of the disease in black men, although diet is one hypothesis with some evidence for it.

Evidence shows that physicians are more likely to refer white men than other patients to what are considered state-of-the-art procedures for diagnosis (Schulman et al. 1999; Ruiz and Verbrugge 1997). In addition, physicians are less likely to refer black women than white women for mammograms (Burns et al. 1996).

Social Discrimination in Breast Cancer Incidence, Diagnosis, and Treatment

Breast cancer has important race, class, and age dimensions. Black women have lower incidence than white women, but higher mortality (Ries et al. 1999). In the 1980s, lower survival rates among black women seemed attributable to less mammography screening (Hunter et al. 1993) and once diagnosed, those women were less likely to receive standard treatment generally recommended for their diagnostic stage (Breen et al. 1999).

A study using 1993–1994 data showed that, among low-income women, blacks reported more mammography screening than whites (Makuc et al. 1999). Nonetheless, although mortality rates dropped on average 1.8% per year from 1989–1995, the figures applied only to white women (Wingo et al. 1999). If low-income or black women are not getting test results and follow-up services, or having a mammogram on a regular schedule, the test would not be effective. Perhaps not enough time has elapsed since black women's mammography use caught up with white women's to show a mortality benefit. Data linking mammography with breast cancer for adequate numbers of individual black and white women are not available to investigate this further.

Monitoring systems do not allow us to link the entire process, beginning with screening, to investigate how race and class contribute to outcomes. Regular screening requires a regular relationship with a health care provider who, in case of diagnosis, can help with treatment choices and care. A class effect is suggested at each point along the continuum of cancer care because, as noted, every aspect of care must be separately negotiated. The class effect cannot be measured, however, because United States cancer registries do not routinely collect socioeconomic status data.

Our knowledge about social inequalities and breast cancer is limited by lack of mammography registries to ascertain whether women received test results and were diagnosed with breast cancer. Data on sequelae to cancer screening were collected for the general population for the first time in 2000. Ideally, mammography registries would be linked to cancer registries, which routinely monitor stage-specific incidence and treatment. Pilot mammography registries do this (Ballard-Barbash et al. 1997), but they do not collect socioeconomic status data.

Cancer registry cases can be linked to socioeconomic status data from the decennial census for small areas, but few analyses of social inequalities by disease site have been published. As data problems are rectified, interdisciplinary collaboration will be necessary to develop and test hypotheses related to social, environmental, and genetic causes of cancer, including their interactions, and systematically to analyze access to care and patterns of service use in diverse populations.

Monitoring Social Discrimination on Population and Individual Health

How differences in health, illness, and death appear as group patterns depends not only on which social factors are measured, but also on the perspective used to organize and interpret the data. Social epidemiology is distinguished from clinical epidemiology by the premise that behavior has to be studied in its social and historical contexts. A few social epidemiologists argue for routine integration of race, class, and gender concepts into social epidemiology studies (Krieger et al. 1993). Practitioners increasingly draw theory from the social sciences and use structural analysis to try to capture a broad range of causes underlying disparities in health and mortality (Blane et al. 1996). This approach expanded research from exclusively individual and medical approaches to include investigations into how populations experience health, illness, and death.

As a result, more than a decade of social epidemiology consistently shows that income equality is associated with long life in a population. This suggests that we should routinely monitor how income distribution is associated with health and mortality. The United States leads high-income countries with the highest measured income gap between rich and poor, shortest average life span, and largest per capita expenditure on health care (Wagstaff et al. 1993). These indicators suggest that spending on health care is inefficient in the richest country in the world. Moreover, findings linking income equality and longevity raise the question of how income distribution affects health.

United States data systems are not constructed to monitor pathways through which hierarchy and inequality might shape health. Social class measures are not routinely collected and race, sex, and age are not regularly reported by socioeconomic status. As a result, health data reporting is limited to the so-called holy trinity of race, age, and gender (Navarro 1990). These data limitations, combined with the historic concentration of blacks at the lower tail of the income distribution, means that variation in health outcomes by social class is often attributed directly and exclusively to race. This practice misrepresents how class and race act separately and interact to influence health outcomes.

Table 9.6 summarizes data reviewed in this chapter by ranking nine important indicators of socioeconomic hierarchy, health care use, and health by sex and racial-ethnic group. Each indicator was ranked independently in descending order. All indicators were summed for an overall ranking by gender for each racial-ethnic group. White men ranked highest overall and among higher-ranked racial-ethnic groups, women ranked below men, as patriarchal theory would predict. However, it is striking that in the two lowest-ranking groups, black and Native men ranked lower than women in their racial-ethnic group.

Population health, as measured by self-reported health status, closely replicates the way wealth, income, and jobs are distributed by race, class, and gender. Social programs in the United States provide more health insurance to women than to men, who in turn use services at higher rates than men. Yet they do not report being as healthy as men.

Medical care alone cannot resolve health problems in a population. Broader social determinants must also be addressed. Such an analysis might also help illuminate why women use more medical services but have worse self-reported health status than men. More research is needed on how women deploy medical care to offset mental and physical stressors caused by patriarchy and a gender division of labor that disadvantages them.

Health-related outcomes can be best understood when race and gender are considered in light of each other and social class. No single category can approximate or summarize the complex set of relations they represent. A key part of the research agenda will be to tease out how these

Table 9.6
Indicators of socioeconomic hierarchy and well-being ranked by race or ethnicity and sex ranked in descending order

Race or ethnicity	Sex	Overall rank	Wealth family assets ≥$10K[a] Age 18+ Rank	Income ≥$25K[b] Age 18+ Rank	Education ≥ college grad[b] Age 25+ Rank	Employed Yes[d] Age 25+ Rank	Job type Supervisor-manager[b] Age 25+ Rank	Insurance Private[a] Age 25+ Rank	Usual source of care Yes[a] Age 18+ Rank	Last check-up within 3 years[a] Age 18+ Rank	Health status EX/VG[c] Age 18+ Rank
White	Male	72	10	9	8	8	9	10	6	3	9
White	Female	71	8	7	7	10	8	9	9	7	6
API	Male	70	9	10	10	7	10	8	2	4	10
API	Female	63	7	8	9	9	4	7	7	5	7
Black	Female	44	1	2	5	5	3	5	10	10	3
Hispanic[e]	Male	41	6	5	6	3	7	4	1	1	8
Black	Male	40	5	3	4	2	5	6	5	6	4
Hispanic[e]	Female	39	4	4	2	6	6	3	4	9	1
Native American, AN	Female	30	3	1	1	4	2	1	8	8	2
Native American, AN	Male	25	2	6	3	1	1	2	3	2	5

API, Asian, Pacific Islander; AN, Alaska native; EX/VG, excellent or very good.
[a] Pooled NHIS 1993–1994 data.
[b] 1990 NHIS data.
[c] Pooled NHIS 1989–1991 data.
[d] 1990 U.S. Census.
[e] Hispanics may be of any race.

interactions shape the range and combinations of gender roles that are associated with women's health.

To evaluate the impact of social policy on population health, it was recommended that policy proposals be asssessed in light of their effect on social justice and social divisions (Wilkinson 1996). This would suggest that employment, tax, and welfare policies should be evaluated for their impact on population health. Two broad questions must be kept in mind: what are the pathways by which particular contexts generate and maintain social inequalities in health? and what actions can be taken to reduce social inequalities? (Macintyre 1997)

Conceptualizing an economic basis for social discrimination is a critical step in the process to monitor health disparities better. Health data should be routinely collected and reported by social class categories for major racial-ethnic groups by gender. Improving our understanding in this area should also help identify promising avenues for interventions to improve health for both individuals and the population. Until we ask the right research questions, we must to monitor the effects of these basic indicators of social inequality.

Notes

1. I thank James Cucinelli, IMS, for expert SUDAAN programming on the National Health Interview Surveys, and James Cucinelli and Ray Chang, IMS, for Excel table construction. Supportive and expert advice on the manuscript content was provided by Constance Nathanson, Laura Montgomery, Elsie Pamuk, Janis Barry-Figueroa, Joan Hoffman, Larian Angelo, Nadine Felton, Patrick Joyce, Martin Brown, Rachel Ballard-Barbash, Carrie Klabunde, and Nancy Moss; and to Freh Kiflemarian for technical assistance. Finally, I express my appreciation to Asha George, Gita Sen, and Piroska Östlin for excellent editorial advice on several drafts.

2. Nonwhite women were mainly black, although detailed categories were not collected.

3. The survey was administered in 1990 during which annual income data for the previous year were collected.

4. L. Montgomery, U.S. National Center for Health Statistics, personal communication.

10

Policy Environments: Macroeconomics, Programming, and Participation[1]

Maggie Bangser

Poverty has always been with us in our communities. It was there in the past, long before Europeans came, and it affected many, perhaps all of us. But it was a different type of poverty. People were not helpless. They acted together and never allowed it to "squeeze" any member of the community. . . But now things have changed. Each person is on their own. A few people who have acquired material wealth are very scared of sliding back into poverty. They do not want to look like us . . . we are left to fight this poverty ourselves. And yet we only understand a little of it. It is only its effects that we can see. The causes we cannot grasp. The forces of poverty and impoverishment are so powerful today. They can only be managed by Governments, or the big churches. So now we feel somewhat hopeless; it is this feeling of helplessness that is so painful, more painful than poverty itself.

—An old woman from Uganda (Community Development Resource Network, 1996 as cited in Brock 1999)

Women living in poverty experience a complex web of persistent inequalities and inequities. Deeply embedded in social, cultural, economic, and political structures, sources of this inequality and inequity represent a form of structural violence, severe deprivation, and sociopolitical marginalization of a significant portion of society (Galtung 1969 cited in Kim et al. 2000). These structures erode women's well-being by restricting their capacity to attain positive health and education outcomes, secure income, and participate in decision making. Structural violence and inequity have broader impacts as well. Limiting women's agency, the processes by which women act to promote change for themselves and catalyze broader social transformation, is a fundamental constraint to achieving human development.

Human Development Reports characterize the face of income-poverty today as that of a woman, child, or elderly person. She is unskilled or works for low wages in an urban area, facing cuts in social welfare brought on by the country's economic stagnation and increasing disparity between rich and poor. Although poor men are also affected by these problems, poor women experience more severe forms of poverty and greater hardship lifting themselves and their children out of the poverty trap. The 1997 Human Development Report notes that "no society treats its women as well as its men" and that gender inequality is strongly associated with human poverty, defined by low levels of life expectancy, health, housing, knowledge, personal security, and participation (UNDP 1997).

Unfortunately, macroeconomic and development policies often exacerbate or fail to improve markedly gender inequalities and inequities. Two policy issues, economic adjustment policies and vertical development programming, constrain poor women, as well as poor men, from achieving equitable health outcomes and realizing their capacities to act as agents for change. Greater gender equity can be achieved by reframing economic and programming policies in terms of women's agency, participation of the poor in agenda setting, and public accountability. Special reference to Africa is made throughout the chapter, but the implications of the findings relate broadly to low-income countries and their relations with high-income countries.

The Macroeconomic Environment: Health, Structural Adjustment, and Debt

"Medicine for the Poor"

Limited government resources in many low-income countries severely compromise the effectiveness and efficiency of the health sector and, coupled with overall poverty, undermine people's capacity to achieve positive health outcomes. The economic fabric of many low-income countries, particularly in Africa, deteriorated in recent decades. Beginning in the 1970s, petro-dollars from oil-producing countries flowed into Western banks. These substantial new monies were used as loans to governments of low-income countries, often funding poorly conceived projects and carrying high interest rates. Volatile world commodity prices and worsening terms of trade undercut the capacity of low-income governments to repay these loans. In the wake of these events, debts were rescheduled at higher interest rates.

This rescheduling came at a steep price. The World Bank[2] (WB) and International Monetary Fund (IMF) mandated compliance with sweeping economic reforms for debtor governments to receive new loans. These reforms, known as structural adjustment programs (SAPs), included policies of privatization, liberalization, and deregulation. This translated into attempts to enhance efficiency by reducing the role of the state relative to the market, allowing prices to be determined by market forces, and integrating national economies into the world economy by lifting barriers to trade and investment (Kim et al. 2000).

By 1992, seventy-five countries had received adjustment loans from the IMF and WB, nearly half of them in Africa. Creditor governments have insisted on compliance with IMF and WB economic adjustment programs as a condition for further aid and debt relief from other donors (Oxfam 1999). Although generally less that 20% of international debt is owed specifically to the IMF, this gatekeeper role between donors and borrowing countries significantly increased the power of the IMF in international financial negotiations.

Unfortunately, "structural adjustment did not reduce debts, cut poverty, nor return countries to the path of growth" (Kim et al. 2000). The IMF's own evaluation of the enhanced structural adjustment facility found that in sub-Saharan Africa average income growth per person fell by 0.5% a year during the first half of the 1990s (Oxfam 1999). In addition, only approximately half of targeted reductions in national budget deficits were achieved, progress in reducing inflation was limited, and savings rates (which determine domestic capacity for investment and growth) were unchanged. "By any standards, this is poor performance. Measured against sub-Saharan Africa's needs, it represents a disaster" (Oxfam 1999).

SAPs did succeed, however, in returning borrowed dollars to wealthy nations. The amount of debt owed to creditors rose from $616 billion in 1980 to roughly $2.2 trillion at the end of 1997. Between 1983 and 1989, poor countries paid $242 billion *more* to creditors than they received in new loans. "The net transfer of resources from developed to developing countries changed from a positive flow of nearly $43 billion in 1981 to a negative flow of $33 billion in 1988" (World Bank 1998a cited in Kim et. al. 2000).

SAPs also built an overhang of debt payments that crippled the capacity of borrower governments to invest in economic and social growth. The human costs of this are staggering, but seem to have little impact on the way the international financial institutions conduct their business. Former chief economist of the IMF, Michael Mussa, stated that "Our programs are like medicine. Some of the medicine has harmful side effects and there are real questions about what the dosage ought to be. The best that can be hoped for is that we are prescribing more or less the right medicine in more or less the right dosage" (Oxfam 1999). If this were a situation of individual medical treatment, the IMF could be held liable for malpractice. However, because borrower governments are largely excluded from substantive policymaking, macroeconomic policies continue to ravage public expenditures for health and development with impunity.

Public pressure to reform debt servicing arrangements has grown in recent years, involving coalitions such as the Jubilee 2000 campaign and such disparate figures as the Pope, rock singer Bono, and economist Jeffrey Sachs. The most recent policy formulation of international financial institutions to address the debt crisis is known as the initiative for heavily indebted poor countries (HIPC), launched in 1996 and amended in 1999 as the enhanced HIPC. Whereas public pressure for debt relief has been relatively successful, considerable disagreement surrounds HIPC's capacity to provide sustainable debt relief and lay the foundation for economic viability. Some critics call for a faster, deeper, and more comprehensive process. Others criticize the fundamental basis of HIPC as overly onerous, calling for complete cancellation of debt for poorest countries.

Governments of low-income countries are poorly represented in, and the voices of the poor almost entirely marginalized from determining macroeconomic policies. The executive board that oversees the IMF includes executive directors from the United States, Japan, Germany, France, and the United Kingdom. In contrast, sub-Saharan Africa has two executive directors representing forty-two countries. On the eve of the world economic forum in January 2000, WBs former chief economist

Joseph Stiglitz stated that the international financial community must "establish a framework in which economic policies are made which affect everybody" and to make sure that all those who are affected, including the poor, "have a voice in those policies" (Friedman 2000).

"All These Look You the Woman in the Face": SAPs, Women, and Ill Health

Both poor men and poor women are affected by SAPs, but women are particularly affected as they generally have less access to financial resources, work longer hours, and have less control over family assets and cash. Throughout debtor countries, uneven distribution of economic growth, erosion of social sector investment due to debt obligations, and impact of SAP-related measures disproportionately reduce poor women's well-being. The impact of these economic measures is felt through negative changes in income, increasing prices of purchases (especially food), worsening working conditions, and decreasing public expenditures including for health care (Gladwin 1991).

For example, policies that emphasize growth in food exports tend to benefit men who have greater access to credit and markets. Women who work largely on small subsistence farms are often worse off as they are made to work double-time on both family farms and their husbands' new farms (Baden 1993). Whereas expansion of the agricultural sector can contribute to increasing women's incomes and status, most women farmers do not have the same access to agricultural inputs or markets as men. They face increased workloads, increased physical and mental strain, and less time for their double duty as childbearers and mothers in the reproductive economy (Elson and Evers 1998). In addition, whereas increased participation of some urban women in the labor force may gain them independent income, introduction of school fees for their children and the general increase in the cost of living means they are not necessarily better off than before (Wratten 1993).

A 1994 consultation between women's organizations and the WB in Tanzania identified specific ways in which structural adjustment and economic reforms had a negative impact on women's financial security and economic base. These included the closing of rural banks, tightening of loan procedures, and increased interest rates. These compounded women's already significant disadvantage as manifest in their unequal access to formal lending institutions, low technical skills in finance, little experience with formal banking procedures, lack of ownership of property, and low incomes. In addition, alternative credit programs were not available throughout the country and in some cases overrepresented wealthier women among beneficiaries in spite of stated low-income target groups (Mbilinyi and Shayo 1996).

A small-scale study in Ghana suggests that women's daily lives and sense of well-being are deeply affected by psychosocial health problems related to economic stress and social pressures. Distress, anxiety, tiredness, and headaches give expression to the pressures poor people experience, particularly poor women, who have little power to shape their personal circumstances. A fundamental root of symptoms was the material and social circumstances of their lives, including expectations to be a "good" woman while facing limited financial security (Avorti and Walters 1999). Declining resources also result in women "swallowing their pride" as they take "demeaning jobs . . . to bring food to the family" (World Bank 2000a). These findings are similar to reports from other poor rural communities such as Brazil, where "nerves" are associated with economic hardship and uncertainty (Rozemberg and Manderson 1998 cited in Avorti and Walters 1999).

Debt and Disinvestment in Social Sectors

By the end of the 1980s, nonoil-producing low-income countries allocated 30 to 70% of export revenues for debt service alone. "Governments required new adjustment loans in order to remain even minimally operative" (Kim et al. 2000). Although critics maintain that confounding variables make it difficult to attribute declining health standards to adjustment policies and debt, it seems evident that economic austerity programs typically undercut expenditures to basic social services. According to a 1995 WB analysis, government spending on the social sectors in all countries undergoing adjustment reforms fell from 5.9% of the budget to 5.3%. Health sector expenditures declined from a mere 1.3% to 1.1% of budgets and real per capita health spending fell by about 15% on average (Christian Aid 1999). In contrast in 1995, countries with a high human development index such as Canada, Sweden, Greece and

Argentina spent an average of 6.1% of gross domestic product on their health sectors (UNDP 1999).

Improved access to basic social services is critical to achieving growth with equity (Oxfam 1999). In turn, disinvestment in social sectors can cause serious decay of primary health care services. This affects all poor people, but particularly women and children, who are the poorest members of communities. In Zimbabwe, a combination of currency devaluations and debt precipitated a drop of more than 30% in health spending. "Allocations to primary health care facilities have fallen, while preventive care budgets, the most cost-effective part of the system, have dropped by a quarter" (Watkins 1998b cited in WEDO 1999). A doctor from Zambia reports: "we have seen things go from being fairly acceptable, where we could admit virtually anybody and be happy to look after them, to being actually scared to look after a patient, because you can't even do the very basic things" (Christian Aid 1999).

The toll of debt servicing on basic social services is staggering (figure 10.1). Nicaragua pays over 50% of government revenue to debt servicing, an amount equal to two and a half times the country's recurrent spending on health and education combined. Debt servicing accounts for more than 30% of government revenue in Tanzania, Malawi and Zambia. In Chad, Mali, Mozambique, Niger, and Rwanda annual debt servicing obligations are in excess of 20% of their government revenue. The $7 per

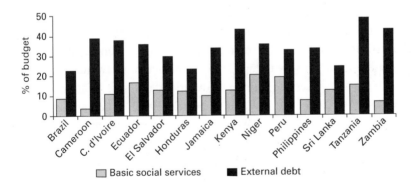

Figure 10.1
Percent of budget on debt vs. basic social services in the late 1990s. (Source: UNICEF and UNDP 1998, analyzed by Vandemoortele 2000.)

capita that sub-Saharan Africa spends each year overshadows per capita health expenditures of $3 to $5 in many of the poorest indebted countries (UNICEF 1999a). In a study compiled by UNICEF, two-thirds of the countries surveyed spend more on external debt servicing than on basic social services. "In sub-Saharan Africa, governments spend about twice as much on complying with their financial obligations vis-à-vis external creditors than on complying with their fundamental social obligations vis-à-vis their people" (Vandemoortele 2000).

Take the case of Tanzania. In 1997, its expenditure on debt servicing absorbed one-third of its entire budget. The country spent nine times as much servicing the debt as it spent on primary health care, and four times as much servicing debt as it spent on primary education (Oxfam 1998). The per capita recurrent health expenditure was lower in 1996 than in 1989, as was the expenditure for education (Lawson 1997). In 1995–1996, Tanzania spent approximately U.S. $2.18 per capita on personnel, drugs, and other recurrent costs of the public health system. This includes curative care, which captures at least 80% of recurrent Ministry of Health costs (Bangser 2000).

The abysmal record of donor countries providing development aid conspires with the debt burden to perpetuate poverty in low-income countries. In 1997, overseas development assistance hit a historic low of 0.22% of combined gross national products in donor countries, far from the already minimal target of 0.7% set by the United Nations (Vandemoortele 2000). Real overseas development assistance declined by more than one-fifth between 1992 and 1997 despite surveys that consistently show public support for international cooperation. Countries hit hardest by these cuts are those with high levels of income-poverty and child mortality and low access to primary education and safe drinking water (OECD/DAC 1996 cited in Vandermoortele 2000). To compound matters, only about 10% of total overseas development assistance is allocated to basic social services. Some critics contend that this could be related to basic social services not typically involving high-level technical advice or sophisticated equipment that create work and contracts for donor country nationals (Vandemoortele 2000). Once again, decreasing donor investment in low-income countries together with ill-advised priorities negatively affect the well-being of the poor.

User Fees and the Gender-Differentiated Impact of Economic Policies

One aspect of economic structural adjustment is the introduction of cost sharing or user fees. These are payments that individuals must contribute to receive health services (as well as education). They often represent the most visible indicator of the transfer in financing responsibility from governments to households (UNICEF 1999a), and they have a disproportionate impact on the poor. This is due in part to the greater impact of fee increases on the poor than on the rich, leading to lower use of health services among the poor (Hsiao 1998). Adding to this burden, formal fees do not include the very real costs of travel and waiting time (Reddy and Vandemoortele 1996).

Imposition of fees severely undercuts the role of preventive care. When rural health facilities in Zimbabwe increased user fees, women limited their antenatal care and began giving birth at home because obstetric care was unaffordable (WEDO 1999; Watkins 1998b; Chinemana and Sanders 1993 cited in Kim et. al. 2000). In 1990–1994, when SAP coincided with a drought, total real health spending, per capita health spending, and wages of health personnel all declined by one-third or more (Marquette 1997). The number of rural women delivering in clinics or hospitals decreased by 20% (Marquette 1997) and the number of women delivering without prenatal care in the country's main hospital more than quadrupled (Illif 1992 cited in Marquette 1997). Similarly, data from Zaria, Nigeria, show that when user charges were introduced, maternal deaths rose by 56% along with a 46% decline in deliveries at the regional hospital (Ekwempu et al. 1990). When fees were introduced in hospitals in Tanzania in 1993, a precipitous decline of 53% outpatient visits was seen in public hospitals studied (Hussein and Mujinja 1997).

Exemption schemes for certain populations such as children under five years old and for maternal-child health services have not been consistently implemented. For example the WB's evaluation of the Zambia user fee experience reports that "legitimate zeal for reforms has unfortunately led to imposing user charges before the necessary safety nets could be put in place. In practice, there is no system in place in clinics and health centers to exempt the poor, as intended in the reform program" (World Bank 1995, unpublished report cited in Christian Aid 1999).

It is the direct impact on individual poor people and the disproportion-ate burden placed on women that require attention in assessing the impact of structural adjustment, debt, and user fees. These economic policies can have a direct and devastating bearing on the lives and health of poor women, as is poignantly illustrated by Teresa (box 10.1).

The Program Environment: Opening Avenues for Inclusive Programming

Poverty, Health, and Vertical Programming

Amartya Sen states "freedom in one area seems to help foster freedom in others" (1999a). Conversely one can hold that lack of freedom in one area can limit freedom in another. Poor people's experience of poverty is complex and rooted in multiple dimensions of powerlessness. Evidence shows that poor people identify strongly with the intangibles of poverty that affect their own agency and ability to change their circumstances. These intangibles include fear, powerlessness, anxiety, hopelessness, lack of respect by others, and isolation. They may not be readily quantifiable, but the poor place a strong emphasis on how they cannot be discounted when considering how best to alleviate poverty (Brock 1999).

Research suggests that people set priorities according to their need to survive. Economic sustainability, transportation, food, and water are high among their priorities. Although health is not unimportant, enabling conditions for survival are often priorities in establishing health and well-being (Bangser 2000). When poor people in Tanzania were asked what they would do with an additional 50,000 shillings (approximately U.S. $75), they ranked paying medical expenses last (Narayan 1997). This suggests that the poor make critical tradeoffs in which they may be forced to compromise their own health in the pursuit of basic survival. For women, who typically are caretakers in families, this trade-off can be particularly acute. They may feel compelled to place the well-being of others over themselves, and have limited options to secure their own health.

The cycle of poverty and ill health is often neglected by health initia-tives that fail to broaden their mandate to incorporate issues of gender equitable social and economic development (Oxaal and Cook 1998; Mal-

Box 10.1
Teresa's struggle for health (Bangser 2000)

Teresa was born in a village in Tanzania in 1974. She finished primary school, married at 18, and moved to her husband's home where she became pregnant. When she went into labor her mother-in-law and husband, rather than a trained provider, assisted her.

Teresa's labor continued for two days before she reached a local hospital. The baby had died and Teresa sustained a severe injury, vesicovaginal fistula, which causes women to leak urine continuously through the vagina. Surgical repair for fistula costs US$200. Given that the average per capita gross national product in Tanzania is $210 (much lower for those in poverty), repair was simply out of reach. Teresa's husband abandoned her, leaving her without economic or social support. She went to her brother's home where she slept separately and was unable to work due to the stigma and smell of leaking urine.

In 1996, her brother scraped together money to take Teresa to Bugando Medical Centre, a referral hospital in Mwanza. Nonetheless, she waited nine months for a repair due to limited hospital capacity and lack of specially trained surgeons. The previous year, the hospital's budget had been drastically cut when Tanzania reduced health expenditures in line with policies of international financial institutions and donor countries. After the cuts, the 800-bed hospital received $1,000 a month for food and $1,000 for drugs.

Teresa had no visitors. Despite the best efforts of doctors, the repair failed and she returned in 1997 for another operation. The day of her operation she was told that surgery was postponed due to an emergency. In resource-limited hospitals, poor people with chronic conditions often come last. Teresa immediately began to weep, since she heard hospitals would soon begin charging fees and she could not possibly afford surgery. The doctors promised she would have the operation, which she did, but it again failed.

Teresa continues to live with her brother and receives periodic care at the hospital through a special fistula project. Interviewed after her most recent operation, Teresa said she had no desire to marry again or try to have children.

hotra and Mehra 1999). For example, programs addressing women's health often focus on reproductive health without necessarily capitalizing on women's capacities to create change for themselves and others (Sen 1999a). Nor do they address socioeconomic element that exacerbate those conditions. Although potentially successful in improving physical health, they do not advance a broader remedy to the economic exclusion that underlies much of women's experience of ill health and powerlessness.

Despite these realities, development agencies and donors typically establish programs that compartmentalize the lives of poor people (World Bank 2000a, Brock 1999; Narayan 1997; Ahonsi and Odaga 2000). Whereas some bilateral European donors[3] have increasingly adopted an overall goal of alleviating poverty in their funding, in practical terms, the money is largely confined to sector-specific streams with little opportunity for intersectoral collaboration. Development planning in silos[4] is manifest in and driven by separate streams of donor funds earmarked for one specific problem a population might face; separate national ministries with staff focusing on one aspect of people's lives; separate needs assessments that guide program goals; separate evaluation instruments that perpetuate an uncoordinated approach to individuals' lives; and priorities and expertise of particular donor and development agencies. Some focused interventions can be highly effective in addressing neglected and socially important issues. Nonetheless, donors and development agencies often fail to develop mechanisms for collaboration, or even discussion, across basic issues that their target groups confront.

Intersectoral Collaboration and Inclusive Programming

Inclusive programming is not a call for development agencies to address all problems, with health professionals now implementing credit programs and educators working on nutrition. In fact, this may achieve only erratic gains (Gonzales et al. 1999). In addition, such homogenization ignores the reality that development professionals (like all professionals) carry a specific set of skills. Instead, inclusive programming would promote selected partnerships across traditionally parallel sectors to catalyze change that addresses social, health, and economic inequities (box 10.2). "For many poor (women), a choice often has to be made between going

Box 10.2
Programming partnerships: selected examples of inclusive programming

---

Society for Women's Action and Training Initiative—India. Builds women's capacity to access institutional credit, strengthen their entrepreneurial skills, improve their reproductive and sexual well-being, and participate in local government.

Mahila Sarvangeen Utkarsh Mandal—India. Links income generation, legal aid, and reproductive health with a focus on violence against women.

Life Vanguards—Nigeria. Links information and education on adolescent reproductive health, entrepreneurial skills and business management, support for youth-owned microenterprises, and leadership training for leaders and members of youth organizations.

Adolescent Health and Information Project, Girls' Power Initiative, and Action Health Inc.—Nigeria. Promote adolescent reproductive health through sexual health awareness raising and gender-leadership training with skills enhancement and career guidance.

Women's Health Action Research Centre—Nigeria. Provides small-business skills training and reproductive health information to poor rural women and links them to credit programs.

Kongwa Women's Credit Programme/Helen Keller Worldwide—Tanzania. Integrates credit and economic livelihood with community education and action for trachoma control.

Planned Parenthood Association of South Africa—South Africa. Integrates sexual health, economic livelihood, business skill development, and arts and culture in programming with adolescents.

Kenya Rural Enterprise Program/Population Council—Kenya. Provides credit and skills training to adolescent girls to strengthen their decision-making capacity, including in sexual health.

World Neighbors—Kenya and Nepal. Combines rural development, savings and credit programs, and education and information on reproductive and sexual health.

---

hungry for a third consecutive day and delaying visiting a doctor to prevent the development of a life-threatening condition. And the choice is not always clear-cut" (Ahonsi 1999). Inclusive programs can bridge this gap, increasing the health status of poor women by implementing strategic partnerships across economic, educational and health programs. Such collaborative programming require expertise of various disciplines and a priority on active communication across them.

Selected inclusive approaches have been tested by several internationally recognized nongovernment organizations (NGOs); for example, the

Bangladesh Rural Advancement Committee (BRAC), demonstrating that "economic empowerment is at the heart of other forms of empowerment" (Abed 1999). Programs that bring together education, health, and credit can promote several ends, such as increasing women's incomes, fostering entrepreneurial skills, reducing family vulnerability during the hungry season, and improving the nutrition status of participants' children. They can also contribute to increasing women's self-confidence and vision of the future (Freedom from Hunger 1998). A Bangladesh study of credit programs reports one woman's experience in this regard: "my husband used to beat me up and take my money. Now he can beat me a thousand times and I won't give him my money. I tell him, 'you had better not beat me too much, I can live without you!'" (Schuler et al. 1996).

Analyzing how poor families decide to use scarce resources could inform the design of inclusive approaches. As indicated by the poverty assessment in Tanzania, poor families make significant trade-offs in determining survival strategies and do not stay within externally delineated program sectors. Analyses of how families decide on expenditures for health and other social services could "help to identify inter-sectoral priorities for achieving better health status and lead to a better understanding of inter-sectoral dynamics" (Elson and Evers 1998).

Working on many issues in an integrated manner can have a synergistic effect. UNICEF (1997), for example, reported that "when micro-credit is linked with access to basic social services and key social development messages, the health and nutrition of borrowers' children, particularly girls, improves; school enrolment increases; safe water and sanitation use broadens." Furthermore, microcredit empowers women by enabling them to make economic decisions and become the source of increased household income (UNICEF 1997).

At the same time, whereas microcredit programs have received attention for lifting women out of poverty and increasing their health and social status, more scrutiny is required to clarify the mechanisms through which such programs achieve economic and other gains for poor women. Some research suggests mixed results of credit programs in promoting women's status and health (Berger 1989; Whitaker 1996; Zeitlin 1997; Gonzales et al. 1999). Critiques cited the need to link women's livelihood efforts strategically to larger business and commercial cycles for initiatives to be financially viable (Berger 1989; Abed 1999). In the social realm, evidence shows that where women's income earning activities have public visibility, women's threat of violence diminishes. In other cases, however, their involvement in income earning opportunities may actually increase their exposure to domestic violence, at least until they "emerge from a period of conflict with a new definition of their roles and status in the household" (Schuler et al. 1996).

NGO programs can point to intersectoral approaches that can be taken to scale in government programs, although larger-scale efforts may be difficult to implement. An attempt in Bangladesh to broaden population and reproductive health programs to a more multisectoral approach illustrates the tremendous institutional and political barriers involved. During the development of the Fifth Population Project in the country, the donor consortium encouraged a more inclusive approach to address broader development and gender concerns. Earlier attempts at multisectoral population initiatives reportedly remained within the population sector only, were not linked to mainstream development programs, and were not scaled up from pilot projects. Noted obstacles to shaping a new multisectoral approach included limited capacity in government ministries to conduct intersectoral programs; lack of a mandate within ministries to act multisectorally; problems of bureaucratic control and ownership; and the lack of nonpopulation expertise in designing these approaches (Population Council 1997). Ultimately, the inter-sectoral approach in Bangladesh was abandoned due to competition and lack of ownership among ministries.[5]

Inclusive Programming and Social Mobilization

Beyond bringing vertical programs together, inclusive programming would highlight the capacity for social change that underlies many successful development programs. Rather than measuring outputs largely by number of services delivered, success would be measured primarily by the extent to which poor people engaged meaningfully in civic decision making and whether social change occurred in communities of marginalized people.

A program developed in 1998 by a women's health and rights organization in Peru illustrates the transformative capacity of inclusive programming from a foundation of social change and women's empowerment. Although it is experimental and evolving, the ReproSalud project of Movimento Manuela Ramos suggests that much can be gained for poor women, men, and communities by addressing health through gender, equity, and community mobilization (Rogow 2000). The Manuela Ramos Movement began in the late 1970s under the leadership of seven women with a commitment to promoting self-esteem, identity, and reproductive health among themselves and with low-income women. They believed that these women could provide vital leadership to the national women's movement in the country.

In the mid-1990s, the women of Manuela Ramos began a visionary and sizeable program to address reproductive health in an integrated manner, through a lens of gender and empowerment. "The underlying theory for this project was that women's reproductive health is closely linked to their social and economic power and that without engagement in dialogue over the central facets of their lives, they have little ability to promote their own health effectively" (Rogow 2000). Three principles guided the project: women would learn about their bodies and translate this knowledge into power; this knowledge would enable women to advocate collectively for change from their local government health providers; and a portion of project funds should be allocated for communal credit programs to give women greater access to cash and enable them to renegotiate matters of their daily life with their husbands.[6]

ReproSalud staff gathered information in each community through participatory diagnostic workshops and selected a local women's organization to help lead the work. The workshops proved to be an intervention in themselves, where women learned that "by working together, they could change the shape of their lives" (Rogow 2000). ReproSalud's program areas included reproductive health, income generation, advocacy for public health services, and overall empowerment of poor women.

The project also included micro- and macroenterprise work. This required a significant investment of time and money to build the initiative, which encouraged staff to limit activities to the project area and not expand them. The sheer size of the overall project, $25 million in four regions of the country, demanded hiring a large number of new staff and developing new management systems.

Local women, not project staff, decided to involve husbands to address gender-related issues. This led to profound discussions between women and men about alcoholism, violence, forced sex, and communication. "Training men to work as educators of other men in their own communities would become one of the most salient facets of ReproSalud's work" (Rogow 2000). The intervention resulted in dramatic decreases in alcohol consumption, domestic violence, and forced sex in all villages visited during the project's evaluation.

The status and influence of the local women's groups increased, as did women's ability to promote their own reproductive health. In terms of family planning specifically (the key issue of concern to the United States donor), "the results indicated an undeniable sea change." One hospital reported a 400% increase in family planning visits by residents of the local ReproSalud community. At the same time the number of visits by residents of the urban center where the hospital is located dropped. Women's self-confidence and self-esteem soared. One coordinator illustrates the impact of the project pointedly: "When I first met these women they were afraid to go to the health center and speak up with the doctor. Now they go straight to the mayor!" (Rogow 2000).

Implications for Future Action: Women's Agency, Participation, and Public Accountability

Participation, Agency, and Equity

By and large, macrolevel economic and development policies that affect the lives of poor women and men are determined with negligible involvement of those actually living in poverty or the governments that represent them. For example, international financial institutions are staffed largely by well-paid professionals from high-income countries, who design SAP programs from offices in Washington, D.C., and European capitals. For poor women, such disenfranchisement from policy setting can be life threatening, as seen from Teresa's story and from the imposition of user fees (Ekwepu et al. 1990; Oxfam 1998). One might ask if cost-sharing policies would be different had poor and marginalized persons from low-income countries been sitting at the table where the user-fee policies were created?

In the 1990s some bilateral donors (particularly those from Scandinavia) began to acknowledge the power imbalance between governments of low-income and high-income countries, and revised their formats for negotiating with recipient countries (Ministry of Foreign Affairs 1999). These overtures toward realigning imbalances are potentially positive signals. At the same time, however, the government of Tanzania must still produce 2,400 quarterly reports each year for its donors, a fact that James Wolfensohn of the World Bank calls "shameful" (Wolfensohn 1999).

Similarly, there is a limited track record of international financial institutions and donor countries actively engaging the voices of poor people to define priorities and approaches to poverty alleviation. The same could also be said for the extent to which most governments of low-income countries engage poor people in development processes. "The lexicon of development has expanded, perhaps irreversibly, to include participation. And as usual with concepts which gain currency, rhetoric has run far, far ahead of understanding, let alone practice" (Chambers 1998).

The World Bank has recently begun to mainstream the concept of participation into its projects (Brock 1999, Chambers 1998), which could serve as a persuasive example to other financial institutions and donors. Nonetheless, "for many of those who work at the grassroots, the social costs of Bank-imposed structural adjustment policies remain a haunting memory. One has to ask what is the Bank's understanding of participation? Is it prepared to re-assess its role and think of creative ways that its systems, procedures, and policy advice might be opened up to facilitate the substantive empowerment of the poor?" (Blackburn and Holland 1998).

Other questions require answers. Is there any hope for fundamentally changing the way that the IMF does business? What principles of engagement will give priority to views of the poor in efforts to reduce poverty and increase equity? How will the particular negative effects on women be addressed? How will donor institutions and governments of low-income countries be held accountable to their commitment to greater inclusion of new voices?

One part of the solution may be to give priority to programs that seek to transform the lives of poor people rather than programs that ameliorate their condition; in other words, to mobilize the agency of the poor rather than pour medicine over their conditions. A focus on agency can catalyze women's capacity to transform their own lives and to create social change more broadly (Sen 1999a). As active agents of change women can promote "social transformations that can alter the lives of *both* women and men" (Sen 1999a). This process would include thinking of development in terms of structural inequality, and moving toward women's increased control in determining access to resources and distribution of benefits (Longwe 1992).[7]

Investing in women's agency, status, and voice can increase women's own relative position in the family, increase their voice in matters of family decision making, raise their confidence, and ease oppressive gender relations. Women's agency also affects children's health and survival, food intake, literacy rates, and overall status of girls in the family (Sen 1999a; Guijt and Shah 1999). The Manuela Ramos experience in Peru is an example of the link between women's agency and these broader payoffs for entire communities. Specific indicators of health and well-being increased dramatically through such an investment, with benefits for poor women and men alike.

Challenges of Inclusion: Participation and Public Accountability

The absence of poor women's voices in policy making strips development strategies of critical information for improving the health of the poor and promotes a disconnect between policy dialogue and health objectives (Rao Gupta 2000). In addition "nothing perhaps is as important for resource allocation in health care as the development of informed public discussion, and the availability of democratic means, for incorporating the lessons of a fuller understanding of the choices that people in every country face" (Sen 1999b). Specifically called for is the primacy of women's voices in setting political, economic, and social goals (Sen 1999a).

In reality, however, challenges to including poor and marginalized voices in designing, implementing and evaluating policies and programs are significant. Participation can be used to describe rudimentary stabs at consultation, and at worst "hide manipulation and even coercion under a cloak of social palatability" (Slocum and Thomas-Slayter 1995 cited in Guijt and Shah 1999).

Engaging people who have typically been marginalized requires moving beyond current trends of stakeholder involvement that focus on officials from ministries and NGOs. Borrowing from the experience of promoting children's political participation (Rajani 1999), a range of mechanisms are needed to ensure that a diversity of poor and underrepresented women are involved in the processes of setting priorities, decision making, and public accountability. These mechanisms include active recruitment of women who tend to be underrepresented. Such mechanisms have to invest actively in building the capability of marginalized women and recognize disparities in ability, preparation, and experience among participants. These processes should guarantee that elite and socially recognized people in communities do not become spokespersons by virtue of their privilege alone.

Informed participation is particularly important in situations of acute poverty where women, families, and communities are taking up the slack of depleted government resources. In Zimbabwe, absence of the poor in the debate over health policy, coupled with increasing demands for households to contribute to health, has been viewed as unfairly shifting health burdens onto already poor individuals (Loewenson 1999). Participation has to be strengthened along two critical dimensions. The first is to create realistic expectations between communities and health services in their respective contributions toward health. The second is to strengthen public governance of health systems, ensuring information exchange, codetermination of plans for resource allocation, cofinancing of services, and monitoring access to services and quality of care.

The Community Working Group on Health in Zimbabwe "consistently noted the dissatisfaction of communities with what was being termed 'participation' in the health sector. To a large extent, this was perceived to mean compliance with state defined programs" (Loewenson 1999). In contrast to this pattern, the working group created mechanisms of participation in health policy decision making that involved a broad cross section of workers, traditional health care providers, people living with a range of health conditions, and members of civic organizations. The group negotiated resource allocation to the health sector through advocacy at the national and district levels to strengthen informed participation in local health planning.

To ensure meaningful participation of marginalized groups and establish ground rules for public accountability, civic organizations of poor people must be strengthened and clear lines of authority delineated with government. Furthermore, participation should be institutionalized "as a matter of course, a regular feature of the functioning" of public institutions or development projects, to ensure that participation is not ad hoc or project based, and that accountability can be monitored (Rajani 1999).

This is particularly true in the case of priority setting and resource allocation that could negatively affect poor women. Involvement of marginalized women could decrease the sustainable inequity (Nyonator and Kutzin 1999) borne of gender-blind policy development and resource allocation. Specific mechanisms of accountability could include, among others, monitoring expenditures to ascertain if poor men or women are disproportionately benefiting or losing out, analyzing gender balance in use of health services and in health outcomes for both users and nonusers of services, and developing gender-aware baseline and indicators that monitor the effect of policy reforms and program deliverables (Elson and Evers 1998).

Conclusion

Macroeconomic policies imposed by international financial institutions on low-income countries have failed to alleviate poverty and in some cases have contributed to greater inequities. More than 1.6 billion people were worse off economically in the late 1990s than they were in the early 1980s. "While most of the world's poor are dying, in the sense of *yearning*, to reap some of the benefits of growth, others are literally dying from the austerity measures imposed to promote it" (Kim et al. 2000).

These policies compromise the effectiveness of the health, human rights, and development communities by undercutting the social and economic environment in which they operate. Pregnant women stop seeking antenatal care because fees are introduced, hospitals cannot provide necessary treatment for poor women because their budgets are slashed, and women caregivers watch family members die of preventable causes because drugs and trained providers are not available.

It is imperative for the health community to challenge directly both international financial institutions and donor governments regarding the economic and human rights failures of their policies. This engagement will require skills in economic literacy, specific terminology, and economic arguments constructed by financial institutions, which may be new ground for health professionals to learn. Engaging effectively in this debate is imperative to undo the consequences of macroeconomic policies affecting the poor.

A first step in this engagement is the question of debt and the enhanced HIPC initiative. Respected human rights and development organizations have endorsed HIPC, which calls for debt relief. Others insist that HIPC is too little, too late, and too cumbersome to implement. In their terms, only a complete write-off of debt obligations can begin to redress the economic and human rights abuses borne of the debt burden. In seeking to alleviate poverty and address gender and health equity, a call for complete debt cancellation is critical.

At the same time, health professionals can shift the focus of their efforts from ameliorating conditions in which the poor live to a focus on the transformative capacity of poor people to create systemic social change. Research methodologies such as participatory rural appraisal contribute to illuminating the reality of poor people's lives, and many community-based programs in poor communities are using approaches that meet the many needs of marginalized groups. Nonetheless, most donor funding continues to segment people's problems into specific funding areas, neglecting the agency of poor people to create lasting social change. Projects and organizations in low-income countries that seek funds from donors must conform to a fragmented pattern of disbursement, limiting the efficacy of programs and donor funds alike to mobilize coherent action for social change.

Macroeconomic and donor policies have not effectively mitigated the marginalization of the very people they are trying to reach. Planning, implementation, monitoring, and evaluation systems typically lack the meaningful participation of the poor. This remains true despite the capacity of participation to catalyze greater equity, creating "conditions which can lead to a significant empowerment of those who at present have little control over the forces that condition their lives" (Blackburn and Holland

1998). It can also, simply, inform more effective, efficient, and accountable service delivery.

Committing to a focus on agency and involving marginalized voices will require financial institutions, donors, and development agencies to reshape the rules of engagement so poor people are meaningfully represented. "Participation has little meaning unless we, and particularly those of us in positions of power, allow others to 'take part', to set agendas, take decisions, manage and control resources" (Blackburn and Holland 1998). Economic, gender, and health inequities are bound to persist if these basic criteria for participation, decision making, and accountability are overlooked.

Notes

1. With appreciation to Rakesh Rajani and Asha George for their thoughtful insights and editorial suggestions, and to Surabhi Kukke for bibliographic assistance.

2. The International Monetary Fund (IMF) was established in 1944 to serve as a permanent institution monitoring currencies worldwide and overseeing international commerce. The World Bank, often viewed as the IMF partner focusing on development, opened in 1946. Its original mandate was to reconstruct economies devastated by World War II. Although, the World Bank is increasingly known for its involvement in social development efforts, the five associated institutions of the World Bank Group principally provide loans and are involved in financing private sector investments. The World Bank Group consists of the International Bank for Reconstruction and Development, the International Development Association, the International Finance Corporation, the Multilateral Investment Guarantee Agency, and the International Center for Settlement of Investment Disputes (www.worldbank.org).

3. For example, the British, Danish, and Swedish international cooperation and development agencies (Reproductive Health Alliance Europe 1999).

4. Thanks to Tom Merrick of the World Bank for pointing out this image to me.

5. T. Merrick, personal communication, 1999.

6. A note about the donor: the ReproSalud project was funded by the United States Agency for International Development (USAID) office in Peru. This grant, by all accounts, was a significant departure from USAID's traditional funding approach. The project overtly addressed issues of women's status and sexuality, which runs counter to USAID's focus on family planning. Manuela Ramos also directly promoted a feminist agenda in the project and committed itself to

community ownership and participation. In contrast to the project officer in Peru who endorsed the Manuela Ramos approach entirely, USAID's director of Health, Population, and Nutrition believed that the agency's program is not meant to focus on social or economic empowerment, but rather to address fertility decline (D. Rogow, personal communication, 1999).

7. Sara Hlupekile Longwe, a gender specialist from Zambia, developed a women's empowerment cycle that examines levels of equality on five consecutive levels: welfare, access, conscientization, participation, and control.

11

Class, Gender, and Health Equity: Lessons from Liberalizing India

Gita Sen, Aditi Iyer, and Asha George

The 1990s were a period of significant macroeconomic and structural changes in the Indian economy. The effects of greater deregulation, privatization, and integration with the global economy were felt in the health sector no less than in others. These changes are echoes of similar transformations occurring at the global level. Some voices in the international health system debates of the 1990s tended to laud privatization as both necessary and inevitable. However, we now have significant evidence from transitional economies and from those where health systems have undergone considerable change, that a well-functioning and wide-ranging system of public health services is the best guarantee of equitable and affordable services for the poor (Bloom 1997; Bloom and Wilkes 1997; Whitehead et al. 2000). When such services are infused with gender sensitivity, the requirement of equity is doubly served (Standing 2000; Sen et al. this volume).

Conversely, poorly regulated privatization may have a negative impact on access and affordability for the poor or for other groups that are socially disadvantaged or discriminated against (McPake and Mills 2000). These changes may be particularly inimical in situations where a history of systematic discrimination already biases health-seeking and health-providing behavior. They could, for example, increase untreated morbidity or exacerbate gender, age, or other biases. They may lead to a kind of forced substitution, by reducing consumption of other essential commodities to accommodate increases in health service costs (Berman 2000). Furthermore, this may not be distributed evenly across members of households. There could also be an increase in household indebtedness, eroding long-term viability or even survival (Liu et al. 1995). The presence of significant socioeconomic inequality thus calls even more strongly for vigorous provision of public health services.

In a country such as India, with a large proportion of the population below the official poverty line,[1] where caste still correlates with economic well-being especially for the poorest in rural areas, and with a long history of gender inequality, the extent to which health services are equitable plays a crucial role in the well-being and indeed survival of those who are disadvantaged. Inequities in health care emanating from colonial policies and politics persisted through five decades of postcolonial governance in India. The (Bhore) Committee (Government of India 1946) acknowledged these inequities and was emphatic that comprehensive health care should be universally accessed by all regardless of their ability to pay.

Despite this, inequalities were widely prevalent in the health sector during the five decades after the country's independence from colonial rule, and the right to health care remains an ideal that largely eludes legal translation[2] (Jesani 1996). Many believe that a major reason for this is that public health services have been much less effective than anticipated by the Bhore Committee. Failures of the system have driven rich and poor toward private health providers. This has made it increasingly difficult to resist and easy to justify pressures for a range of more recent privatization and deregulation measures.

As a result, more than three-fourths of India's estimated total health expenditure consists of out-of-pocket payments made by individual households (Berman 1995). One argument could be that the trend toward greater privatization is not only inevitable given the failure of public provisioning, but may actually be beneficial even for the poor. At least services are available (which is more than can be said for public services), and competition may ensure reductions in cost and improvements in quality. An opposite argument is that unbridled privatization will lead to increasing inequity. Compared with better-off people, the poor have a more critical need for preventive and curative care, tend to pay proportionately more for health care (Makinen et al. 2000), and are less able to absorb the financial risks that health emergencies entail (Liu et al. 1995).

Key dimensions that determine the extent of equity are access, cost, and range and quality of services available to different economic classes, genders, and other groups. This chapter attempts to assess the evidence in this regard, with particular focus on the recent decade of privatization and deregulation.[3] Assessing the magnitude, direction, and impact of changes in the health sector in India during the 1990s is complex. Not only did many changes at both micro- and macrolevels affect aspects ranging from health financing to health-related behavior, but the data are fragmentary and disparate in their reliability and scope. Analysts to date therefore tended to address partial aspects and often had to hypothesize rather than confirm.

Data with the widest coverage are from two surveys of morbidity done by the National Sample Survey (NSS) in the mid-1980s and 1990s. We use them, together with empirical findings of other studies, to put forward some results of significant changes that appear to have occurred in the 1990s, especially in relation to health equity. The focus is essentially on the impact of growing privatization and deregulation on morbidity prevalence and treatment, on use of health services, and on the cost of care.

As we will see, NSS data from the mid-1980s already showed striking differences across the economic class spectrum in the extent of untreated illness, as well as in expenditures on inpatient and outpatient care. Such differences held true for gender also. Women had higher rates of untreated morbidity than men, and community surveys show that the average spent on them for inpatient as well as outpatient care tended to be significantly less. These results corroborate studies showing that households in India tend to postpone seeking health services and spend less on health care of girls and women than of boys and men (Das Gupta 1987; Khan et al. 1983). They point to a systematic pattern of preexisting inequity in access to health services in terms of both gender and economic class.

We also hoped to analyze caste-related differences and cross-match them with gender and economic class. In India scheduled castes and tribes are at the bottom of the caste hierarchy and have been subject to affirmative action regulations since the country's independence. Despite positive discrimination, however, a wide gulf exists between them and other castes because of large economic distinctions and continuing social discrimination, particularly in rural areas. The NSS survey for the mid-1990s provides some basic caste-related data differentiating among scheduled castes, scheduled tribes, and others. Corresponding data are not available for the mid-1980s so it is not possible to compare the two periods. Caste data for the mid-1990s present a mixed picture that is difficult to interpret, and hence we do not discuss this further.

Socioeconomic Inequality and Its Implications for Health Services in the 1980s

Gender and economic class are two major dimensions of socioeconomic inequality and injustice in India. Whereas each one interacts with and cross-cuts the other, they are by no means congruent in terms of how they work or in their effects. Each therefore has to be analyzed both separately and in relation to the other to obtain a fuller picture of causes or consequences of inequality. In addition, the gap between rural and urban areas in terms of development resources and services is striking, and has persisted despite half a century of development efforts after independence.

Rural-Urban Differences

Health services are grossly skewed in distribution. Urban areas and economically developed regions attract a larger share of health resources than warranted by their share in the total population, whereas economically backward and remote areas remain consistently underserved. In 1991, only 32% of all hospitals, 20% of hospital beds, and no more than an estimated 41% of all trained doctors were in rural areas, where over 70% of the population still lives (Duggal et al. 1995a). The extent of the rural disadvantage varies from one state to the other. States such as Kerala, Punjab, Goa, Manipur, and Mizoram, which have invested more in rural public health services, were able to reduce the rural-urban gaps, unlike Bihar, Jammu and Kashmir, Haryana, Rajasthan, and Himachal Pradesh (Duggal et al. 1995a).

Rural areas received a declining share of qualified practitioners between 1961 and 1981, even as medical education in the country expanded, mainly in private colleges recognized by different medical councils (Jesani with Ananthraman 1993). In Ahmednagar district of Maharashtra state, even in rural areas, average population-to-doctor ratios were 812:1 and 1806:1 in developed and underdeveloped talukas (subdivisions of the district), respectively (Sule 1999). The bias against rural areas is heightened by types of doctors available in them. In the economically backward areas of Satara district, trained allopaths and homeopaths constituted a minuscule 5% and 9% respectively, of all health practitioners. The so-called Indian Systems of Medicine accounted for 41% and unqualified practitioners constituted 45% (Nandraj and Duggal 1997).

Gender Biases

High and persistent rural-urban differences in the scope and quality of available health services are symptomatic of an approach to health service provision that has been unable to redress or counteract the core problems of inequality of access and continuing biases against particular groups in the population. The prevalence of gender biases in access to nutrition and health care, working to the detriment of girls and women, has long been known (Das Gupta 1987). Households, particularly in the northern belt of the country, discriminate against girls and women in terms of the amount and quality of food they receive, by delaying their access to quality health care, and by spending less on girls than on boys (Miller 1981). Women all too often suffer ill health silently, particularly when it is related to sexuality or reproduction (Bang et al. 1989). Whereas considerable variations in this regard exist across states, gender bias is significant in all but a few areas.

The government's approach to providing public health services has been geography based and has paid little attention until very recently[4] to the need to tackle biases systematically at household and community levels. Such biases remained significant therefore, as attested by the NSS all-India survey in 1986–1987 on morbidity and use of medical services (National Sample Survey Organization 1992). In 1986–1987, untreated morbidity was 15% to 21% higher among women and girls than in men and boys (table 11.1). This figure does not include the reservoir of untreated sexual and reproductive illnesses that neither the NSS survey of 1986–1987 nor that of 1995–1996 was able to capture.[5]

Morbidity rates as such were not very different between rural men and women in 1986–1987, but were higher for urban women than for men. However, reporting of female morbidity is particularly sensitive to study

Table 11.1
Gender differences in rates of morbidity and untreated morbidity, India, 1986–1987 (National Sample Survey Organisation 1992)[a]

	Rural	Urban
Morbidity rates (No. of ailing persons/1,000)		
Male	64	30
Female	63	33
Totals	64	31
F:M ratio	0.98	1.10
Untreated morbidity rates[b] (No. of untreated persons per 1000 ailing people)		
Male	172.4	98.1
Female	198.0	118.9
Totals	184.8	108.6
F:M ratio	1.15	1.21

[a] Statement 10, p. 65; Statement 11, p. 66.
[b] Untreated morbidity = (100,000 − rate of treated morbidity)/100.

methodologies and techniques of data collection. In contrast to the NSS, a district-level study (Madhiwalla et al. 2000) incorporated gender perspectives in its methodology and analysis of data. Morbidity rates were significantly higher for both men and women but especially for women. It appears that the full extent of women's morbidity becomes evident only when women are addressed one-to-one by women researcher-interviewers after initial rapport building.

Through long years of socialization and reinforced by competing demands on their time and energy, women often do not acknowledge their own health problems. Chronic backache and persistent weakness are two examples from a long list that also includes reproductive tract infections, among other conditions. Careful gender-sensitive probing increased reporting of female morbidity by 124% (Madhiwalla et al. 2000). We can therefore conclude that rates as elicited in the NSS surveys are probably gross underestimates of the full extent of women's illness.

Economic Class Differences

Just as gender bias is an inherent part of the health-related behavior of households, economic class differences are also striking. These differences

Table 11.2
Class gradients by gender in morbidity, untreated morbidity, and costs of care,
India, 1986–1987 (National Sample Survey Organisation 1992)[a]

	Rural	Urban
Morbidity rates (no./1,000)		
Male	1.25	−0.18
Female	2.29	0.79
Totals	1.82	0.25
Untreated morbidity rates (no./1,000 ailing persons)		
Male	−13.44[b]	−0.04
Female	−24.47[b]	−15.79[c]
Totals	−18.74[b]	−8.27[c]
Average expenditure on hospitalization (in rupees)		
Male	NA	NA
Female	NA	NA
Totals	42.50[b]	143.37[b]
Average expenditure on outpatient care (in rupees)		
Male	NA	NA
Female	NA	NA
Totals	5.17[c]	9.83[b]

NA, not available. Gradients in this chapter were estimated by fitting trend lines
for the variable across different fractiles of monthly per capita consumption expenditure.
[a] Statement 10, p. 65; Statement 11, p. 66; table 5.00, p. S-418; table 11.00,
p. S-516.
[b] Significance 1%.
[c] Significance 5%.

affect the amount of treatment households receive and how much they
spend on it. Table 11.2 provides evidence of the failure of the health
system in this regard.

The NSS surveys provide data tabulated across monthly per capita
expenditure (MPCE) fractiles of households. With these as a rough proxy
for economic class,[6] we use the gradient across fractiles as a simple
measure of the extent of inequality. The NSS survey shows a positive
class gradient for morbidity rates in the rural areas, but neither the rural
nor the urban slope is significantly different from zero. Nonetheless it is
worth noting that a positive gradient means that the better-off have

higher morbidity than the poor. This holds a fortiori for women in the NSS survey, as inequality in morbidity among women was greater than among men. Positive gradients for morbidity fly in the face of common-sense understanding of the probability of ill health given differences in nutrition levels, anemia, and environmental and occupational conditions between poor and rich. Such findings are not, however, peculiar to NSS surveys alone.

District level studies illustrate the relationship between reported morbidity and socioeconomic indicators (Duggal with Amin 1989; George et al. 1997; Madhiwalla and Jesani 1997). Reported morbidity rates are often positively associated with socioeconomic status. But does this reflect more illness among the rich, or a reporting bias among the poor who may not be able or willing to acknowledge their own ill health?

Those who believe the latter to be true point out that the need for and access to health services reflect a process with several stages. At its core lies a health concern that may not always be recognized. Once a problem is identified and recognized as a need, social dynamics within households and communities endorse or constrain health-seeking behavior. At a third level lie questions of availability, quality, and affordability of care. It is only when all these gateways are crossed that morbidity is nearly certain to be reported (Chatterjee 1988).[7]

The class gradient for untreated morbidity was highly significant and negative in both rural and urban areas in 1986–87. This means that the poor were less likely to be treated than the rich. The extent of inequality among women in this regard was even worse than among men in both rural and urban areas. Indeed almost all of the urban class differences in untreated morbidity were due to differences among women; the class gradient among urban males was not significantly different from zero. Furthermore, when they were treated, the poor tended to spend less on both outpatient and inpatient care (as shown by positive and highly significant gradients) than the better-off.

This discussion shows that, at least until the mid-1980s, the health service system had not done away with either class or gender inequity in access. Untreated morbidity had both an economic class gradient and significant gender inequality even without including untreated reproductive ill health. Furthermore, class differences among women in terms of untreated morbidity were higher than among men. Qualitative and microsurvey evidence corroborates some of these findings, pointing to a pattern of poor access to and poor quality of public health services.

The Public-Private Mix in the 1980s

The demand for health care services from the private sector can be highly inelastic in the absence of a functioning public health system as a base. Unless people have an alternative, they may be compelled to pay high prices or be forced to opt out of services altogether. The consequences of opting out are increased burdens of untreated morbidity and often hidden costs of women's time and labor as health care providers of first and last resort. Public services therefore play a critical role in the health of the poor and especially poor women.

The public sector includes an elaborate system of primary health centers (PHCs), subcenters, community health centers (CHCs), dispensaries, and public hospitals in most states. But they tended to be located in the more developed and accessible villages (ICMR 1991). This is seen even in states that can claim to have achieved national norms of coverage[8] and distance[9] in aggregate terms.

A well-functioning public health system not only ensures effective services to those at the lower ends of the socioeconomic hierarchy, but can also set a ceiling for prices and a norm for quality in the private sector. It can therefore be a major anchor for equity overall. Interstate comparisons in India appear to confirm this, as states with better public health services have lower prices in the private sector (Krishnan 1995). A study of public hospitals in seven sub-Saharan African countries found that, although curative health spending was not well targeted, it was still progressive. The subsidy that did reach the poor constituted a larger proportion of their household expenditure compared with the rich (Castro-Leal et al. 2000).

Table 11.3 shows the public-private mix in terms of outpatient and inpatient use of services, and table 11.4 the relative costs of public and private health services based on the mid-1980s NSS survey. By the mid-1980s, over 70% of outpatient care was in the private sector, the bulk

Table 11.3

Public-private sector use for medical care, India, 1986–1987 (National Sample Survey Organisation 1992)[a]

Health sectors	Outpatient care (%)		Inpatient care (%)	
	Rural	Urban	Rural	Urban
Share of public sector	25.6	27.2	59.7	60.3
Public hospital	17.7	22.6	55.4	59.5
PHC/CHC	4.9	1.2	4.3	0.8
Public dispensary	2.6	1.8		
ESI doctor	0.4	1.6		
Share of private sector	74.5	72.9	40.3	39.7
Private hospital	15.2	16.2	32.0	29.6
Nursing home	0.8	1.2	4.9	7.0
Charitable institution	0.4	0.8	1.7	1.9
Private doctor	53.0	51.8		
Others	5.2	2.9	1.7	1.2
Totals	100.1	100.0	100.0	100.0

PHC, primary health center; CHC, community health center; ESI, employees state insurance.

[a] Statements 13R and 13U, pp. 67–68; Statements 2R and 2U, pp. 53–54.

provided by private doctors. This was true in both rural and urban areas. However, the public sector still accounted for 60% of all inpatient care, the bulk provided by public hospitals in rural and urban areas.

The cost differential (as measured by average total expenditure) between public and private outpatient care was only 5% in rural services and 8% in urban services.[10] Given that the survey did not include a range of costs such as bribes, tips, and the like that are known to be rampant in the public sector, one can safely conclude that there was practically no cost difference between public and private outpatient services. In these circumstances, patients appear to have gone overwhelmingly to the private sector. On the other hand, the cost difference between public and private inpatient care was much higher (table 11.4). Rural private hospitalization was over twice as expensive and urban private hospitalization over three times as expensive as public hospitals. Thus, where private costs were relatively higher, that is, for inpatient treatment in both rural

Table 11.4
Average expenditure on medical care, India, 1986–1987 (National Sample Survey Organisation 1992)[a]

| | Rupees per illness episode/hospitalization | | |
	Rural	Urban	Urban:rural ratio[b]
Outpatient care			
Public sector	73	74	1.01
Private sector	77	80	1.04
Totals	76	79	1.04
Private:public ratio[c]	1.05	1.08	
Inpatient care			
Public sector	320	385	1.20
Private sector	733	1206	1.64
Totals	597	933	1.56
Private:public ratio[c]	2.29	3.13	

[a] Source table 11.00, p. S-516, Statement 6, p. 59.
[b] Measures the urban-rural differential in average expenditure.
[c] Measures the private-public differential in average expenditure.

Table 11.5
Class gradients for inpatient care by facility, India, 1986–1987 (National Sample Survey Organisation 1992)[a]

Health care facility	Rural	Urban
Public hospitals	−0.60	−1.50
PHCs	−1.29	−1.28
Private hospitals	0.82	0.15
Nursing homes	1.09	0.97
Charitable institutions	0.56	−0.98
All hospitals	−0.08	−0.81

PHC, primary health center.
[a] Source table 2.00, p. S-137–S-146, S-149–S-150.

and urban areas, the share of the private sector was lower. This may explain why public hospitals continued to be more popular than private hospitals in the 1980s.

These survey data allow us to explore economic class implications only for inpatient care, and do not provide corresponding gender breakdowns. Whereas gradients across MPCE fractiles for both public hospitals and PHCs in rural and urban areas were negative, indicating greater use by the poor, and the gradient for private hospitals was positive, none of these gradients was statistically significant (table 11.5). On balance, the gradient for all hospitalizations was near zero, indicating relatively low inequality in overall use in both rural and urban areas.

To summarize, whereas patients increasingly resorted to the private sector for outpatient services, public hospitals were dominant providers of inpatient care, especially for the poor. Although this varied considerably across states, public hospitals provided an important alternative to the private sector and at significantly lower cost.

Privatization and Deregulation in the 1990s

Deteriorating Public Services

Despite its continuing importance for inpatient care, the public sector was beset with quality problems by the late 1980s that continued in the 1990s. Public financing of health services, which is mostly borne by state governments, was inadequate and irrationally distributed (Iyer and Sen 2000). The share of health in the government's (combined center and state) revenue expenditure, which was 2.7% in 1950–51, peaked at 5.1% in 1960–61 and then began to decline. The decline was particularly evident in the first half of the 1990s; by 1994–95, it had, infact, fallen to 2.6% (Duggal et al. 1995a).

As the Indian Council of Medical Research (1991) admitted, even such facilities as did exist in the public health system tended to be located in the more developed and accessible villages in the rural areas. Operational problems, such as inadequate transport and mismatch between working hours of PHCs and frequency of buses, further limited access to a few villages and hamlets in their immediate vicinity (ICMR 1988; Awasthi et al. 1993).

Furthermore, the referral system is poorly developed in most states. The CHCs are inaccessible because there are too few of them[11] and they are poorly equipped. One major problem that they and the PHCs face is attracting and retaining qualified practitioners with basic and specialist qualifications. At the end of 1992, for example, as many as 82% of posts sanctioned for obstetricians and gynecologists in Uttar Pradesh were vacant. Similarly, at the end of March 1993, some 68% of all posts earmarked for pediatricians in Gujarat were unoccupied (Central Bureau of Health Intelligence various years). Lack of trained medical staff in health centers led to greater dependence on lower-level health workers, especially auxiliary nurse midwives, who are socially vulnerable, ill supported, and unable to provide more than a selective and narrow range of services (Iyer and Jesani 1999).

These inadequacies and allocative inefficiencies resulted in acute shortfalls in even the most essential drugs and equipment in public health institutions, particularly in rural areas (Phadke et al. 1995). The few resources sent to the PHC for distribution to subcenters are sometimes used at the PHC itself, leaving the subcenters with virtually nothing (ICMR 1988, 1991). In Satara district of Maharashtra, some public health facilities had only 3% of required drugs available for 90% of the year (Phadke et al. 1995).

These weaknesses are clearly not independent of investment patterns. Improving standards of care and access of the public to information are clearly also necessary to strengthen the functioning of the public health system. Public policy tends, however, to move in a different direction. Despite the noted importance of (especially) public hospitals for the poor, debate on the direction of the health service sector pits those in favor of strengthening the public sector[12] and more effectively regulating the private sector, against those who hold that privatization is the route to follow. Changes in the 1990s appear to have favored the latter.

An Expanding Private Health Sector
Although 1991 is typically bracketed as the year in which India formally launched reforms aimed at greater deregulation, liberalization, and privatization, the health sector began to move in this direction in the 1980s. During the 1990s, however, the impetus for these changes grew.

The declining share of public hospitals and dispensaries in public health expenditures since the 1980s (Iyer and Sen 2000) coincided with a growing number of private hospitals that received state support through public financial assistance and tax exemptions. This type of public subsidy to the private sector further skewed the urban bias in health resources. Private health services tend to be clustered around places that are better provisioned with public health facilities and infrastructure. This is usually in urban or more economically advanced areas (Sule 1999).

An estimated 85% to 93% of all qualified doctors now work in the private sector, largely as solo practitioners (Jesani and Ananthraman 1993; Sule 1999). According to official data, an estimated 67% of hospitals are privately owned. However, they are generally small, and taken together do not exceed an estimated 35% of all hospital beds (Central Bureau of Health Intelligence 1994). A number of corporate hospitals have been set up since the 1980s, but these are not as numerous as the hugely disparate subset of nursing homes.

State support for privatization, which began in the late 1970s and 1980s, grew with public-private cooperation in health care delivery and took various modes (Gill et al. 1997; Purohit and Mohan 1996; Bhatia and Mills 1997; Bennett and Muraleedharan 2000). This included orienting and training private practitioners for rational management of priority health problems such as tuberculosis, acute respiratory infections, and diarrhea, and in national programs such as the National Immunization Program and the Reproductive and Child Health Program.

In some places this also led to contracting the services of private specialists and hospitals for first referral services. For example, several states (Rajasthan, Punjab, Uttar Pradesh) began hiring the services of women gynecologists to hold regular clinics in government health centers. In other instances, retail outlets and private practitioners were enlisted to market contraceptives. Contracting services of private companies for nonmedical essential services (laundry, equipment maintenance, catering) in government hospitals also grew.

Such measures may help to improve the availability and quality of services. But concern for equity requires that standards of care and standardization of charges must be addressed, plus the question of accountability to patients using government facilities. Qualifications of these private practitioners as well as their prescribing practices, including information about contraindications and side effects, charges for treatment, and the continuing role of government services in the area, must be carefully reviewed to ensure quality of care and equity.

Other privatization measures involve transferring government facilities to private voluntary organizations or under a corporate umbrella. This happened, for instance, when the Punjab Health Systems Corporation was set up bringing 150 public hospitals under its purview (Gill 1996). Whereas this may improve managerial efficiency, it may not of itself solve the problem of access in remote areas. Furthermore, unless criteria for corporatization are clearer than at present, its impact on equity will remain unknown.

The government also set up autonomous societies to facilitate easier disbursement of funds and to put into operation programs such as AIDS control, blindness control, and reproductive and child health programs. Coordination of the activities of these organizations with the government, the quality of leadership, and issues of political interference would crucially affect the success of these schemes. Equally important, and at present uncertain, is the question of financial and programmatic accountability of these bodies to the government and to people.

On the whole some attempts at cooperation between public and private health services are innovative and have the potential for improving quality and access. However, many of our concerns about the private sector remain unresolved. Close monitoring of the effects of these changes is therefore essential if their effect on health equity is to be assessed effectively.

Quality Concerns in the Private Sector

The government's role in regulating the location of private health services and their quality has been minimal. Absence of comprehensive legislation or regulation over their functioning means no standardization or assurance of quality, or affordable pricing of care (Nandraj 1994). Lack of a database on the formal and informal private sector in terms of volume, distribution, and competence also poses an enormous challenge to policy initiatives.

Physical standards in terms of space, light, hygiene, water supply, adequacy of equipment, and safe disposal methods are variable. In cities such as Bombay, where real estate prices are exorbitant, nursing homes tend to be small, cramped, and grossly deficient in terms of all indicators of physical quality (Nandraj 1994). Process standards also vary in terms of adequacy of medical and paramedical personnel and modes of their interaction with patients (Nandraj and Duggal 1997; Muraleedharan 1999). Also, private doctors do not feel morally compelled to treat patients who suffer from stigmatized diseases. About 20% of 106 general practitioners in three slum areas of Bombay were reluctant to treat patients with leprosy for fear that their practice would be adversely affected (Uplekar and Cash 1991).

"Cut practice," meaning kickbacks from specialists, diagnostic, and radiologic facilities to referring general practitioners, was estimated to be as high as 30% to 40% of fees charged (Nandraj 1994). This may well motivate some general practitioners to recommend tests and specialist consultations even when they may be unnecessary. Similarly, the need to recover the costs of recently acquired medical technology may inflate the cost of care. According to a study of four very large corporate hospitals in Madras, 43% to 60% of their total investment was in medical equipment (Sukanya 1996).

Aside from low quality and unethical pricing, a problem of medical competence exists. As many as 68% of ayurveds and homeopaths and 77% of unqualified healers mainly practiced allopathy for which they were not certified (Nandraj and Duggal 1997). Even though these practitioners have no formal training in allopathy, many are motivated to prescribe allopathic drugs to facilitate quick cures that will satisfy their clients (Sule 1999).

This contributes to the finding that the proportion of undesirable and/or irrational drugs prescribed was quite high for all types of doctors, but significantly higher among private doctors. As a result as much as 69% of resulting expenditure was unnecessary (Phadke et al. 1995). A study of antituberculosis treatment prescribed by 100 private practitioners unearthed a total of 80 different regimens, most of which were inappropriate and expensive (Uplekar and Shepard 1991). Sale of drugs without prescriptions in private pharmacies is extremely common. Often the people behind the pharmacy counter recommend medicines on the basis of what appears to be popular and with no regard for possible side effects.

Knowledge about the prices of drugs and, more important, their side effects is unreliable and variable, especially among those in the private sector who receive continuing education from medical representatives of pharmaceutical companies. Sales representatives tend to focus on doctors who prescribe frequently, especially in cities, leading to highly skewed dissemination of information. Most important, information about side effects or the prices of alternatives is not routinely provided.

Many of these quality-related problems are obviously the result of an inadequate system of regulation of the private sector. As such all consumers, both the poor and the better-off, are potentially affected. But the poor, especially in a country such as India where poverty, illiteracy, and gender and caste oppression go hand in hand, have fewer resources to circumvent these problems or to challenge health practitioners or institutions on their own. Inequity thus is locked in.

Deregulation of Drugs

Systematic deregulation of pricing of drugs as well as radical changes to the country's patent regime are two significant changes that had a bearing on the quality and costs of health care in the 1990s. Until the late 1960s, virtually no regulations governed the pharmaceutical industry,[13] which was dominated by transnational corporations. The government sought to break some of the dependency on imports by actively encouraging local innovation. In 1970 it passed the Indian Patents Act, which disallowed product patents, granted patents for processes for five to seven years, and introduced compulsory licensing in the public interest. It also passed a drug (price control) order that defined, for the first time, a ceiling on the prices of all drugs. The constitution of the Hathi Committee (Government of India 1975) calling for major changes in the working of the drug industry was a third milestone. This committee provided inspiration for the drug policy of 1978, although its more radical recommendations[14] never saw light of day.

Since the committee's report in 1975, there have been several drug price control orders, as well as two drug policy statements. Each of these further liberalized the scope of price control in terms of the number of drugs that are included and the extent to which the government can control the import, retention, and common sale prices of bulk drugs, as well as retail and ceiling prices of scheduled formulations. In 1970, all drugs were targeted for price control. In 1979, the number came down to 347; in 1987, it was 163; and by 1995, it was reduced to a mere 73 (Rane 1998; Srinivasan 1999; Bidwai 1995).

One major reason why the government failed to regulate prices and production of drugs adequately is overt and covert resistance from the drug industry, consisting initially of transnational corporations and later including Indian firms and wholesale and retail traders. A second reason is that policies governing the industry come under the purview of the Ministry of Chemicals and Fertilizers and not the Ministry of Health. Hence the industry was directly affected by changes occurring in India's overall industrial policy. The effects of general industrial deregulation began to be felt in the 1980s (Bidwai 1995) and continued and accelerated in the 1990s. Thus, absence of a regulatory list of essential drugs means that the market is flooded with irrational drugs. Nonadoption of generic names led to excessive branding and different pricing, which consumers are in no position to assess.

The impact of liberalization of the pharmaceutical industry is starkly evident in spiraling costs of drugs since the 1980s. Between 1980 and 1995 the 778 drugs selected for study had a 197% increase overall. The sharpest increases averaging 336% were evident for anticancer drugs, many of which are imported, and also for those drugs that have a near monopoly. Several drugs that have to be taken over long periods of time, such as those for thyroid disorders, had increases of over 500%. The prices of inessential drugs and irrational combinations such as balms, antidiarrheals, antiobesity drugs, laxatives, enzymes, food products, and some nutritional additives also increased (Rane 1996). The impact of India's recent acceptance of a new product patent regime under World Trade Organization rules may well lead to substantial increases in the prices of newer patented drugs. India's ability to sell drugs at lower prices than in other countries will be severely tested in the coming years.

Health Inequity in the 1990s

Trends toward greater privatization and deregulation provide the backdrop for examining health care use and costs in the 1990s and their implications for gender and class inequity.

Patterns of Health Services Use

How have use patterns been affected by privatization in the health sector? Among people who sought outpatient care in 1995–1996, more than 80% did so in the private sector (table 11.6). This represents a further increase in the already dominant share of the private sector in outpatient care. What is also striking is the fall in public sector use even in poorer states such as Rajasthan, Assam, Orissa, and Madhya Pradesh (Iyer and Sen 2000).

Comparing tables 11.6 and 11.3 shows that the increase in use of the private sector and decline in the public sector are not uniform across

Table 11.6
Public-private sector use for medical care, India, 1995–1996 (National Sample Survey Organisation 1992)[a]

Health sectors	Outpatient care (%)		Inpatient care (%)	
	Rural	Urban	Rural	Urban
Share of public sector	19.0	19.0	45.2	43.1
Public hospital	11.0	15.0	39.9	41.8
PHC, CHC	6.0	1.0	4.8	0.9
Public dispensary	2.0	2.0	0.5	0.4
ESI doctor	0.0	1.0		
Share of private sector	80.0	81.0	54.7	56.9
Private hospital	12.0	16.0	41.9	41.0
Nursing home	3.0	2.0	8.0	11.1
Charitable institution	0.0	1.0	4.0	4.2
Private doctor	55.0	55.0		
Others	10.0	7.0	0.8	0.6
Totals	99.0	100.0	99.9	100.0

PHC, primary health center; CHC, community health center; ESI, employees state insurance.
[a] Table 4.10, p. 22; table 4.16, p. 28.

subcategories. The bulk of decline in public sector use of outpatient services was in hospitals, whose share in rural areas fell from 17.7% to 11% of the total, and from 22.6% to 15% in urban areas between the two NSS survey periods. In rural areas, the share of private hospitals also declined, while the share of PHCs and CHCs in the public sector, and of nursing homes, private doctors, and others in the private sector increased. To the extent that lower-level institutions such as PHCs and CHCs are picking up some of the patients who earlier would have gone without a referral directly to a hospital, this may be a trend in the direction of greater efficiency of use of public sector institutions. However, clearly not all of the decline in the public hospitals was due to such shifts.

Furthermore, whereas a small increase occurred in hospitalizations in urban areas, a sharp drop was seen in rural areas from 28 per 1,000 ailing persons in 1986–1987 to just 13 per 1,000 in 1995–1996 (National Sample Survey Organization 1998:25). The general public-private mix for inpatient care is significantly different from the mid-1980s when the public sector was dominant. In 1995–1996, 55% and 57%, respectively, of those who were hospitalized went to private sector institutions in rural and urban areas, respectively, compared 40% in 1986–1987. The private sector clearly became the dominant provider of inpatient care during the decade. This may be linked to narrowing of the cost gap between the sectors.

Comparing tables 11.5 and 11.7 shows significant changes toward greater inequality in use of health facilities by inpatients by economic class (MPCE) in the mid-1990s. In rural areas the class gradient for inpatient use of public hospitals, which was insignificant in the mid-1980s, turned positive and statistically significant. This means that even public hospitals were used more by the better-off in the 1990s. Although PHC use was not significantly unequal, the gradient for private hospitals, nursing homes, and charitable institutions, which was already positive, became steeper and statistically significant. The overall gradient for hospital use went from near zero (indicating not too much inequality overall) to a highly significant positive number. In urban areas, inequality in use of public facilities did not worsen significantly, but inequality in use of private facilities did.

Table 11.7
Class gradients for inpatient care by facility, India, 1995–1996 (National Sample Survey Organisation 1998)[a]

Health care facility	Rural	Urban
Public hospitals	3.11[c]	0.35
PHCs	0.93	−1.25
Private hospitals	5.64[b]	3.44[b]
Nursing homes	4.38[b]	3.89[b]
Charitable institutions	3.04[c]	3.28[c]
All hospitals	4.14[b]	2.11[c]

PHC, primary health center.
[a] Source table 12, p. A-65, A-170.
[b] Significance at 1%.
[c] Significance at 5%.

Some of this increase in inequality in use of hospital facilities may be the result of attempts by both public and private health institutions to attract more paying customers who can cross-subsidize services to the poor. The pressure on institutions to do this certainly increased in the climate of fiscal stringency prevalent in the 1990s. This would not be a problem if it made it more possible in fact for hospitals to offer inpatient services to the poor. However, the steep fall in rural hospitalization rates, combined with increased use by the better-off, suggests instead that the poor are being squeezed out.

Use of the private sector is often directly related to the purchasing power of households (Duggal with Amin 1989; Sundar 1995; George et al. 1997; National Sample Survey Organisation 1998). Debilitated public health institutions may not only have a negative impact on use by the poor, but may also severely affect women's access to and use of care. National- and state-level studies indicate that inequalities within households mediate the distribution of benefits to certain groups. Significantly low sums of money are spent on treatment of women and girls in the household for both inpatient and outpatient care (Das Gupta 1987; Sundar 1995; National Sample Survey Organisation 1998; Batliwala et al. 1998).

For women, considerations such as affordability, time, work, distances to be traveled, and faith in the abilities of health providers determine

Table 11.8

Class gradients by gender for inpatient care by facility, India, 1995–1996 (National Sample Survey Organisation 1998)[a]

Health care facility	Rural		Urban	
	Male	Female	Male	Female
Public hospitals	3.23[b]	2.95[c]	0.60	0.08
PHCs	1.40	0.58	1.19	−3.58[c]
Private hospitals	5.71[b]	5.53[b]	3.63[b]	3.23[b]
Nursing homes	4.68[b]	3.99[b]	3.85[b]	3.90[b]
Charitable institutions	3.59[c]	2.48[c]	3.64[b]	2.82
All hospitals	4.33[b]	3.92[b]	2.26[c]	1.91

PHC, primary health center.
[a] Source table 12, p. A-65, A-170.
[b] Significance at 5.1.
[c] Significance at 1.1.

their access to and use of care (Gupte et al. 1999; Shatrugna et al. 1993; Sundar 1995). These considerations are not mutually exclusive. A group of rural women in a drought-prone area of Maharashtra, for instance, spoke of distance and time in terms of money they would have to pay for transport or lose as wages (Gupte et al. 1999). In Haryana the presence of public facilities had a positive impact on women's use of care (Rajeshwari 1996) because that entailed fewer demands on household resources.

Table 11.8 shows gender class gradients for inpatient care by types of rural and urban institutional facilities in the mid-1990s. Such data were not available in the 1986–1987 survey. The table shows significant inequality in the use of facilities (except PHCs and urban public hospitals) for both women and men. Of interest, inequality among men in this regard appears to be somewhat higher than among women.

Cost of Care

Costs that are incurred in treating ailments are medical fees, costs of drugs, diagnostic facilities, institutional care, and travel to the facility. There may also be a range of hidden costs such as those for tips, bribes, and so on. Opportunity cost in terms of wages lost ought to be included.

Table 11.9
Average expenditure on medical care, India, 1995–1996 (National Sample Survey Organisation 1998)

	Rural		Urban		Urban:rural ratio[b]
	1995–1996	Change % 1986–1996	1995–1996	Change % 1986–1996	1995–1996
Outpatient care					
Public sector	129	77	166	124	1.29
Private sector	186	142	200	150	1.08
Totals	176	132	194	146	1.10
Private:public ratio[c]	1.44		1.20		
Inpatient care					
Public Sector	2080	549	2195	470	1.06
Private Sector	4300	486	5344	343	1.24
Totals	3202	436	3921	320	1.22
Private:public ratio[c]	2.07		2.43		

[a] Table 4.19, p. 32; table 4.21, p. 33.
[b] Measures the urban-rural differential in average expenditure.
[c] Measures the private-public differential in average expenditure.

As mentioned, direct, indirect, and opportunity costs force a proportionally higher burden on the poor and on disadvantaged women, as they have less security and control over their resources.

Compared with the mid-1980s, costs of both outpatient and inpatient care rose in rural and urban areas.[15] Between 1986–1987 and 1995–1996, in rural areas, private outpatient costs went up by 142% as against 77% in the public sector (table 11.9). In urban areas, private outpatient costs increased by 150% compared with 124% in the public sector. The urban-rural price difference for outpatient care rose from 1.04 in 1986–1987 to 1.10 in 1995–1996.

Trends in costs of in-patient care between 1986 and 1996 are more dramatic. Average costs spiraled by 436% in rural and by 320% in urban areas. This significantly larger rise in rural areas resulted in narrowing the urban-rural expenditure differential from 1.56 to 1.22. Spiraling costs of inpatient care were also particularly evident in institutions in the public sector in contrast to the private sector in both rural and urban areas. There are opposing trends in the private-public cost ratio for outpatient and inpatient care. Between 1986–1987 and 1995–1996, ratio for outpatient care increased from 1.05 to 1.44 in rural areas and from 1.08 to 1.20 in urban areas. For inpatient care in contrast, the ratio actually fell from 2.29 to 2.07 in rural areas and from 3.13 to 2.43 in urban areas.

Whereas costs of all care went up significantly during the period, it is worth noting that costs of private outpatient care and of public inpatient care went up in comparative terms. In a sense this was a double blow for the poor, since private outpatient care was not much more expensive than public care earlier, and public inpatient care used to be much less costly compared with private care. It may also partly explain the relative increase in the share of the private sector in inpatient care, as the public sector becomes more costly in relative terms.

Lending added support to this argument is the fact that hospitalization costs to the poor in government hospitals appeared to be significantly higher in 1995–1996 than in other hospitals in the rural areas (National Sample Survey Organisation 1998). The average total expenditure per hospitalization in the so-called free wards of government hospitals is more than 20% higher than in other hospitals. The cost in paying general wards is about the same.

A major contributor to rising costs of outpatient and inpatient care is escalation of drug prices. This is a result not only of increases in the actual prices of drugs, but is also affected by prescribing practices of private practitioners who provide most outpatient care. As mentioned, private practitioners receive most of their continuing education about drugs and therapeutics from pharmaceutical sales and medical representatives who do not provide information about side effects and costs unless specifically asked. Thus, older drugs that may be as effective and less inexpensive tend to be substituted needlessly by newer and more expensive ones.

Taken together, these rises in costs of all types of care impose heavy burdens on people, especially those with few means. The proportion of household spending on treatment by the poorest income groups in five major states rose sharply between 1961 and 1987 and was higher than the average health expenditure for all income groups (Prabhu et al. 1995). District surveys in Maharashtra and Madhya Pradesh during the late 1980s and early 1990s showed that expenditure on health as a proportion of total household consumption expenditure was higher among groups belonging to lower socioeconomic classes (Duggal with Amin 1989; George et al. 1997).

On the basis of these findings, one could hypothesize that the cost of accessing health care may have had a range of possible effects in the 1990s. These could include cutbacks on other areas of social consumption such as food, which itself directly affects health status; increased indebtedness, especially among the poor; growing untreated morbidity; and growing gender and possibly age biases in health-seeking behavior. The first two outcomes were evidenced by a community-level study of the impact of structural adjustment on poor households in Rajasthan (ASTHA 1998). Costs and affordability also crucially determine women's access to care, especially in poorer groups. In the face of rising costs of care, it is likely that women may find it increasingly difficult to access formal care and may experience recurring untreated morbidity.

Untreated Morbidity
As noted earlier, the quality of morbidity data in the NSS surveys leaves a lot to be desired. Both overall rates and rates for women are suspiciously low when compared with community-level studies (Madhiwalla et al. 2000). Smaller studies report significantly higher rates of untreated morbidity. They also show that nontreatment tends to be highest in reproductive-age groups. Women tend to leave untreated conditions that are chronic but not incapacitating, such as reproductive problems, mental stress, weakness, and aches and pains (Madhiwalla et al. 2000; Shatrugna et al. 1993; Bhatia and Cleland 1995; Bang et al. 1989). These health problems are, however, poorly treated by the NSS as noted. Despite this caveat, data on untreated morbidity point to some trends that bear further investigation (table 11.10).

The mid-1990s survey shows higher morbidity rates for both women and men, possibly due to better counting. Untreated morbidity as such, both rural and urban, continued to be significantly higher for women. The female to male ratio in untreated rural morbidity was practically unchanged at 1.14, whereas the urban ratio fell somewhat to 1.08.

Somewhat surprising, untreated morbidity rates were lower overall than in the mid-1980s. This aggregate fall, however, conceals absolute increases in untreated morbidity in the bottom MPCE fractiles in both

Table 11.10
Gender differences in rates of morbidity and untreated morbidity, India, 1995–1996
(National Sample Survey Organisation 1998)[a]

	Rural		Urban	
	1995–1996	Change (%) 1986–1996	1995–1996	Change (%) 1986–1996
Morbidity rates (no. of ailing persons/ 1,000 people)				
Men	83	30	79	163
Women	87	38	88	167
Totals	85	33	83	168
Women:men ratio	1.05	6	1.11	1
Untreated morbidity rates[b] (no. of untreated persons/ 1,000 ailing people)				
Men	162	−6	90	−8
Women	184	−7	97	−18
Totals	173	−6	93	−14
Women:men ratio	1.14	−1	1.08	−11

The morbidity rates for 1995–1996 (with a 30 day recall period) are estimates by the NSS (NSSO 1998). NSS 1995–1996 (30 days) = NSS 1995–1996 (15 days) + PPC (15 days), where PPC is the number of persons reporting any ailment (acute or nonacute) during the 15-day recall period. Calculated ratios are slightly lower than NSS estimates because of nonavailability of PPC for non-acute ailments.
[a] Source tables 1.2 and 9.2, pp. A-21, A-53, A-126, A-158; source table 8.2, pp. A-46, A-151.
[b] Untreated morbidity = (1000 − rate of treated morbidity).

rural and urban areas. This is particularly sharp for men, whereas the pattern for women is more mixed across the fractiles.

Rates of untreated morbidity among men showed substantial increases between 1986 and 1996 in the lowest fractile groups. In the lowermost fractile, rates went up by as much as 39% and 61% in rural and urban areas, respectively. In the next lowest fractile, increases were to the extent of 20% and 18%. The trend begins to be reversed in the middle fractiles and this is heightened in the topmost group where rates actually fell by 17% to 18%. Since morbidity rates appear to be undercounted among the poor, the decline in untreated morbidity among the rich led to the observed fall in the rate overall (table 11.11).

Table 11.11
Class gradients by gender in morbidity, untreated morbidity and costs of care, India, 1995–1996 (National Sample Survey Organisation 1998)[a]

	Rural	Urban
Morbidity rates (no./1,000 persons)		
Men	8.82[b]	5.00[b]
Women	10.82[b]	6.64[b]
Totals	9.61[b]	5.68[b]
Untreated Morbidity Rates (no./1,000 ailing persons)		
Men	−26.50[b]	−15.04
Women	−22.82[b]	−20.25[b]
Totals	−24.75[b]	−17.57[c]
Average expenditure on hospitalization (in rupees)		
Men	889.89[c]	1437.40[c]
Women	532.39[c]	1245.60[c]
Totals	736.86[c]	1354.40[c]
Average expenditure on outpatient care (in rupees)		
Men	20.21[b]	26.39[b]
Women	19.96[b]	25.46[b]
Totals	20.11[b]	26.04[b]

[a] Source tables 1.2 and 9.2, p. A-21, A-53, A-126, A-158; source table 8.2, p. A-46, A-151; source table 19, p. A-92, A-197; source table 22.2, p. A-103, A-208.
[b] Significance at 1%.
[c] Significance at 5%.

Greater inequality across economic classes is evidenced by increases in gradients for the extent of untreated morbidity and expenditures on outpatient and inpatient care. Class gradients for untreated morbidity became significantly worse for both men and women in urban areas; there appears to have been little change in the class gradient for rural women. Worsening of the class gradient appears to have been sharper for men in both rural and urban areas.

The suspicion that health care is becoming increasingly difficult for poorer classes to access is borne out by reasons that were offered for no treatment (table 11.12). Compared with 1986–1987, the proportion of those who were unable to access care because of financial reasons went up significantly in both rural and urban areas, as did the proportion who

Table 11.12
Reasons for no treatment, India, 1986–1996 (National Sample Survey Organisation 1998)[a]

Reason for no treatment	Rural (%)		Urban (%)	
	1986–1987	1995–1996	1986–1987	1995–1996
No medical facility	3	9	0	1
No faith in medicine	2	4	2	5
Long waiting	0	1	1	1
Financial reasons	15	24	10	21
Illness not "serious"	75	52	81	60
Other reasons	5	10	6	12
Totals	100	99	100	101

[a] Table 4.9, p. 21.

said that no medical facility was available. Correspondingly, the proportion of those who did not consider their health problems to be serious enough went down considerably.

Summary

The subject of health equity is a complex one with many determinants and various levels and dimensions. Although we suspect that morbidity in general, and particularly for poor men and possibly all women, was undercounted in the NSS surveys, and despite the fact that data by economic class and gender are incomplete, this analysis shows some alarming results.

No one would seriously contend that health services were equitable in the country before the 1990s. Gender and economic class inequities were severe. Despite attempts to develop a wide-ranging set of institutions and to provide a floor of basic services through the public system to meet the goals of affordable and accessible health care for all, the reality was rather different. Public health services were poor in terms of access and quality. As a result, by the 1980s the bulk of health expenditure was out of pocket, and a largely unregulated private sector was becoming increasingly dominant. Gender and class inequity in access and cost continued to be severe. Nevertheless the public sector, and especially public hospitals, did provide an important if inadequate alternative, especially for the poor.

Key changes during the 1990s, eroded health equity even further. These included further deregulation of drug production and prices, deterioration in public hospitals combined with growing subsidies to private hospitals, and a range of other privatization measures with mixed and at present uncertain effects.

By the mid-1990s, the private sector was dominant in terms of both outpatient and inpatient services, and the average cost of all care (and particularly of inpatient care) went up significantly. Although the extent of untreated morbidity overall appears to have declined, this may be partly a statistical artifact resulting from undercounting of morbidity among the poor and declines in untreated morbidity among the rich. Untreated illness among the poor clearly increased. Inequity by economic class appears to have worsened, and the divide between rich and poor in terms of untreated illness and expenditures on health services, as well in the use of both public and private health care institutions, grew. The rich are now the major users of not only private but also public hospitals.

Thus class-based inequalities in access to health services clearly worsened for both men and women. Gender inequity, particularly in untreated morbidity, remains severe. However, the change in class gradients for both untreated morbidity and hospital use was somewhat sharper for men. This relative worsening of access for poor men, even though they continue to be better off than poor women, may imply that poor households are now really stretched to the breaking point in terms of access and affordability of health services. It may reflect the worst kind of catching up in terms of gender equality.

Notes

1. At the end of 1997, rural poverty stood at 36.47% and urban at 29.02% (headcount index) (Datt 1999). According to World Bank estimates, 53% of India's population lived below an internationally comparable purchasing power of a dollar a day per head in 1992.

2. Its status as a Directive Principle of State Policy in the Indian Constitution means that it could become an inviolate fundamental right if it is appropriately legislated, but this has not happened so far.

3. This paper extends the analysis in Iyer and Sen (2000).

4. Some change in mind-set appears to have occurred after the international conference on population and development in Cairo in 1994, but actual change on the ground is very slow.

5. Both surveys correctly decided that normal pregnancy and childbirth should not be treated as illness. The NSS (1986–1987) also excluded expenditures related to abortions and miscarriages. The later survey was meant to include complications around pregnancy and childbirth, but how well it did so is not clear. Neither survey made a special attempt to ensure that information on reproductive ill health was systematically collected from women; in the absence of such attempts, it is now generally known that, at least in this regard, women do not easily reveal their suffering.

6. Growing literature, particularly in Europe, indicates that the economic class of male and female household members may not be the same because of differences in control over and access to income and other social support systems. The NSS data do not allow us to explore such distinctions here.

7. The appendix provides a discussion of the methodology used in the NSS surveys.

8. The PHCs and subcenters are entrusted with populations of 30,000 and 5,000, respectively, whereas CHCs are expected to cater to the needs of a 1,00,000-strong population. District hospitals in contrast do not have any clearly defined catchment areas. In 1992, subcenters and PHCs were catering to their designated population sizes; however, CHCs were dealing with three times the expected population load (Central Bureau of Health Intelligence 1992).

9. All India data show that the maximum radial distance covered by a CHC was 22.03 km in 1992; PHCs covered 6.92 km and subcenters covered 2.76 km (Central Bureau of Health Intelligence 1992).

10. These comparisons do not of course take into account the possibility that patients may go to public and private services for different sets of health problems that may be intrinsically different in terms of cost. This cannot be tested with these data.

11. The CHCs are ideally expected to play the role of a first referral unit for four PHCs. Instead, at the end of 1992, the ratio of PHCs to CHCs was 10:1 (Central Bureau of Health Intelligence 1992). In states such as Uttar Pradesh, this number was as high as 15, but in Tamil Nadu it was an even higher 20.

12. After 1994, the attempt to transform the existing Family Welfare Program through the Reproductive and Child Health Program and a target-free approach in family planning may be seen as a move toward strengthening public health services, but its results have been mixed to date (Sen et al. 1998).

13. There was no legislation governing the prices, production, quality, and supply of drugs and pharmaceuticals. There were no standard dosages, no effective labeling regulations. Nor was it obligatory for manufacturers to provide informa-

tion on indications, contraindications, adverse reactions, or side effects (Bidwai 1995).

14. These include the call for a change from brand names to generic names, for the state to take complete responsibility for supporting research to develop new drugs, for a phased imposition of bans on the import of bulk drugs, and for related measures to encourage indigenous manufacturing.

15. These figures have not been deflated for changes in inflation because of difficulties in identifying and constructing an appropriate price deflator. However, the implicit price deflator for the gross domestic product during the 1990s grew at 8.6% per year (World Bank 2000b). If costs of health services had simply kept up with this rate of inflation, in the mid-1990s they would have been around 230% of what they were a decade earlier. As can be seen, the increases in costs of outpatient care were less than this, but increases for inpatient care were considerably higher.

12

Measuring Up: Gender, Burden of Disease, and Priority Setting[1]

Kara Hanson

The 1993 World Development Report (World Bank 1993) introduced a number of new terms into the language of international health policy. Phrases such as the "global burden of disease" (GBD), "priority setting," "minimum package of clinical services," and DALYs (disability-adjusted life-years) increasingly appeared in health policy discussions, and associated methodologies were advocated as tools for planning in the health sector. The Global Burden of Disease and Injury series, a multivolume work presenting aggregate estimates of the burden of disease arising from different causes in 1990, represents an extraordinary effort to gather demographic and epidemiological information. The series also includes a number of specialist volumes, one of which is concerned with health dimensions of sex and reproduction (Murray and Lopez 1998). More recently, GBD estimates for 1999 were presented in the 2000 World Health Report (WHO 2000).

Whereas the GBD methodology and use of DALYs to measure the burden arising from different health problems were widely applied, considerable controversy arose around their use (Anand and Hanson 1997, 1998; Arnesen and Nord 1999; Barker and Green 1996; Nygaard 2000; Paalman et al. 1998). They also raised a number of issues that are of concern from a gender perspective (Sundby 1998, 1999; WHO 1998h).

More broadly, both measuring disease burden and determining priorities for resource allocation raise issues for equity (Anand and Hanson 1997, 1998). Any process for allocating resources among disease priorities necessarily requires values and judgments, since it ultimately involves allocation of resources among individuals. Furthermore, allocation processes frequently take place in political arenas, where values may not be made explicit and objectives may be unclear or mutually conflicting. However, even the positive exercise of measuring the disease burden will also embody values and therefore raises issues of equity.

A number of factors may introduce a gender bias into the measurement of health using the GBD approach. Some of these are related to data availability and are thus amenable to technical fixes; others are conceptual issues related to the measurement and valuation of ill health. In addition, gender issues raise particular challenges for cost-effectiveness analysis and resource allocation, both because of the gender processes that contribute to ill health, and because of the narrow focus of cost-effectiveness analysis on a limited range of health interventions.

Approaches to Measuring Ill Health

For a number of reasons we might be interested in knowing the aggregate quantity of ill health, its distribution among population subgroups, and relative contributions of different diseases and conditions to the total. Such knowledge is useful for understanding the scale of health problems and their distribution among individuals, countries, regions, and socioeconomic groups. It might also form the basis for policies aimed at reducing ill health, such as setting priorities among alternative health interventions and for measuring the success of such policies.

Measuring of health status raises a number of ethical issues. First, any measure will incorporate a valuation of different health states: there is no such thing as a purely objective measure. Valuation also enters in the choice of what to include and exclude, for example, whether the burden should be that of the individual alone or take into account second-order health or other effects on caregivers or dependents.

A distinction has to be made between measuring the disease burden of an individual and measuring ill health at the population level. An individual's burden can be captured through disease or body system-specific measure of illness, such as pain scales, attack rates, or one of the large number of specialized tools that are available (Bowling 1995). For conditions that are always fatal and for which the main health consequence is premature death, life-years lost could be used to measure an individual's illness burden. However, more complex problems occur when a population perspective is taken. This requires a method for aggregating across individuals whose ill health is caused by a range of different problems with different consequences (premature death, different forms of disability, pain).[2]

Early approaches to measuring the health of populations, such as potential years of life lost, infant mortality, and life expectancy at birth, looked only at mortality and thus focused on the main causes of death, failing to capture the significant amount of ill health that results in disability or morbidity. During the 1960s and 1970s, efforts were initiated to measure nonfatal health outcomes at the individual level, and a huge literature now exists on measurement of health-related quality of life (HRQL). For comparisons of individuals, three main groups of instruments can be identified (Fox-Rushby 1994). First, generic measures allow comparisons across contexts and disease groups (McMaster Health Index Questionnaire, Sickness Impact Profile, SF-36, Nottingham Health Profile). A second group is made up of disease-specific measures (scales for assessing cancers, psychiatric conditions, neurological conditions, etc.). The third group comprises composite indicators that combine mortality and morbidity (quality-adjusted life years, QALYs) (Weinstein and Stason 1976), and Euroqol (Euroqol Group 1990).

QALYs adjust time spent in less than perfect health using quality weights that range from one (perfect health) to zero (death). They have been used to assess the effectiveness of interventions and to compare the cost-effectiveness of health interventions that have different profiles of effects on morbidity and mortality. They have not been used to measure the health of populations, although some have advocated their use for this purpose (Williams 1999).

Three major efforts have attempted to measure the quantity of ill health at the population level and include both premature mortality and nonfatal health outcomes. The first was the Ghana Health Assessment project (Ghana Health Assessment Project Team 1981), which developed a method to estimate quantitatively the health impact of different diseases to compare the potential effect on population health of various intervention programs. The unit of measurement was number of days of healthy life lost due to a disease, which included both mortality and morbidity. Although quite widely known, the method does not appear to have been adopted by other researchers. One reason may be the scale of data collection that is required. It is also not clear whether the results had any impact on policy and resource allocation.

The next major effort was the Global Burden of Disease study, which was developed as an input into the 1993 World Development Report *Investing in Health,* and was jointly undertaken by the World Bank and the WHO. Subsequently a series of volumes was published (Murray & Lopez 1996, 1998) containing revised and refined estimates of the GBD in 1990.

The unit of measurement for the burden of disease in the GBD exercise is the disability-adjusted life-year (DALY). The DALY, like the QALY, is a composite measure of health that combines the time lost to premature mortality (years of life lost, YLLs) and years lived with a disability (YLDs). Time lost to premature death is measured in relation to a standard expectation of life (80 for men, 82.5 for women), using model life tables. Time lived with disability is translated into an equivalent time loss using a set of weights that reflects reduction in functional capacity.

DALYs incorporate four values in their construction:

• Choice of expectation of life at each age that, for purposes of GBD, reflects life expectancy in a low-mortality setting;

• Sex gap in life expectancy (part of the gap that is assumed to be related to biological differences in longevity between sexes);

• Value of a year of life lived at each age (age weights)

• Value of time lived at different time periods (discounting)

The first three carry direct gender implications and should be analyzed from a gender perspective. Discounting also has gender implications through its indirect effect on both the sex gap in life expectancy and age weighting.

The most recent health indicator is disability-adjusted life expectancy (DALE). Designed to be directly comparable with life expectancy, DALE weights expected years of ill health by their severity and subtracts these from overall life expectancy to give equivalent years of healthy life (WHO 2000). Unlike DALYs and the GBD, DALE is not typically decomposed into different causes: it is primarily intended as a summary measure. The

2000 World Health Report presents DALE for each country disaggregated by sex.

Estimated GBD in 1990[3]

The total number of DALYs lost in 1990 was estimated to be 1,379,238 thousand. Of these, 52% were lost by men and 48% by women. The GBD exercise divides causes of death into three groups: group I consists of communicable, maternal, perinatal, and nutritional conditions; group II is made up of noncommunicable diseases; and group III is injuries, including intentional and unintentional ones. In terms of total DALYs lost, group I constitutes 44%, group II 41%, and group III the remaining 15% of the total disease burden.

Breaking down these aggregate figures by sex provides additional insights into relative burdens of women and men (figure 12.1). Women have a relatively greater burden arising from group I conditions (which make up 48% of the total female burden vs. 41% of the male burden) and similar contributions from group II diseases (41% vs. 40%). Injuries make up a smaller proportion of the total female disease burden (11% vs. 19% in males).

Further disaggregating DALYs into its two subcomponents, premature mortality (YLLs) and disability (YLDs), provides additional insight into gender differences in the burden of ill health (table 12.1). Overall, the number of years lost to premature mortality is greater for males than

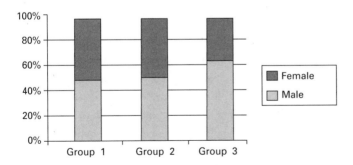

Figure 12.1
Total DALYs lost, all regions, by disease group, 1990 (Murray and Lopez 1996).

Table 12.1
Relative contributions of premature mortality and disability in 1990, all regions, by main disease group (Murray and Lopez 1996)

Years of life lost (YLLs) ('000) no. (%)	Men	Women	Totals
Totals	486,937 (54)	419,565 (46)	906,501
Group I	246,875 (50)	243,713 (50)	490,588
Group II	152,937 (54)	130,458 (46)	283,395
Group III	87,125 (66)	45,394 (34)	132,519
Years lost to disability (YLDs), ('000) no. (%)			
Totals	235,096 (50)	237,641 (50)	472,736
Group I	47,300 (41)	68,072 (59)	115,372
Group II	139,689 (50)	141,548 (50)	281,237
Group III	48,107 (63)	28,021 (37)	76,128
YLDs as a percentage of total DALYs, by disease group			
Totals	33	36	34
Group I	16	22	19
Group II	48	52	50
Group III	36	38	36

females. For group I conditions, the shares are approximately equal, however, for groups II and III, the male share of total mortality is higher. In contrast, whereas the total number of years lived with disability is approximately equal for men and women, females experience a higher share of total disability arising from group I conditions (59% vs 41%). For group II the distribution is approximately equal, but men contribute the greater share of disability arising from group III conditions.

The third panel of table 12.1 shows the contribution of disability (YLDs) to total DALYs lost by each sex in each of the three main disease groups. Overall, disability contributes about one-third of total DALYs lost, but women experience higher levels of disability than men in all three groups, with the difference being most marked for group I conditions (22% of total DALYs vs. 16%), reflecting the burden of reproductive-related disability. This is consistent with the observation that women live longer than men but experience more morbidity.

Table 12.2
DALYs lost/100,000 population in 1990, by region (Murray and Lopez 1996)

	Men	Women	Totals
Established market economies	14,029	10,830	12,396
Former socialist countries of Europe	21,615	14,661	17,977
India	32,390	35,500	33,892
China	18,573	18,203	18,394
Other Asia and Islands	27,563	24,345	25,961
Sub-Saharan Africa	61,350	54,532	57,901
Latin America and the Caribbean	24,197	19,986	22,087
Middle East crescent	30,309	29,659	29,990

Relative inequalities in health across regions are shown by analyzing differences in the aggregate disease burden. One way of making crude comparisons across regions is DALYs per 100,000 population (table 12.2). Here, the burden of ill health associated with poverty is very clear. The highest absolute burden is found in sub-Saharan Africa, where DALYs per 100,000 population is over four times higher than in established market economies. The next highest burdens are found in India (nearly three times higher than high-income countries) and the Middle East crescent (2.4 times higher than high-income countries).

In terms of composition of the burden, there are also regional differences (table 12.3). For example, group I conditions (communicable, maternal, perinatal, and nutritional) account for only 7% to 10% of all DALYs lost in established market economies and in the former socialist countries of Europe. However, they make up over 50% of all DALYs lost in India and sub-Saharan Africa, and almost 50% in other Asia and Pacific islands, and in the Middle East crescent. In all regions, group I disorders account for a greater share of the burden for women than for men. In contrast, group III conditions (accidents and injuries) are consistently a greater share of burden for men than for women. Considerable regional variations are apparent, with accidents and injuries accounting for nearly 25% of men's disease burden in the former socialist countries of Europe, in sub-Saharan Africa, and in Latin America and the Caribbean.

The GBD volume provides more disaggregated data on deaths and disability due to specific causes. Tables 12.4 and 12.5 show the ten leading

Table 12.3

Regional patterns in percentage of DALYs lost by disease group, for men and women separately (Murray and Lopez 1996)

	Group I		Group II		Group III	
	Men	Women	Men	Women	Men	Women
Established market economies	7	8	78	85	16	7
Former socialist countries of Europe	7	11	68	79	25	10
India	54	59	30	28	17	13
China	22	27	58	58	20	15
Other Asia and Islands	42	48	40	42	18	10
Sub-Saharan Africa	62	70	18	20	20	10
Latin America and the Caribbean	33	39	45	52	22	10
Middle East crescent	45	51	39	40	16	9

Row totals may not add up to 100% because of rounding.

causes of DALYs for adults in low- and high-income regions. Tuberculosis and iron-deficiency anemia are relatively more important causes of women's ill health in low-income regions, and a number of the other leading causes are related to reproductive health. For men, the top ten causes reflect a considerable burden related to behavioral factors (accidents, violence, alcohol, injury). The burden of mental health conditions is apparent in both regions, but more pronounced in high-income countries.

The emphasis of the GBD is distinctly global in nature, with a focus on national level data-collection efforts (Gwatkin and Guillot 2000; Gwatkin et al. 1999). In general, little or no data on disease burden are available for population subgroups (WHO 2000). This is in contrast to earlier epidemiologic work that focused on measuring the ill health of the poor. The GBD's global orientation is potentially problematic because health problems of the poor differ from those of the rich in nature as well as in magnitude. To the extent that concern with global aggregates leads to a focus on noncommunicable disease, attention may be diverted away from the greater burden of communicable diseases experienced by the poor.

The GBD methodology is used by those authors to calculate the burden of disease of the global poor (defined as the 20% of the global population

Table 12.4
Ten leading causes of DALYs lost by men and women (age 15–44 yrs) in 1990 for developing regions (Murray and Lopez 1996)

Women	DALYs ('000)	Cumulative %	Men	DALYs ('000)	Cumulative %
All causes	177,227	100	All causes	180,211	100
Unipolar major depression	22,740	12.8	Unipolar major depression	12,658	7.0
Tuberculosis	8,703	17.7	Road traffic accidents	11,387	13.3
Iron-deficiency anemia	7,135	21.8	Tuberculosis	10,747	19.3
Self-inflicted injuries	6,526	25.5	Violence	9,844	24.8
Obstructed labor	6,033	28.9	Alcohol use	8,420	29.4
Chlamydia	5,364	31.9	War	7,448	33.6
Bipolar disorder	5,347	34.9	Bipolar disorder	5,601	36.7
Maternal sepsis	5,226	37.8	Self-inflicted injuries	5,478	39.7
War	4,934	40.6	Schizophrenia	5,068	42.5
Abortion	4,856	43.4	Iron-deficiency anemia	4,898	45.3

Table 12.5
Ten leading causes of DALYs lost by men and women (age 15–44 yrs) in 1990 for developed regions (Murray and Lopez 1996)

Women	DALYs ('000)	Cumulative %	Men	DALYs ('000)	Cumulative %
All causes	24,674	100	All causes	36,943	100
Unipolar major depression	4,910	19.8	Alcohol use	4,677	12.7
Schizophrenia	1,450	25.7	Road traffic accidents	4,167	23.9
Road traffic accidents	1,137	30.3	Unipolar major depression	2,664	31.1
Bipolar disorder	1,106	34.7	Self-inflicted injuries	2,072	36.8
Obsessive-compulsive disorders	933	38.5	Schizophrenia	1,578	41.0
Alcohol use	801	41.7	Drug use	1,404	44.8
Osteoarthritis	783	44.9	Violence	1,196	48.1
Chlamydia	599	47.3	Ischemic heart disease	1,160	51.2
Self-inflicted injuries	569	49.6	Bipolar disorder	1,135	54.3
Rheumatoid arthritis	549	51.8	HIV infection	911	56.7

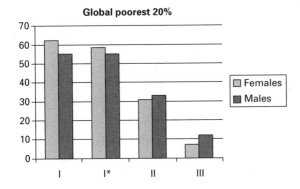

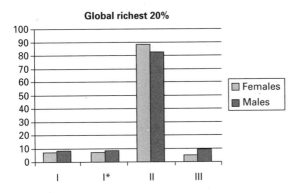

Figure 12.2
Causes of death by gender, 1990. (Source: Gwatkin and Guillot 2000.) Group I:
Communicable, maternal, perinatal, and nutritional conditions. Group I*: (Less
maternal conditions): Communicable, perinatal, and nutritional. Group II: Noncommunicable diseases. Group III: Injuries.

living in countries with the world's lowest average per capita incomes)
and the global rich (20% of the population living in the richest countries).
In addition to providing evidence that supports their contention, disaggregation by sex provides some interesting insights (figure 12.2). First,
the communicable disease group (I) is a relatively greater source of ill
health for poor women than for poor men, even after excluding maternal
conditions. The burden of noncommunicable disease is slightly greater
for poor men than for poor women; however, among the rich these differences disappear. There is very little sex difference in the burden of communicable disease, and noncommunicable diseases become more
important for women than for men.

Gender Issues and the GBD: How Does It Measure Up?

The amount of information presented in the GBD represents an enormous and impressive effort to collect and present epidemiological and demographical data. Nonetheless, a certain amount of caution is required in interpreting the findings. Specifically, we must ask whether the data contain potential biases and whether the methods might obscure gender differences in health. For example, if disability is more difficult to measure (and therefore potentially less reliable) than mortality, the greater burden of disability among women seen in figure 12.3 may be understated. Furthermore, some of those conditions that are more likely to result in disability for women than for men (e.g., violence) may also be prone to

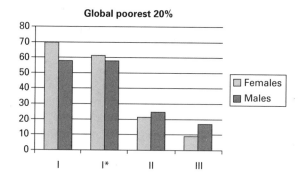

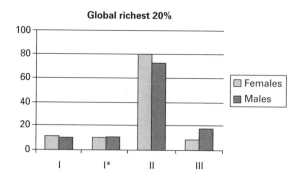

Figure 12.3
Causes of DALY loss by gender, 1990. (Source: Gwatkin and Guillot 2000.) Group I: Communicable, maternal, perinatal, and nutritional conditions. Group I*: (Less maternal conditions): Communicable, perinatal, and nutritional. Group II: Noncommunicable diseases. Group III: Injuries.

underreporting, leading to a general understatement of the burden of women relative to that of men.

I categorize the main gender issues relating to burden of disease measurement into three groups. First are conceptual issues related to what is being measured. Second are biases that arise through the estimation of disease prevalence and incidence. The third set of issues relates to the biases that arise from the methods for measuring and valuing ill health. I maintain that whereas problems in the second category can be resolved by collecting more complete, disaggregated data, those in the first and third categories pose more thorny conceptual challenges to methods for measuring health.

What Is Being Measured?

DALYs measure disease, not health. They measure ill health as a shortfall from a maximum achievable level of health, and attribute this shortfall to a single disease. This is consistent with the intended use of this analysis, which is to direct resources toward health interventions (often, but not always provided through health services) that will reduce or eliminate the burden.

Measures of Disease versus Measures of Health   A tool for measuring disease may not be ideal for planning in the health sector, and may introduce a particular form of gender bias into the process. This is because so many of women's activities and women's health services are about producing health rather than treating disease.[4] For example, 20% of hospital admissions in Tanzania are related to pregnancy and childbirth. Whereas some fraction of these would contribute to the burden of disease through complications leading to maternal conditions, most of this use of health services is aimed at promoting health by ensuring access to obstetric interventions in case of complications.

In The Netherlands, women's higher visiting rates for screening and diagnostics (e.g., cervical smears) and preventive purposes (e.g., contraception) explained more than 25% of the overall gender difference in reported health problems, a category used in the analysis that is highly correlated with use (Gijsbers van Wijk et al. 1995). In a subsequent study, significant gender differences were found in use of prevention and diagnostics in all age groups under sixty-five years. The authors concluded that "up to the age of 65 . . . preventive health behavior is put into practice to a much larger degree by women than by men" (Gijsbers van Wijk et al. 1996). In contrast to women, men tend to seek health care only after identifying a particular problem.

Attribution of the Full Shortfall to a Single Disease   A second issue relates to assumptions about the causes of ill health that are implied by the disease focus. By attributing the whole shortfall from age at death or onset of a disabling condition to a single disease, the method implicitly assumes that the lost stream of healthy life would be lived in a state of perfect health. However, particularly in high-mortality regions, averting a death (e.g., a child death from malaria) means that the individual continues to be vulnerable to other diseases. This is particularly problematic for calculations of the cost-effectiveness of interventions, where the assumed health gain may be overestimated. But it also may overstate the true burden of illness due to particular causes.

The Burden of Disease and Underdevelopment   Using the same standard life expectancy across all countries causes further problems for attribution of burdens to particular diseases. The standard that is used in DALYs (life expectancy at birth of 80 years for men and 82.5 years for women, and a West model life table[5]) was chosen to reflect the highest life expectancy observed at a national level (Japan). The equity underpinnings of using a common life expectancy for all countries are clear. It ensures that a premature death, say at the age of fifty-five, contributes the same amount to the GBD whether it occurred to a poor woman in Bangladesh or a rich woman in the suburbs of a United States city (Murray 1994).

Nonetheless, the use of a standard life expectancy implies that health interventions alone would increase life expectancy to high-income country levels. In fact, a multitude of factors and processes contribute to the premature death of a woman in Bangladesh, only some of which could be influenced by the provision of health services. In addition, DALYs lost will be attributed to only one disease since multiple causes are not handled in the analysis. It would thus seem more appropriate to call the burden being measured using such a yardstick "the burden of disease and underdevelopment" rather than the burden of disease alone (Anand and Hanson 1997).

Is Disability the Appropriate Measure of Burden?   In the terminology of the International Classification of Impairment, Disease, and Handicap (ICIDH), the GBD exercise seeks to measure disability,[6] which reflects impact on an individual's performance independent of the social environment.[7] An alternative would be to consider the amount of handicap caused by a nonfatal health outcome, which would take into account overall consequences of an impairment as influenced by the individual's circumstances. Handicap-adjusted life-years (HALYs) were used to calculate the burden of trachotomous disease (Evans and Ranson 1995). To the extent that illness is associated with either stigma or consequences that vary with social context (e.g., infertility[8]), handicap may be a better measure of the burden of ill health, and in some cases may be a more appropriate outcome when allocating health care (and other) resources. Introducing local information about the context, however, will undermine the global nature of the estimates.

Burden for Whom?   The burden that the GBD measures is the burden of ill health as experienced by the individual. Social consequences of illness in the form of emotional loss to others are intended to be captured through use of age weights (Musgrove 2000). However, by using the same age-weighting function for men and women, no account is taken of women's caring roles and their predominant responsibility for reproduction. The problem caused by this underestimation of the burden to women of ill health will also carry through to any analysis of the cost effectiveness of interventions for alleviating this burden.

Issues in Estimating Incidence and Prevalence

At a global level, an effort to measure the loss of healthy life and to classify this loss among disease groupings requires significant data on both mortality and disability. For the GBD study, estimates of mortality by cause were constructed from a number of different sources (Murray and Lopez 1996). Where good vital registration data are available, estimates use deaths coded by the vital registration system to the International Classification of Diseases, Version 9 (ICD-9). For India and China, sample registration systems were used. Data from population laboratories were used when available. Other sources were epidemiological estimates, cause of death models, and studies by disease experts, which generated assessments of incidence, prevalence, remission, and case fatality rates.

The aggregation of mortality due to individual diseases arrived at mortality levels exceeding total mortality as estimated by various demographic methods. To constrain the aggregate level of mortality due to individual diseases to the upper bound for mortality for each age and sex group, an algorithm was applied by the series editors to reduce cause-specific mortality estimates (AbouZahr 1998; Rowley and Berkley 1998). The process for compressing or squeezing mortality estimates for individual causes to make them fit an aggregate estimate of mortality is somewhat opaque, and raises concerns about the implications of this process for the final distribution of deaths among causes.

Much fewer data are available for nonfatal compared with fatal health outcomes. To estimate YLDs, disease experts or groups (largely men from high-income countries) were identified for 100 conditions. Estimates were made of disease and disability incidence, remission, case fatality rates, and prevalence distribution by severity class of disability, drawing on published and unpublished studies. The estimates were reviewed for consistency and then revised and subject to international review and rereview (Murray and Lopez 1996).

Given extensive data requirements and complex process of arriving at estimates of the burden of individual diseases, where might we be concerned about gender bias or inaccuracy in the measurement of GBD?

Conditions Likely to Be Underreported Systematically   Some conditions may be systematically underreported and thus underestimated. For example, for conditions such as deaths from induced abortions and suicides, fear or stigma may discourage reporting either in surveys or in routine statistics. Violence against women is another example. There are few population-based data on the incidence of violence against women and its physical and mental health consequences (Heise et al. 1994; WHO 1998b).

In the GBD framework, gender-based violence is a risk factor rather than a disease itself. In other words, its effect is to increase the incidence of a range of health outcomes. Estimates of the health consequences of rape and domestic violence were produced for the 1993 WDR. The health consequences considered were sexually transmitted infections (STIs), human immuno deficiency virus (HIV) infection, abortion, depression, alcohol dependence, drug dependence, posttraumatic stress disorder, unintentional injuries, suicide, homicide, and intentional injury. It is estimated that rape and domestic violence account for 5% of DALYs lost by women of reproductive age in demographically developing countries and 19% in high-income countries (World Bank 1993; Heise et al. 1994). The difference between estimates for high- and low-income countries could itself be due to gender bias and underestimation of these causes in the latter.

Other health conditions might be systematically underreported because women are more likely to be asymptomatic. For example, 50% to 80% of STIs in women have either no symptoms or symptoms that are not easily recognized. Where women's illness is more likely to be asymptomatic, both health service statistics and population-based information tend to be biased unless the latter includes medical or laboratory examinations.

For the GBD study, prevalence of STIs was estimated for each region from a review of the medical literature, restricting the focus to studies in low-risk populations after 1985 (Rowley and Berkley 1998). The duration of infection was estimated using an algorithm incorporating assumptions about the probability the individual is symptomatic and the probability of treatment. A probability mapping of disease to sequelae was created, focusing on the effects of major complications with and without treatment. A number of complications were allocated to other sections of the study (ectopic pregnancy, neonatal pneumonia, low birthweight, infertility). Miscarriage and spontaneous abortions were excluded. By excluding these complications the direct burden of STIs can be only partially estimated.

Rowley and Berkley (1998) raised a number of other concerns and limitations of their study:

• Prevalence was estimated from a literature survey, and thus was limited by the data available. In particular, availability of data varied considerably by region.

• Duration was estimated using average access to health care and did not necessarily take account of different access for men and women.

• Only three pathogens were examined, of the more than forty that are known. Available information was insufficient to include other STIs, although they are known to be linked to adverse outcomes, HIV infection, and premature delivery.

• Estimates of the burden of STIs exclude social and economic consequences, such as those of infertility, which may include anxiety, depression, and abandonment.

Differences in health-seeking behavior (in particular between high- and low-income countries) may also bias data on disease prevalence and incidence. In many low-income countries women use health services less than men. This may be because the burdens of their domestic roles mean that they do not have time to visit health services, because resources required to attend facilities are not available to them, or because of poor interpersonal relations with (often male) health providers.

This can have a significant impact on the validity of epidemiological databases. Significant sex differences were seen in attendance at malaria clinics in Thailand (6:1 in favor of males); yet according to population-based surveys, there were no sex differences in infection rates (Ettling et al. 1989). It is very difficult to estimate the burden associated with unmet health needs.

Men's illness may also be underreported. For example, the focus of public sector primary health care services on maternal and child health-family planning services may discourage men from seeking care. In rural Bangladesh, men with symptoms of STIs were much more likely to use private sources of care, including traditional and less than fully qualified practitioners, and hardly used the public sector infrastructure (Hawkes 1998). Care sought from these providers hardly ever appears as part of routine utilization statistics. In high-income countries, men also tend to use health services less than women.

Underuse of health services may also arise where women feel the services have little to offer. For example, services may not have the capacity or resources to respond to needs for surgery to repair rectovaginal fistulas, so women may not attend them. Population-based surveys may be conducted to detect prevalence of such conditions, but even this approach may not be effective if stigma prevents women from reporting the condition.

Sex Differences in Health Consequences   A number of diseases have different health consequences for men and women. Where these are unknown or unmeasured, sex-specific estimates of disease burden will be biased. There is surprisingly little knowledge of sex differences in the natural history of disease and sequelae. This lack may be due to gender bias in the selection of both research topics and research subjects (Freedman and Maine 1993). Even where women and men are both affected by a particular illness, the tendency is to ignore the potential for differences between them in diagnosis, symptoms, prognosis, and effectiveness of alternative treatments (WHO 1998b). For instance, despite the importance of cardiovascular disease in women's mortality, and evidence of important differences between men and women, nearly all of the most important cohort studies of causes and treatment looked only at men. As a consequence, doctors tend to extrapolate the results to women, even though they have no clinical evidence to support this (Freedman and Maine 1993).

Similarly, women are likely to be excluded from research studies on HIV infection and AIDS, leaving unanswered many questions about biological differences in the effects on men and women (WHO 1998b). Women in both rich and poor countries have a shorter life expectancy after a diagnosis of AIDS, a difference that is attributed to the combination of unequal access to health care, and lack of information about the disease in women (Anastos and Vermund 1993; de Bruyn 1992; Richie 1990 cited in WHO 1998b). It is not clear whether these differences in longevity have been taken into account in the GBD estimates of the burden of HIV infection.

Finally, until recently there has been little study of ways in which sex (and gender) affect tropical disease transmission and risk of infection, recognition, and response to signs of infection, access to health care, and symptoms. Where these differences are recognized, they tend to be restricted to the effects of tropical disease on fertility and pregnancy outcomes (Manderson et al. 1993; Vlassoff and Bonilla 1994). Women tend to have higher antibody responses to malaria (Vlassoff and Bonilla 1994), but immunity is compromised during pregnancy. As a consequence, malaria in pregnancy is associated with abortion, stillbirth, and low birthweight, factors that should be taken into account when evaluating the burden of malaria and its different effects on women and men. Gender biases in medical knowledge may lead to misreporting of the incidence and underestimation of the health impact (and thus the disease burden) of such conditions for women.

Gender Differences in Susceptibility and Responses to Ill Health   Gender roles may influence susceptibility to illness, responses to illlness, and consequences of ill health for well-being. These gender roles and their effects have to be understood to capture true disease burdens. For example, discriminatory practices in the allocation of food occur in South Asia (Jacobson 1993; Chen et al. 1981), and nutritional deficiency is associated with lower immunity and thus greater susceptibility to a range of infectious diseases such as leprosy. The consequences of illness may also differ for women and men because of differential access to and use of health services. In some parts of the world, households spend less on health care for women and girls due to preference for sons (Das Gupta 1987; Chen et al. 1981; Hossain and Glass 1988). Other barriers may include cultural practices that deny women the right to travel alone or to consult male health workers (WHO 1998b).

Even with access to services, care may be insufficiently sensitive to constraints facing women. For example, women may be less likely to benefit from syndromic management of STIs, as they may be unaware of their partner's exposures, or may be more unwilling than men to share this information with a health worker because of confidentiality concerns and fear of social disapproval. They may consequently be more likely to suffer from untreated STIs than men.[9] In addition, because untreated STIs are more likely to become asymptomatic in women, women are likely to suffer more disabling sequelae such as pelvic inflammatory disease and infertility.

Although gender differences in the social consequences of ill health are excluded from the burden of disease calculations, they may influence health outcomes in significant ways. For example, women may suffer greater social consequences of disfiguring illness such as leprosy and lymphatic filariasis. As a result, they may seek care later for fear of stigmatization (WHO 1998b), which may in turn lead to greater disability or disfigurement, as in leprosy (Ulrich et al. 1993).

Women's Health Conditions that Are Excluded Because of Lack of Data

A final broad class of bias arises for the range of women's health conditions where data simply are not available on dimensions, causes, and consequences (WHO 1998b). Many obstetric, gynecological, and contraceptive morbidities are particularly difficult to measure, and as a result have been excluded from estimates of the GBD. For example, whereas bacterial vaginosis is a very common reason for seeking health care among women where STI prevalence is relatively low, no estimates are included in the GBD (Sarah Hawkes, personal communication).

A WHO report listed a range of conditions that should be considered for inclusion in any GBD revisions. These include indirect obstetric complications, such as preexisting conditions aggravated by pregnancy; a range of excluded gynecological morbidities: other STIs, reproductive tract infections, menstrual disorders, female genital mutilation and harmful practices and violence; contraceptive morbidity; psychological morbidity; infertility; morbidities attributable to HIV infection; interlinkages between HIV and STIs; and stillbirths (WHO 1998b).

Problems of the Valuation of Ill Health

Many of the issues discussed could be addressed through improved data-gathering processes, structuring them to be sensitive to sex and gender dimensions. However, a broader set of concerns arises in relation to the methods used to assign values to ill health in the GBD calculations.

Sex Gap in Life Expectancy   In addition to the choice of standard against which losses are measured is the issue of how to treat sex differences in longevity. In most societies women live longer than men. In some countries, notably those of the former Soviet Union, life expectancy at birth is as much as thirteen years greater for women than for men (World Bank 1998b). Women's biological advantage is believed to account for part of this difference: rates of spontaneous abortion and stillbirth are higher for male fetuses in all societies, and excess male mortality persists during the first six months of life (WHO 1998b). Reasons for this may include differences in chromosomal structure, possibly a slower maturing of boys' lungs due to the effects of testosterone (Waldron 1986), and biological protection against ischemic heart disease afforded by endogenous estrogens (WHO 1998b). That part of the difference in longevity that is attributable to biological differences is not (at least at present) amenable to intervention.

However, an important component to sex differentials in life expectancy is socially determined by factors heavily influenced by gender roles. In most countries, social factors reinforce the female biological advantage, with males experiencing greater exposure to risk factors such as smoking and occupational hazards, and higher levels of dangerous behaviors associated with masculine roles that tend to involve risk-taking behavior (WHO 1998b), a process that is itself highly gendered. In contrast, in some countries females (especially girls) are at particular disadvantage in terms of allocations of food, health care and access to education (e.g., South Asia, China).

The health costs of these gender-determined behaviors should be captured in any estimation of the burden of disease. This can be accomplished by using a sex gap in life expectancy that represents an estimate of only the biological component of the sex difference. In constructing DALYs, a sex gap of 2.5 years is used, which is an estimate of the biological gap derived from observed differences in life expectancy among populations with relatively lower exposure to risk factors such as smoking and occupational hazards (Murray 1994). The choice of gap has implications for the estimation of women's disease burden relative to that of men's. If 2.5 years overestimates the real sex difference in life expectancy, the burden of disease of women will be underestimated relative to that of men. The reverse will arise if the true gap is less than 2.5 years (Anand and Hanson 1997).

Valuation of Nonfatal Health States   In calculating the burden of disease, DALYs assign a value of one for premature mortality (before age weighting and discounting). For nonfatal health outcomes, time spent in that health state receives a disability weight ranging between zero and one, which is meant to reflect loss of functioning associated with disabling sequelae.

The approach to estimating disability weights taken in the GBD study was revised after the 1992 estimates (Murray 1996). Where previously groups of experts assigned weights on the basis of descriptors of different levels of functional disability, the new protocol involved the Person Trade-Off (PTO) method[10] in a deliberative process. The protocol was designed to be used with health care providers, who were asked to evaluate "the average individual with the condition described taking into account the average social response or milieu" (Murray 1996).

However, it is not at all clear that (mostly male) health professionals' assessments of disability weights are more valid than, for example, those of individuals who have experienced the health problem or of their family members. Others challenged the use of health professionals' assessments. It is well recognized that different groups (health professionals, patients, patients' families, general public) tend to assess the same health state in different ways (Nord 1992).

Differences between GBD disability weights and weights obtained from forty poor women age seventeen to fifty-four in Phnom Penh, Cambodia, were studied using a visual analogue scale (table 12.6; Sadana 1998). Although strictly speaking, the weights are not directly comparable as they were elicited by different methods, a number of interesting issues emerge. In eight of twelve health states that were common to both studies, women gave higher disability weights. In particular, disorders associated with stigma and shame for women in Cambodia are associated with higher disability weights than those given by Geneva experts. These conditions include infertility and vitiligo. This finding is consistent across age groups, education levels, and type of health problem that the individual was experiencing at the time of the interview. From these findings, it was concluded that it is essential to consider community and population values in resource allocation processes; that it is not surprising that different health state values arise in different contexts; and that improving the validity and reliability of values obtained in such exercises should not be pursued at the expense of suppressing conflict and different perspectives.

Different weightings that Cambodian women attach to different disease conditions raises the question of whether it is meaningful to use the same disability weights for all countries. The need to use a common weighting system derives from the desire to calculate the burden of disease at the global level, and to ensure that differences among regions arise from differences in disease prevalence, incidence, and onset, and not from differences in the valuation of disability states. However, if it can be shown that different societies place very different weights on nonfatal health outcomes, this undermines the validity and meaning of such global

Table 12.6
Comparison of disability weights: Cambodia Reproductive Health Study versus GBD (Sadana 1998)

	Reproductive health study, Cambodia	GBD study, Geneva
HIV infection, AIDS	0.936	
Active psychosis	0.909	0.722
Maternal death	0.906	1 (all deaths)
Blindness	0.818	0.642
Quadriplegia	0.800	0.895
Dementia	0.757	0.762
Deafness	0.696	0.333
Infertility	0.650	0.191
Severe eclampsia	0.647	
Below-the-knee amputation	0.632	0.281
Prolapse	0.604	
Rectovaginal fistula	0.577	0.373
Severe pain during sex	0.567	
Vitiligo on face	0.536	0.020
Fetal death 7 months	0.487	
Severe anemia	0.482	0.111
Unipolar depression	0.451	0.619
PID with symptoms	0.437	
Abortion 3 months, hemorrhage/sepsis	0.419	
Sad, chills, weak postnatal (local condition named toas)	0.416	
No satisfactory contraception	0.390	
Miscarriage 3 months	0.344	
Unable to breastfeed	0.284	
Moderate cramps/low pack pain during period	0.282	
Moderate dizziness	0.187	
Bright skin, regular period, good family relations	0.015	

GBD, global burden of disease; PID, pelvic inflammatory disease.

measures. It suggests that such analyses may more appropriately be made at the regional, country, or subcountry level where there is sufficient agreement on relative weights attached to these health states.

Other Values Incorporated in Construction of DALYs   Two additional values are incorporated in DALYS: discounting and age weighting. Arguments against discounting of life-years are fully presented in Anand and Hanson (1997). From a gender perspective, discounting has the effect of compressing the gender gap in life expectancy, because the additional years lived by women occur in the future, where they receive relatively less weight. This further reduces the estimated sex gap in the burden of disease.

Age weighting assigns a different value to a year of life lost or lived with disability, depending on the age at which it is lived. The specific age-weighting function that is used in DALYs attaches greater value to a year of young or middle-aged life than to a year lived by young children or the elderly. The main justification appears to be based on a notion of welfare interdependence, which "clearly exists as some individuals play a critical role in providing for the well-being of others—consider parents and their young children" (Murray 1996). The same age-weighting function is used for both men and women. However, it is not clear that the welfare transfers implied by the function are actually the same for both sexes. In particular, young girls in many societies have extensive responsibilities for child care and food preparation, and it is not clear that women's responsibilities for the welfare of others decline as they reach old age. The fact that these economic activities of young women are often not marketed reinforces gender bias in the economic paradigm. This casts doubt on the validity of using the same age-weighting function for men and women. In general, arguments in support of age weighting are rather weak (see Anand and Hanson 1997 for a full discussion).

Priority Setting and Cost-Effectiveness Analysis

Most of the recent international health movements (Primary Health Care, Selective PHC, Child Survival and Development Revolution, Safe Motherhood, Better Health through Family Planning) were aimed at reshaping health priorities (Murray 1990). Priority setting in the health sector using principles of cost-effectiveness analysis is not new (Walsh and Warren 1979, Ghana Health Assessment Team 1981, and Walsh 1988 all cited in Murray 1990). However, analyses presented in the World Bank's Disease Priority Review (Jamison et al. 1993) and the 1993 World Development Report significantly raised the profile of these approaches. As a consequence the term priority setting has become almost synonymous with cost-effectiveness analysis to determine the allocation of health sector resources among interventions.

Principles of cost-effectiveness analysis as used with GBD are straightforward. It is assumed that the overriding aim of health services is to minimize the aggregate burden of ill health. Given a fixed health budget, this is accomplished by allocating resources to interventions that provide the maximum health improvement per dollar. This requires a comparison of the costs of an intervention with its consequences in terms of reduction of disease burden (measured as the burden with and without intervention) to produce a cost-effectiveness ratio. Interventions are then ranked by this ratio and resources allocated beginning with the best buy, gradually moving down the list as the benefits of each intervention are exhausted. League tables of cost-effectiveness rankings appear in the 1993 World Development Report, were considered in the Oregon Medicaid reform proposals, and were occasionally discussed in the context of United Kingdom Regional Health Authority health service purchasing (Allen et al. 1989).

Of course, this is only one possible use. Cost-effectiveness analysis can also be used to evaluate different alternatives for prevention and treatment of a particular illness at the individual or program level, or to investigate costs of reaching specific population subgroups.

General Critique of Cost-Effectiveness Approach

The cost-effectiveness framework has a number of general limitations. First, it considers only health benefits of health sector interventions and does not usually look at the health benefits of interventions outside the sector. Thus, even with the narrowly defined objective of burden minimization, the restricted perspective of analysis can lead to sub-optimal resource allocation (Anand and Hanson 1997).

Second, the exercise is neutral to distribution of benefits: preventing ten years of burden for one person is equivalent to averting one year for each of ten people, and a benefit to a rich person is identical to a benefit to a poor one. Minimizing the burden of ill health is purely an efficiency criterion. Whereas equity weights were proposed to accommodate such distributional issues (Kabeer 1994), this would require the incorporation of additional information about individuals, such as income or poverty status. Such variables are strictly not part of the information that is collected as part of the GBD exercise, nor do they usually appear in epidemiological data sets.

Gender Issues

In addition to general limitations of priority setting using cost-effectiveness approaches, a range of gender issues exists.

Estimating the Costs of Treatment   A relatively technical issue is the problem of valuation of the costs of health interventions. Women's time inputs are frequently ignored (Leslie 1989); this may have the effect of orienting health services toward interventions that are particularly demanding in terms of women's time, without full recognition of costs. At the same time, efforts to value such nonmarketed inputs may be more difficult to the extent that gender processes keep women out of formal labor markets (Kabeer 1994).

Interdependent Risks and Vulnerabilities   Certain diseases are risk factors for other diseases. From the disease-measurement point of view, this means that a simple calculation of mortality by immediate cause of death will not reflect a true picture of ill health due to a particular disease. One example is diabetes mellitus, which has its own sequelae, but which is also associated with increased risk of ischemic heart disease and cerebrovascular disease (Murray and Lopez 1996). Interdependence is also important from an intervention point of view, in that prevention of a primary case of diabetes will also prevent other disorders attributable to diabetes. Unless such interdependencies are taken into account, cost-effectiveness analysis will underestimate the benefits from intervention.

The GBD volumes treat a short number of risk factors in this way (tuberculosis, hepatitis B and C, STIs, Chagas disease, onchocerciasis, trachoma, diabetes mellitus, unipolar major depression, glaucoma, cataracts). However, a number of other such interactions, many of which are mediated by gender-related factors, should be taken into account in further work. Undernutrition was mentioned as a gender-related condition that increases the likelihood of contracting a range of infectious diseases. The interaction between HIV infection and malaria is another area requiring further research.

Risk Factors and Gendered Processes That Generate Ill Health   Reduction of disease burden can take the form of preventing and treating the disease itself, or preventing or reducing exposures that may be the underlying cause (Murray and Lopez 1996). Three types of risk factors are distinguished in the GBD study: exposures in the classic epidemiological sense, physiological states, such as hypertension or undernutrition, and social states such as poverty and inequality. Risk factors included in the GBD study all fit into the first two categories. However, data required for a gender analysis of such risk factors are not available, so the epidemiological parameters being estimated ("attributable burden") are likely to be underestimated.

For example, in the absence of data on the relative risk of mortality from undernutrition of adults, only children from birth to age five years were included in estimates of excess mortality and morbidity attributable to undernutrition (Murray and Lopez 1996). Data on occupation-related injuries come primarily from high-income countries (exceptions are Mexico and, for some causes, China), where gender patterns of work may differ substantially from those in low-income countries. Finally, the focus of the disease burden attributable to air pollution is measures of total suspended particulates and sulfur dioxide. Indoor cooking will contribute to observed aggregate levels of these pollutants, but no mechanism exists for recording womens' differential exposure, which arises from their gendered household roles.

Social states as risk factors are not examined.[11] One reason for excluding an analysis of social states as risk factors in the GBD work is that it would almost certainly require going beyond the narrow confines of the health sector and the interventions it alone can deliver. It would require what the current British government calls "joined-up" thinking, involving multisectorial policy initiatives. At a very minimum, this must be based on a broader vision of health policy, rather than the current narrow focus on health services.

Gender issues may also underpin a variety of these and other risk factors. It is necessary to look at how gender roles contribute to the causes of ill health among women (and men). To the extent that such roles are important underlying risks, a focus on health interventions alone is unlikely to produce enduring improvements in health. For example, women may be differently exposed to the risk of contracting a range of diseases by virtue of their domestic responsibilities (water collection and link with schistosomiasis; respiratory problems and indoor smoke from cooking). At the same time, certain gendered patterns of behavior may also protect against infection, such as the requirement to dress in certain ways may reduce the risk of mosquito bites. Women's work outside the house may impose risks for ill health. Nursing is a profession with a predominance of women; however, nurses have high rates of preterm and low-birthweight babies, and factors contributing to these outcomes are well known: standing, lifting, moving heavy loads, and strains of night shifts (Oakley 1994). The point is that with appropriately gender-disaggregated data, it should be possible to measure the health burdens arising from these roles, but the focus on health interventions to minimize this burden will not resolve the fundamental causes of differential exposure to such risks.

These approaches should not be limited to the health of women. The excess burden of male deaths due to accidents and injuries is also traced partly to gender roles. This is true for unintentional injuries such as occupational accidents, as men are employed in more dangerous industries, as well as for intentional injuries, which are closely connected to social constructions of masculine behavior (WHO 1998b). A focus on health interventions as a way to reduce the burden of these events surely takes us far away from its root causes.

Priority-setting approaches, with their biomedical and individualist foundations, cannot adequately address gendered processes that generate ill health. Even the narrowly defined goal—minimizing the burden of disease—cannot be achieved without taking account of gender-related factors. It will not be enough simply to provide an essential package of cost-effective health services if women's access to them is restricted. Priority-setting approaches have to broaden their perspective beyond what services to offer, and incorporate concerns about the gender-related factors that will influence their use. Women's access to health services may be limited by time constraints, issues of intrahousehold resource allocation and decision making, or legal and sociocultural constraints (Oxaal and Cook 1998).

If the goal of health service planning is broadened to include equity considerations, limitations of the cost-effectiveness approach become even more pronounced. Improving health equity may require specific efforts to focus on measures that will achieve health gains for disadvantaged groups; a simple efficiency criterion will not suffice. This raises two different issues. First, additional information is required to identify those who are relatively disadvantaged, and not just in health terms. And second, more focus is required on the processes that underlie poor health: this will almost certainly involve reaching beyond the limits of biomedical individualism (Fee and Krieger 1993) looking at the social and historical forces generating disadvantage, and looking beyond the individual to the level of groups.

Summary

Burden of disease measurement and priority setting are powerful tools for supporting decision making in the health sector. They make explicit a number of value choices that were often obscured in previous attempts to shift priorities. However, they continue to be opaque in a number of areas, and create room for gender bias.

Gender bias may arise in three broad areas. The first concerns issues relating to the availability of data, in particular accurate measures of disease incidence or prevalence, for men and women. These are problems that could, in practice, be resolved with adequate sensitivity to the potential for gender bias and sufficient resources devoted to collection of data.

The second set of problems relates to issues that are subject to continued debate and cannot be fixed by technical solutions. These include an appropriate concept of burden and choice of whose values should be used to assign burden .weights for nonfatal illness.

Finally, some fundamental problems are associated with cost-effectiveness analysis as a tool for priority setting in the health sector. First, although analytically convenient, it is not clear that the same indicator (DALYs) should be used for both measuring disease burden and resource allocating resources to minimize that burden, as this ignores important equity concerns in health sector resource allocation. For example, in measuring the aggregate burden of disease it may be desirable to use the minimal information set of DALYs (age, sex, disability status, time period). However, if an objective of resource allocation is to improve health equity, we have to know about other characteristics of individuals who are ill, including their disadvantages in other spaces, such as income or broader measures of socioeconomic status, and their access to health and other public services.

A second problem with the GBD priority-setting approach is its focus on individual outcomes and health interventions. If allocation of resources is to improve health and health equity, it has to address the processes that generate ill health and influence access to health care resources. Some of these are gendered processes, and others relate to broader structures of inequality and disadvantage.

These concerns point to two areas of action for those involved with gender and health equity. First, within the broad GBD approach, it is necessary to collect better data about women's and men's health. This means that more effort must be expended to investigate disease prevalence and incidence; to support research that examines the consequences of ill health for women and identify where these differ from the consequences for men; to identify and explore interactions among different diseases; and to ensure that the range of stakeholders involved in valuing nonfatal health outcomes is as broad as possible. Second, a broader effort is required to improve the measurement of women's health, rather than disease. A closer dialogue between experts in women's health and experts in disease measurement and health economics must take place to integrate ideas and concepts relating to health measurement that have been developed in parallel. Such an effort should be sensitive to uses that will be made of such data, particularly in planning health services. This might imply disentangling issues of activities that promote health versus those that treat disease. It also has to be sensitive to differences in health consequences and burdens across settings, and to grapple with some of the thornier issues of what burden to measure and how it should be valued. For instance, more attention could be paid to the particular burdens of women as caretakers of people who are ill.

The GBD study provides a rich source of information on mortality and morbidity in both high- and low-income regions of the world. It is a potentially powerful tool for women's health advocates in mobilizing for reallocation of health resources. However, effort is necessary to strengthen its conceptual and technical basis to make it more sensitive to issues of gender and health, so that its value as a tool for health sector analysis can be increased.

Notes

1. For helpful suggestions and ideas, I thank Charlotte Watts, Patrick Vaughan, Sarah Hawkes, and Sarah Cook. Extremely useful comments on early drafts were provided by Asha George, Piroska Östlin, and Gita Sen. Kara Hanson is employed by the Health Economics and Financing Program at LSHTM, which is funded by the United Kingdom Department for International Development (DFID). The views expressed are those of the author and do not necessarily reflect DFID policy.

2. This desire to aggregate across different health states may be misguided: death and disability may simply be incommensurable, and not be put on the same scale at all (Anand and Hanson 1997).

3. Estimates of the global burden of disease in 1999 are published in the World Health Report (WHO 2000), and summary tables are also available at http://www.who.int/whr/2000/en/statistics.htm. At the time the final manuscript was being prepared, DALY figures disaggregated by sex were not available to update the tables.

4. I am grateful to Patrick Vaughan for discussions on this issue.

5. The advantage of using a life-table approach, which incorporates expectation of life at each age (rather than, for example, potential years of life lost, which fixes the maximum at an arbitrary limit) is that in populations where life expectancy at birth exceeds this standard, life expectancy at any age (particularly ages over 80 for men and 82.5 for women) will still be positive, allowing some shortfall from perfect health to be captured.

6. The ICIDH classification defines impairment at the level of the organ system, disability as the impact on the individual's performance, and handicap as the overall consequences of the disease, which depends on the social environment.

The example given in Murray (1994) is helpful in clarifying the distinctions between the three: ". . . the loss of a finger or an eye is an impairment. The consequent disability may be the loss of fine motor function or sight . . . the loss of fine motor function may be a greater handicap, in this terminology, for a concert violinist than for a bank-teller."

7. Although Murray (1996) noted that the method for eliciting disability weights probably results in ratings that correspond to the average level of handicap.

8. In the GBD, infertility is included as a sequela of Chlamydia infection, gonorrhea, maternal sepsis, and abortion. It receives a disability weight of 0.180.

9. I am grateful to Patrick Vaughan for pointing out this gender difference.

10. One form of PTO asks participants to trade off life extension of healthy individuals and life extension of individuals in a given health state; for example, taking the perspective of a decision maker, would you prefer to purchase interventions that will provide one year of life for 1000 perfectly healthy individuals or 2000 blind individuals? The second form asks participants to trade off between raising the quality of life of those in a given health state (state i) to perfect health for one year and extending life for healthy individuals for one year. Both forms arrive at preference weights for the health state being considered (Murray 1996).

11. Risk factors studied are malnutrition, poor water supply, sanitation and personal and domestic hygiene practices, unsafe sex, tobacco, alcohol, occupation, hypertension, physical inactivity, illicit drugs, and air pollution.

13

Frameworks for Understanding Health Sector Reform

Hilary Standing

What Does Health Sector Reform Mean?

Health sector reform is a moving target. In many countries the health sector has constantly undergone change (Kutzin 1995). However, in its more recent sense, it has become associated with a particular set of policy prescriptions focused on institutional and financial reforms. In regions where donor influence is particularly strong, such as sub-Saharan Africa, where donors fund much of the health sector recurrent costs, most countries have health sector reform programs in place.

It is clear from international experience that the concept of health sector reform has very different meanings in different national and regional contexts. Many financial and political drivers are the same, but options adopted vary from country to country and region to region. For instance, reform has a quite different flavor in the Americas than in sub-Saharan Africa. This reflects partly the objectively different conditions in the two continents, and partly the degree to which reform is donor driven. But it means also that the issues raised for gender equity are not the same everywhere.

For instance, health sector reform in the Americas is focused strongly on two types of institutional change: decentralization and reform of social security systems. These are taking place in the context of relatively strong states. There is also a thriving civil society and basis for negotiating citizen participation, including very strong women's advocacy groups active in health issues in many countries. In sub-Saharan Africa, on the other hand, reforms are taking place against a background of severe crisis in health sector budgets, weak state capacity to manage and regulate the health sector in sustainable and equitable ways, and limited civil society involvement. Reforms there heavily emphasize different financing mechanisms, the role of the private sector, and improvement of human resource management.

Health sector reform is also embedded in larger macroeconomic and political shifts that took place over the 1980s and 1990s. This in turn affects ways in which gender issues were related to the reforms. Much of the relatively small amount of policy-relevant work on gender that relates directly to international health policy concentrated not on the health sector itself but on consequences of structural adjustment for women's health and well-being and for gender inequalities. This discussion begins, therefore, with the chronology of reforms in, or affecting, the health sector. The chronology encompasses structural adjustment programs, the Bamako Initiative, health sector reforms, and sector-wide approaches (SWAps). Gender issues are configured in different ways at different chronologic moments (table 13.1). Like all chronologies this is

Table 13.1
Chronology of institutional and financial reforms

Policies on or influencing health sector	Macroeconomic-political climate	Institutional points of articulation
Structural adjustment programs early 1980s on	Economic crisis, neoliberal responses, "state failures"	IMF, World Bank
Bamako initiative 1987	Crisis in health sector spending, need to protect the most vulnerable	UNICEF, WHO, African health ministers
Health sector reform late 1980s-early 1990s	Public sector reform and governance, efficiency-effectiveness agenda, controlling government expenditure	World development report 1993, U.S. and U.K. health reforms
Sectorwide approaches 1997 on	Development assistance as "partnership" with national governments, defining priorities within a sound macroeconomic and institutional framework	WHO, European bilaterals, World Bank (Sector Investment Programs)

not very nuanced but it makes it possible to trace some important debates in relation to gender and health.

Gender and Health in the Context of Various Reforms

Structural Adjustment Programs

In the area of health reforms, gender analysts have paid the most attention to structural adjustment programs (SAPs; Afshar and Dennis 1992). This is perhaps not surprising, as the package of measures national governments are required to implement includes major demand restraint elements. One aim of adjustment policies is to reduce public expenditure. In the public sector, real wages have been held down or cut and subsidies on, for example, essential goods such as foodstuffs have been removed or reduced. Much of the critique of structural adjustment, therefore, focuses on its impact on the social sector, which is heavily dependent on public financing.

Gender analysts are particularly critical of structural adjustment programs, locating them as the cause of the deteriorating state of the health and education sectors of adjusting countries. According to Stewart (1992), there were "significant falls in real expenditure per head in these sectors in about two thirds of the countries of sub-Saharan Africa and Latin America in the early 1980s." Real health expenditure in Jamaica is said to have fallen by 20% between 1980–1985, and by 22% in Zambia between 1982–1986 (Stewart 1992). These cuts, directly attributable to SAPs, were concentrated on nonwage recurrent and capital expenditure. As up to 80% of health budgets is spent on salaries, this means that services, maintenance, equipment, and facilities are severely hit.

These cuts affect women particularly in two ways. First, women are biological reproducers, and any deterioration in provision of reproductive health services affects them disproportionately. Second, women carry out the bulk of the tasks of social reproduction: caring for children and dependents and managing the care of sick family members. This is especially relevant in two contexts. One is the increasing burden of care in areas with high levels of human immunodeficiency virus (HIV) infections. The other is where the demographic transition is placing greater demands on households for managing the consequences of aging. Reductions in health sector expenditure have major knock-on effects for the informal care economy, which is largely managed by women.

The debate on structural adjustment is complex and has led to well-defended but opposing orthodoxies. Partly at issue is how to assign cause and effect in the general crisis enveloping many developing countries in the early 1980s, especially sub-Saharan Africa. Whereas gender analysts on the whole saw SAPs as directly responsible, others suggested that there are deeper problems. For instance, World Bank economists Van der Gaag and Barham (1998) stated that it was the effects of existing unsustainable economic policies, rather than the SAPs themselves, that produced the crisis in the social sector. These policies included high levels of borrowing that created major burdens of debt servicing, high rates of public expenditure on military hardware, and maintaining loss-making state enterprises. They take issue with critics of SAPs, contending that evidence shows that real per capita expenditure in the social sector did not decline under SAPs.

Serious methodological issues must be disentangled on both sides. A particular problem is measurement. For instance, Van der Gaag and Barham used highly aggregated data mainly at national level as evidence for their case. Feminists and gender analysts were more inclined to use experience on the ground from users and service providers at the sharp end of declining services. Also, whereas real per capita expenditure may not have fallen in adjusting countries, in many countries it has not risen either. This has negative consequences when one takes into account rising needs and depreciation of existing infrastructure. Furthermore in health, as noted, costs are relatively fixed, with salary costs making up the bulk of sector expenditure. Therefore any increase in the total salary budget will squeeze all other costs. Effectively, this means that social sector expenditure is reduced.

What is not in doubt is the severity of the crisis in many low-income countries. Health facilities are often in a chronic state of disrepair and essential equipment is missing or broken. Service quality is frequently poor and many facilities lack health staff. Users increasingly rely on an unregulated market of providers with few or no checks on competence. The costs of health care, particularly for the poor, are very high. In a number of countries in sub-Saharan Africa, the burden of HIV infection is placing intolerable strains on existing health infrastructure.

The crisis produced two important but related lines of critique and policy concern in relation to gender equity and health in the context of structural adjustment. First, a substantive critique focused on the adverse impact of public expenditure cuts on women (and also children), particularly the decline in social sector spending (Stewart 1992; Whiteford 1993; Vlassof 1994). Second, feminist economists drew attention to adverse policy consequences of hidden conceptual bias in economic theories underpinning structural adjustment. Represented as gender neutral, they are in fact gender blind in disregarding nonmarket work carried out substantially by women (Elson 1992; Palmer 1992). The economic crisis and the increasing interconnectedness of the world economy (globalization) are reshaping the relationships among markets, states, and households, as well as that between market and nonmarket spheres (Sen 1996).

Health Implications Commentaries on the effects of SAPs on health outcomes drew attention to both direct and indirect effects on women. In terms of direct effects, most attention was paid to (hypothesized) effects of user charges for health care and deterioration in the quality of services after cuts in health sector budgets. Better-documented examples relate to maternity care. In a number of countries, there appear to have been increases in home deliveries and delays in seeking care, leading to worse maternal and infant outcomes (Kutzin 1995; Ekwempu et al. 1990; Stewart 1992).

A wide range of probable indirect effects on women's and children's health was described. Falling real incomes in poor households, which were linked to SAPs, may disproportionately affect women as they are often concentrated in the poorer percentiles of the population. Removal of food subsidies, for instance, the price of the staple maize meal doubled in Zambia, would have particularly affected nutritional intake in poor urban households (Stewart 1992).

Health effects associated with increasing poverty in adjusting economies may include rises in the incidence of communicable diseases, worsening infant and child mortality rates, and increases in the proportion of low-birthweight babies (Antrobus 1988, cited in Whiteford 1993). In the Dominican Republic, although it did not produce a large-scale increase in mortality, the economic crisis did reverse a previous upward trend in health improvement manifest in such indicators as maternal and infant mortality (Whiteford 1993).

Also noted as a significant gendered impact of SAPs is the effect on women's work burdens brought about by reductions in social sector support. Women are generally the main household carers and informal producers of health care. For example, reductions in length of affordable inpatient stays, and avoidance of hospital care and increases in self-treatment over treatment by service providers tend to impose greater time and labor costs on women (Leslie 1992).

Gender Issues   SAPs stimulated a major critique by feminist economists of the pervasive conceptual bias in the language and tools of economics. Elson (1992) noted the way in which orthodox economics ignores the sexual division of labor, women's unpaid household labor, and relationships between paid and unpaid work. This has serious policy repercussions in two areas. First, in sub-Saharan African countries, where women are major food producers, neglect of trade-offs that women producers make between market and nonmarket sectors has major implications for policies to promote greater production for the market. For instance, a Zambian woman explained that she had missed the whole planting season because she had to accompany a family member to hospital and take care of the person (Evans and Young 1988, cited in Elson 1992).

Second, not counting of (mainly) women's household and community-based unremunerated work led to ill-thought-out prescriptions for more decentralization of responsibilities for health and community development activities to communities (Elson 1992). This was done on the assumption that women are an underoccupied workforce who will just pick up the extra burden.

One conceptual critique of economic approaches to adjustment emphasized economic inefficiencies resulting from not taking gender into account in planning adjustment programs (Palmer 1992). SAPs represent a disinvestment in human capital, which creates a reproduction tax on women through withdrawal of social sector investment. This in turn influences the way time and resources are allocated, reducing women's remunerative activities with associated effects on household-level incomes and on macroeconomic policies. Women are more vulnerable to these than men as they are more heavily represented among the poor.

Feminist commentators thus generally saw SAPs as associated with poor outcomes for women's health and well-being. However, the debate was heavily characterized by assumptions from first principles rather than by empirical evidence, and was stronger on critique than policy options (Vlassof 1993; Whiteford 1993). Issues raised mainly concerned what kinds of distributional policies would protect women against the worst consequences of such programs. Examples are special measures to target women and poor households through tax and subsidy systems, such as special social funds (Marquette 1997).

Approaches for promoting equity through targeting have limitations (Gilson 1998). Among other things, they entail a technocratic approach that does not take sufficient account of the social and political contexts within which policies are delivered. Sen (1996) provides a conceptual framework and research agenda that poses wider questions about the link between women's well-being and economic transformation. She notes the importance of strengthening regulatory roles of states and of civil society organizations in monitoring adverse gender effects.

The Bamako Initiative

The Bamako initiative was largely a crisis response to plummeting public sector budgets and increasing failure of basic health service delivery in the 1980s in much of sub-Saharan Africa. It originated in a meeting of African health ministers, together with UN caring agencies in Bamako, Mali, in 1987. It has since been implemented in a number of east and west African countries. The initiative stressed the need to protect the health of women and children, which is most vulnerable to economic shocks. Its recommendations addressed particularly the issue of drug shortages through the development of revolving drug funds to support the purchase and distribution of regular supplies. The development of community-based health financing schemes was emphasized, together with the need for greater community participation in the health sector. Although confined to Africa, this is an important precursor of what then becomes labeled health sector reform.

Gender Issues   It is difficult to assess the outcome of the Bamako initiative from a policy point of view, as reviews of outcomes looked at impact on the poor as a general category, without disaggregating by gender. The general finding was that the initiative improved matters for most rural poor but did little for the very poorest (Gilson 1998).

Mechanisms through which the Bamako initiative is supposed to operate raise two main concerns with respect to gender and health. The first relates to wider concerns that were expressed in the context of the child survival revolution spearheaded by UNICEF. Several components, such as oral rehydration and immunization, are highly dependent on women's time for their realization (Leslie 1992). Yet the time burden is rarely factored into policy considerations in the area of child health. This is highlighted in a review of the impact of the first four years of the Bamako initiative on maternal and child health services by the following comment:

Mothers are a key target group as they are the ones who invariably bring children to the health services, and as such their health knowledge, attitudes and practices, especially at home, need to be aggressively addressed. (Jarret and Ofosu-Amaah 1992)

This kind of stance ignores both the competing demands on women's time from productive as well as reproductive activities, and the more contextual question of whether mothers always have the most influence over health practices.

The second concern was raised specifically in the context of the Bamako initiative. The main mechanism of community participation was local level health committees. Experience of these suggests that they tend to be bureaucratic rather than participatory structures, set up at the behest of governments and international agencies. One review of the impact of the initiative on five countries noted that women were virtually absent from local health committees, despite emphasis on promoting the health of women and children (McPake et al. 1993). From a gender perspective, therefore, community participation looks like an increase in health-related time burdens for women and lack of voice in related decision-making processes.

Health Sector Reform

Health sector reform became the dominant theme some time during the late 1980s. It was associated with a set of activities and objectives being implemented in high- and low-income countries and across the political spectrum, and addressed in particular financing, resource allocation, and management issues. Health reforms in the United Kingdom were particularly influential, especially the move to general management rather than clinician-led decision making, and the separation of purchasing from providing functions in health care.

Reform is therefore an amalgam of a number of regional and international trends and is a response to the following structural problems (Nabarro and Cassels 1994)

• The need to place limits on health sector expenditure and use resources in a more efficient and effective way. Examples are the persistent bias to tertiary care, poor accountability and monitoring of expenditure, rigidity in resource use, poor cost effectiveness in the public sector, and poor systems management.

• Failure of service delivery access, particularly in relation to the poor, and despite the rhetoric of primary health care.

• Poor quality of services in many countries as a result of poor human resources management, lack of incentives to improve public services, and poor treatment of users.

To this could be added:

• Increasing acknowledgment of the substantial role of the nonpublic sector in providing health care, (such as private practice, pharmacies, NGOs, and indigenous practitioners, and the need to take account of this in health sector planning.

A number of classic statements of health sector reform (Berman 1993; Cassels 1995) particularly emphasize it as a process of institutional reform. It involves redefining the relationships between sets of institutional actors involving the state, service providers, other health-related organizations such as hospital boards, health insurance providers, and users. Reform can therefore be seen as an amalgamation of both economic efficiency and public sector–good governance international agendas. Elements, particularly those concerned with controlling health sector expenditure, relate to economic crisis and structural adjustment policies. Other elements, particularly those connected to public sector and institutional reform, are related to governance issues and the role of the state as the overall regulatory body.

Despite continual protestations from those who write that the prescriptions of reform must be context sensitive, it has become associated with a particular menu. These components are noted below in the context of the gender implications that they raise.

Gender Issues   Standing (1997) attempts to consider each agenda component in terms of both potential impact and implications for women's health inequalities in both consumption and production of health. She includes the otherwise neglected dimension of women as formal producers of health care. Some key issues are summarized here.

Many countries are attempting to tackle human resource issues in the health sector. Civil service reform aspects are aimed at improving the efficiency of human resources by reducing numbers, reworking terms and conditions, changing skill mix, and improving monitoring of performance. On the whole, little attention has been paid to gender. However, the health sector workforce is very female, particularly in nursing and in some areas of community health staffing. This raises issues of equal opportunities. If reforms are not sensitive to the gender composition of the workforce, women health workers may be inadvertently disadvantaged if, for example, retrenchment is concentrated in their sectors.

As important, disregard of the gender dimensions creates inefficiencies. It is assumed that women and men employees respond to the same incentives and that prevailing male patterns of work and career structures are appropriate to both sexes. Evidence on the ground suggests that such assumptions should be rethought and that human resource management would be more effective if made more sensitive to gender issues (Standing 2000b).

Health sector reform has been concerned with improving the functioning of health ministries by developing more effective financial and management systems and defining cost-effective interventions, such as minimum basic packages. A key issue is whether techniques used for priority setting and monitoring, such as cost-effectiveness analysis, can incorporate gender equity concerns within their methodologies. For example, disability-adjusted life-years (DALYs) were criticized for taking a very narrow view of health outputs. They measure disease burdens only, excluding the process of care as well as its quality dimensions

(Zwi and Mills 1995). Informal care burdens borne disproportionately by women are invisible in current mainstream forms of measurement (Hanson 1999)

Decentralization is a key plank of many health sector reform programs, entailing the devolution of management and service provision to district or other local bodies. It raises some big questions about the balance between central (national) and local decision making and resource allocation. If district-level or community-based management structures make allocational decisions that result in worsening gender equity, what if any mechanisms are available to attempt to redress the balance?

We still know little about the gender impacts of decentralization. However, the question was explored from the point of view of effects on reproductive health services (Aitken 1998). Commitments by governments to the 1994 Cairo agenda implied significant changes to the way services are delivered. Under decentralization, national policies often failed to be implemented locally either because budgets were not allocated at local level, or because implementing agents disapproved of a policy and did not carry it out. This was particularly the case with minority services such as management of incomplete abortions and sexual health services for adolescents. Conservative attitudes can be powerfully expressed and legitimated where implementation depends on local will.

Health sector reform programs particularly involved developing new financing and cost-recovery options, such as user fees, community financing schemes, insurance, and vouchers. Most concern focused on the impact of user fees on women's access to care. This is a continuation of the structural adjustment–economic crisis critique. However, very few hard data are available mainly because few studies of the impact of user charges provided gender-disaggregated data.

Broadening health financing options raises three main gender issues:

• Are women more disadvantaged by particular modes of payment (or are they better able to manage some modes over others)?

• Does cost recovery, particularly levying user charges at point of delivery, have an adverse effect on women's health?

• How do different types of cost recovery affect access to services by gender?

Evidence on each issue is anecdotal. Factors that influence the capacity of women to pay directly for health services, or indirectly through different kinds of prepayment schemes, include access to an independent cash income and control over its use, the extent to which households discriminate in favor of males/senior members in health expenditure, and employment patterns. Where health benefits are dependent on the social wage, women can lose out because their employment histories may be fragmented due to domestic responsibilities.

Studies of the impact of user charges tended to focus on the poor, with no disaggregation by gender. Most evidence on the impact of user charges on women's health comes from sub-Saharan Africa in the 1980s. For example, when user charges were introduced in Nigeria, maternal deaths in the Zaria region rose by 56%, along with a decline of 46% in the number of deliveries in the main hospital (Ekwempu et al. 1990). Use of maternal and child health services in Zimbabwe in the early 1990s declined when user charges were more strongly enforced (Kutzin 1995).

As noted, access to services is strongly influenced by gender. Concern about cost recovery focused mainly on household-level capacity and willingness to pay for health care. Yet evidence suggests that important gender differences exist in household health expenditures (Beall 1995). According to a survey of household expenditure in Zambia, expenditure on health care for women was less than one-third of that on men. This finding is not replicated everywhere, but it is a significant issue in some contexts, such as south Asia.

It could be maintained that user charges must be seen as part of a broader question of how services are funded nationally and how financing strategies affect women and men differently. Increasingly, in poor and even middle-income countries, the same segmentation of populations emerges in terms of how health care needs are met. Formal sector workers tend to be covered by public or private insurance, the moderately poor may have access to basic health insurance or community financing, and the very poor are targeted for microcredit and funds for catastrophic illness. Each of these has specific gender implications, but in the context of broader gender equity issues, women will be disproportionately represented in the third category, given the prevailing distribution of poverty.

Reform programs also promoted working with the private sector, creating competition between providers and establishing regulatory and health service contracting-out systems. Again, we have little hard evidence on the gender impact, if any, of attempts to develop regulatory and contracting mechanisms for working with the nongovernment sector. One less-considered issue is the role of this sector in providing preventive services. Many low-income countries have a strong bias toward curative services and drug sales. This is particularly strong in the private sector, as providers' incomes tend to be dependent on these. Can the private sector be harnessed in support of preventive health services? Arguably, such services are of particular importance to women. As major providers of informal health care, women absorb much of the burden of environmental health problems.

Studies of private sector provision suggest that significant barriers must be overcome if this is to happen (Uplekar 2000). Whereas private sector practitioners are often preferred because of their proximity, convenience, and often more friendly attitudes, clinical standards are frequently erratic. A public health ethos is largely absent, and strong regulatory regimes and accompanying incentives would be required to change this. More has to be done to test what services could appropriately be contracted to private providers and how incentives on, for example, reaching minority groups could be incorporated into contracts.

Sector-Wide Approaches

SWAps are a coordinated approach by donors to health sector funding in which donors relinquish specific project funding in return for a voice in the development of the national sectoral strategy as a whole (Cassels 1997; Walt et al. 1999). They represent a continuation of several elements of the classic health sector reform agenda, notably reforming health management systems and ministries of health, and setting clear priorities for the public sector. They also represent a significant shift in some aspects of donor thinking in relation to reform.

The first shift is in the acknowledgment of the importance of national ownership of reforms and thus of the pivotal role of governments in these processes (World Bank 1997; Evans and Moore 1998). A second shift is from the wholly supply-driven agenda to concern with the demand side and whether institutional reforms actually improve access to health care and health outcomes for the poor. A third shift is in emphasis on involving a wider range of stakeholders in negotiating strategic plans for the health sector. These include NGOs, the private sector, and groups in civil society.

A gap exists between rhetoric and operational experience, as SWAps are relatively new and experience of their implementation is limited. However, they represent an accelerating trend in donor funding in the health sector. They are currently sector focused, but it is likely that the future will see moves toward multisectoral funding, allowing for enlargement of the traditional scope of the health sector.

Gender Issues   As SWAps are quite new, evidence on their gender impact is also limited. The first examination of them from a gender point of view stated that gender-aware health sector programs are more cost effective than ones that do not take gender into account, so gender should be mainstreamed at all policy levels (Elson and Evers 1998).

The authors noted two particular concerns with the way SWAps are formulated. The first is continuing lack of recognition in policy and planning of women's unpaid reproductive work in the health care economy. The second is the way in which program monitoring continues to stress more easily quantifiable indicators of institutional performance (e.g., how many people were trained?), rather than the kinds of qualitative indicators that are necessary to assess the gender impact of reforms (e.g., quality of care in health facilities).

Case studies of SWAps are beginning to appear.[1] The only one to focus on gender looked at the experience in Bangladesh (Evers and Kroon 2000). Quite serious efforts were made to integrate gender issues into the design of the SWAp. This did not prove easy and raised some key points. First, gender specialists involved in the SWAp themselves had to switch from a microlevel approach to a more institutional and macrounderstanding of how gender bias operates in sector and other institutions, and how it influences, for instance, health sector budgets and patterns of resource allocation. Second, and closely related to this, is the need to move from seeing gender issues as narrowly about service delivery to poor women, to a broader concept of gender and reform. Areas such as human resources issues, where women form a major part of the low-status, low-paid health workforce, and their lack of decision-making power in organizations proved much more difficult to put on the agenda. Third was lack of leadership for gender both nationally and among donors. This highlights the need for organizational support to develop gender analysis and planning capacity, and the importance of having an institutional focus for work on these issues, not simply a commitment in principle.

A further key issue relates to the need and potential for incorporating women as stakeholder voices in the policy process. It remains to be seen whether the promise of such involvement can be borne out in practice, or whether SWAps will remain an essentially bureaucratic negotiation between donors and governments. There is also the question of which stakeholders are able to obtain a place at the table. Who will speak for (which) women, and with what kind of accountability?

Despite recognition of the importance of demand side issues, SWAps continue to be heavily focused on the supply side (Foster 1999). More attention is still required on issues such as health-seeking behavior and the views of the poor themselves. The management information system in Bangladesh now takes into account views of community stakeholders with gender expertise, resulting in recording of women's violence-related injuries (Evers and Kroon 2000).

Conceptual, Empirical, and Methodological Issues

Conceptual Problems

Debates about gender and health policy contain a minefield of difficult issues. The literature describes various problems of conceptual confusion, conceptual adequacy, and conceptual hegemony. The health sector reform literature is particularly prone to conceptual confusion. In its characterization of human behavior, it tends to veer between the neoliberal and the sociologically heroic. For example, debates about incentives for improving health worker performance rest on instrumental (and ungendered) assumptions about the relationship between individual behavior and incentives. Evidence suggests that financial reward is not the only motivator of employees and that men and women may also value different kinds of incentives (Standing 1997). At the same time, heavy stress is placed on devolving greater responsibilities onto communities, with corresponding assumptions about their collective altruism. In responding with a more gendered analysis it is important to watch out for these underlying conceptual biases.

Debates express conceptual inadequacy particularly in relation to limited conceptualization of the nonmarket sphere and of links between market and nonmarket. Given the significant role played by households, familial, and other nonmarket relations in the production and consumption of health, failure to bring these more fully into the analysis of the health sector is serious (Bloom and Standing 1999).

Development of a serious discourse around gender and health generated both greater conceptual sophistication and some tendency to conceptual hegemony. One standard distinction is between impact on women approaches and gendered approaches. Gender is the preferred term for a range of conceptually respectable reasons; it is both relational and can encompass masculinity and men's health issues. This resulted in the proponents of a gender and health analysis tending to appropriate the conceptual high ground for themselves.

But it is important to recognize that gender actually stands for quite an eclectic conceptual mix and that this is not necessarily a bad thing. We must avoid the temptation of seeing the discourse as unified or asserting that there is one correct way of doing gender analysis. For example, both Ingrid Palmer and Diane Elson offer a gender analysis of the health sector, but the former pursues a neoclassical approach to gender equity and the latter gives an institutional one.

The distinction between impact on women and gender impact is more complex than conceptual hegemony allows for. Discussions about health effects on women may position women in a number of ways:

• As more likely to be part of the poorest (hence, policy issues relate to antipoverty strategies, safety nets, etc.)

• As epidemiologically more vulnerable (policy issues relate to access to appropriate health services)

• As socially burdened through responsibility for children, the elderly, the sick, and so on (policy issues relate to unintended effects of interventions in increasing care burdens)

Similarly, gender approaches can encompass:

• Social and structural gender inequalities in access to services (policy issues relate to improving access for the disadvantaged gender)

• Addressing men's health profiles and behaviors as well as women's (policy issues relate to addressing power issues in sexual relations, appropriate interventions for reaching men)

• Redressing male bias in institutions and in policy formulation (policy issues relate to mainstreaming gender at the institutional level)

Although there is an understandable demand for simple formulas and tools for gender analysis, we do a disservice to planners struggling to understand gender if we present it as more conceptually unified than it is.

Problems of Evidence

Substantiated argument in both gender and international health policy is seriously lacking. Proponents of particular stances on the role of the market or the state neglect analytical insights from political economy (Reich 1994). In the case of gender, the tendency is to fall back on first principles (women suffer greater ill health than men) or global generalizations (men have greater access to formal health care than women), or to write prescriptively (health sector reform policies should . . . , etc.).

There are two main predisposing factors for this. First, gender disaggregated data in the health sector continues to be lacking *at the level where it is needed.* That is, many countries have some routine disaggregation, often at facilities level, but they make little or no use of it for policy purposes and it is difficult to excavate for research. Second, the appropriate questions are not being asked before research is carried out. Discussions thus tend to take place retrospectively, questions raised remain rhetorical, and debate is often conducted at an exclusively normative level.

Methodological Problems

These are also closely linked to the problem of evidence, and what counts as evidence. But there are also some obvious methodological traps that gender analysis should strive to avoid.

First, much of the debate is conducted at too high a level of abstraction for substantive gender issues to be meaningfully inserted into policy debate. Debates about women's access to health care have to go beyond assertions of gender disadvantage and examine *which* women, in *which contexts* suffer disadvantage, and *what desired policy outcomes* should follow?

Second, a great deal of facile extrapolation is made from a limited range of case studies. Randomly selected studies widely separated in time and space, employing different methodologies, and with no quality controls, are put together and a pattern is forced out of them. This makes it all too easy to select cases that suit the thesis and not seek out counter cases.

Third, health commentators have a strong disposition to make one case study stand for a universal relationship, especially where it fits the commentator's agenda. A study in Jamaica commissioned by the World Bank found no health or social sector disadvantage among children living in female-headed households (Louat et al. 1993). This became the basis for a new orthodoxy asserting that female-headed households are a poor predictor of poverty. However, this form of false generalization is also unfortunately encountered in gender analysis too, with substantive evidence of gender disadvantage in one context being translated into a gender universal.

Fourth, insufficient attention is paid to other variables interacting with gender, such as poverty, ethnicity, and age. More multivariate analysis is necessary. For example, a study of age and gender in patterns of illness revealed a significant relationship between the two variables (Collier 1993). Data were reproduced from a survey of households in rural Tanzania, collected in 1983, designed to identify which groups in the population were most prone to illness. Just using gender alone, the survey found that 18.1% of men were ill during the reference period, compared with 19.4% of women. However, when age and symptom severity variables were added in, a strong gender effect was found. Women age sixteen to forty-nine were 33% more likely to be ill than men of the same age group, and 43% more likely to suffer from fever, diarrhea, and vomiting. Men, on the other hand, were more likely to suffer from pulmonary illnesses (probably as a consequence of smoking). These findings clearly have significant public health implications.

Developing a Conceptual-Policy Framework for Gender and Health Sector Reform

What might a framework for incorporating gender issues into health reform policies look like? Work on this is relatively new, but broadly, two main ways might push the debate forward. Of these, only gender mainstreaming has been developed to any significant extent. Like all frameworks, they have both advantages and limitations. The aim is not to suggest that one is preferable to the other but rather to explore the implications of two somewhat different ways of conceptualizing gender issues in the context of the health sector.

Gender Mainstreaming

Gender mainstreaming is the major institutional response by national donors and international organizations to perceived gender inequities in the development process. We can understand what this means in several ways. It broadly refers to a move from women-specific projects and organizational responses to one of integrating gender concerns into funded activities, as well as at all levels of the organization's staff and functions (Razavi and Miller 1995). Some of the impetus for mainstreaming came through U.N. World Conferences on Women, such as resolutions from the 1995 Beijing conference. It it has also an increasingly important theme among multilateral and bilateral agencies.

The health sector has not figured either prominently or substantively in the debate about mainstreaming until recently. Now, however, agencies such as WHO are beginning to develop approach. A number of bilateral donors have mainstreaming policies that relate specifically to the health sector (CIDA 1996; DANIDA 1996). The most comprehensive attempt is the work of Elson and Evers (1998) on defining gender-aware policies for sector program support. Whereas its particular focus is on sector-wide approaches, the analysis has general relevance to gender mainstreaming in health policy.

A macro-meso-micro framework was employed to examine issues that a national policy framework should address. From this, a comprehensive checklist was developed for a gender-sensitive national sector framework (Elson and Evers 1998). At macrolevel it includes incorporating households and disaggregated gender-age information into planning, sensitizing planning tools in relation to the role of unpaid reproductive labor, assessing the gender balance of personnel in key strategic and financial roles, and assessing institutional capacity in gender planning. At the meso-level, it includes assessing gender balance in health sector employment, identifying stakeholders to ensure that women's voices are represented, and assessing gender differences in access to services. At the microlevel, it involves examining access to resources and decision making within households, and determining whether households operate in ways that impede access to resources by gender.

This framework enables gender issues to be factored in at several levels simultaneously and appropriate actions to be proposed at each level. It can ensure that gender-aware indicators are incorporated into monitoring and evaluation and highlight the need to develop gender-sensitive training for health care providers.

Such a framework has considerable advantages. Gender issues are not marginalized. It provides a systematic way of addressing key gender issues in epidemiology, service provision, and employment. It also has some limitations as it can become very mechanistic. Gender is assumed always to occupy the same analytical space, possibly to the detriment of examining other serious forms of social disadvantage, such as class and race. It predisposes to checklist management, ticking off issues without serious commitment to their substance. It is probably ineffective unless senior bureaucrats have existing commitment and ownership. Although it addresses stakeholder interests, it does so from an essentially bureaucratic stance.

Developing Contextual-Situational Frameworks

The impetus for thinking about this arose partly with dissatisfaction with gender mainstreaming approaches, particularly those noted above. It seems vital, given the complex nature of health as a social good, to embed gender more firmly within other sets of social relations, such as class, households, and generation. But it was also stimulated by concern over the ways in which a particular health sector reform menu is now a universal technical prescription for the diverse problems of the health sectors of low-income and transitional countries. Health sector reform is not one agenda, but many agendas that are tied to different political economies, including the level of state capacity and the role played by external agents such as donors.

In much of sub-Saharan Africa suffering prolonged economic crisis, the emphasis has been on how to deliver minimal basic health services through means such as basic health packages and locally administered revolving drug funds. There has also been emphasis on decentralization, but in the context of weak state capability. Regardless of much talk of private sector involvement, the reality is a very weak private sector and severely limited capacity to contract in and regulate it. In many Latin American countries, on the other hand, one main focus has been on financing reforms and reform of social security systems to bring in more private sector involvement. The private sector plays a strong role. The other major focus has been on decentralization in the context of reasonably strong state capability. This meant quite high levels of stakeholder involvement, including a strong women's health movement. These different profiles mean that gender issues and priorities have to be contextualized rather than assumed to be similar across all reforming countries.

One challenge is that gender is part of a complex nexus of actions and behaviors taking place within some kind of household arrangement. And households themselves exist within a wider political and social economy of differentiation. Gender is thus more to the fore in some kinds of decisions than others, but it is also linked intrinsically to time and generational dynamics of households, and to the household level of security. Feminist analysis rightly emphasized the need to disaggregate the household, to look inside it, and to understand the ways in which gender is a powerful principle in determining a hierarchy of resources and entitlements. Hitherto, health sector reform has paid little attention to the demand side, but if it is to deliver anything to those who need it most, it will have to address these dynamics.

This is also a plea for reaggregating the household in terms of acknowledging its critical role as a socioeconomic and cultural mediator of health decision making. In particular, decisions made at this level often reflect more fundamental concerns to manage risk and secure the economic and social viability of households over the short, medium, and long term (for a related but analytically different take on the household, see Berman et al. 1994). In talking about households, this does not imply that they should be seen as structured in the same way. Households come in diverse forms and carry different meanings. But the key point is that people generally live in entities culturally defined as households.

Gender analysis thus has at its heart something of a paradox in relation to equity debates. It is a principle extrapolated from the wider social arena, as we can talk about gender relations as analytically separable from other kinds of social relations. For example, emphasis on disaggregating gender relations within the household enables us to ask questions about gender inequalities in consumption of health resources. At the same time, gender relations are also embedded in those same social relations, and gender finds its expression within household and other relations. Given this interdependence, how do we address the dynamics of household-level choices to give nutrition or health treatment preference to a male earner in the context of thinking about equity? How distinct in practice are the interests of poor women and poor men in relation to their mutual interests in household survival?

What this implies is that rather than starting from a view that gender carries the same significance in all contexts, this approach would attempt to analyze gender and health issues within wider decision-making units, such as households, and in the temporal dynamics of health decision making. The empirical significance of gender will therefore depend on two things. First, it will reflect the particular configurations of gender relations in a given context and their intersection with other key markers of inequality (age, class, etc.). Second, it has to be set against the background of what is happening in the health sector itself, for instance, problems of access to services will not be equally significant everywhere. The matrix (table 13.2) is only suggestive of the kind of analysis that might be undertaken. The contents of columns 3 and 4, and to some extent 2, are context specific.

Part of the aim of developing a more contextualized framework for gender analysis and health is to move away from bureaucratic approaches to gender mainstreaming. However, this brings its own problems. There are two prerequisites for developing such a framework. One is to commission a situational analysis to inform policy making, as opposed to acting on cheaper and quicker off-the-shelf assumptions about the rela-

Table 13.2
Contextual-situational matrix for gender and health policy

1 Household, temporal perspective	2 Actions related to this	3 Policy level	4 Gender issues, priorities
Short term	Treatment, advice-seeking behavior for acute illness	Access to services, availability of appropriate and affordable service providers, regulation of provider competence, drug availability, etc.	e.g., Can women access services when and where they need them, and can they afford them? Do they have information necessary to obtain treatment for themselves, family members?
Medium term	Preventive health-seeking behaviors: antenatal care, vaccinations, clean water and sanitation; managing risk such as from serious or long-term illness	Public health interventions, cost-recovery mechanisms, insurance schemes, fiscal measures, safety nets, microcredit, schemes for improving women's entitlements	e.g., Burden of infectious diseases on carers; gender inequalities in household and employment financial entitlements
Long term	Investing in education of specific children, nutrition of main earners–potential earners	Cross-sectoral, social sector support strategies, safety nets, gender targeting: getting and keeping girls in school	e.g., Culturally sanctioned discrimination against women, girls

tionship of gender, health, and equity. The second is a commitment to stakeholder and participatory approaches to determining people's needs. This is an inherently messy business as it entails negotiating a way through competing claims and finding a way for less privileged voices to be heard. As a process, it is thus more complex to operationalize.

However, as a process, it has considerable potential for brokering between planners and planned for, as the following example might illustrate. Considerable attention is paid to the possible impact on women's time burdens of policy interventions in the health sector. Debate about this, however, remains at the level of a critique. It is not at all clear what should follow from this critique. Should any intervention that might affect women's time be lobbied against? What has rarely been asked is how women themselves experience these demands. Do they see them as burdensome? What kinds of trade-offs do they think are acceptable and what other kinds of support might be appropriately given? Unless these questions are asked of those on the receiving end, we run the risk of creating well-meant but mechanistic prescriptions that bear only a contingent relationship to people's realities.

Summary

Gender and health issues have been raised by gender analysts in the context of a range of approaches to reforming the health sector. The lines of analysis draw attention to various policy dimensions. In particular, gender critiques of structural adjustment programs and economic crisis noted both direct and indirect effects of social sector expenditure cuts on women's health and caring burdens, and the pervasive conceptual bias in economics that causes women's unpaid productive and reproductive work to be discounted.

Gender analysis of health sector reform programs stresses the importance of understanding women's role as both producers and consumers of health care, of identifying inequalities in health resources and health needs between women and men, and of ways in which institutional reforms can have gender implications. In examining these implications of sectorwide approaches, analysts propose taking a gender mainstreaming approach to policy development, and incorporating women's voices as stakeholders in the policy process.

A number of methodological issues have policy implications. A pervasive problem is lack of sufficient gender-disaggregated data, as is the need to improve health information systems to take account of this. It is necessary to get away from stating generalities and be more specific in policy discourse about which women and in which contexts. The importance of factoring in variables that intersect with gender, such as age, class, and race, is also emphasized.

More provocatively, a challenge is made to bureaucratic approaches to gender mainstreaming. This requires a more context-sensitive approach to bringing gender issues into policy analysis. This analysis has to move away from the presumption that gender always has the same significance in all contexts to a more empirically informed approach. This approach would pay closer attention to household-level dynamics and the interests of both women and men in maintaining household viability over time. Policy analysis therefore must look at the ways in which households respond to or are likely to be affected by institutional and financial reforms in the light of their short-, medium-, and long-term management of health risks. Gender will be variously significant in these dynamics.

For this kind of policy analysis to be carried out, a shift must be made from bureaucratic approaches to mainstreaming based on checklists of issues, to one that engages actively with stakeholders in households and communities. This means more use of participatory and other qualitative approaches to understanding demand-side behavior, and greater willingness to develop political engagement with civil society stakeholders and advocacy groups in planning the health sector.

Note

1. A recent issue of *Health Policy and Planning* (Walt et al. 1999) was devoted to SWAps. However, none of the studies touched on gender issues.

References

Abas, M. A. and J. C. Broadhead. 1997. Depression and anxiety among women in an urban setting in Zimbabwe. *Psychological Medicine* 27: 59–71.

Abbot, J. and R. Johnson. 1995. Domestic violence against women. Incidence and prevalence in an emergency department population. *Journal of the American Medical Association* 273(22): 1763–1767.

Abed, F. H. 1999. *The BRAC Story: Development and Change in Bangladesh.* David E. Bell Lecture. Cambridge: Harvard Center for Population and Development Studies.

Abeyesekera, J. D. A. and H. Shahnavaz. 1988. Ergonomic aspects of personal protective equipment: Its use in industrially developing countries. *Journal of Human Ecology* 17(1): 67–69.

AbouZahr, C. 1998. Maternal mortality overview. In *Health Dimensions of Sex and Reproduction,* eds. C. J. L. Murray and A. D. Lopez. Boston: Harvard School of Public Health on behalf of the World Health Organization and the World Bank.

AbouZahr, C. and E. Ahman. 1998. Unsafe abortion and ectopic pregnancy. In *Health Dimensions of Sex and Reproduction,* eds. C. J. L. Murray and A. D. Lopez. Boston: Harvard School of Public Health on behalf of the World Health Organization and the World Bank.

AbouZahr, C. and P. Vaughan. 2000. Assessing the burden of sexual and reproductive ill-health. *Bulletin of the World Health Organization* 78(5): 655–666.

Abrahamsen, R. 1997. Gender Dimensions of AIDS in Zambia. *Journal of Gender Studies* 6(2): 177–189.

Acierno, R., Resnick, H. S., and D. G. Kilpatrick. 1997. Health impact of interpersonal violence. 1. Prevalence rates, case identification, and risk factors for sexual assault, physical assault, and domestic violence in men and women. *Behavioral Medicine* 23: 53–64.

Adler, N. E., Boyce, T., Chesney, M. A., Cohen, S., Folkman, S., Kahn, R. L., and S. L. Syme. 1994. Socioeconomic status and health. The challenge of the gradient. *American Psychologist* 49(1): 15–24.

Afshar, H. and C. Dennis. 1992. *Women and Adjustment Policies in the Third World*. Basingstoke: Macmillan.

AHCPR. 1992. *Minorities: Health Insurance Coverage*. Intramural research highlights 10. Rockville, MD: Association for Health Care Policy and Research.

Ahlborg, G., Bodin, L., and C. Hogstedt. 1990. Heavy lifting during pregnancy: A hazard to the fetus? A prospective study. *International Journal of Epidemiology* 9(1): 90–97.

Ahonsi, B. 1999. Reproductive health programming response to the feminization of poverty associated with economic globalization in Nigeria. Paper for the Ford Foundation, New York.

Ahonsi, B. and A. Odaga. 2000. Partnership Case Study: Nigeria. Paper prepared for the Ford Foundation, New York.

Aitken, I. 1998. Implications of decentralization as a reform strategy for the implementation of reproductive health programs. Report of the meeting on the implications of health sector reform on reproductive health and rights. Washington, DC: Center for Health and Gender Equity and the Population Council.

Alan Guttmacher Institute. 1999. *Sharing Responsibility: Women, Society and Abortion Worldwide*. New York: Alan Guttmacher Institute.

Albelda, R. 1985. "Nice work if you can get it": Segmentation of white and black women workers in the post-war period. *Review of Radical Political Economics* 17(3): 72–85.

Albers, P. and N. Breen. 1996. Gender parity and American Indian reservations. *Race, Gender and Class* 3(2): 75–95.

Alderete, E. W. 1999. *Health of Indigenous Peoples* (WHO/SDE/HSD/99.1). Geneva: World Health Organization.

Alfredsson, L., Spetz, C-L., and T. Theorell. 1985. Type of occupation and near-future hospitalization for myocardial infarction and some other diagnoses. *International Journal of Epidemiology* 14: 378–388.

Allen, D., Lee, R. H., and K. Lowson. 1989. The use of QALYs in health service planning. *International Journal of Health Planning and Management* 4: 261–273.

Allen, L. M., Nelson, C. J., Rouhbakhsh, P., Scifres, S. I., Greene, R. L., Kordinak, S. T., Davis, L. J. Jr., and R. M. Morse. 1998. Gender differences in factor structure of the self administered alcoholism screening test. *Journal of Clinical Psychology* 54: 439–445.

Alvesson, M. and Y. D. Billing. 1997. *Understanding Gender and Organisations*. London: Sage.

American Medical Association on Scientific Affairs. 1992. Violence against women: Relevance for medical practitioners. *Journal of the American Medical Association* 267: 3184–3189.

Amick, B. C., Levine, S., Tarlov, A. R., and D. C. Walsh. 1995. *Society and Health*. New York: Oxford University Press.

Amott, T. L. and J. A. Matthaei. 1991. *Race, Gender and Work—A Multicultural Economic History of Women in the United States.* Boston: South End Press.

Anand, S. and K. Hanson. 1997. Disability-adjusted life years: A critical review. *Journal of Health Economics* 16: 685–702.

Anand, S. and K. Hanson. 1998. DALYs: Efficiency versus equity. *World Development* 26(2): 307–310.

Anastos, K. and S. Vermund. 1993. Epidemiology and natural history. In *Until the Cure: Caring for Women with HIV,* ed. A. Kurth. London and New Haven: Yale University Press.

Anderson, M. 1992. The history of women and the history of statistics. *Journal of Women's History* 4(1): 14–36.

Angell, M. 2000. The pharmaceutical industry—To whom is it accountable? *New England Journal of Medicine* 342: 1902–1904.

Aniansson, A., Zetterberg, C., Hedberg, M., and K. G. Henriksson. 1984. Impaired muscle function with aging. A background factor in the incidence of fractures of the proximal end of the femur. *Clinical Orthopaedics* 191: 193–201.

Anker, R. 1998. *Gender and Jobs: Sex Segregation of Occupations in the World.* Geneva: International Labour Organization.

Annandale, E. and K. Hunt. 2000. Gender inequalities in health: Research at the crossroads. In *Gender Inequalities in Health,* eds. E. Annandale and K. Hunt. Buckingham: Open University Press.

Ansar Ahmed, S., Hissong, B. D., Verthelyi, D., Donner, K., Becker, K., and E. Karpuzoglu-Sahin. 1999. Gender and risk of autoimmune disease: Possible role of estrogenic compounds. *Environmental Health Perspectives* 107(S5): 681–686.

Antonovsky, A. 1967. Social class, life expectancy and overall mortality. *Milbank Memorial Fund Quarterly* 45(2): 31–73.

Antrobus, P. quoted by Safa, H. I. 1988. Women and the debt crisis in the Caribbean. Draft used with permission of the author.

Arber, S. 1997. Comparing inequalities in women's and men's health: Britain in the 1990s. *Social Science and Medicine* 44(6): 773–787.

Arber, S. 2000. Gender differences in social support in relation to health and disability in later life. Presentation at workshop on gender analysis of health. Geneva: World Health Organization.

Arber, S. and H. Cooper. 1999. Gender difference is health in later life: The new paradox? *Social Science and Medicine* 48(1): 61–76.

Arber, S. and J. Ginn. 1991. *Gender and Later Life: A Sociological Analysis of Resources and Constraints.* London: Sage.

Arber, S. and H. Thomas. 2000. From women's health to a gender analysis of health. In *Comparative Medical Sociology,* ed. W. C. Cockerham. Oxford: Blackwell.

Arnesen, T. and E. Nord. 1999. The value of DALY life: Problems with ethics and validity of disability-adjusted life years. *British Medical Journal* 319: 1423–1425.

Arnold, D., ed. 1988. *Imperial Medicine and Indigenous Societies.* Manchester: Manchester University Press.

Arnold, D., ed. 1996. *Warm Climates and Western Medicine.* Amsterdam and Atlanta: Editions Rodopi B.V.

Ashton, J., ed. 1992. *Healthy Cities.* Buckingham: Open University Press.

Aspray, T. J., Prentice, A., and T. J. Cole. 1995. The bone mineral content of weight-bearing bones is influenced by the ratio of sitting to standing height in elderly Gambian women. *Bone* 17(3): 261–263.

Aspray, T. J., Prentice, A., Cole, T. J., Sawo, Y., and J. Reeve. 1996. Low bone mineral content is common but osteoporotic fractures are rare in elderly rural Gambian women. *Journal of Bone and Mineral Research* 11(7): 1019–1025.

Astbury, J. 1996. *Crazy for You: The Making of Women's Madness.* Melbourne: Oxford University Press.

Astbury, J. 1999. *Gender and Mental Health.* Working paper 99.18. Cambridge: Harvard Center for Population and Development Studies.

ASTHA. 1998. *Voices from the Roots of the Grass. Impact of SAP and the New Economic Policy on the Poor in Rajasthan (A Study: First Phase).* Rajasthan, India: Astha.

Austin, J. B. and J. Dankwort. 1999. The impact of a batterers' program on battered women. *Violence Against Women* 5: 25–42.

Avotri, J. Y. and V. Walters. 1999. You just look at our work and see if you have any freedom on earth: Ghanaian women's accounts of their work and their health. *Social Science and Medicine* 48: 1123–1133.

Awasthi, R., Gupte, M., Sinha, R., Morankar, S. N., Sonak, S., and S. Pungaliya. 1993. *Strengthening Health Education Services. An Action Research Study.* Pune, India: Foundation for Research in Community Health.

Baca Zinn, M. and B. Thornton Dill. 1998. Theorizing difference from multiracial feminism. In *Women, Culture and Society: A Reader,* eds. B. J. Balliet and P. McDaniel. New York: Norton.

Backlund, E., Sorlie, P. D., and N. J. Johnson. 1996. The shape of the relationship between income and mortality in the United States. *Annals of Epidemiology* 6(1): 12–20.

Baden, S. 1993. *Gender and Adjustment in Sub-Saharan Africa.* BRIDGE Report 8. Brighton: Institute of Development Studies.

Bailey, J. E., Kellermann, A. L., Somes, G. W., Banton, J. G., Rivara, F. P., and N. P. Rushford. 1997. Risk factors for violent death of women in the home. *Archives of Internal Medicine* 157(7): 777–782.

Balasubrahmanyan, V. 1987. Women and the burden of child health. *Economic and Political Weekly* February 28: 363–364.

Balfour, A. and H. Scott. 1924. *Health Problems of the Empire, Past, Present and Future.* London: W. Collins.

Ballard-Barbash, R., Taplin, S. H., Yankaskas, B. C., Ernster, V. L., Rosenberg, R. D., Carney, P. A., Barlow, W. E., Geller, B. M., Kerlikowske, K., and B. K. Edwards. 1997. Breast cancer surveillance consortium: A national mammography screening and outcomes database. *American Journal of Roentgenology* 169: 1001–1008.

Bandarage, A. 1997. *Women, Population and Global Crisis.* London: Zed.

Bang, R. A., Bang, A. T., Baitule, M., Choudhary, Y., Sarmukkadam, S., and O. Tale. 1989. High prevalence of gynaecological diseases in rural Indian women. *Lancet* 1(8629): 85–88.

Bangser, M. 2000. Reproductive health in Tanzania post-ICPD. In *Promoting Reproductive Health: Investing in Health for Development,* eds. S. Forman and R. Ghosh. Boulder, CO: Lynne Rienner.

Barker, C. and A. Green. 1996. Opening the debate on DALYs. *Health Policy and Planning* 11(2): 179–183.

Barker, G. 1999. Working with adolescent boys: A review of international literature and a survey of programs working with adolescent boys in health and health promotion. Unpublished manuscript prepared for the World Health Organization.

Barnett, R. and G. Baruch. 1987. Social roles, gender and psychological distress. In *Gender and Stress,* eds. R. Barnett, L. Biener, and G. Baruch. New York: Free Press.

Batliwala, S., Anitha, B. K., Gurumurthy, A., and C. S. Wali. 1998. *Status of Rural Women in Karnataka.* Bangalore: National Institute of Advanced Studies.

Bayne-Smith, M. 1996. Health and women of color: A contextual overview. In *Race, Gender, and Health,* ed. M. Bayne-Smith. London: Sage.

Beaglehole, R. 1999. Mama, listen! Raising a child without violence: A handbook for teen parents. Los Angeles.

Beall, J. 1995. In sickness and in health: Engendering health policy for development. *Third World Planning Review* 17(2): 213–222.

Behera, D., Dash, S., and S. P. Yadav. 1991. Carboxyhaemoglobin in women exposed to different cooking fuels. *Thorax* 46: 344–346.

Behrman, J. 1980. *Tropical Diseases: Response of Pharmaceutical Companies.* Washington, DC: American Enterprise Institute for Public Policy Research.

Beil, E. 1992. Miscarriage: The influence of selected variables on impact. *Women and Therapy* 12: 161–173.

Bejerot, E. and A. Härenstam. 1995. To combine paid work and family. In *On the Way to Healthy Work,* ed. G. Westlander. Solna: National Institute of Working Life [in Swedish].

Belle, D. 1990. Poverty and women's mental health. *American Psychologist* 45: 385–389.

Ben Salem, B. and K. J. Beattie. 1996. *Facilitative Supervision: A Vital Link in Quality Reproductive Health Service Delivery.* AVSC working paper 10. New York: EngenderHealth.

Bennett, S. and V. R. Muraleedharan. 2000. New public management and health care in third world. *Economic and Political Weekly* January 8–14.

Berer, M. 1993. *Women and HIV/AIDS: An International Resource Book.* London: Pandora.

Berer, M. 2000. Making abortions safe: A matter of good public health policy and practice. *Bulletin of the World Health Organization* 78(5): 580–592.

Berger, M. 1989. Giving women credit: The strengths and limitations of credit as a tool for alleviating poverty. *World Development* 17(7): 1017–1032.

Bergman, B. and B. Brismar. 1991. Suicide attempts by battered wives. *Acta Psychiatrica Scandinavica* 83: 380–384.

Berkley, S. 1998. Unsafe sex as a risk factor. In *Health Dimensions of Sex and Reproduction,* eds. C. J. L. Murray and A. D. Lopez. Boston: Harvard School of Public Health on behalf of the World Health Organization and the World Bank.

Berkman, L. F. and S. L. Syme. 1979. Social networks, host resistance, and mortality: A nine year follow up study of Alameda County residents. *American Journal of Epidemiology* 109: 186–204.

Berkman, L. F. and L. Breslow. 1983. *Health and Ways of Living: The Alameda County Study.* New York: Oxford University Press.

Berman, P. 1993. Health sector reform: Framing the issues. Paper presented at the conference on health sector reform in developing countries: Issues for the 1990s, Department of Population and Public Health, Durham, NH, September 10–13.

Berman, P. 1995. Financing of rural health care in India: Estimates of the resources available and their distribution. Paper prepared for International Workshop on Health Insurance in India. Bangalore, September 20–22.

Berman, P. 2000. Organization of ambulatory care provision: A critical determinant of health system performance in developing countries. *Bulletin of the World Health Organization* 78(6): 791–801.

Berman, P., Kendall, C., and K. Bhattacharyya. 1994. The household production of health: Integrating social science perspectives on micro-level health determinants. *Social Science and Medicine* 38(2): 205–215.

Bertell, R. 1999. Environmental influences on the health of children. In *Risk, Health and Environment,* ed. M. E. Butter. Nongovernmental organization background document for the Third Ministerial Conference on Environment and Health and parallel Healthy Planet Forum. London, June 16–18. Groningen: Science Shop for Biology, University of Groningen.

Bhatia, J. C. and J. Cleland. 1995. Self reported symptoms of gynecological morbidity and their treatment in south India. *Studies in Family Planning* 26(4): 203–216.

Bhatia, J. C., Cleland, J., Bhagavan, L., and N. S. Rao. 1997. Levels and determinants of gynecological morbidity in a district of south India. *Studies in Family Planning* 28(2): 94–103.

Bhatia, M. and A. Mills. 1997. Contracting out of dietary services by public hospitals in Bombay. In *Private Health Providers in Developing Countries: Serving in Public Interest?*, eds. S. Bennett, B. McPake, and A. Mills. London: Zed.

Bhuiya, A. and S. Ansary. 1998. Status of health and health equity in Bangladesh. Report prepared for the Global Health Equity Initiative meeting, Dhaka, December 11–17.

Bidwai, P. 1995. One step forward, many steps back. Dismemberment of India's national drug policy. *Development Dialogue* 1: 193–222.

Bigsby, R., Chapin, R. E., Daston, G. P., Davis, B. J., Gorski, J., Earl Gray, L., Howdeshell, K. L., Zoeller, R. T., and F. S. vom Saal. 1999. Evaluating the effects of endocrine disruptors on endocrine function during development. *Environmental Health Perspectives* 107(Suppl 4): 613–618.

Bird, H. A. and J. Hill. 1992. Repetitive strain disorder: Towards diagnostic criteria. *Annals of the Rheumatic Diseases* 51: 974–977.

Bisgrove, E. Z. and B. M. Popkin. 1996. Does women's work improve their nutrition: Evidence from the urban Philippines. *Social Science and Medicine* 40: 1475–1488.

Black, D., Cummings, S., and D. Karpf. 1996. Randomised trial of effect of alendronate on risk of fracture in women with existing vertebral fractures. *Lancet* 7(348): 1535–1541.

Blackburn, J. and J. Holland. 1998. *Who Changes?: Institutionalizing Participation in Development*. London: Intermediate Technology Publications.

Blake, S. M., Klepp, K. I., Pechacek, T. F., Folsom, A. R., Luepker, R. V., Jacobs, D. R., and M. B. Mittelmark. 1989. Differences in smoking cessation strategies between men and women. *Addictive Behavior* 14(4): 409–418.

Blanc, A. K., Wolff, B. N., Gage, A. J., Ezeh, A. C., Neema, S., and J. Ssekamatte-Ssebuliba. 1996. *Negotiating Reproductive Outcomes in Uganda*. Kampala: Institute of Statistics and Applied Economics; Calverton, MD: Macro International.

Blane, D., Brunner, E., and R. Wilkinson. 1996. The evolution of public health policy: An anglocentric view of the last fifty years. 1996. In *Health and Social Organization: Towards a Health Policy for the 21st Century,* eds. D. Blane, E. Brunner, and R. Wilkinson. New York: Routledge.

Blau, F. D. and M. A. Ferber. 1986. *The Economics of Women, Men, and Work*. Englewood Cliffs, NJ: Prentice-Hall.

Blau, F. D., Simpson, P., and D. Anderson. 1998. Continuing progress? Trends in occupational segregation in the United States over the 1970s and 1980s. *Feminist Economics* 4(3): 29–71.

Blehar, M. C. and D. A. Oren. 1995. Women's increased vulnerability to mood disorders: Integrating psychobiology and epidemiology. *Depression* 3: 3–12.

Blendon, R. J., Aiken, L. H., Freeman, H. E., and C. R. Corey. 1989. Access to medical care for black and white Americans: A matter of continuing concern. *Journal of the American Medical Association* 261(2): 278–281.

Bloom, G. 1997. *Primary Health Care Meets the Market: Lessons from China and Vietnam.* IDS working paper 53. Brighton: Institute of Development Studies.

Bloom, G. and H. Standing. 1999. Meeting health needs in contexts of social change: Pluralism and marketisation in the health sector. Paper for the social policy conference, Institute of Development Studies, Brighton, October 28–29.

Bloom, G. and A. Wilkes, eds. 1997. Health in transition: Reforming China's rural health services. *IDS Bulletin* 28(1).

Bloom, G., Lucas, H., Edun, A., Lenneiye, M., and J. Milimo. 2000. *Health and Poverty in Sub-Saharan Africa.* IDS working paper 103. Brighton: Institute of Development Studies.

Blumel, D. K. et al. 1993. *Who Pays? The Economic Costs of Violence against Women.* Queensland, Australia: Women's Policy Unit, Office of the Cabinet.

Bongaarts, J. and J. Bruce. 1996. The causes of unmet need for contraception and the social content of services. *Studies in Family Planning* 26(2): 57–75.

Bonjour, J. P., Burckhardt, P., Dambacher, M., Kraenzlin, M. E., and C. Wimpfheimer. 1997. Epidemiology of osteoporosis. *Schweizerische Medizinische Wochenschrift* 127(16): 659–667 [in German].

Booth, B. and M. Verma. 1992. Decreased access to medical care for girls in Punjab, India: The roles of age, religion and distance. *American Journal of Public Health* 82: 1155–1157.

Bott, S. 2000. Unwanted pregnancy and induced abortion among adolescents in developing countries: Findings from WHO case studies. In *Sexual and Reproductive Health: Recent advances, future directions,* eds. C. O. Puri and P. F. A. Van Look. New Delhi: New Age Limited. Vol. 1.

Bowling, A. 1995. *Measuring Disease.* Buckingham and Philadelphia: Open University Press.

Boyer, D. and D. Fine. 1992. Sexual abuse as a factor in adolescent pregnancy and child maltreatment. *Family Planning Perspectives* 24(1): 4–11.

Brabant, C. 1992. Heat exposure standards and women's work: Equitable or debatable? *Women's Health* 18(3): 49–65.

Brabin, B. J. 1991. *The Risks and Severity of Malaria in Pregnant Women.* Applied field research in malaria report 2. UNDP/World Bank/WHO Special Program for Research and Training in Tropical Diseases. Geneva: World Health Organization.

Bracke, P. 2000. The three year persistence of depressive symptoms in men and women. *Social Science and Medicine* 51: 51–64.

Bradley, C. 1988. Wife-beating in Papua New Guinea: Is it a problem? *Papua New Guinea Medical Journal* 31: 257–268.

Bradley, H. 1989. *Men's Work, Women's Work.* Cambridge: Polity Press.

Breen, N. 2000. *Social Class and Health. Understanding Gender and Its Interaction with Other Social Determinants.* Working paper 00.03. Cambridge: Harvard Center for Population and Development Studies.

Breen, N. and J. B. Figueroa. 1996. Stage of breast and cervical cancer diagnosis in disadvantaged neighborhoods: A prevention policy perspective. *American Journal of Preventive Medicine* 12(5): 319–326.

Breen, N., Kessler, L. G., and M. L. Brown. 1996. Breast cancer control among the underserved: An overview. *Breast Cancer Research and Treatment* 40: 105–115.

Breen, N., Wesley, M. N., Merrill, R. M., and K. Johnson. 1999. The relationship of socio-economic status and access to minimum expected therapy among female breast cancer patients in the National Cancer Institute black-white cancer survival study. *Ethnicity and Disease* 9: 111–125.

Brisson, C., Vinet, A., and M. Vezina. 1989. Disability among female garment workers. A comparison with a national sample. *Scandinavian Journal of Work and Environmental Health* 15(5): 323–328.

Broadhead, J. C. and M. A. Abas. 1998. Life events, difficulties and depression among women in an urban setting in Zimbabwe. *Psychological Medicine* 28: 29–38.

Brock, K. 1999. It's not only wealth that matters, it's peace of mind too: A review of participatory work on poverty and ill being. Paper for the Institute of Development Studies, Brighton.

Broom, D. 1986. Occupational health among houseworkers. *Australian Feminist Studies* 2: 15–33.

Brown, G. and T. Harris. 1978. *Social Origins of Depression: A Study of Psychiatric Disorder in Women.* London: Tavistock.

Brown, G. W. 1998. Genetic and population perspectives on life events and depression. *Social Psychiatry and Psychiatric Epidemiology* 33: 363–372.

Brown, G. W., Harris, T. O., and C. Hepworth. 1995. Loss and depression: A patient and non-patient comparison. *Psychological Medicine* 25: 7–21.

Brown, G. W., Harris, T. O., and M. J. Eales. 1996. Social factors and comorbidity of depressive and anxiety disorders. *British Journal of Psychiatry* 168(Suppl 30): 50–57.

Bru, E., Mykletun, R. J., and S. Svebak. 1994. Assessment of musculoskeletal and other health complaints in female hospital staff. *Applied Ergonomics* 25(2): 101–105.

Brunette, M. and R. E. Drake. 1998. Gender differences in homeless persons with schizophrenia and substance abuse. *Community Mental Health Journal* 34: 627–642.

Bullard, R. D. 1999. Dismantling environmental racism in the USA. *Local Environment* 4(1): 5–19.

Bullock, L. and J. McFarlane. 1989. The battering low-birthweight connection. *American Journal of Nursing* 89: 1153–1155.

Burdekin, B. 1993. *Report of the National Inquiry into the Human Rights of People with Mental Illness.* Canberra: Australian Government Publishing Service.

Burdorf, A. 1992. Exposure assessment of risk factors for disorders of the back in occupational epidemiology. *Scandinavian Journal of Work and Environmental Health* 18(1): 1–9.

Bureau of Labor Statistics. 1999. URL: bls.gov: CPS labor force statistics, specified as follows: Employment and unemployment. Access to historical data for the "A" tables of the employment situation release. Black and white women age 20 years and older (not seasonally adjusted) all years. Washington, DC: U.S. Department of Labor.

Burns, R. B., McCarthy, E. P., Freund, K. M., Marwill, S. L., Shwartz, M., Ash, A., and M. A. Moskowitz. 1996. Black women receive less mammography even with similar use of primary care. *Annals of Internal Medicine* 125(3): 173–182.

Butter, M. E., ed. 1999a. *Sustainable Development and Women's Health.* Groningen: Science Shop for Biology, University of Groningen.

Butter, M. E., ed. 1999b. *Risk, Health and Environment.* Nongovernment organization background document for the Third Ministerial Conference on Environment and Health and parallel Healthy Planet Forum. London, June 16–18. Groningen: Science Shop for Biology, University of Groningen.

Byrne, C. A., Resnick, H. S., Kilpatrick, D. G., Best, C. L., and B. E. Saunders. 1999. The socioeconomic impact of interpersonal violence on women. *Journal of Consulting and Clinical Psychology* 67: 362–366.

Caldwell, J., ed. 1996. The international conference on population and development, Cairo 1994. Is its *Plan of Action* important, desirable, feasible? *Health Transition Review* 6: 71–122.

Caldwell, J. C., Findley, S. E., Caldwell, P., Santow, G., Cosford, W., Braid, J., and D. Broers-Freeman, eds. 1990. What we know about health transition: The cultural, social and behavioural determinants of health. *Health Transition Series 2,* Vols. 1 and 2. Canberra: Australian National University.

Callahan, E. J., Bertakis, K. D., Azari R., Helms, L. J., Robbins, J., and J. Miller. 1997. Depression in primary care: Patient factors that influence recognition. *Family Medicine* 29: 172–176.

Campbell, C. A. 1995. Male gender roles and sexuality: Implications for women's AIDS risk and prevention. *Social Science and Medicine* 41(2): 197–210.

Campbell, J. C. 1985. Beating of wives: A cross-cultural perspective. *Victimology* 10: 174–185.

Campbell, J. C., Kub, J. E., and L. Rose. 1996. Depression in battered women. *Journal of the American Women's Association* 51(3): 106–110.

Canadian Panel on Violence Against Women. 1993. *Changing the Landscape: Ending Violence, Achieving Equality.* Ottawa: Minister of Supply and Services.

Carrasquillo, O., Himmelstein, D. U., Woolhandler, S., and D. H. Bor. 1999a. A reappraisal of private employers' role in providing health insurance. *New England Journal of Medicine* 340(2): 109–114.

Carrasquillo, O., Himmelstein, D. U., Woolhandler, S., and D. H. Bor. 1999b. Trends in health insurance coverage, 1989–1997. *International Journal of Health Services* 29(3): 467–483.

Carrin, G. and Politi, C. 1997. *Poverty and Health: An Overview of Basic Linkages and Public Policy Measures.* WHO Task Force on Health Economics. Geneva: World Health Organization.

Cassels, A. 1995. Health sector reform: Key issues in less developed countries. *Journal of International Development* 7(3): 329–347.

Cassels, A. 1997. *A Guide to Sector-Wide Approaches for Health Development, Concepts, Issues, and Working Arrangements.* Geneva: World Health Organization.

Castro-Leal, F., Dayton, J., and K. Mehra. 2000. Public spending on health care in Africa: Do the poor benefit? *Bulletin of the World Health Organization* 78(1): 66–74.

Cauley, J. and M. Danielson. 2000. Osteoporosis. In *Women and Health,* eds. M. B. Goldman and M. C. Hatch. Burlington: Academic Press.

Cauley, J., Seeley, D., and K. Ensrud. 1995. Estrogen replacement therapy and fractures in older women. *Annals of Internal Medicine* 122(1): 9–16.

Center, J., Nguyen, T., and D. Schneider. 1999. Mortality after all major types of osteoporotic fracture in men and women: An observational study. *Lancet* 353: 878–882.

Central Bureau of Health Intelligence. 1992. *Bulletin of Rural Health Statistics.* New Delhi: Government of India.

Central Bureau of Health Intelligence. 1994. *Health Information of India,* New Delhi: Government of India.

Central Bureau of Health Intelligence. Various years. *Health Information of India.* New Delhi: Government of India.

Chambers, R. 1998. *Who Changes? Institutionalizing Participation in Development.* London: Intermediate Technology Publications.

Chapko, M. K., Somsé, P., Kimball, M., Hawkins, R. V., and M. Massanga. 1999. Predictors of rape in the Central African Republic. *Health Care for Women International* 20: 71–79.

Chapman, K. S. and G. Hariharan. 1996. Do poor people have a stronger relationship between income and mortality than the rich? Implications of panel data for health-health analysis. *Journal of Risk and Uncertainty* 12: 51–63.

Chatterjee, M. 1988. *Access to Health.* New Delhi: Manohar.

Chavalitsakulchai, P. and H. Shahnavaz. 1993. Musculoskeletal disorders of female workers and ergonomics problems in five industries of a developing country. *Journal of Human Ergonomics* 22(1): 29–43.

Chen, L., Huq, E., and S. D'Souza. 1981. Sex bias in the family allocation of food and health care in rural Bangladesh. *Population and Development Review* 7(1): 55–70.

Chenet, L. 2000. Gender and socioeconomic inequalities in mortality in central and eastern Europe. In *Gender Inequalities in Health,* eds. E. Annandale and K. Hunt. Buckingham: Open University Press.

Chin, K., Evans, M. C., Cornish, J., Cundy, T., and I. R. Reid. 1997. Differences in hip axis and femoral neck length in premenopausal women of Polynesian, Asian and European origin. *Osteoporosis International* 7(4): 344–347.

Chinemana, F. and D. Sanders. 1993. Health and structural adjustment in Zimbabwe. In *Social Change and Economic Reform in Africa,* ed. P. Gibbon. Uppsala: Scandinavian Institute of African Studies.

Christian Aid. 1999. *Millennium Lottery: Who Lives, Who Dies in an Age of Third World Debt?* London: Christian Aid.

Christie, J. 1876. *Cholera Epidemics in East Africa.* London: Macmillan.

CIDA. 1996. *Strategy for Health. Draft Consultation Document.* Quebec: Canadian International Development Agency.

CIOMS. 1993. *International Ethical Guidelines for Biomedical Research Involving Human Subjects.* Geneva: Council for International Organizations of Medical Sciences.

Clarke, E. H. 1874. *Sex in Education or a Fair Chance for the Girls.* Boston: James R. Osgood.

Clarke, J. N. and A. K. Gerlak. 1998. Environmental racism in the sunbelt? A cross-cultural analysis. *Environmental Management* 22(6): 857–867.

Clatts, M. C. 1995. Disembodied acts: On the perverse use of sexual categories in the study of high risk behavior. In *Culture and Sexual Risk: Anthropological Perspectives on AIDS,* eds. H. ten Brummelhuis and G. Herdt. Amsterdam: Overseas Publishers Association.

Cline, A. D., Jansen, G. R., and C. L. Melby. 1998. Stress fractures in female army recruits: Implications of bone density, calcium intake and exercise. *Journal of the American College of Nutrition* 17(2): 128–135.

Cohen, S. and A. Zazri. 1997. Reproductive tract infections/sexually transmitted diseases among women of reproductive age attending outpatient clinics in three hospitals in South Kalimantan, Indonesia. Paper presented at the workshop on international reproductive health: international shared experience, Population Council, Indonesia.

Cohen, S. and C. Richards. 1994. The Cairo consensus: Population, development and women. *Family Planning Perspectives* 26(6): 272–277.

Colborn, T., Dumanoski, D., and J. P. Myers. 1996. *Our Stolen Future: Are We Threatening Our Fertility, Intelligence and Survival?* New York: Dutton.

Collier, P. 1993. The impact of adjustment on women. In *Understanding the Social Effects of Policy Reform,* eds. L. Demery, M. Ferroni, C. Grootaert, with J. Wong-Valle. Washington, DC: World Bank.

Collumbien, M. and S. Hawkes. 2000. Missing men's messages: Does the reproductive health approach respond to men's sexual health needs? *Culture, Health and Sexuality* 2(2): 135–150.

Commonweal, WEDO, and Greenpeace. 1999. Understanding the impact of persistent organic pollutants on women and the environment. *POPs Primer* www.wedo.org.

Community Development Resource Network. 1996. A study of poverty in selected districts of Uganda. Report commissioned for the Uganda Participatory Poverty Assessment Programme. Kampala, Uganda.

Condon, J. T. 1993. The assessment of antenatal emotional attachment: Development of a questionnaire instrument. *British Journal of Medical Psychology* 66: 167–183.

Congdon N., West S., Vitale S., Katala S., and B. B. Mmbaga. 1993. Exposure to children and risk of active trachoma in Tanzanian women. *American Journal of Epidemiology* 137(3): 366–372.

Cook, G. C. 1988. *Communicable and Tropical Diseases*. Guildford: Biddles, Let.

Cook, R. C. 1997. UN human rights committees advance reproductive rights. *Reproductive Health Matters* 10: 151–153.

Cook, R. C. and B. M. Dickens. 2000. *Considerations for Formulating Reproductive Health Laws* (WHO/RHR/100.1). Geneva: World Health Organization.

Cooper, C., Campion, G., and L. J. Melton. 1992. Hip fractures in the elderly: A world-wide projection. *Osteoporosis International* 2(6): 285–289.

Coser, L. 1974. *Greedy Institutions*. New York: Free Press.

Costi, A. 1998. Environmental justice and sustainable development in central and eastern Europe. *European Environment* 8(4): 107–112.

Counts, D. A., Brown, J. K., and J. C. Cambell. 1992. *Sanctions and Sanctuary: Cultural Perspectives on the Beating of Wives*. Boulder, CO: Westview Press.

Crawford, M. 1991. *Women killing: Intimate femicide in Ontario 1974–1990*. Unpublished document.

Crowell, A. N. and A. Burgess, eds. 1996. *Understanding Violence Against Women*. Washington, DC: National Academy Press.

Cumming, R. G., Cummings, S. R., and M. C. Nevitt 1997a. Calcium intake and fracture risk: Results from the study of osteoporotic fractures. *American Journal of Epidemiology* 145(10): 926–934.

Cumming, R. G., Nevitt, M. C., and S. R. Cummings. 1997b. Epidemiology of hip fractures. *Epidemiologic Reviews* 19(2): 244–257.

Cummings, S. R. 1985. Are patients with hip fractures more osteoporotic? *American Journal of Medicine* 78: 487–494.

Cummings, S. R., Phillips, S. L., and M. E. Wheat. 1988. Recovery of function after hip fracture. The role of social supports. *Journal of the American Geriatric Society* 36(9): 801–806.

Cundy, T., Cornish, J., Evans, M. C., Gamble, G., Stapleton, J., and I. R. Reid. 1995. Sources of interracial variation in bone mineral density. *Journal of Bone and Mineral Research* 10(3): 368–373.

DANIDA. 1996. *Uganda Health Sector Support Programme*. Copenhagen: Danish International Development Assistance, Ministry of Foreign Affairs.

Das Gupta, M. 1987. Selective discrimination against female children in rural Punjab, India. *Population and Development Review* 13(1): 77–100.

Datt, G. 1999. Has poverty declined since economic reforms? Statistical data analysis. *Economic and Political Weekly* December 11: 3516–3518.

Davis, J., Ross, P., Nevitt, M., and R. Wasnich. 1997. Incidence rates of falls among Japanese men and women living in Hawaii. *Journal of Clinical Epidemiology* 50(5): 589–594.

Davis, R. M. 1987. Current trends in cigarette advertising and marketing. *New England Journal of Medicine* 316(12): 725–732.

Day, T. 1995. *The Health Related Costs of Violence against Women in Canada: The Tip of the Iceberg*. London, Ontario, Canada: Center for Research on Violence against Women and Children.

de Bruyn, M. 1992. Women and AIDS in developing countries. *Social Science and Medicine* 34(3): 249–262.

De la Rosa, J. 1999. Five years and beyond. In *Whose World Is It Anyway?*, eds. J. W. Foster and A. Anand. Ottawa: United Nations Association in Canada.

De Laet, C. E. D. H., van Hoit, B. A., Burger, H., Hofman, A., and H. A. P. Pols. 1997. Bone density and risk of hip fracture in men and women: Cross-sectional analysis. *British Medical Journal* 315: 221–225.

Degni-Segui, R. 1996. *Report on the Situation of Human Rights in Rwanda Submitted by the Special Rapporteur for the Commission of Human Rights (E/CN.4/1996/68)*. Geneva: United Nations High Commissioner for Human Rights.

Dehne, K. and R. Snow. 1999. *Integrating STI Management into Family Planning Services: What Are the Benefits?* (WHO/RHR/99.10). Geneva: World Health Organization.

Dekoning, H. W., Smith, K. R., and J. M. Last. 1985. Biomass fuel combustion and health. *Bulletin of the World Health Organization* 63: 11.

Dennerstein, L. 1995. Mental health, work and gender. *International Journal of Health Services* 25(3): 503–509.

Dennerstein, L., Dudley, E., and H. Burger. 1997. Well-being and the menopausal transition. *Journal of Psychosomatic Obstetrics and Gynecology* 18: 95–101.

DHS. 1994. *Philippine Safe Motherhood Survey 1993*. Calverton, MA: National Statistics Office and MACRO International Inc.

DHS. 1995a. *Encuesta nacional de demografía y salud 1995*. Colombia: PROFAMILIA and Demographic Health Surveys/Institute for Resource Development and Macro International.

DHS. 1995b. *Egypt Demographic and Health Survey*. Cairo: National Population Council and Macro International.

DHS. 1997. *Encuesta Nacional de Demografía y Salud Reproductiva, 1995–1996.* Asunción, Paraguay: Centro Paraguayo de Estudios de Población, US Centers for Disease Control and US Agency for International Development.

DHS. 1998. *Encuesta de Salud Reproductiva 1995–1996. Resumen de los Hallazgos.* Puerto Rico: Departmento de Salud y la Escuela de Salud Pública de la Universidad de Puerto Rico and US Centers for Disease Control.

Diaz Curiel, M., Carrasco de la Pena, J. L., Honorato Perez, J., Perez Cano, R., and A. Rapado. 1997. Study of bone mineral density in lumbar spine and femoral neck in a Spanish population. Multicentre research project on osteoporosis. *Osteoporosis International* 7(1): 59–64.

Diniz, S. G. and A. F. d'Oliveira. 1998. Gender violence and reproductive health. *International Journal of Gynaecology and Obstetrics* 1(Suppl): S33–S42.

Diwan, V. K., Thorson, A., and A. Winkvist. 1998. *Gender and Tuberculosis: An International Workshop.* Report from an international research workshop at the Nordic School of Public Health, May 24–26. Göteborg: Nordic School of Public Health.

Dixon-Mueller, R. 1993. The sexuality connection in reproductive health. *Studies in Family Planning* 24(5): 269–282.

Dixon-Mueller, R. and A. Germain. 1992. Stalking the elusive "unmet need" for family planning. *Studies in Family Planning* 23(5): 330–335.

Dobash, R. P. and R. E. Dobash. 1992. *Women, Violence and Social Change.* London: Routledge.

Dolin, P. 1998. Tuberculosis epidemiology from a gender perspective. In *Gender and Tuberculosis*, eds. V. K. Diwan, A. Thorson, and A. Wikvist. Report from an international research workshop at the Nordic School of Public Health, May 24–26. Göteborg: Nordic School of Public Health.

Doty, P. 1987. Health status and health services use among older women: An international perspective. *World Health Statistical Quarterly* 40: 279.

Douma, W. and H. Van den Hombergh. 1993. Biodiversity conservation and women's empowerment: Local dilemmas and regional challenges. *Vena Journal* 5(2): 31–35.

Doyal, L. 1979. *The Political Economy of Health.* London: Pluto Press.

Doyal, L. 1995. *What Makes Women Sick. Gender and the Political Economy of Health.* London: Macmillan.

Doyal, L. 2000. Gender equity in health: Debates and dilemmas. *Social Science and Medicine* 51(6): 931–939.

Dresner-Pollak, R., Ginsberg, G., Cohen, A., and J. Stessman. 1996. Characteristics of falls in 70-year-olds in Jerusalem. *Israel Journal of Medical Sciences* 32: 625–628.

Dressler, W. W. 1990. Lifestyle, stress, and blood pressure in a southern black community. *Psychosomatic Medicine* 52(2): 182–198.

Drossman, D. A., Talley, N. J., Lesterman, J., Olden, K. W., and M. A. Barreiro. 1995. Sexual and physical abuse and gastrointestinal illness. Review and recommendations. *Annals of Internal Medicine* 123(10): 782–794.

Duggai, R. with S. Amin. 1989. *Cost of Health Care: A Household Survey in an Indian District.* Bombay: Foundation for Research in Community Health.

Duggal, R., Nandraj, S., and A. Vadair. 1995a. Health expenditure across states. Part I. *Economic and Political Weekly* April 15: 834–844.

Duggal, R., Nandraj, S., and A. Vadair. 1995b. Health expenditure across states. Part II. *Economic and Political Weekly* April 22: 901–908.

Duncan, M. E., Tibaux, G., Pelzer, A., and L. Mehari. 1994. A socioeconomic, clinical and serological study in an African city of prostitutes and women still married to their first husband. *Social Science and Medicine* 39(3): 323–333.

Dunlop, J., Kyte, R., and M. MacDonald. 1996. Redrawing the map: The world after the Beijing and Cairo conferences. *SAIS Review* 16(1): 153–165.

EcoForum. 1999. Proceedings of the Pan European ECO conference in public participation, Chisinau, Moldova, April 17–18.

Edelson, J. F. 1999. The overlap between child maltreatment and woman battering. *Violence Against Women* 5(2): 134–154.

Edleson, J. L. 1990. Judging the success of interventions with men who batter. In *Family Violence: Research and Public Policy Issues,* ed. D. J. Beshrov. Washington, DC: American Enterprise Institute.

Ejobi, F., Kanja, L. W., Kyule, M. N., Nyeko, J., and J. Opuda-Asibo. 1998. Some factors related to sum-DDT levels in Ugandan mothers' breast milk. *Public Health* 112(6): 425–427.

Ekwempu, C. C., Maine, D., Olorukoba, M. B., Essien, E. S., and M. N. Kisseka. 1990. Structural adjustment and health in Africa [letter]. *Lancet* 336(8706): 56–57.

Eller, T. J. and W. Fraser. 1993. *Asset Ownership of Households.* Current population reports. Household economic studies (P70–47). Washington, DC: U.S. Department of Commerce.

Ellis, D. and W. S. Dekeseredy. 1997. Rethinking estrangement, interventions and intimate femicide. *Violence Against Women* 3(6): 590–609.

Ellsberg, M. 1997. *Candies in Hell. Domestic Violence Against Women in Nicaragua.* Thesis, Umea University, Sweden.

Ellsberg, M., Peña, R., Herrera, A., Winkvist, A., and G. Hullgren. 1999. Domestic violence and emotional distress among Nicaragua women: Results from a population-based study. *American Psychologist* 54: 30–36.

Ellsberg, M., Winkvist, A., Pena, R., and H. Stenlund. 2001. Women's strategic responses to violence in Nicaragua. *Journal of Epidemiology and Community Health* 55(8): 547–555.

Elmstahl, S., Gullberg, B., Janzon, L., Johnell, O., and B. Elmstahl. 1998. Increased incidence of fractures in middle-aged and elderly men with low intakes of phosphorus and zinc. *Osteoporosis International* 8(4): 333–340.

Elson, D. 1992. Male bias in structural adjustment. In *Women and Adjustment Policies in the Third World,* eds. H. Afshar and C. Dennis. Basingstoke: Macmillan.

Elson, D. and B. Evers. 1998. *Sector Programme Support: The Health Sector, a Gender Aware Analysis.* Manchester: University of Manchester, Genecon Unit.

El-Zanaty, F., Hussein, E. M., Shawky, G. A., Way, A. A., and S. Kishor. 1996. *Egypt Demographic and health Surveys III.* Cairo: National Population Council; Calverton, MD: Macro International.

Engberg, L. 1993. Women and agricultural work. *Occupational Medicine* 8(4): 869–882.

Ettling, M. B., Krongthong, T., Krachaklin, S., and P. Bualombai. 1989. Evaluation of malaria clinics in Maesot, Thailand: Use of serology to assess coverage. *Transactions of the Royal Society of Tropical Medicine and Hygiene* 83(3): 325–330.

Etzioni, R., Legler, J. M., Feuer, E. J., Merrill, R. M., Cronin, K., and B. F. Hankey. 1999. Interpreting trends in prostate cancer. Part III. Quantifying the link between population PSA testing and recent declines in prostate cancer mortality. *Journal of the National Cancer Institute* 91(12): 1033–1039.

Euroqol Group. 1990. Euroqol: A new facility for the measurement of health-related quality of life. *Health Policy* 16: 199–208.

Evans, A. and M. Moore, eds. 1998. The bank, the state and development: Dissecting the 1997 World Development Report. *Institute of Development Studies Bulletin* 29(2).

Evans, A. and K. Young. 1988. *Gender issues in household labour allocation: The case of Northern Province, Zambia.* ODA/ESCOR Research Report. London: Overseas Development Assistance.

Evans, R. G., Barer, M. L., and T. R. Marmor, eds. 1994a. *Why Are Some People Healthy and Others Not? The Determinants of Health of Populations.* New York: Aldine De Gruyter.

Evans, R. G., Hodge, M., and I. B. Pless. 1994b. If not genetics, then what? Biological pathways and population health. In *Why Are Some People Healthy and Others Not? The Determinants of Health of Populations,* eds. R. G. Evans, M. L. Barer, and T. R. Marmor. New York: Aldine De Gruyter.

Evans, T. G. and M. K. Ranson. 1995. The global burden of trachomatous visual impairment. Part II. Assessing burden. *International Ophthalmology* 19: 271–280.

Evers, B. and M. Kroon. 2000. Integrating gender into sector wide programmes: The health sector in Bangladesh. Confidential draft supplied by the authors.

Ezeh, A. C., Seroussi, M., and H. Raggers. 1996. *Men's Fertility, Contraceptive Use and Reproductive Preferences.* Demographic and health surveys comparative studies 18. Calverton, MD: Institute for Resource Development/Macro Systems, Inc.

Fair, E., Islam, M. A., and S. A. Chowdhury. 1997. *Tuberculosis and Gender: Treatment Seeking Behaviour and Social Beliefs of Women with Tuberculosis in Rural Bangladesh.* Working paper 1. Dhaka: Bangladesh Rural Advancement Committee.

Farmer, P. 1996. Social inequalities and emerging infectious diseases. *Emerging Infectious Diseases* 2(4): 259–269.

Farmer, P. 1997a. Social scientists and the new tuberculosis. *Social Science and Medicine* 44(3): 347–358.

Farmer, P. 1997b. On suffering and structural violence: A view from below. In *Social Suffering,* eds. A. Klienman, V. Das, and M. Lock. Berkeley: University of California Press.

Farr. W. 1839. Letter to the Registrar General. *First Annual Report of the Registrar General.* London: His Majesty's Stationary Office.

Fathalla, F. 1994. Launching a second contraceptive technology revolution. In *Challenges in Reproductive Health Research. Biennial Report 1992–1993,* eds. J. Khanna, P. F. A. Van Look, and P. D. Griffin. Geneva: World Health Organization.

Fee, E. and N. Krieger. 1993. Understanding AIDS: Historical interpretations and the limits of biomedical individualism. *American Journal of Public Health* 83(10): 1477–1486.

Feldmeier, H., Poggensee, G., and I. Krantz. 1993. A synoptic inventory of needs for research on women and tropical parasitic diseases. Part II. Gender-related biases in the diagnosis and morbidity assessment of schistosomiasis in women. *Acta Tropica* 55: 139.

Felitti, V. J., Anda, R. F., Nordenberg, D., Williamson, D. F., Spitz, A. M., Edwards, V., Koss, M. P., and J. S. Marks. 1998. Relationship of childhood abuse and household dysfunction to many of the leading causes of death in adults. *American Journal of Preventive Medicine* 14: 245–258.

Ferguson, A. 1986. Women's health in a marginal area of Kenya. *Social Science and Medicine* 23(1): 17–29.

Ferrari, S., Rizzoli, R., and J. P. Bonjour. 1998. Heritable and nutritional influences on bone mineral mass. *Aging* 10: 205–213.

Feskanich, D., Weber, P., and W. C. Willett. 1999. Vitamin K intake and hip fractures in women: A prospective study. *American Journal of Clinical Nutrition* 69(1): 74–79.

Feskanich, D., Willett, W. C., Stampfer, M. J., and G. A. Colditz. 1997. Milk, dietary calcium, and bone fractures in women: A 12-year prospective study. *American Journal of Public Health* 87(6): 992–997.

Figueroa, J. G. 1998. Algunos elementos para interpretar la presencia de los varones en los procesos de salud reproductiva. *Revista de Cuadernos de Salud Publica* 14(Suppl 1): 87–96.

Finkelhor, D., Hotaling, D., Lewis, G., and I. A. Smith. 1990. Sexual abuse in a national survey of adult men and women: Prevalence, characteristics and risk factors. *Child Abuse and Neglect* 14: 19–28.

Finkler, K. 1997. Gender, domestic violence and sickness in Mexico. *Social Science and Medicine* 45: 1147–1160.

Fisher, B., Bauer, M., Margolese, R., and C. Redmond. 1985. Five-year results of a randomized clinical trial comparing total mastectomy and segmental mastectomy with or without radiation in the treatment of breast cancer. *New England Journal of Medicine* 312(11): 665–673.

Flegal, K. M., Carroll, M. D., Kuczmarski, R. J., and C. L. Johnson. 1998. Overweight and obesity in the United States: Prevalence and trends, 1960–1994. *International Journal of Obesity Related Metabolic Disorders* 22: 39–47.

Foley, J. D. 1991. *Uninsured in the United States: The Non-Elderly Population without Health Insurance.* Report SR-10.91. Washington, DC: Employee Benefit Research Institute.

Fonn, S., Xaba, M., Tint, K. S., Conco, D., and S. Varkey. 1998. Reproductive health services in South Africa: From rhetoric to implementation. *Reproductive Health Matters* 6(11): 22–31.

Forrest, B. D. 1991. Women, HIV and mucosal immunity. *Lancet* 337: 835–836.

Foster, M. 1999. Lessons of experience from sector-wide approaches in health. Paper prepared for the Inter-Agency Working Group on Sector-Wide Approaches and Development Cooperation. Geneva: World Health Organization.

Fox-Rushby, J. A. 1994. The relationship between health economics and health-related quality of life. In *Quality of Life Assessment: International Perspectives,* eds. J. Orley and W. Kuyken. Berlin and Heidelberg: Springer-Verlag.

Frankenhaeuser, M., Lundberg, U., and M. Chesney. 1991. *Women, Work and Health: Stress and Opportunities.* New York: Plenum Press.

Frankenhaeuser, M., Lundberg, U., Fredrikson, B. M., Toumisto, M., and A. L. Myrsten. 1989. Stress on and off the job as related to sex and occupational status in white-collar workers. *Journal of Organizational Behaviour* 10: 321–346.

Franks, P., Clancy, C. M., and M. R. Gold. 1993. Health insurance and mortality. Evidence from a national cohort. *Journal of the American Medical Association* 270(6): 737–741.

Freedman, L. and D. Maine. 1993. Women's mortality: A legacy of neglect. In *The Health of Women: A Global Perspective,* eds. M. Koblinsky, J. Timyan, and J. Gay. Boulder, CO: Westview Press.

Freedom from Hunger. 1998. *Impact of Credit with Education on Mothers and Their Young Children's Nutrition.* Davis, CA: Freedom from Hunger.

Freemantle, F. 1911. *Monograph on Health and the Empire.* London: Ouseley.

Freidman, A. 2000. World Bank dissenter sticks to his guns. *International Herald Tribune.* January 27: p. 1.

Frieze, I. and A. Browne. 1989. Violence in marriage. In *Family Violence,* eds. L. Ohlin and M. Tonry. Chicago: University of Chicago Press.

Fuchs, V. R. 1988. *Women's Quest for Economic Equality*. London: Harvard University Press.

Fujita, T. and M. Fukase. 1992. Comparison of osteoporosis and calcium intake between Japan and the United States. *Proceedings of the Society for Experimental Biology and Medicine* 200(2): 149–152.

Fujiwara, S., Kasagi, F., Yamada, M., and K. Kodama. 1997. Risk factors for hip fracture in a Japanese cohort. *Journal of Bone and Mineral Research* 12(7): 998–1104.

Furstenberg, A. L. and M. D. Mezey. 1987. Differences in outcome between black and white elderly hip fracture patients. *Journal of Chronic Disease* 40(10): 931–938.

Gabe, J. and M. Calnan. 1989. The limits of medicine, women's perception of medical technology. *Social Science and Medicine* 28: 223–231.

Gallagher, S. 1991. Acceptable weights and physiological costs of performing combined manual handling tasks in restricted postures. *Ergonomics* 34(7): 939–952.

Galtung, J. 1969. Violence, peace, and peace research. *Journal of Peace Research* 6(3): 167–191.

Garenne, M. and M. Lafon. 1998. Sexist diseases. *Perspectives in Biology and Medicine* 41(2): 176–189.

Gater, R., Tansella, M., Korten, A., Tiemens, B. G., Mavreas, V. G., and M. O. Olatawura. 1998. Sex differences in the prevalence and detection of depressive and anxiety disorders in general health care settings. *Archives of General Psychiatry* 55: 405–413.

Gazmararian, J. A., Lazorick, S., Spitz, A. M., Ballard, T. J., Saltzman, L. E., and J. S. Marks. 1996. Prevalence of violence against pregnant women. *Journal of the American Medical Association* 275: 1915–1920.

George, A., Shah, I., and S. Nandraj. 1997. Morbidity, health care utilization and expenditure, Madhya Pradesh 1990–91. In *Household Health Expenditure in Two States. A Comparative Study of Districts in Maharashtra and Madhya Pradesh*. Pune/Mumbai: Foundation for Research in Community Health.

Germain, A., Holmes, K. K., Piot, P., and J. N. Wasserheit, eds. 1992. *Reproductive Tract Infections: Global Impact and Priorities for Women's Reproductive Health*. New York: Plenum Press.

Ghana Health Assessment Project Team. 1981. A quantitative method of assessing the health impact of different diseases in less developed countries. *International Journal of Epidemiology* 10(1): 73–80.

Gijsbers van Wijk, C. M. T., Kolk, A. M., van den Bosch, W. J., and H. J. van den Hoogen. 1995. Male and female health problems in general practice: The differential impact of social position and social roles. *Social Science and Medicine* 40(5): 597–611.

Gijsbergs van Wijk, C. M. T., Van Vliet, K. P., and A. M. Kolk. 1996. Gender perspectives and quality of care: Towards appropriate and adequate health care for women. *Social Science and Medicine* 43:707–720.

Gilbert, P. and S. Allan. 1998. The role of defeat and entrapment (arrested flight) in depression: an exploration of an evolutionary view. *Psychological Medicine* 28: 585–598.

Gilks, C., Floyd, K., Haran, D., Kemp, J., Squire, B., and D. Wilkinson. 1998. *Sexual Health and Health Care: Care and Support for People with HIV/AIDS in Resource Poor Settings.* DFID Health and Population occasional paper. Liverpool: Liverpool School of Tropical Medicine.

Gill, S. S. 1996. Punjab: Privatising health care. *Economic and Political Weekly* January 6: 18–19.

Gill, S., Iyer, A., and M. Uplekar. 1997. Models of co-ordination and co-operation between NGOs, private and public health care services in the Reproductive and Child Health Programme. A paper to aid discussion. Produced for InDevelop, Uppsala AB, Sweden (unpublished).

Gilligan, C. 1992. *In a Different Voice: Psychological Theory and Women's Development.* Cambridge: Harvard University Press.

Gillioz, L., De Puy, J., and V. Ducret. 1997. *Domination et Violences Envers les Femmes dans le Couple.* Lausanne: Editions Payot.

Gilsanz, V., Skaggs, D. L., Kovanlikaya, A., Sayre, J., and M. L. Loro. 1998. Differential effect of race on the axial and appendicular skeletons of children. *Journal of Clinical Endocrinology and Metabolism* 83(5): 1420–1427.

Gilson, L. 1998. In defence and pursuit of equity. *Social Science and Medicine* 47(12): 1891–1896.

Gitlin, M. J. and R. O. Pasnau. 1989. Psychiatric syndromes linked to reproductive function: A review of current knowledge. *American Journal of Psychiatry* 146: 1413–1422.

Gladen, B. C. and W. J. Rogan. 1995. DDE and shortened duration of lactation in a northern Mexican town. *American Journal of Public Health* 85(4): 504–548.

Gladwin, C., ed. 1991. *Structural Adjustment and African Women Farmers.* Gainesville: University of Florida Press.

Glenn, E. N. 1985. Racial ethnic women's labor: The intersection of race, gender and class oppression. *Review of Radical Political Economics* 17(3): 86–108.

Glenn, E. N. 1999. The social construction and institutionalization of gender and race: An integrative framework. In *Revisioning Gender,* eds. J. Lorber, M. M. Ferree, and B. Hess. Newbury Park, CA: Sage.

Goldman, M. B. and M. C. Hatch, eds. 2000. *Women and Health.* San Diego: Academic Press.

Gonzalez, F., Dearden, K., and W. Jimenez. 1999. Do multi-sectoral development programmes affect health? A Bolivian case study. *Health Policy and Planning* 14(4): 400–408.

Gordon, D. M. 1996. *Fat and Mean: The Corporate Squeeze of Working Americans and the Myth of Managerial "Downsizing."* New York: Free Press.

Gottschalk, P. and B. Wolfe. 1993. United States. In *Equity in the Finance and Delivery of Health Care: An International Perspective,* eds. A. Wagstaff, E. van Doorslaer, and F. Ruter. New York: Oxford University Press.

Government of India. 1946. *Report of the Health Survey and Development Committee,* Vols. 1–4 (Bhore committee). New Delhi: Superintendent of Government Printing.

Government of India. 1975. *Report of the Committee on Drugs and Pharmaceuticals* (Hathi committee). New Delhi: Government of India.

Gready, M., Klugman, B., Makhosazana, X., Boikanyo, E., and H. Rees. 1997. South African women's experiences of contraception and contraceptive services. In *Beyond Acceptability: Users' Perspectives on Contraception,* eds. T. K. S. Ravindran, M. Berer, and J. Cottingham. London: Reproductive Health Matters.

Greaves, L., Hankivsky, O., and J. Kingson-Riechters. 1995. *Selected Estimates of the Costs of Violence against Women.* London, Ontario, Canada: Center for Research on Violence against Women and Children.

Green, C. J., Bassett, K., Foerster, V., and A. Kazanjian. 2000. Beyond the clinical effectiveness of bone mineral density testing in British Colombia: A comprehensive approach to health technology assessment. Presentation at the building bridges conference, British Columbia Office of Health Technology Assessment, Victoria, April 28–May 1.

Green, L. A. and M. T. Raffin. 1993. Differences in management of suspected myocardial infarction in men and women. *Journal of Family Practice* 36: 389.

Greene, M. and A. Biddlecom. 1997. *Absent and Problematic Men: Demographic Accounts of Male Reproductive Roles.* Policy Research Division working paper 103. New York: Population Council.

Grembowski, D., Andersen, R., and M. Chen. 1989. A public health model of the dental care process. *Medical Care Review* 46(4): 439–496.

Grisso, J. A., Schwarz, D. F., Miles, C. G., and J. H. Holmes. 1996. Injuries among inner-city minority women: A population-based longitudinal survey. *American Journal of Public Health* 86: 67–70.

Gritz, E. R. 1987. Which women smoke and why? In *Proceedings of Not Far Enough: Women vs. Smoking.* A workshop for women's group and women's health leaders. Boston: Harvard University Institute for the Study of Smoking Behavior and Policy.

Gruenbaum, E. 1996. The cultural debate over female circumcision: The Sudanese are arguing this one out for themselves. *Medical Anthropological Quarterly* 10(4): 455–475.

Guijt, I. and M. K. Shah, eds. 1999. *The Myth of Community: Gender Issues in Participatory Development.* London: Intermediate Technology Publications.

Guillette, E. A. 1994. Balancing reproductive rights and agricultural rights. Paper presented at the VI International Congress on Women's Health Issues, Gaberone, Botswana, June 28–July 1.

Guillette, E. A., Meza, M. M., Aquilar, M. G., Solo, A. D., and I. E. Garcia. 1998. An anthropological approach to the evaluation of preschool children exposed to pesticides in Mexico. *Environmental Health Perspectives* 106(6): 347–353.

Gullberg, B., Johnell, O., and J. A. Kanis. 1997. World-wide projections for hip fracture. *Osteoporosis International* 7(5): 407–413.

Gupta, G. R. and E. Weiss. 1993. Women's lives and sex: Implications for AIDS prevention. *Culture, Medicine and Psychiatry* 17: 399–412.

Gupta, R. K. and A. K. Srivastava. 1988. Study of fatal burn cases in Kanpur, India. *Forensic Science International* 37: 88.

Gupte, M., Bandewar, S., and H. Pisal. 1999. Women's perspective on the quality of general and reproductive health care: Evidence from rural Maharashtra. In *Improving the Quality of Care in India's Family Welfare Programme: The Challenge Ahead,* eds. M. A. Koenig and K. E. Khan. New York: Population Council.

Guralnick, J. M., Leveille, S. G., Hirsch, R., Ferrucci, L., and L. P. Fried. 1997. The impact of disability in older women. *Journal of American Medical Women's Association* 52: 113–120.

Gwatkin, D. R. and M. Guillot. 2000. *The Burden of Disease among the Global Poor: Current Situation, Future Trends and Implications for Strategy.* Washington, DC: World Bank.

Gwatkin, D. R., Guillot, M., and P. Heuveline. 1999. The burden of disease among the global poor. *Lancet* 354(9178): 586–589.

Haan, M., Kaplan, G., and S. Syme. 1989. Old observations and new thoughts. In *Pathways to Health: The Role of Social Factors,* eds. J. Bunker, D. Gomby, and B. Kehrer. Menlo Park, CA: Henry J. Kaiser Family Foundation.

Haavio-Mannila, E. 1986. Inequalities in health and gender. *Social Science and Medicine* 22(2): 141–149.

Hacker, A. 1992. *Two Nations: Black and White, Separate, Hostile, Unequal.* Old Tappan, NJ: Simon & Schuster.

Hailey, D., Sampietro-Colom, L., and D. Marshall. 1998. The effectiveness of bone density measurement and associated treatments for prevention of fractures: An international collaborative review. *International Journal of Technology Assessment in Health Care* 14(2): 237–254.

Haj-Yahia, M. M. 1998. *The Incidence of Wife-Abuse and Battering and some Sociodemographic Correlates as Revealed in Two National Surveys in Palestinian Society.* Ramallah: Besir Center for Research and Development.

Halbreich, U. and L. A. Lumley. 1993. The multiple interactional biological Processes that might lead to depression and gender differences in its appearance. *Journal of Affective Disorders* 29: 159–173.

Hall, E. M. 1989. Gender, work control and stress: A theoretical discussion and empirical test. *International Journal of Health Services* 19: 725–745.

Hall, E. M. 1990. Women's work: An inquiry into the health effects of invisible and visible labor. Ph.D. dissertation, Karolinska Institute, Stockholm.

Halpérin, D. S., Bouvier, P., Jaffe, P. D., Mounoud, R. L., Pawlak, C. H., Laederach, J., Wicky, H. R., and F. Astie. 1996. Prevalence of child sexual abuse among adolescents in Geneva: Results of a cross-sectional survey. *British Medical Journal* 312(7042): 1326–1329.

Hambrecht, M., Maurer, K., and H. Hafner. 1993. Evidence for a gender bias in epidemiological studies of schizophrenia. *Schizophrenia Research* 8: 223–231.

Hammarström, A., Härenstam, A., and P. Östlin. 2001. Gender and health: Concepts and explanatory models. In *Gender Inequalities in Health: A Swedish Perspective,* eds. P. Ostlin, M. Danielson, F. Diderichsen, A. Härenstam, and G. Lindberg. Cambridge, MA: Harvard Center for Population and Development Studies with Harvard University Press.

Handley, A. 1996. Acute stress disorder in parents of preterm infants. Honors thesis, University of Melbourne.

Handwerker, W. P. 1993. Gender power differences between parents and high-risk sexual behaviour by their children: AIDS/STD risk factors extend to a prior generation. *Journal of Women's Health* 2: 310–316.

Hanson, K. 1999. *Measuring up: Gender, Burden of Disease, and Priority Setting Techniques in the Health Sector.* Working paper 99.12. Cambridge: Harvard Center for Population and Development Studies.

Hansson, S. O. 1998. The neglect of women in occupational toxicology. In *Women's Health at Work,* eds. Å. Kilbom, K. Messing, and C. Bildt Thorbjörnsson. Solna: National Institute of Working Life.

Harding, S. 1987. *Feminism and Methodology.* Bloomington: Indiana University Press.

Hartigan, P. 1999. *Communicable Diseases, Gender, and Equity in Health.* Working paper 99.08. Cambridge: Harvard Center for Population and Development Studies.

Hawkes, S. 1998. Why include men? Establishing sexual health clinics for men in rural Bangladesh. *Health Policy and Planning* 13(2): 121–130.

Hedlin, M., Bengtsson, B., Norell, M., and H. Malker. 1994. *Reported Occupational Skin Diseases.* Solna: National Board of Occupational Safety and Health [in Swedish].

Heise, L. 1993. Violence against women: The missing agenda. In *The Health of Women. A global perspective,* eds. M. Koblinsky, J. Timyan, and J. Gay. Boulder, CO: Westview Press.

Heise, L. 1998. Violence against women: An integrated, ecological framework. *Violence Against Women* 4(3): 262–290.

Heise, L., Ellsberg, M., and M. Gottemoeller. 1999. *Ending Violence Against Women.* Population reports. Baltimore: Population Information Program, Johns Hopkins University School of Public Health.

Heise, L., Pitanguy, J., and A. Germain. 1994. *Violence Against Women: The Hidden Health Burden.* World Bank discussion paper 255. Washington, DC: World Bank.

Held, P. J., Pauly, M. V., Bovbjerg, R. R., Newmann, J., and O. Salvatierra. 1988. Access to kidney transplantation, has the United States eliminated income and racial differences? *Archives of Internal Medicine* 148: 2594.

Hendrick, V., Altshuler, L. L., Gitlin, M. J., Delrahim, S., and C. Hammen. 2000. Gender and bipolar illness. *Journal of Clinical Psychiatry* 61: 393–396.

Henwood, D. 1999. Jail and jobs. *Left Business Observer* 88: 8.

Heston, T. F. and L. M. Lewis. 1992. Gender bias in the evaluation and management of acute nontraumatic chest pain. The St. Louis Emergency Physicians' Association research group. *Family Practice Research Journal* 12: 383.

Hibbard, H. and C. Pope. 1993. The quality of social roles as predictors of morbidity and mortality. *Social Science and Medicine* 36(3): 217–225.

Hickey, C. A., Cliver, S. P., Goldenberg, R. L., McNeal, S. F., and H. J. Hoffman. 1997. Low prenatal weight gain among low-income women: What are the risk factors? *Birth* 24(2): 102–108.

Hintikka, J., Saarinen, P., Tanskanen, A., Koivumaa-Honkanen, H., and H. Viinamaki. 1999. Gender differences in living skills and global assessment of functioning among outpatients with schizophrenia. *Australian and New Zealand Journal of Psychiatry* 33: 226–231.

Ho, S. C., Woo, J., Chan, S. S., Yuen, Y. K., and A. Sham. 1996. Risk factors for falls in the Chinese elderly population. *Journal of Gerontology. Series A, Biological Sciences and Medical Sciences* 51(5): M195–198.

Hodgson, D. and S. Cotts Watkins. 1997. Feminists and neo-Malthusians: Past and present alliances. *Population and Development Review* 23(3): 469–523.

Hofer, T. P. and S. J. Katz. 1996. Healthy behaviors among women in the United States and Ontario: The effect on use of preventive care. *American Journal of Public Health* 86: 1755–1759.

Hoffman, K. L., Demo, D. H., and J. N. Edwards. 1994. Physical wife abuse in a non-Western society: An integrated theoretical approach. *Journal of Marriage and the Family* 56: 131–146.

Holmboe-Ottesen, G. and M. Wandel. 1988. Women's role in food production and nutrition: Implications for their quality of life. *Food and Nutrition Bulletin* 10(3): 8–15.

Holmes, M. M., Resnick, H. S., Kilpatrick, D. G., and C. L. Best. 1996. Rape-related pregnancy: Estimates and descriptive characteristics from a national sample of women. *American Journal of Obstetrics and Gynecology* 175(2): 320–324.

Hooper, K., Chuvakova, T., Kazbekova, G., Hayward, D., Tulenova, A., Petreas, M. X., Wade, T. J., Benedict, K., Cheng, Y., and J. Grassman. 1999. Analysis of breastmilk to assess exposure to chlorinated contaminants in Kazakhstan: Sources of 2,3,7,8-TCD exposures in an agricultural region of southern Kazakhstan. *Environmental Health Perspectives* 107(6): 447–456.

Hossain, M. M. and R. I. Glass. 1988. Parental son preference in seeking medical care for children less than five years of age in a rural community in Bangladesh. *American Journal of Public Health* 78(10): 1349–1350.

Hotaling, G. T. and D. B. Sugarman. 1986. An analysis of risk markers in husband to wife violence: The current state of knowledge. *Violence and Victims* 1: 101–125.

Howson, C. P., Harrison, P. F., Hotra, D., and M. Law, eds. 1996. *In Her Lifetime: Female Morbidity and Mortality in Sub-Saharan Africa.* Washington, DC: National Academy Press.

Hsaio, W. 1998. *Health Care Financing in Developing Nations: A Background Paper.* Boston: Harvard School of Public Health.

Huang, Z. and J. H. Himes. 1997. Bone mass and subsequent risk of hip fracture. *Epidemiology* 8(2): 192–195.

Huang, Z., Himes, J. H., and P. G. McGovern. 1996. Nutrition and subsequent hip fracture risk among a national cohort of white women. *American Journal of Epidemiology* 144(2): 124–134.

Hubbard, R. 1995. *Profitable Promises: Essays on Women, Science and Health.* Monroe, MA: Common Courage Press.

Hudelson, P. 1996. Gender differentials in tuberculosis: The role of socioeconomic and cultural factors. *Tubercle and Lung Disease* 77: 391–400.

Hughes, W. 1996. *Essentials of environmental toxicology.* London: Taylor & Francis.

Human Rights Watch. 1997. *South Africa. Violence against Women and the Medico-Legal System.* New York: Human Rights Watch.

Human Rights Watch. 2000. *Federal Republic of Yugoslavia. Rape as a Weapon of Ethnic Cleansing.* New York: Human Rights Watch.

Hunter, C. P., Redmond, C. K., Chen, V. W., Austin, D. F., Greenberg, R. S., Correa, P., Muss, H. B., Forman, M. R., Wesley, M. N., and R. S. Blacklow. 1993. Breast cancer: Factors associated with stage at diagnosis in black and white women. Black/white cancer survival study group. *Journal of the National Cancer Institute* 85: 1129–1137.

Hussein, A. K. and P. G. M. Mujinja. 1997. Impact of user charges on government health facilities in Tanzania. *East African Medical Journal* 74(12): 751–776.

ICMR. 1988. *Utilisation of Health and Family Planning Services in Bihar, Gujarat and Kerala. A Task Force Study.* New Delhi: Indian Council of Medical Research.

ICMR. 1991. *Evaluation of Quality of Family Welfare Services at Primary Health Centre Level. A Task Force Study.* New Delhi: Indian Council of Medical Research.

Illif, P. 1992. A case for exempting maternity patients from health services charges. Harare: University of Zimbabwe Medical School.

Indigenous Environmental Network and Greenpeace. 1999. *Drumbeat for Mother Earth* [leaflet and video]. Amsterdam.

Institute of Medicine. 1993. *Access to Health Care in America.* Washington, DC: National Academy Press.

Institute of Medicine. 1998. *Gender Differences in Susceptibility to Environmental Factors: A Priority Assessment.* Washington, DC: National Academy Press.

International Clinical Epidemiology Network. 2000. IndiaSAFE and WorldSAFE disseminate findings. *INCLEN News* 21(1): 4–7.

IWMI. 1999. *Water Scarcity and Poverty.* Water brief 3. Colombo: International Water Management Institute.

Iyer, A. and A. Jesani. 1999. Barriers to quality of care: The experience of auxiliary nurse-midwives in rural Maharashtra. In *Improving Quality of Care in India's Family Welfare Programme. The Challenge Ahead,* eds. M. Koenig and M. E. Khan. New York: Population Council.

Iyer, A. and G. Sen. 2000. Health sector changes and health equity in the 1990s. In *Health and Equity: Effecting Change,* ed. S. Raghuram. Humanist Institute for Cooperation with Developing Countries technical report series 1.8. Bangalore: National Printing Press.

Jacobsen, S. J., Goldberg, J., Miles, T. P., Brody, J. A., Stiers, W., and A. A. Rimm. 1990. Hip fracture incidence among the old and very old: A population-based study of 745,435 cases. *American Journal of Public Health* 80: 871–873.

Jacobsen, S. J., Goldberg, J., Milist, P., Brody, J. A., Stiers, W., and A. A. Rimm. 1992. Race and sex differences in mortality following fracture of the hip. *American Journal of Public Health* 82: 1147–1150.

Jacobson, J. 1993. Women's health, the price of poverty. In *The Health of Women: A Global Perspective,* eds. M. Koblinsky, J. Timyan, and J. Gay. Boulder, CO: Westview Press.

Jaffe, P. G., Wolfe, D. A., and S. K. Wilson. 1990. Children of battered women. In *Developmental Clinical Psychology and Psychiatric,* Vol. 1. Newbury Park, CA: Sage.

Jaglal, S. B., Kreiger, N., and G. A. Darlington. 1993. Past and recent physical activity and risk of hip fracture. *American Journal of Epidemiology* 138(2): 107–118.

Jaglal, S. B., Kreiger, N., and G. A. Darlington. 1995. Lifetime occupational physical activity and risk of hip fracture in women. *Annals of Epidemiology* 5(4): 321–324.

Jahan, R. 1995. *The Elusive Agenda: Mainstreaming Women in Development.* London: Zed.

James, S. A., Hartnett, S. A., and W. D. Kalsbeek. 1983. John Henryism and blood pressure differences among black men. *Journal of Behavioral Medicine* 6(3): 259–278.

Jamison, D. H. et al., eds. 1993. *Disease Control Priorities in Developing Countries.* Oxford: Oxford University Press for the World Bank.

Jarrett, S. W. and S. Ofosu-Amaah. 1992. Strengthening health services for MCH in Africa: The first four years of the Bamako initiative. *Health Policy and Planning* 7(2): 164–176.

Järvholm, B., ed. 1996. *Working Life and Health. A Swedish Survey.* Solna: National Board of Occupational Safety and Health, National Institute of Working Life and Swedish Council for Work Life Research.

Jazairy, I., Alamgir, M. and T. Panuccio. 1992. *The State of World Rural Poverty.* New York: New York University Press/ International Fund for Agricultural Development.

Jeejeebhoy, S. 1998. Associations between wife beating and fetal and infant death: Impressions from a survey in rural India. *Studies in Family Planning* 29: 300–308.

Jesani, A. 1996. *Law and Health Care Providers. A Study of Legislations and Legal Aspects of Health Care Delivery.* Mumbai: Centre for Enquiry into Health and Allied Themes [mimeo].

Jesani, A. with S. Ananthraman. 1993. *Private Sector and Privatisation in the Health Care Services. A Review Paper for the ICSSR-ICMR Joint Panel on Health, August 1990.* Mumbai: Foundation for Research in Community Health.

Jewkes, R., Penn-Kekana, L., Levin, J., Ratsaka, M., and M. Schrieber. 1999. *"He Must Give Me Money, He Mustn't Beat Me." Violence Against Women in Three South African Provinces.* Pretoria: Centre for Epidemiological Research in South Africa, Medical Research Council.

Johannisson K. 1995. *Den mörka kontinenten. Kvin nan, Medicinen och fin-descècle.* Stockholm: Norstedt.

Johansson, E., Long, N. H., Diswan, V. K., and A. Winkvist. 1999. Attitudes to compliance with tuberculosis treatment among women and men in Vietnam. *International Journal Tubercle and Lung Disease* 3(10): 862–868.

Johnson, H. 1996. *Dangerous Domains. Violence Against Women in Canada.* Nelson, Canada: International Thomson Publishing.

Johnson, H. 1998. Rethinking survey research on violence against women. In *Rethinking Violence Against Women,* eds. R. P. Dobash and R. E. Dobash. London: Sage.

Johnson, J. 1846. *The Influence of Tropical Climates on European Constitutions.* New York: S. S. and Wood.

Joint Work Environment Council for the Government Sector. 1997. *Reflections on Women in Working Life*. Stockholm: SAN.

Jones, A. H. 1980. *Wealth of a Nation to Be: The American Colonies on the Eve of the Revolution*. New York: Columbia University Press.

Jones, B. A. P. 1983. The economic status of black women. In *The State of Black America*. Washington, DC: National Urban League.

Jordan, J., Kaylan, A., and J. L. Surrey. 1991. *Women's Growth in Connection: Writings from the Stone Centre*. New York: Guilford Publications.

Kaastad, T. S., Meyer, H. E., and J. A. Falch. 1998. Incidence of hip fracture in Oslo, Norway: Differences within the city. *Bone* 22(2): 175–178.

Kabakian-Khasholian, T., Campbell, O., Shediac-Rizkallah, M., and F. Ghorayeb. 2000. Women's experiences of maternity care: Satisfaction or passivity? *Social Science and Medicine* 51: 103–113.

Kabeer, N. 1994. *Reversed Realities: Gender Hierarchies in Development Thought*. New Delhi: Kali for Women; London: Verso.

Kaluzny, A. D. and R. B. Warnecke. 1996. *Managing a Health Care Alliance*. San Francisco: Jossey-Bass.

Kamat, S. R. and V. B. Deshi. 1987. Sequential health effect study in relation to air pollution in Bombay. *European Journal of Epidemiology* 3: 265–277.

Kandrack, M., Grant, K. R., and A. Segall. 1991. Gender differences in health related behaviour: Some unanswered questions. *Social Science and Medicine* 31(5): 579–590.

Kannus, P., Parkkari, J., Sievänen, H., Heinonen, A., and I. Vuori. 1996. Epidemiology of hip fractures. *Bone* 18(Suppl 1): 57–63.

Kanthak, J., Bernstorff, A., and N. Jayaraman. 1999. *Ships for Scrap: Steel and Toxic Wastes for Asia. A Fact-Finding Mission to the Indian Shipbreaking Yards in Alang and Bombay*. Hamburg: Greenpeace.

Kaplan, G. A., Pamuk, E. R., Lynch, J. W., Cohen, R. D., and J. L. Balfour. 1996. Inequality in income and mortality in the United States: Analysis of mortality and potential pathways [Published erratum appears in BMJ 1996; 312(7041): 1253.] *British Medical Journal* 312(7037): 999–1003.

Kaplan, H. I. and B. J. Sadock. 1988. *Synopsis of Psychiatry, Behavioural Sciences, Clinical Psychiatry*. Baltimore: Williams & Wilkins.

Karasek, R. 1979. Job demands, job decision latitude and mental strain: Implications for job redesign. *Administrative Science Quarterly* 24: 285–308.

Karasek, R. and T. Theorell. 1990. *Healthy Work*. New York: Basic Books.

Karim, Q. A. and S. S. A. Karim. 1999. Epidemiology of HIV infection in South Africa. *International AIDS Society Newsletter* 4–7.

Kaslow, N. J. and M. P. Thompson. 1998. Factors that mediate and moderate the link between partner abuse and suicidal behavior in African American women. *Journal of Consulting and Clinical Psychology* 66(3): 533–540.

Katz, S. J. and T. P. Hofer. 1994. Socioeconomic disparities in preventive care persist despite universal coverage. Breast and cervical cancer screening in Ontario and the United States. *Journal of the American Medical Association* 272: 530–534.

Katz, S. J., Hofer, T. P., and W. G. Manning. 1996. Hospital utilization in Ontario and the United States: The impact of socioeconomic status and health status. *Canadian Journal of Public Health* 87(4): 253–256.

Kaufert, P. A. 1998. Women, resistance, and the breast cancer movement. In *Pragmatic Women and Body Politics.*, eds. M. Lock and P. A. Kaufert. New York: Cambridge University Press.

Kaur, V. 1997. General considerations: Tropical diseases and women. *Clinics in Dermatology* 15: 171–178.

Kawachi, I., Kennedy B. P., and R. Glass. 1999. Social capital and self-rated health: A contextual analysis. *American Journal of Public Health* 89: 1187–1193.

Kemp, J., Squire, S. B., Nyasulu, I., and F. M. L. Salaniponi. 1996. Is tuberculosis diagnosis a barrier to care? *Transactions of the Royal Society of Tropical Medicine and Hygiene* 90: 472.

Kendie, S. B. 1992. Survey of water use behaviour in rural north Ghana. *Natural Resources Forum* 16: 126–131.

Kennedy, B. P., Kawachi, I., Glass, R., and D. Prothrow-Stith. 1998. Income distribution, socioeconomic status and self rated health in the United States: Multilevel analysis. *British Medical Journal* 317(7163): 917–921.

Kerr, R. and J. McLean. 1996. *Paying for Violence: Some of the Costs of Violence against Women in B.C.* British Colombia, Canada: Ministry of Women's Equality.

Kessler, R. C., McGonagle, K. A., Zhao, S., Nelson, C. B., Hughes, M., Eshleman, S., Wittchen, H. U., and K. S. Kendler. 1994. Lifetime and 12 month prevalence of DSM-III-R psychiatric disorders in the United States. *Archives of General Psychiatry* 51: 8–19.

Kessler, R. C., Sonnega, A., Bromet, E., Hughes, M., and C. B. Nelson. 1995. Posttraumatic stress disorder in the national comorbidity survey. *Archives of General Psychiatry* 52: 1048–1060.

Kettel, B. 1996. Women, health and the environment. *Social Science and Medicine* 42(10): 1367–1379.

Khan, M. E., Ghosh Dastidar, S., and S. Bairathi. 1983. Women and health: A case study in sex discrimination. Paper presented at the ICMR-Ford Foundation workshop on child health, nutrition and family planning, Bangalore.

Khattab, H., Younis, N., and H. Zurayk. 1999. *Women, Reproduction and Health in Rural Egypt: The Giza Study.* Cairo: American University in Cairo Press.

Kiel, D. P., Myers, R. H., and A. Cupples. 1997. The Bsm 1 vitamin D receptor restriction fragment length polymorphism (bb) influences the effect of calcium intake on bone mineral density. *Journal of Bone and Mineral Research* 12: 1049–1057.

Kiessling, K. L., ed. 1999. *Alleviating the Consequences of an Ecological Catastrophe. Women, Children, Environment and Health: Conference on the Aral Sea.* Stockholm: Swedish UNIFEM Committee.

Kim, J. and M. Motshei. 2002. "Women enjoy punishment": Attitudes and experiences of gender violence among primary health care nurses in rural South Africa. *Social Science and Medicine* 54: 91–102.

Kim, J. Y., Millen, J. V., Irwin, A., and J. Gershman. 2000. *Dying for Growth: Global Inequality and the Health of the Poor.* Monroe, MA: Common Courage Press.

Kim, K. and Y. Cho. 1992. Epidemiological survey of spouse abuse in Korea. In *Intimate Violence: Interdisciplinary Perspectives,* ed. C. Viano. Washington, DC: Hemisphere.

Kin, K., Lee, J. H. E., and K. Kushida. 1993. Bone density and body composition on the Pacific Rim: A comparison between Japan-born and U.S.-born Japanese-American women. *Journal of Bone and Mineral Research* 8: 861–869.

Kirmani, M. N. and D. Munyakho. 1996. The impact of structural adjustment programs on women and AIDS. In *Women's Experience with HIV/AIDS: An International Perspective,* eds. L. D. Long and E. M. Ankrah. New York: Columbia University Press.

Kitagawa, E. M. and P. M. Hauser. 1973. *Differential Mortality in the United States.* Cambridge: Harvard University Press.

Kjellberg, A. 1998. Men, work and health. In *Women's Health at Work,* eds. Å. Kilbom, K. Messing, and C. Bildt Thorbjörnsson. Solna: National Institute of Working Life.

Klabunde, C. N., Potosky, A. L., Harlan, L. C., and B. S. Kramer. 1998. Trends and black/white differences in treatment for nonmetastatic prostate cancer. *Medical Care* 36(9): 1337–1348.

Kleerekoper, M. 1994. Detecting osteoporosis. Beyond the history and physical examination. *Postgraduate Medicine* 103(4): 45–47.

Klugman, B. 2001. A critical review of tools for mainstreaming gender analysis and their application and usefulness in health. Gender Working Group. Geneva: World Health Organization.

Kochanek, K. D., Maurer, J. D., and H. M. Rosenberg. 1994. Why did black life expectancy decline from 1984 through 1989 in the United States? *American Journal of Public Health* 84(6): 938–944.

Kogevinas, M. and M. Porta. 1997. Socioeconomic differences in cancer survival: A review of the evidence. In *Social Inequalities and Cancer,* eds. M. Kogevinas, N. Pearce, M. Susser, and P. Boffetta. IARC Scientific publications 138. Lyon: International Agency for Research on Cancer.

Kogevinas, M., Pearce, N., Susser, M., and P. Boffetta. 1999. *Social Inequalities and Cancer.* Lyon: International Agency for Research on Cancer.

Koller, D. L., Rodriguez, L. A., and J. C. Christian. 1998. Linkage of a QTL contributing to normal variation in bone mineral density to chromosome 11q12-13. *Journal of Bone and Mineral Research* 13(12): 1903–1908.

Koppe, J. G. 1995. Nutrition and breast-feeding. *European Journal of Obstetrics, Gyneacology and Reproductive Biology* 62(1): 73–78.

Koppe, J. G., Ten Tusscher, G., and P. De Boer. 1999. Background exposure to dioxins and PCBs in Europe and resulting health effects. In *Sustainable Development and Women's Health,* ed. M. E. Butter. Groningen: Science Shop for Biology, University of Groningen.

Koss, M. 1990. The women's mental health research agenda: Violence against women. *American Psychologist* 45: 374–380.

Koss, M. and L. Heslet. 1992. Somatic consequences of violence against women. *Archives of Family Medicine* 1: 53–59.

Koss, M. P. 1993. Detecting the scope of rape. A review of prevalence research methods. *Journal of Interpersonal Violence* 8(2): 198–222.

Koss, M. P. 1994. The negative impact of crime victimization on women's health and medical use. In *Reframing Women's Health,* ed. A. Dan. Thousand Oaks, CA: Sage.

Koss, M. P. and T. E. Dinero. 1989. Discriminant analysis of risk factors for sexual victimization among a national sample of college women. *Journal of Consulting and Clinical Psychology* 57: 242–250.

Koss, M. P., Koss, P. G., and W. Woodruff. 1991. Deleterious effects of criminal victimization on women's health and medical utilization. *Archives of Internal Medicine* 151: 342–347.

Kramer, B. S., Brown, M. L., Prorok, P. C., Potosky, A. L., and J. K. Gohagan. 1993. Prostate cancer screening: What we know and what we need to know. *Annals of Internal Medicine* 119(9): 914–923.

Krieger, N. 1990. Racial and gender discrimination: Risk factors for high blood pressure? *Social Science and Medicine* 30(12): 1273–1281.

Krieger, N. and E. Fee. 1994. Man-made medicine and women's health: The biopolitics of sex/gender and race/ethnicity. *International Journal of Health Services* 24(2): 265–283.

Krieger, N. and S. Sidney. 1997. Prevalence and health implications of anti-gay discrimination: A study of black and white women and men in the CARDIA cohort. *International Journal of Health Services* 27(1): 157–176.

Krieger, N., Rowley, D. L., Herman, A. A., Avery, B., and M. T. Phillips. 1993. Racism, sexism, and social class: Implications for studies of health, disease, and well-being. *American Journal of Preventive Medicine* 9: 82–122.

Krishnan, T. N. 1995. Access to health and burden of treatment in India. An inter-state comparison. Paper presented at the international workshop on health insurance in India, Bangalore, September 20–22.

Kumanyika, S. K. and S. M. Krebs-Smith. 2000. *Preventive Nutrition Issues in Ethnic and Socioeconomic Groups in the United States.* Totowa, NJ: Humana Press.

Kutner, N. G. and Brogan, D. 1990. Sex stereotypes and health care: The case of treatment for kidney failure. *Sex Roles* 24: 279.

Kutzin, J. 1993. *Obstacles to Women's Access: Issues and Options for More Effective Interventions to Improve Women's Health.* Human resources development and operations policy Working paper. Washington, DC: World Bank.

Kutzin, J. 1995. *Experience with Organizational and Financing Reform of the Health Sector.* Current concerns SHS paper 8 (SHS/CC/94.3). Geneva: World Health Organization.

La Vecchia, C., Negri, E., Levi, F., and J. A. Baron. 1991. Cigarette smoking, body mass and other risk factors for fractures of the hip in women. *International Journal of Epidemiology* 20(3): 671–677.

Labunska, I., Stephenson, A., Brigden, K., Stringer, R., Santillo, D., Johnston, P. A., and J. M. Ashton. 1999. *Toxic Hotspots: A Greenpeace Investigation of Gujarat Industrial Estates. Organic and Heavy Metal Contaminants in Samples Taken at Three Industrial Estates in Gujarat, India.* Exeter: Greenpeace Research Laboratories, Department of Biological Sciences, University of Exeter.

Lahelma, E. and S. Arber. 1994. Health inequalities among men and women in contrasting welfare states. *European Journal of Public Health* 4: 213–226.

Lane, S. D. and A. I. Meleis. 1991. Roles, work, health perceptions and health resources of women: A study in an Egyptian delta hamlet. *Social Science and Medicine* 33(10): 1197–1208.

Lanting, C. I. 1999. Effects of perinatal PCB and dioxin exposure and early feeding mode on child development. Ph.D. dissertation, University of Groningen, Groningen.

Larme, A. C. 1998. Environment, vulnerability and gender in Andean ethnomedicine. *Social Science and Medicine* 47(8): 1005–1015.

Larrain, S. 1993. *Estudio de frecuencia de la violencia intrafamiliar y la condición de la mujer en Chile.* Santiago: Pan American Health Organisation.

Larsson, S., Eliasson, P., and L. I. Hansson. 1989. Hip fractures in northern Sweden 1973–1984. A comparison of rural and urban populations. *Acta Orthopaedica Scandinavica* 60(5): 567–571.

Lassen, P. M. and I. M. Thompson. 1994. Treatment options for prostate cancer. *Urology Nursing* 14: 12–15.

Lau, E., Donnan, S., Barker, D. J., and C. Cooper. 1988. Physical activity and calcium intake in fracture of the proximal femur in Hong Kong. *British Medical Journal* 297(6661): 1441–1443.

Lau, E. M. C. 1996. The epidemiology of hip fracture in Asia: An update. *Osteoporosis International* 6(Suppl. 3): 19–23.

Lau, E. M. C. and C. Cooper. 1996. The epidemiology of osteoporosis. *Clinical Orthopedics* 323: 65–74.

Lauderdale, D. S., Jacobsen, S. J., and S. E. Furner. 1997. Hip fracture incidence among elderly Asian-American populations. *American Journal of Epidemiology* 146(6): 502–509.

Laurence, L. and R. Spalter-Roth. 1996. *Measuring the Costs of Domestic Violence Against Women and the Cost-Effectiveness of Interventions: An Initial Assessment and Proposals for Further Research.* Washington, DC: Institute for Women's Policy Research.

Law, M. R., Wald, N. J., and T. W. Meade. 1991. Strategies for prevention of osteoporosis and hip fracture. *British Medical Journal* 303(6800): 453–459.

Lawson, A. 1997. *Tanzania: Public Expenditure Review, Budgeting Priorities in the Social Sectors.* Oxford: Oxford Policy Management.

Le Boff, M. S., Kohlmeier, L., and S. Hurwitz. 1999. Occult vitamin D deficiency in postmenopausal US women with acute hip fracture. *Journal of the American Medical Association* 281(16): 1505–1511.

Lean Lim, L. 1996. *More and Better Jobs for Women. An Action Guide.* Geneva: International Labour Office.

Lee, W. T., Leung, S. S., Ng, M. Y., Wang, S. F., and Y. C. Xu. 1993. Bone mineral content of two populations of Chinese children with different calcium intakes. *Bone and Mineral* 23(3): 195–206.

Legler, J. M., Feuer, E. J., Potosky, A. L., Merrill, R. M., and B. S. Kramer. 1998. The role of prostate-specific antigen (PSA) testing patterns in the recent prostate cancer incidence decline in the United States. *Cancer Causes Control* 9(5): 519–527.

Lehto, J. and A. Ritsatakis. 1999. Health impact assessment as a tool for intersectoral health policy. Discussion paper for a conference on health impact Assessment: From theory to practice, Gothenburg. (POLCO1 02 01/6). WHO Regional Office for Europe.

Leibenluft, E. 1997. Women with bipolar illness: Clinical and research issues. *American Journal of Psychiatry* 153: 163–173.

Leibenluft, E. 2000. Women with bipolar illness: An update. *Bulletin of the Menninger Clinic* 64: 5–17.

Leonard, H. J. 1989. *Environment and the Poor: Development Strategies for a Common Agenda.* New Brunswick, NJ: Transaction Books.

Lerner, D. J. and W. B. Kannel. 1986. Patterns of coronary heart disease morbidity and mortality in the population. *American Heart Journal* 111(2): 383–390.

Leslie, J. 1989. Women's time: A factor in the use of child survival technologies? *Health Policy and Planning* 4(1): 1–16.

Leslie, J. 1992. Women's time and the use of health services. *Institute of Development Studies Bulletin* 23(1): 4–7.

Levins, R. 1995. Preparing for uncertainty. *Ecosystem Health* 1: 47–54.

Levinson, D. 1989. *Family Violence in Cross Cultural Perspective*. Newbury Park, CA: Sage.

Levy, F. 1995. Incomes and income inequality. In *State of the Union*, ed. R. Farley. New York: Russell Sage Foundation.

Lieberman, U., Weiss, S., and J. Bröll. 1995. Effect of oral alendronate on bone mineral density and the incidence of fractures in postmenopausal osteoporosis. *New England Journal of Medicine* 333(22): 1437–1443.

Liefooghe, R. 1998. Gender differences in beliefs and attitudes towards tuberculosis and their impact on tuberculosis control: What do we know. In *Gender and Tuberculosis*, eds. V. K. Diwan, A. Thorson, and A. Wikvist. Report from an International research workshop at the Nordic School of Public Health, May 24–26. Göteborg: Nordic School of Public Health.

Lillie-Blanton, M. and T. LaVeist. 1996. Race/ethnicity, the social environment and health. *Social Science and Medicine* 43(1): 83–91.

Lillie-Blanton, M., Martinez, R. M., Taylor, A. K., and B. G. Robinson. 1993. Latina and African American women: Continuing disparities in health. *International Journal of Health Services* 23(3): 555–584.

Lindamer, L. A., Lohr, J. B., Harris, M. J., McAdams, L. A., and D. V. Jeste. 1999. Gender-related clinical differences in older patients with schizophrenia. *Journal of Clinical Psychiatry* 60: 61–67.

Linzer, M., Spitzer, R., Kroenke, K., Williams, J. B., Hahn, S., Brody, D., and F. de Gruy. 1996. Gender, quality of life and mental disorders in primary care: Results from the PRIME-MD 1000 study. *American Journal of Medicine* 101: 526–533.

Lips, P. 1997. Epidemiology and predictors of fractures associated with osteoporosis. *American Journal of Medicine* 103(2A): 3–8.

Liu, Y. L., Hsiao, W. C., Li, Q., Liu, X. Z., and M. H. Ren. 1995. Transformation of China's rural health care financing. *Social Science and Medicine* 41(8): 1085–1093.

Livingstone, A. M. 1995. *A Study of the Links Between Gender and Health in the Upper West Region*. Ghana: Ministry of Health, Upper West Region.

Lock, M. and D. Gordon, eds. 1998. *Biomedicine Examined*. Dordrecht: Kluwer Academic Publishers.

Lock, M. and N. Scheper-Hughes. 1990. A critical-interpretive approach in medical anthropology: Rituals and routines of discipline and dissent. In *Medical Anthropology: Contemporary Theory and Method*, eds. T. M. Johnson and C. F. Sargent. New York: Praeger.

Loewenson, R. 1995. Occupational health in small-scale industries in Africa. *African Newsletter*. (2). www.occuphealth.fi/e/info/anl/295/loewe.htm.

Loewenson, R. 1999. *Public Participation in Health: Making People Matter*. IDS Working paper 84. Brighton: Training and Research Support Centre (Zimbabwe) and Institute of Development Studies.

Loewenson, R., Laurell, A. C., and C. Hogstedt. 1999. Participatory approaches in occupational health research. In *Health and Work*, eds. N. Daykin and L. Doyal. Hundmills, Basingstoke, Hampshire, and London: Macmillan.

London, L. and R. Bailie. 1998. Improving surveillance for acute pesticide poisoning in the western Cape, South Africa. *African Newsletter* (1). www.occuphealth.fi/e/info/anl/198/london.htm.

Long, N. H., Johansson, E., Lonnroth, K., Eriksson, B., Winkvist, A., and V. K. Diwan. 1999. Longer delays in tuberculosis diagnosis among women in Vietnam. *International Journal of Tubercle and Lung Disease* 3(5): 388–393.

Longwe, S. H. 1992. A framework for understanding women's empowerment. Paper prepared for UNICEF workshop on women's empowerment, Gaberone, Botswana.

Loring, M. and B. Powell. 1988. Gender, race, and DSM-III: A study of the objectivity of psychiatric diagnostic behavior. *Journal of Health and Social Behavior* 29: 1–22.

Louat, F., Grosh, M. E., and J. van der Gaag. 1993. *Welfare Implications of Female Headship in Jamaican Households*. Living standards measurement study working paper 123. Washington, DC: World Bank.

Luehmann, D., Kohlmann, T., Lange, S. and H. Raspe. 2000. Die rolle der Osteodensitometrie im Rahman der Primaer-, Sekundaer-, und Tertaerpraevention/Therapie der Osteoporose. Aufbau einer Datenbasis "Evaluation medizinischer Verfahren und Technologien in der Bundesrepublick." Luebeck: Institut fuer Sozialmedizin, Medizinische Universitaet Luebeck.

Lufkin, E. G., Wahner, H. W., and W. M. O'Fallon. 1992. Treatment of postmenopausal osteoporosis with transdermal estrogen. *Annals of Internal Medicine* 117: 1–9.

Lundberg, U. 1998. Work and stress in women. In *Women, Stress, and Heart Disease*, eds. K. Orth-Gomér, M. Chesney, and N. K. Wenger. Hillsdale, NJ: Lawrence Erlbaum.

Lupton, D. 1994. *Medicine as Culture: Illness, Disease and the Body in Western Societies*. London: Sage.

Luschen, G., Geling, O., Janssen, C., Kunz, G., and O. Von dem Knesebeck. 1997. After unification: Gender and subjective health status in East and West Germany. *Social Science and Medicine* 44(9): 1313–1323.

Lynch, J. W. and G. A. Kaplan. 1997. Understanding how inequality in the distribution of income affects health. *Journal of Health Psychology* 2(3): 297–314.

Macintyre, S. 1986. The patterning of health by social position in contemporary Great Britain: Directions for sociological research. *Social Science and Medicine* 23(4): 393–415.

Macintyre, S. 1997. The Black report and beyond: What are the issues? *Social Science and Medicine* 44(6): 723–745.

Macintyre, S., Hunt, K., and H. Sweeting. 1996. Gender differences in health: Are things really as simple as they seem? *Social Science and Medicine* 42(4): 617–624.

Macintyre, S., Maciver, S., and A. Sooman. 1993. Area, class and health: Should we be focusing on places or people? *Journal of Social Policy* 22(2): 235–242.

Macran, S., Clarke, L., and H. Joshi. 1996. Women's health: Dimensions and differentials. *Social Science and Medicine* 42(9): 1203–1216.

Madhiwalla, N. and A. Jesani. 1997. Morbidity among women in Mumbai City: Impact of work and environment. *Economic and Political Weekly* October 25: WS-38–WS-44.

Madhiwalla, N., Nandraj, S., and R. Sinha. 2000. *Health, Households and Women's Lives. A Study of Illness and Childbearing among Women in Nashik District, Maharashtra.* Mumbai: Centre for Enquiry into Health and Allied Themes.

Makinen, M., Waters, H., Rauch, M., Almagambetova, N., Bitran, R., Gilson, L., McIntyre, D., Pannarunothai, S., Prieto, A. L., Ubilla, G., and S. Ram. 2000. Inequalities in health care use and expenditures: Empirical data from eight developing countries or countries in transition. *Bulletin of World Health Organization* 78(1): 55–65.

Makuc, D. M., Breen, N., and V. Freid. 1999. Low income, race and the use of mammography. *Health Services Research* 34(1 Pt 2): 229–239.

Makuc, D. M., Freid, V. M., and P. E. Parsons. 1994. Health insurance and cancer screening among women. *Advance Data* 254(3): 1–11.

Males, M. 1997. Adolescents: Daughters or alien sociopaths? *Lancet.* 349(Suppl I): SI13-SI16.

Malhotra, A. and R. Mehra. 1999. *Fulfilling the Cairo Commitment: Enhancing Women's Economic and Social Options for Better Reproductive Health.* Washington, DC: International Center for Research on Women.

Maman, S., Campbell, J., Sweat, M. D., and A. C. Gielen. 2000. The intersections of HIV and violence: Directions for future research and interventions. *Social Science and Medicine* 50: 459–478.

Manh Loi, V., Tuan Huy, V., Huu Minh, N., and C. Clement. 1999. *Gender Based Violence: The Case of Vietnam.* Washington, DC: World Bank.

Manderson, L., Jenkins, J., and M. Tanner. 1993. Women and tropical diseases: Introduction. *Social Science and Medicine* 37(4): 441–444.

Marmot, M. and A. Feeney. 1997. General explanations for social inequalities in health. In *Social Inequalities and Cancer,* eds. M. Kogevinas, N. Pearce, M. Susser, and P. Boffetta. International Agency for Research on Cancer Scientific publication 138. Lyon: International Agency for Research on Cancer.

Marmot, M. G. 1991. Health inequalities among British civil servants in the Whitehall II study. *Lancet* 337: 1387–1393.

Marmot, M. G., Kogevinas, M., and M. A. Elston. 1987. Social/economic status and disease. *Annual Review of Public Health* 8: 111–135.

Marmot, M. G., Shipley, M. J., and G. Rose. 1984. Inequalities in death: Specific explanations of a general pattern? *Lancet* 1: 1003–1006.

Maroni, M., Colosio, C., Fait, A., and S. Visentin. 1999. Occupational exposure to pesticides in the developing world: Health effects and strategies for prevention. *African Newsletter* (1). www.occuphealth.fi/e/info/anl/199/developing04.htm.

Marottoli, R. A., Berkman, L. F., Leo-Summers, L., and L. M. Cooney. 1994. Predictors of mortality and institutionalization after hip fracture: The New Haven EPESE cohort. *American Journal of Public Health* 84: 1807–1812.

Marquette, C. 1997. Current poverty, structural adjustment, and drought in Zimbabwe. *World Development* 25(7): 1141–1149.

Marshall, D., Johnell, O., and H. Wedel. 1996. Meta-analysis of how well measures of bone mineral density predict occurrence of osteoporotic fractures. *British Medical Journal* 312: 1254–1259.

Martin, E. 1990. Science and women's bodies: Forms of anthropological knowledge. In *Body/Politics: Women and the Discourses of Science,* eds. M. Jacobus, E. Fox Keller, and S. Shuttleworth. New York: Routledge.

Martin, E. 1996. The egg and the sperm: How science has constructed a romance based on stereotypical male-female roles. In *Gender and Health: An International Perspective,* ed. C. Sargent. Englewood Cliffs, NJ: Prentice-Hall.

Mastroianni, A. C., Faden, R., and S. Federman. 1994. *Women and Health Research: Ethical and Legal Issues of Including Women in Clinical Studies.* Washington, DC: Institute of Medicine, National Academy Press.

Matamala, M. I. 1998. Gender-related indicators for the evaluation of quality of care in reproductive health services. *Reproductive Health Matters* 6(11): 10–21.

Maticka-Tyndale, E., Elkins, D., Haswell-Elkins, M., and D. Rujkarakorn. 1997. Contexts and patterns of men's commercial sexual partnerships in northeastern Thailand: Implications for AIDS prevention. *Social Science and Medicine* 44(2): 199–213.

Mazza, D., Dennerstein, L., and V. Ryan. 1996. Physical, sexual and emotional violence against women: A general practice-based prevalence study. *Medical Journal of Australia* 164(1): 14–17.

Mbilinyi, M. and R. Shayo. 1996. Gender responsiveness of World Bank programmes in Tanzania. Final report on a workshop on gender responsiveness in World Bank programmes in Tanzania, Dar es Salaam, March.

Mbizvo, M. 1996. Gender dynamics and the challenges for HIV prevention. *Central African Journal of Medicine* 42(12): 351–354.

McDonald, D. A. 1998. Three steps forward, two steps back: Ideology and urban ecology in South Africa. *Review of African Political Economy* 75: 73–88.

McFarlane, J., Cristoffel, K., Bateman, L., Miller, V., and L. Bullock. 1991. Assessing for abuse: Self-report versus nurse interview. *Public Health Nursing* 8(4): 245–250.

McFarlane, J., Parker, B., and K. Soeken. 1996. Abuse during pregnancy: Associations with maternal health and infant birth weight. *Nursing Research* 275: 1915–1920.

McGrath, E., Keita, G. P., and B. R. Strickland, eds. 1990. *Women and Depression. Risk Factors and Treatment Issues.* Washington, DC: American Psychological Association.

McIntosh, C. A. and J. L. Finkle. 1995. The Cairo conference on population and development: A new paradigm? *Population and Development Review* 21(2): 223–260.

McKinlay, J. B. 1996. Some contributions from the social system to gender inequalities in heart disease. *Journal of Health and Social Behavior* 37: 1–26.

McKinney, M. M. and K. M. Marconi. 1992. Legislative interventions to increase access to screening mammography. *Journal of Community Health* 17: 333–349.

McMichael, A. J. 1995. The health of persons, populations and planets: Epidemiology comes full circle. *Epidemiology* 6(6): 633–636.

McNeill, W. H. 1976. *Plagues and People.* Garden City, NY: Doubleday.

McPake, B. and A. Mills. 2000. What can we learn from international comparisons of health systems and health system reform? *Bulletin of the World Health Organization* 78(6): 811–820.

McPake, B., Hanson, K., and A. Mills. 1993. Community financing of health care in Africa: An evaluation of the Bamako initiative. *Social Science and Medicine* 36(11): 1383–1395.

Meding, B. 1998. Work-related skin disease. In *Women's Health at Work*, eds. Å. Kilbom, K. Messing, and C. Bildt Thorbjörnsson. Solna: National Institute of Working Life.

Mehretu, A. and C. Mutambirwa. 1992. Time and energy costs of distance in rural life space of Zimbabwe: Case study in the Chiduku communal area. *Social Science and Medicine* 34: 17–24.

Meikle, J. 2000. March of superbugs must be halted. *Guardian* June 13.

Melhus, H., Michaelsson, K., and A. Kindmark. 1998. Excessive dietary intake of vitamin A is associated with reduced bone mineral density and increased risk for hip fracture. *Annals of Internal Medicine* 129(10): 770–778.

Melkas, H. and R. Anker. 1998. *Gender Equality and Occupational Segregation in Nordic Labour Markets.* Geneva: International Labour Office.

Memon, A., Pospula, W. M., and A. Y. Tantawy. 1998. Incidence of hip fracture in Kuwait. *International Journal of Epidemiology* 27(5): 860–865.

Menchik, P. L. 1993. Economic status as a determinant of mortality among black and white older men: Does poverty kill? *Population Studies* 47: 427–436.

Messerschmidt, J. 1993. *Masculinities and Crime: Critique and Reconceptualization of Theory.* Lanham, MD: Rowman & Littlefield.

Messing, K. 1993. Prostitutes and chimney sweeps both have problems: Towards full integration of both sexes in the study of occupational health. *Social Science and Medicine* 36: 47–55.

Messing, K. 1998. *One-Eyed Science. Occupational Health and Women Workers.* Philadelphia: Temple University Press.

Messing, K. and Å. Kilbom. 1998. Equally Different. Identifying biological specificities or relevance to work related health. In *Women's Health at Work,* eds. Å. Kilbom, K. Messing, and C. Bildt Thorbjörnsson. Solna: National Institute of Working Life.

Meyer, H. E., Tverdal, A., and C. Henriksen. 1996. Risk factors of femoral neck fractures in Oslo. *Tidsskrift for den Norske Laegeforening* 116(22): 2656–2659.

Michell, L. and A. Amos. 1997. Girls, pecking order and smoking. *Social Science and Medicine* 44(12): 1861–1869.

Michelson, E. H. 1993. Adam's rib awry? Women and schistosomiasis. *Social Science and Medicine* 37(4): 493–501.

Miller, B. 1981. *The Endangered Sex: Neglect of Female Children in Rural North India.* Ithaca, NY: Cornell University Press.

Miller, B. A., Ries, L. A. G., Hankey, B. F., Kosary, C. L., Harras, A., Devesa, S. S., and B. K. Edwards, eds. 1993. *SEER Cancer Statistics Review: 1973–1990.* National Cancer Institute, NIH publication 93-2789. Rockville, MD: National Institute of Health.

Miller, J. D. 1996. Food-borne natural carcinogens: Issues and priorities. *African Newsletter* (Suppl 1). www.occuphealth.fi/e/info/anl/1966/miller.htm.

Ministry of Foreign Affairs. 1999. Making partnerships work on the ground. Ministry of Foreign Affairs, Government of Sweden report of a workshop, Stockholm.

Mirlees-Black, C. and C. Byron. 1999. *Domestic Violence: Findings from the BCS Self-Completion Questionnaire.* Research findings 86. London: Home Office.

Mishel, L. and J. Bernstein. 1994. *The State of Working America 1994–95.* Armonk, NY: M.E. Sharpe.

Mishra, V., Retherford, R. D., and K. R. Smith. 1997. *Effects of Cooking Smoke on Prevalence of Tuberculosis in India.* East-West center working papers population series 92. Honolulu, HI: East West Center.

Mishra, V. N., Malhotra, M., and S. Gupta. 1990. Chronic respiratory disorders in females of Delhi. *Journal of the Indian Medical Association* 88: 77–80.

Mishra, V. N., Retherford, R. D., and K. R. Smith. 1999. Biomass cooking fuels and prevalence of blindness in India. *Journal of Environmental Medicine* 1(4): 189–199.

Moeller, D. W. 1997. *Environmental Health,* revised ed. Cambridge: Harvard University Press.

Moen, P. H., Robinson, J., and V. Fields. 1994. Women's work and caregiving roles: A life course approach. *Journal of Gerontology* 36: 913–917.

Momeni, K. A., Peña, R., Ellsberg, M. C., and L. A. Persson. 1999. Violence against women increases the risk of infant and child mortality. A case-referent study in Nicaragua. In *Infant Mortality in Transitional Nicaragua*. Doctoral thesis, Umea University, Sweden.

Montgomery, L. E. and O. Carter-Pokras. 1993. Health status by social class and/or minority status: Implications for environmental equity research. *Toxicological and Industrial Health* 9(5): 729–773.

Mooney, J. 1993. *The Hidden Figure: Domestic Violence in North London*. London: Middlesex University, School of Sociology and Social Policy.

Morrison, A. and M. B. Orlando. 1997. The socio-economic impact of domestic violence against women in Chile and Nicaragua. In *Too Close to Home. Domestic Violence in the Americas,* eds. R. A. Morrison and M. L. Biehl. Washington, DC: Inter-American Development Bank (distributed by Johns Hopkins University Press).

Morse, L. H. and L. J. Hinds. 1993. Women and ergonomics. *Occupational Medicine: State of the Art Reviews* 8(4): 721–731.

Mort, F. 1987. *Dangerous Sexualities: Medico-Moral Politics in England since 1830*. London: Routledge and Kegan Paul.

Mullen, P. E., Martin, J. L., Anderson, J. C., Romans, S. E., and G. P. Herbison. 1993. Childhood sexual abuse and mental health in adult life. *British Journal of Psychiatry* 163: 721–732.

Mullen, P. E., Romans-Clarkson, S. E., Walton, V. A., and G. P. Herbison. 1988. Impact of sexual and physical abuse on women's mental health. *Lancet* 1(8590): 841–845.

Munger, R. G., Cerhan, J. R., and B. C. Chiu. 1999. Prospective study of dietary protein intake and risk of hip fracture in postmenopausal women. *American Journal of Clinical Nutrition* 69(1): 147–152.

Muraleedharan, V. R. 1999. *Characteristics and Structure of the Private Hospital Sector in Urban India: A Study of Madras City*. Small applied research paper 5. Partnerships for Health Reform Project. Bethesda, MD: Abt Associates.

Murray, C. J. L. 1990. Rational approaches to priority setting in international health. *Journal of Tropical Medicine and Hygiene* 93(5): 303–311.

Murray, C. J. L. 1994. Quantifying the global burden of disease: The technical basis for disability-adjusted life-years. *Bulletin of the World Health Organization* 72: 495–501.

Murray, C. J. L. 1996. Rethinking DALYs. In *The Global Burden of Disease,* Vol. 1, eds. C. J. L. Murray and A. D. Lopez. Boston: Harvard School of Public Health on behalf of the World Health Organization and the World Bank.

Murray, C. J. L. and A. D. Lopez. 1996. *The Global Burden of Disease: A Comprehensive Assessment of Mortality and Disability from Diseases, Injuries and Risk Factors in 1990 and projected to 2020. Summary*. Boston: Harvard School of Public Health on behalf of the World Health Organization and the World Bank.

Murray, C. J. L. and A. D. Lopez. 1998. Quantifying the health risks of sex and reproduction. In *Health Dimensions of Sex and Reproduction,* eds. C. J. L. Murray and A. D. Lopez. Boston: Harvard School of Public Health on behalf of the World Health Organization and the World Bank.

Musgrove, P. 2000. A critical review of "A critical review." *Health Policy and Planning* 15(1): 110–115.

Musselman, D. L., Evans, D. L., and C. B. Nemeroff. 1998. The relationship of depression to cardiovascular disease. *Archives of General Psychiatry* 55: 580–592.

Mussolino, M. E., Looker, A. C., and J. H. Madans. 1998. Risk factors for hip fracture in white men: The NHANES I epidemiologic follow-up study. *Journal of Bone and Mineral Research* 13(6): 918–924.

Mwenesi, H., Harpham, T., and R. Snow. 1995. Child malaria treatment practices among mothers in Kenya. *Social Science and Medicine* 40(9): 1271–1277.

Myntti, C. and J. Cottingham. 1998. Gender analysis in sexual and reproductive health: A conceptual framework and practical tool. Unpublished manuscript prepared for the UNDP/UNFPA/WHO/World Bank Special Programme of Research, Development and Research Training in Human Reproduction, and its collaborators.

Nabarro, D. and A. Cassels. 1994. *Strengthening Health Management Capacity in Developing Countries.* London: Overseas Development Administration

Nair, D., George, A., and K. T. Chacko. 1997. Tuberculosis in Bombay: New insights from poor urban patients. *Health Policy and Planning* 12(1): 77–85.

Najman, J. M. 1993. Health and poverty: Past, present and prospects for the future. *Social Science and Medicine* 36: 157–166.

Nandraj, S. 1994. Beyond the law and the Lord. Quality of private health care. *Economic and Political Weekly* July 2: 1680–1685

Nandraj, S. and R. Duggal. 1997. *Physical Standards in the Private Health Sector. A Case Study of Rural Maharashtra.* Mumbai: Centre for Enquiry into Health and Allied Themes.

Narayan, D. 1997. *Voices of the Poor: Poverty and Social Capital in Tanzania.* Washington, DC: World Bank.

Narayana, G. 1996. Family violence, sex and reproductive health behavior among men in Uttar Pradesh, India. Unpublished.

Nathanson, C. A. 1975. Illness and the feminine role: A theoretical review. *Social Science and Medicine* 9: 57–62.

Nathanson, C. A. and A. D. Lopez. 1987. The future of sex mortality differentials in industrialized countries: A structural hypothesis. *Population Research and Policy Review* 6(2): 123–136.

National Cancer Institute. 1991. *Strategies to Control Tobacco Use in the United States: A Blueprint for Public Health Action in the 1990s.* NIH publication 92-3316. Washington, DC: U.S. Department of Health and Human Services.

National Center for Health Statistics. 1997. *Health, United States 1996–97 and Injury Chartbook*. Publication 97-1232. Hyattsville, MD: U.S. Department of Health and Human Services.

National Sample Survey Organisation. 1992. Morbidity and utilisation of medical services (NSS 42nd round 1986–87). *Sarvekshana* 52(XV).

National Sample Survey Organisation. 1998. *Morbidity and Treatment of Ailments*. Report 441, NSS Fifty-second round, July 1995–June 1996. New Delhi: Department of Statistics, Government of India.

Navarro, V. 1990. Race or class versus race and class: Mortality differentials in the United States. *Lancet* 336: 1238–1240.

Ndoye, F. J. 1998. Pesticide management and control in the Gambia. *African Newsletter* (1).

Nelson, E. and C. Zimmerman. 1996. *Household Survey on Domestic Violence in Cambodia*. Cambodia: Ministry of Women's Affairs, Project against Domestic Violence.

Nermo, M. 1994. The uncompleted equality. In *Conditions of Everyday Life,* eds. J. Fritzell and O. Lundberg. Stockholm: Brombergs [in Swedish].

Neuhauser, D. 1999. Foreword. *Medical Care* 37(6): JS8-JS9.

Nguyen, T. V., Eisman, J. A., Kelly, P. J., and P. N. Sambrook. 1996. Risk factors for osteoporotic fractures in elderly men. *American Journal of Epidemiology* 144(3): 255–263.

Norbeck, J. S. 1984. Modification of life event questionnaires. *Research in Nursing and Health* 7: 61–71.

Nord, E. 1992. Methods for quality-adjustment of life years. *Social Science and Medicine* 34: 559–569.

Norton, A. and B. Bird. 1998. *Social Development Issues in Sector Wide Approaches*. Social development division working paper 1. London: Department for International Development.

Nygaard, E. 2000. Is it feasible or desirable to measure burdens of disease as a single number? *Reproductive Health Matters* 8(15): 117–127.

Nyonator, F. and J. Kutzin. 1999. Health for some? The effects of user fees in the Volta region of Ghana. *Health Policy and Planning* 14(4): 329–341.

Nystrom, M. 1995. *Focus: Kitchen Design, a Study of Housing in Hanoi*. Lund: Lund University Press.

Oakley, A. 1994. Who cares for health? Social relations, gender, and the public health. *Journal of Epidemiology and Community Health* 48: 427–434.

O'Campo, P., Xue, X., Wang, M. C., and M. Caughy. 1997. Neighborhood risk factors for low birth weight in Baltimore: A multilevel analysis. *American Journal of Public Health* 87(7): 1113–1118.

OECD. 1999. *Development Advisory Committee: Meeting the Goals of S-21: Gender Equality and Environment*, Vol. III. (DCD/DAC/WID/99.3). Paris: Organization for Economic Cooperation and Development.

OECD/DAC. 1996. *Shaping the 21st century: The contribution of development cooperation.* Paris: Organization for Economic Cooperation and Development.

Offer, S. N. and M. Sabshin. 1984. *Normality and the Life Cycle: A Critical Integration.* New York: Basic Books.

Onyango Ouma, W., Laisser, R., Mbilima, M., Araoye, M., Pittman, P., Agyepong, I., Zakari, M., Fonn, S., and C. Vlassoff. 2001. The impact of *Health Workers for Change* in 7 settings: A useful management and health system development tool. *Health Policy and Planning* 16(Suppl 1): 33–39.

Östlin, P. 1997. Gender, social class and health. In *Equity in Health through Public Policy,* eds. E. Ollila, M. Kiovusalo, and T. Partonen. Helsinki: STAKES.

Östlin, P. 1998. Presentation on Gender and Occupational Health. Workshop on Gender and Health Equity, Harvard Center for Population and Development Studies. Cambridge.

Östlin, P., Alfredsson, L., Hammar, N., and C. Reuterwall. 1998. Myocardial infarction in male and female dominated occupations. *Occupational and Environmental Medicine* 55(9): 642–644.

Östlin, P., George, A., and G. Sen. 2001a. Gender, health and equity: The intersections. In *Challenging Inequities in Health: From Ethics to Action,* eds. T. Evans, M. Whitehead, F. Diderichsen, A. Bhuiya, and M. Wirth. New York: Oxford University Press.

Östlin, P., M. Danielsson, A. Härenstam, F. Diderichsen, and G. Lindberg, eds. 2001b. *Gender and Inequalities in Health.* Cambridge: Harvard Center for Population and Development Studies, Harvard University Press.

Owusu, W., Willett, W. C., and D. Feskanich. 1997. Calcium intake and the incidence of forearm and hip fractures among men. *Journal of Nutrition* 127(9): 1782–1787.

Oxaal, Z. and S. Cook. 1998. *Health and Poverty Gender Analysis.* BRIDGE report 46. Brighton: Institute of Development Studies.

Oxfam. 1998. *Debt Relief for Tanzania: An Opportunity for a Better Future.* International position paper. Oxford: Oxfam International.

Oxfam. 1999. *The IMF: Wrong Diagnosis, Wrong Medicine.* Oxford: Oxfam International.

Paalman, M., Bekedam, H., Hawken, L., and D. Nyheim. 1998. A critical review of priority-setting in the health sector: The methodology of the 1993 world development report. *Health Policy and Planning* 13(1): 13–31.

PAHO. 1998. *Health in the Americas,* Vol. I. Scientific publication 569. Washington, DC: Pan American Health Organization.

Pai, M. 2000. Unnecessary medical interventions: Caesarean sections as a case study. *Economic and Political Weekly* July 29: 2755–2761.

Pakkari, J., Kannus, P., and S. Niemi. 1994. Increasing age-adjusted incidence of hip fractures in Finland: The number and incidence of fractures in 1970–

1991 and prediction for the future. *Calcified Tissue International* 55: 342–345.

Palmer, I. 1992. Gender equity and economic efficiency in adjustment programmes. In *Women and Adjustment Policies in the Third World,* eds. H. Afshar and C. Dennis. Basingstoke: Macmillan.

Pamuk, E., Makuc, D., Heck, K., Reuben, C., and K. Lochner. 1998. *Health, United States, 1998 with Socioeconomic Status and Health Chartbook.* (DHHS publication (PHS) 98-1232). Hyattsville, MD: National Center for Health Statistics.

PANAP. 1998. Pesticide dump sickens Pakistan residents. *Pesticide Monitor* 7(3–4). www.poptel.org.uk/panap/pm/nfa-pm7.htm.

Paolisso, M. and J. Leslie. 1995. Meeting the changing health needs of women in developing countries. *Social Science and Medicine* 40: 55–65.

Pappas, G., Queen, S., Hadden, W., and G. Fisher. 1993. The increasing disparity in mortality between socioeconomic groups in the United States, 1960 and 1986. *New England Journal of Medicine* 329: 103–109.

Parker, R. 1993. "Within four walls": Brazilian sexual culture and HIV/AIDS. In *Sexuality, Politics and AIDS in Brazil: In Another World?* eds. H. Daniel and R. Parker. London: Falmer Press.

Partanen, T., Mbakaya, C., Ohay-Mitoko, G., Ngowi, A. V. E., and D. Mfitumukiza. 1999. East Africa pesticide network: Progress, results and impact. *African Newsletter* (1). www.occuphealth.fi/e/info/anl/199/east02.htm.

Paspati, I., Galanos, A., and G. P. Lyritis. 1998. Hip fracture epidemiology in Greece during 1977–1992. *Calcified Tissue International* 62(6): 542–547.

Patandin, S. 1999. Effects of environmental exposure to polychlorinated biphenyls and dioxins on growth and development in young children: A prospective follow-up study of breast-fed and formula-fed infants from birth until 42 months of age. Ph.D. dissertation, Erasmus University, Rotterdam.

Patel, D. N., Pettifor, J. M., and P. J. Becker. 1993. The effect of ethnicity on appendicular bone mass in white, coloured and Indian schoolchildren. *South African Medical Journal* 83: 847–853.

Patel, V., Araya, R., de Lima, M., Ludermir, A., and C. Todd. 1999. Women, poverty and common mental disorders in four restructuring societies. *Social Science and Medicine* 49: 1461–1471.

Patel, V., Simunyu, E., and F. Gwanzura. 1995. Kufungisisa (thinking too much): A Shona idiom for non-psychotic mental illness. *Central African Journal of Medicine* 41: 209–215.

Pearson, V. 1995. Goods on which one loses: Women and mental health in China. *Social Science and Medicine* 41(8): 1159–1173.

Persson, I., Naessen, T., and H. O. Adami. 1992. Reduced risk of hip fracture in women with endometrial cancer. *International Journal of Epidemiology* 21(4): 636–642.

Peterson, R. 1997. Women, environments and health: Overview and strategic directions for research and action. In *International Perspectives on Environment, Development and Health: Towards a Sustainable World,* eds. G. S. Shahi, B. S. Levy, A. Binger, T. Kjellström, and R. Lawrence. New York: Springer.

Petley, G. W., Cotton, A. M., Murrills, A. J., Taylor, P. A., and C. Cooper. 1996. Reference ranges of bone mineral density for women in southern England: The impact of local data on the diagnosis of osteoporosis. *British Journal of Radiology* 69(823): 655–660.

Phadke, A., Fernandes, A., Sharda, L., and A. Jesani. 1995. *A Study of Drug Supply and Use of Pharmaceuticals in Satara District.* Mumbai: Foundation for Research in Community Health.

Phillips, K. A., Fernyak, S., Potosky, A. L., Schauffler, H. H., and M. Egorin. 2000. Use of preventive services by managed care enrollees: An updated perspective. *Health Affairs* 19(1): 102–116.

Piccinelli, M. and F. G. Homen. 1997. *Gender Differences in the Epidemiology of Affective Disorders and Schizophrenia.* Geneva: World Health Organization.

Pilgrim, D. and A. Rogers. 1993. *A Sociology of Mental Health and Illness.* Buckingham: Open University Press.

Piot, P. 1999. HIV/AIDS and violence against women. UNAIDS speech to the Commission on the Status of Women, 43rd session, panel on women and health, New York, March 1–19, 1999.

Pittman, P. 1997. *Equidad de Género en la Dimensión Socioemocional de la Calidad de Atención en Salud.* Washington, DC: Pan American Health Organization.

Pittman, P. and P. Hartigan. 1996. Gender inequity: An issue for quality assessment researchers and managers. *Health Care for Women International* 17(5): 469–486.

Pitts, M., Brown, M., and J. McMaster. 1995. Reactions to repeated STD infections: Psychological aspects and gender issues in Zimbabwe. *Social Science and Medicine* 40(9): 1299–1304.

Polych, C. and D. Sabo. 1995. Gender politics, pain, and illness: The AIDS epidemic in North American prisons. In *Men's Health and Illness: Gender, Power and the Body,* eds. D. Sabo and D. Gordon. Thousand Oaks, CA: Sage.

Popay, J., Bartley, M., and C. Owen. 1993. Gender Inequalities in health: Social position, affective disorders and minor physical morbidity. *Social Science and Medicine* 36(1): 21–32.

Pope, C. A. III, and X. P. Xu. 1993. Passive cigarette smoke, coal heating, and respiratory symptoms of non-smoking women in China. *Environmental Health Perspectives* 101(4): 314–316.

Population Council. 1997. *What Can Be Done to Foster Multisectoral Population Policies?* Summary report of a seminar. New York: Population Council.

Potosky, A. L., Kessler, L., Gridley, G., Brown, C. C., and J. W. Horm. 1990. Rise in prostatic cancer incidence associated with increased use of transurethral resection. *Journal of the National Cancer Institute* 82(20): 1624–1628.

Prabha, R. 1983. Just one more queue: Women and water shortage in Tamil Nadu. *Manushi* June/July.

Prabhu, S., Uplekar, M. W., and N. H. Antia. 1995. *Health Care Financing in India*. A status paper prepared for the ICMR-ICSSR Joint Panel for Health. Mumbai: Foundation for Research in Community Health.

Prasad, S. 1999. Medicolegal response to violence against women in India. *Violence Against Women* 5(5): 478–506.

Prevention of the Maternal Mortality Network. 1992. Barriers to treatment of obstetric emergencies in rural communities of West Africa. *Studies in Family Planning* 23(5): 279–291.

Prindeville, D. M. and J. G. Bretting. 1998. Indigenous women activists and political participation: The case of environmental justice. *Women and Politics* 19(1): 39–58.

Proctor, E. K., Morrow-Howell, N., and L. Chadiha. 1997. Physical and cognitive functioning among chronically ill African American and white elderly in home care following hospital discharge. *Medical Care* 35(8): 782–791.

Province, M. A., Hadley, E. C., and M. C. Hornbrook. 1995. The effects of exercise on falls in elderly patients: A preplanned meta-analysis of the FICSIT trials. Frailty and injuries: Cooperative studies of intervention techniques. *Journal of the American Medical Association* 273: 1341–1347.

Puentes-Markides C. 1992. Women and access to health care. *Social Science and Medicine* 35: 619–626.

Pugliesi, K. 1995. Work and well-being: Gender differences in the psychological consequences of employment. *Journal of Health and Social Behavior* 36: 57–71.

Punnett, L. and W. M. Keyserling. 1987. Exposure to ergonomic stressors in the garment industry: Application and critique on job site work analysis methods. *Ergonomics* 30(7): 1099–1116.

Purohit, B. C. and R. Mohan. 1996. New directions for public health financing. *Economic and Political Weekly* February 24: 450–453.

Rahman, O., Strauss, J., Gertler, P., Ashley, D., and K. Fox. 1994. Gender differences in adult health: An international comparison. *Gerontological Society of America* 34(4): 463–469.

Raikes, A. 1990. *Pregnancy, Birthing and Family Planning in Kenya: Changing Patterns of Behaviour: A Health Service Utilization Study in Kisii District*. Copenhagen: Centre for Development Research.

Rajani, R. 1999. *Promoting Strategic Adolescent Participation: A Discussion Paper for UNICEF*. New York: United Nations Children's Fund.

Rajeshwari. 1996. Gender bias in utilisation of health care facilities in rural Haryana. *Economic and Political Weekly* February 24: 489–494.

Ramirez Rodriguez, J. C. and P. N. Vargas Becerra. 1996. Una espada de doble filo: La salud reproductiva y la violencia doméstica contra la mujer. Presentacion seminario salud reproductiva en América Latina y el Caribe: Temas y problemas, Brazil.

Randall, M. and L. Haskell. 1995. Sexual violence in women's lives: Findings from the women's safety project, a community-based survey. *Violence Against Women* 1(1): 6–31.

Rane, W. 1996. Analysis of drug prices, 1980–1995. *Economic and Political Weekly* August 24–31: 2331–2980.

Rane, W. 1998. Price control on drugs is essential. *Economic and Political Weekly* October 17–24: 2697–2698.

Rangan, S. and M. Uplekar. 1998. Gender perspectives of access to health and tuberculosis care. In *Gender and Tuberculosis,* eds. V. K. Diwan, A. Thorson, and A. Wikvist. Report from an international research workshop at the Nordic School of Public Health, May 24–26. Göteborg: Nordic School of Public Health.

Rao Gupta, G. 2000. Commentary on "health inequalities and the health of the poor." *Bulletin of the World Health Organization* 78(1): 81–82.

Rashed, S., Johnson, H., Dongier, P., Moreau, R., Lee, C., Crepeau, R., Lambert, J., Jefremovas, V., and C. Schaffer. 1999. Determinants of the permethrin impregnated bednets (PIB) in the Republic of Benin: The role of women in the acquisition and utilisation of PIBs. *Social Science and Medicine* 49(8): 993–1005.

Rathgeber, E. M. and C. Vlassoff. 1993. Gender and tropical diseases: A new research focus. *Social Science and Medicine* 37(4): 513–520.

Ratner, P. 1993. The incidence of wife abuse and mental health status in abused wives in Edmonton, Alberta. *Canadian Journal of Public Health* 84: 246–249.

Ravindran, T. K. S. 1992. The untold story: How the health care systems in developing countries contribute to maternal mortality. *International Journal of Health Services* 22: 513–528.

Razavi, S. ed. 2000. *Gendered Poverty and Well Being.* Oxford: Blackwell.

Razavi, S. and C. Miller. 1995. *Gender Mainstreaming. A Study of Efforts by the UNDP, the World Bank and the ILO to Institutionalize Gender Issues.* Geneva: United Nations Research Institute for Social Development.

Reddy, S. and Vandemoortele, J. 1996. *User Financing of Basic Social Services: A Review of Theoretical Arguments and Empirical Evidence.* New York: United Nations Children's Fund.

Reich, M. 1994. The political economy of health transitions in the third world. In *Health and Social Change in International Perspective,* eds. L. Chen, A. Kleinman, and N. Ware. Boston: Harvard School of Public Health.

Reich, M. 2000. The global drug gap. *Science* 287(5460): 1979–1981.

Rengam, S. V. 1994. Women and pesticides in Asia: Campaign for change. *Global Pesticide Campaigner* 4(3). http://www.igc.org/panna/resources/-pestis/PESTIS.burst.711.html.

Repetti, R. L., Matthews, K. A., and I. Waldron. 1989. Effects of paid employment on women's mental and physical health. *American Psychology* 44:1394.

Reproductive Health Alliance Europe. 1999. Profile of European donors prepared by Peter Hall, London.

Resnick, H. S., Acierno, R., and D. G. Kilpatrick. 1997. Health impact of interpersonal violence. 2. Medical and mental health outcomes. *Behavioral Medicine* 23(2): 65–78.

Resnick, S., Gottesmann, I., and M. McGue. 1993. Sensation-seeking in opposite-sex twins: An effect of prenatal hormones? *Behavior Genetics* 23(4): 323–329.

Restrepo, M., Munoz, N., Day, N. E., Parra, J. E., de Romero, L., and X. Nguyen-Dinh. 1990. Prevalence of adverse reproductive outcomes in population occupationally exposed to pesticides in Colombia. *Scandinavian Journal of Work, Environment and Health* 16(4): 232–238.

Reynolds, P. and G. A. Kaplan. 1990. Social connections and risk for cancer: Prospective evidence from the Alameda County study. *Behavioral Medicine* 16(3): 101–110.

Richie, B. 1990. AIDS: In living color. In *The Black Women's Health Handbook*, ed. E. White. Seattle: Seal Press.

Richters, J. 1994. *Women, Culture and Violence: A Development, Health and Human Rights Issue.* Leiden: The Netherlands Women and Autonomy Centre.

Ries, L. A. G., Kosary, C. L., Hankey, B. F., Miller, B. A., and B. K. Edwards. 1999. *SEER Cancer Statistics Review, 1973–1996.* Bethesda, MD: National Cancer Institute.

Rittenhouse, A. C. 1991. The emergence of premenstrual syndrome as a social problem. *Social Problems* 38(3): 49–56.

Roberts, G. L., Lawrence, J. M., Williams, G. M., and B. Raphael. 1998. The impact of domestic violence on women's mental health. *Australian and New Zealand Journal of Public Health* 22: 796–801.

Rodgers, K. 1994. Wife assault: The findings of a national survey. *Juristat Service Bulletin of the Canadian Centre for Justice Statistics* 14(9): 1–22.

Rodwin, M. A. 1994. Patient accountability and quality of care: Lessons from medical consumerism and the patients' rights, women's health and disability rights movements. *American Journal of Law and Medicine* 20: 147–167.

Rogers, R. G. 1992. Living and dying in the U.S.A.: Sociodemographic determinants of death among blacks and whites. *Demography* 29: 287–303.

Rogmark, C., Sernbo, I., Johnell, O., and J. A. Nilsson. 1999. Incidence of hip fractures in Malmo, Sweden, 1992–1995. A trend-break. *Acta Orthopaedica Scandinavica* 70(1): 19–22.

Rogow, D. 2000. Alone you are nobody, together we float: The Manuela Ramos movement. *Qualite/Calidad/Quality* Vol. 10. New York: Population Council.

Roman, C. 1992. *Working Life and Family Life. A Study on Women in Working Life.* Uppsala: Uppsala University, Department of Sociology [in Swedish].

Römkens, R. 1997. Prevalence of wife abuse in The Netherlands. *Journal of Interpersonal Violence* 12(1): 99–125.

Rorsman, B., Gräsbeck, A., Hagnell, O., Lanke, J., Öhman, R., Öjesjö, L., and L. A. Otterbeck. 1990. Prospective study of first-incidence depression. The Lundby study, 1957–72. *British Journal of Psychiatry* 156: 336–342.

Rosales, J. and E. Loaiza. 1999. *Encuesta Nicaraguense de Demografia y Salud 1998.* Managua: Instituto Nacional de Estadisticas y Censos.

Rosen, G. 1958. *A History of Public Health.* New York: MD Publications.

Rosenberg, L. 1993. Hormone replacement therapy: The need for reconsideration. *American Journal of Public Health* 83: 1670–1673.

Ross, P. D., Orimo, H., Wasnich, R. D., Vogel, J. M., and C. J. MacLean. 1989. Methodological issues in comparing genetic and environmental influences on bone mass. *Bone and Mineral* 7(1): 67–77.

Rowley, J. and S. Berkley. 1998. Sexually transmitted diseases. In *Health Dimensions of Sex and Reproduction,* eds. C. J. L. Murray and A. D. Lopez. Boston: Harvard School of Public Health on behalf of the World Health Organization and the World Bank.

Royce, J., Corbett, K., Sorensen, G., and J. Ockene. 1997. Gender, social pressure and smoking cessations: The community intervention trial for smoking cession at baseline. *Social Science and Medicine* 44(3): 359–370.

Royston, E. and S. Armstrong, eds. 1989. *Preventing Maternal Deaths.* Geneva: World Health Organization.

Rozemburg, B. and L. Manderson. 1998. "Nerves" and tranquilizer use in rural Brazil. *International Journal of Health Services* 28(1): 165–181.

Ruiz, M. T. and L. M. Verbrugge. 1997. A two way view of gender bias in medicine. *Journal of Epidemiological and Community Health* 51(2): 106–109.

Rupich, R. C., Specker, B. L., Lieuw-a-Fa, M., and M. Ho. 1996. Gender and race differences in bone mass during infancy. *Calcified Tissue International* 58(6): 395–397.

Russel-Aulet, M., Wang, J., Thornton, J. C., Colt, E. W., and R. N. Pierson. 1993. Bone mineral density and mass in a cross-sectional study of white and Asian women. *Journal of Bone and Mineral Research* 8(5): 575–582.

Russo, N. F. 1990. Overview: Forging research priorities for women's health. *American Psychologist* 45: 368–373.

Sadana, R. 1998. A closer look at the WHO/World Bank Global Burden of Disease Study's methodologies: How do poor women's values in a developing country compare with international public health experts? Conference presentation at the Public Health Forum, Reforming Health Sectors, London School of Hygiene and Tropical Medicine, April 21–24.

Saleh, S., Fortney, S. J. A., Rogers, S. M., and D. M. Potts. 1986. Accidental burn deaths to Egyptian women of reproductive age. *Burns, Including Thermal Injuries* 12: 241.

Salmond, K., Howden-Chapman, P., Woodward, A., and C. Salmond. 1999. Setting our sights on justice: Contaminated sites and socio-economic deprivation. *International Journal of Environmental Health Research* 9(1): 19–29.

Saltzman, L. E. and D. Johnson. 1996. CDC's family and intimate violence prevention team: Basing programs on science. *Journal of the American Medical Women's Association* 51: 83–86.

Sartorius, N., Jablensky, A., Korten, A., Ernberg, G., Anker, M., Cooper, J. E., and R. Day. 1986. Early manifestations and first-contact schizophrenia in different cultures. *Psychological Medicine* 16: 909–928.

Saunders, D. G. and K. Hamberger. 1993. Indicators of woman abuse based on chart review at a family practice centre. *Archives of Family Medicine* 2: 537–543.

Schneider, H. and L. Gilson. 1999. Impact of free maternal health care in South Africa. In *Safe Motherhood Initiatives: Critical Issues,* eds. M. Berer and T. K. S. Ravindran. London: Reproductive Health Matters.

Schneiderman, J. S. 1997. The common interest of earth science, feminism and environmental justice. *NWSA-Journal* 9(3): 124–137.

Schoepf, B. G. 1988. Women, AIDS, and economic crisis in Central Africa. *Canadian Journal of African Studies* 22(3): 625–644.

Schor, J. B. 1991. *The Overworked American: The Unexpected Decline of Leisure.* New York: Basic Books.

Schuler, M. ed. 1992. *Freedom from Violence: Women's Strategies from Around the World.* New York: UNIFEM.

Schuler, S. R., Hashemi, S. M., Riley, A. P., and S. Akhter. 1996. Credit programs, patriarchy and men's violence against women in rural Bangladesh. *Social Science and Medicine* 43(12): 1729–1742.

Schulman, K. A., Berlin, J. A., Harless, W., Kerner, J. F., Sistrunk, S., Gersh, B. J., Dube, R., Taleghani, C. K., Burke, J. E., and S. Williams. 1999. The effect of race and sex on physicians' recommendations for cardiac catheterization. *New England Journal of Medicine* 340(8): 618–626.

Schurch, M. A., Rizzoli, R., and B. Mermillod. 1996. A prospective study on socioeconomic aspects of fracture of the proximal femur. *Journal of Bone and Mineral Research* 11(12): 1935–1942.

Scott-Collins, K., Schoen, C., and S. Joseph. 1999. *Health Concerns across a Woman's Lifespan: The Commonwealth Fund 1998 Survey of Women's Health.* New York: Commonwealth Fund.

Seeman, E. 1997. Osteoporosis: Trails and tribulations. *American Journal of Medicine* 103(2A): 74S–89S.

Sen, A. 1999a. *Development as Freedom.* New York: Knopf.

Sen, A. 1999b. Health in development. Keynote address to the fifty-second World Health assembly, Geneva.

Sen, G. 1996. Gender, markets, and states: A selective review and research agenda. *World Development* 24(5): 821–829.

Sen, G. and S. Batliwala. 2000. Empowering women for reproductive rights. In *Women's Empowerment and Demographic Processes: Moving Beyond Cairo,* eds. H. Presser and G. Sen. Oxford: Oxford University Press.

Sen, G., Germain, A., and L. Chen, eds. 1994. *Population Policies Reconsidered: Health, Empowerment and Rights.* Cambridge: Harvard Center for Population and Development Studies with Harvard University Press.

Sen, G., Gurumurthy, A., and H. Sudarshan. 1999. Karnataka. In *The Community Needs-Based Reproductive and Child Health in India: Progress and Constraints.* Jaipur: HealthWatch Trust.

Sen, G., Mukherjee, V., Ramachandran, V., and A. Gurumurthy. 1998. Reproductive health and rights in India after ICPD: An assessment. Case study prepared for DAWN for the ICPD+5 assessment.

Sen, G. and R. Snow, eds. 1994. *Power and Decision: The Social Control of Reproduction.* Cambridge: Harvard Center for Population and Development Studies with Harvard University Press.

Shapiro, S., Venet, W., Strax, P., Venet, L., and R. Roeser. 1982. Ten- to fourteen-year effect of screening on breast cancer mortality. *Journal of the National Cancer Institute* 69: 349–355.

Shatrugna, V., Vidyasagar, P., Sujata, T., and G. Vasanthi, eds. 1993. *Women's Work and Its Impact on Child Health and Nutrition.* Hyderabad: National Institute of Nutrition.

Shaw, J. M. and C. M. Snow. 1998. Weighted vest exercise improves indices of fall risk in older women. *Journal of Gerontology* 53(1): M53–M58.

Shelton, B. A. 1992. *Women, Men and Time: Gender Differences in Paid Work, Housework and Leisure.* New York: Greenwood Press.

Shipman, K. L., Rossman, B. B. R., and J. C. West. 1999. Co-occurrence of spousal violence and child abuse: Conceptual implications. *Child Maltreatment* 4(2): 93–102.

Shkolnikov, V. M. 1997. *The Russian Health Crisis of the 1990s in Mortality Dimensions.* Working paper 97.01. Cambridge: Harvard Center for Population and Development Studies.

SIDA. 1996. *A Gender Perspective in the Water Resources Management Sector.* Department for Natural Resources and the Environment. Publications on water resources 6. Stockholm: Swedish International Development Agency.

SIECUS. 1991. *Guidelines for Comprehensive Sexuality Education.* New York: Sex Information and Education Council of the United States.

Silbergeld, E. K. 2000. Environmental Exposures. In *Women and Health,* eds. M. Goldman and M. Hatch. New York: Academic Press.

Simoni-Wastila, L. 2000. The use of abusable prescription drugs: The role of gender. *Journal of Women's Health and Gender Based Medicine* 9: 289–297.

Sims, J., ed. 1994. *Women, Health and Environment: An Anthology*. (WHO/EHG/94.11). Geneva: World Health Organization.

Sims, J. 1997. *Women, Health and Environment*. Paper prepared for the Regional Conference of Parliamentarians on Women, Health and Environment, Bangkok, August 4–6. New Delhi: WHO South East Asian Regional Office.

Slocum, R. and B. Thomas-Slayter. 1995. Participation, empowerment and sustainable development. In *Power, Process and Participation: Tools for Change*, eds. R. Slocum and L. Wichart. London: Intermediate Technology Publications.

Small, R., Astbury, J., Brown, S., and J. Lumley. 1994. Depression after childbirth. Does social context matter? *Medical Journal of Australia* 161: 473–477.

Smith, G. D. and M. J. Shipley. 1991. Confounding of occupation and smoking: Its magnitude and consequences. *Social Science and Medicine* 32(11): 1297–1300.

Smith, K. R. 1987. *Biofuels, Air Pollution and Health: A Global Review*. London: Plenum Press.

Smith, K. R. 1990. The risk transition. *International Environmental Affairs* 2(3): 227–251.

Soda, M. Y., Mizunuma, H., Honjo, S., Okano, H., and Y. Ibuki. 1993. Pre- and postmenopausal bone mineral density of the spine and proximal femur in Japanese women assessed by dual-energy x-ray absorptiometry: A cross-sectional study. *Journal of Bone and Mineral Research* 8(2): 183–189.

Soliday, E., McCluskey-Fawcett, K., and M. O'Brien. 1999. Postpartum affect and depressive symptoms in mothers and fathers. *American Journal of Orthopsychiatry* 69: 30–38.

Sorlie, P., Rogot, E., Anderson, R., Johnson, N. J., and E. Backlund. 1992. Black–white mortality differences by family income. *Lancet* 340: 346–350.

Sorlie, P. D., Backlund, E., and J. B. Keller. 1995. US mortality by economic, demographic, and social characteristics: The national longitudinal mortality study. *American Journal of Public Health* 85(7): 949–956.

Sow, A. 1994. African women and pesticides: More exposed to risks, less informed about danger. *Global Pesticide Campaigner* 4(3). www.igc.org/panna/resources/-pestis/PESTIS.burst.710.html.

Spicer, P. E. and R. K. Kereu. 1993. Organochlorine insecticide residues in human breastmilk. A survey of lactating mothers from a remote area in Papua New Guinea. *Bulletin of Environmental Contamination and Toxicology* 50(4): 540–546.

Spitz, A. M., ed. 2000. Special issue: Violence and reproductive health. *Maternal and Child Health Journal* 4(2): 77–154.

Srinivasan, S. 1999. How many aspirins to the rupee? Runaway drug prices. *Economic and Political Weekly* February 27: 514–518.

Stack, C. B. 1974. *All Our Kin: Strategies for Survival in a Black Community.* Rockleigh, NY: Harper & Row.

Standing, G. 1989. Global feminization through flexible labor. *World Development* 17: 1077–1096.

Standing, H. 1997. Gender and equity in health sector reform programmes: A review. *Health Policy and Planning* 12(1): 1–18.

Standing, H. 1999. *Frameworks for Understanding Gender Inequalities and Health Sector Reform: An Analysis and Review of Policy Issues.* Working paper 99.06. Cambridge: Harvard Center for Population and Development Studies.

Standing, H. 2000a. Gender impacts of health reforms. The current state of policy and implementation. Paper presented at the Asociación Latinoamericana de Medicina Social meeting of Havana, Cuba, July 3–7.

Standing, H. 2000b. Gender: A missing dimension in human resource policy and planning for health reforms. *Human Resources for Health Development Journal* 4(2) (online at http://www.moph.go.th/hrdj/).

Stanko, E. A., Crisp, D., Hale, C., and H. Lucraft. 1998. *Counting the Costs: Estimating the Impact of Domestic Violence in the London Borough of Hackney.* London: Crime Concern.

Stansfeld, S. A., Head, J., and M. G. Marmot. 1998. Explaining social class differentials in depression and well-being. *Social Psychiatry and Psychiatric Epidemiology* 33: 1–9.

Statistics Canada. 2000. Family violence in Canada: A statistical profile. www.statcan.ca.

Stefansson, C. G. 1991. Long term unemployment and mortality in Sweden 1980–86. *Social Science and Medicine* 32: 419–424.

Stein, J. 1997. *Empowerment and Women's Health: Theory, Methods and Practice.* London: ZED.

Steiner, J. F., Kramer, A. M., Eilertsen, T. B., and J. C. Kowalsky. 1997. Development and validation of a clinical prediction rule for prolonged nursing home residence after hip fracture. *Journal of the American Geriatrics Society* 45(12): 1510–1514.

Stenberg, B. and S. Wall. 1995. Why do women report "sick building symptoms" more often than men? *Social Science and Medicine* 40(4): 491–502.

Stellman, J. M. and A. Lucas. 2000. Women's occupational health: International perspectives. In *Women and Health,* eds. M. Goldman and M. Hatch. New York: Academic Press.

Stewart, F. 1992. Can adjustment programmes incorporate the interests of women? In *Women and Adjustment Policies in the Third World,* eds. H. Afshar and C. Dennis. Basingstoke: Macmillan.

Stewart, M. 1994. Gynecologic morbidity is high for Egyptian women in a pair of rural villages. *International Family Planning Perspectives* 20(1): 40–41.

Stijkel, A. 1995. On managing reproductive risks of occupational exposure to chemicals. Ph.D. dissertation, University of Amsterdam, The Netherlands.

Stoppe, G., Sandholzer, H., and C. Huppertz. 1999. Gender differences in the recognition of depression in old age. *Maturitas* 32: 205–212.

Straus, M. A., Hamby, S. L., Boney-McCoy, S., and D. B. Sugarman. 1996. The revised conflict tactics scale (CTS2)—Development and preliminary psychometric data. *Journal of Family Issues* 17(3): 283–316.

Stronks, K., van de Mheen, H. D., Looman, C. W. N., and J. P. Mackenbach. 1996. Behavioural and structural factors in the explanation of socio-economic inequalities in health: An empirical analysis. *Sociology of Health and Illness* 18(5): 653–674.

Stronks, K., van de Mheen, H. D., and J. P. Mackenbach. 1998. A higher prevalence of health problems in low income groups: Does it reflect relative deprivation? *Journal of Epidemiological and Community Health* 52(9): 548–557.

Sukanya, S. 1996. Investment in medical equipment: Study of private hospitals in Madras City. *Radical Journal of Health* 3(1): 9–25.

Sule, M. 1999. Health manpower in the district. In *Health Resources, Investment and Expenditure. A Study of Health Providers in a District in India,* ed. S. Kavadi. Pune: Foundation for Research in Community Health.

Sundar, R. 1995. *Household Survey of Health Care Utilisation and Expenditure.* NCAER working paper 53. New Delhi: National Council of Applied Economic Research.

Sundby, J. 1998. *A Gender Perspective on Disability Adjusted Life Years and the Global Burden of Disease* [mimeo]. Geneva: World Health Organization.

Sundby, J. 1999. Are women disfavored in the estimation of disability-adjusted life years and the global burden of disease? *Scandinavian Journal of Public Health* 27: 279–285.

Sutherland, C., Bybee, D., and C. Sullivan. 1998. The long-term effects of battering on women's health. *Women's Health* 4: 41–70.

Sweeney, E. P. 2000. Recent studies indicate that many parents who are current or former welfare recipients have disabilities or other medical conditions. Report from the Center on Budget and Policy Priorities, Washington, DC.

Swiss, S. and J. E. Giller. 1993. Rape as a crime of war: A medical perspective. *Journal of the American Medical Association* 270: 612–615.

Syme, S. L. 1998. Social and economic disparities in health: Thoughts about intervention. *Milbank Memorial Fund Quarterly* 76(3): 493.

Syme, S. L. and L. F. Berkman. 1976. Social class, suspectibility and sickness. *American Journal of Epidemiology* 104(1), 1–8.

Taha, T. E. and R. H. Gray. 1993. Agricultural pesticide exposure and perinatal mortality in central Sudan. *World Health Organization Bulletin* 71(3–4): 317–321.

Tanner, M. and C. Vlassoff. 1998. Treatment seeking behavior for malaria: A typology based on edemicity and gender. *Social Science and Medicine* 46(4–5): 523–532.

Tavani, A., Negri, E., and C. La Vecchia. 1995. Calcium, dairy products, and the risk of hip fracture in women in northern Italy. *Epidemiology* 6(5): 554–557.

Thaddeus, S. and D. Maine. 1994. Too far to walk: Maternal mortality in context. *Social Science and Medicine* 38(8): 1091–1110.

Theobald, S. 1999. Embodied contradictions: Organisational responses to gender and occupational health interests in the electronics industries of northern Thailand. Ph.D. thesis, School of Development Studies, University of East Anglia.

Thomas, D. B., Ray, R. M., Pardthaisong, T., Chutivongse, S., Koetsawang, S., Silpisomkosoi, S., Virutamasen, P., Christopherson, W. M., Melnick, J. M., Meirik, O., Farley, T. M. M., and G. Riotton. 1996. Prostitution, condom use and invasive squamous cell cervical cancer in Thailand. *American Journal of Epidemiology* 143(8): 779–786.

Thorslund, M., Lundberg, O., and M. Parker. 1993. Class and ill-health among the elderly. *Journal of the Swedish Medical Association* 90: 3547–3553 [in Swedish].

Ton, P., Tovignan, S., and S. D. Vedouhé. 2000. Endosulfan deaths and poisonings in Benin. *Pesticides News* 47: 12–14.

Townsend, J. 1996. Price and consumption of tobacco. *British Medical Bulletin* 52(1): 132–142.

Townsend, P., Davidson, N., and M. Whitehead. 1992. *Inequalities in Health: The Black Report and the Health Divide*. London: Penguin.

Trichopoulos, D., Li, F. P., and D. J. Hunter. 1996. What causes cancer? *Scientific American* (special edition) 275(3): 80–84.

Tsouderos, Y., Bauza-Canellas, C., Decassin, P., Denis, M., and B. Cusset. 1994. Bone mineral density of the femoral neck, a cross-sectional study of normal values in 827 French women aged 36 to 86 years. *Revue du Rhumatisme* 61(6): 439–446.

Turan, C., Zorlu, C. G., Ekin, M., Hancerkiogullari, N., and F. Saracoglu. 1996. Urinary incontinence in women of reproductive age. *Gynecologic and Obstetric Investigation* 41(2): 132–134.

Ulrich, M., Zulueta, A-M., Caceres-Dittmar, G., Sampson, C., Pinardi, M-E., Rada, E-M., and N. Aranzazu. 1993. Leprosy in women: Characteristics and repercussions. *Social Science and Medicine* 37(4): 445–456.

UNAIDS. 1999. *Gender and HIV/AIDS: Taking Stock of Research Programmes*. Geneva: Joint United Nations Programme on HIV/AIDS.

UNAIDS. 2000. http://www.unaids.org/.

UNAIDS and WHO. 1999. *AIDS Epidemic Update: December 1999*. Geneva: Joint United Nations Programme on HIV/AIDS and the World Health Organization.

UNCHS. 1996. *An Urbanizing World: Global Report on Human Settlements.* Oxford: Oxford University Press.

UNDP. 1995. *Human Development Report.* New York: Oxford University Press.

UNDP. 1997. *Human Development Report.* New York: Oxford University Press.

UNDP. 1998a. *Human Development Report.* New York: Oxford University Press.

UNDP. 1998b. *Overcoming Human Poverty.* New York: United Nations Development Program.

UNDP. 1999. *Human Development Report.* New York: Oxford University Press.

UNECE. 1998. *Convention on Access to Information, Public Participation and Decision-making and Access to Justice in Environmental Matters.* Aarhus, Denmark. Geneva: United Nations Economic Commission for Europe.

UNEP. 1999a. *Report on the Intergovernmental Negotiations for an Internationally Legally Binding Instrument for Implementing International Action of Certain Persistent Organic Pollutants on the Work of the Third Session.* Geneva: United Nations Environmental Program.

UNEP. 1999b. *Global Environment Outlook 2000: Millennium Report on the Environment.* London: Earthscan Publications.

UNESCO. 1996. *Living with Radiation after Chernobyl.* UNESCO Chernobyl program. Paris: United Nations Education, Science, and Cultural Organization.

UNGASS. 1999. Key actions for further implementation of the Program of Action of the International Conference on Population and Development, 21st special session, New York. New York: United Nations.

UNHCR. 1996. *Concluding Observations: Peru* (CCPR/C/70/add.72, para.15). Geneva: United Nations High Commission for Human Rights.

UNICEF. 1997. *Give Us Credit: How Access to Loans and Basic Social Services Can Enrich and Empower People.* New York: United Nations Children's Fund.

UNICEF. 1999a. *Children in Jeopardy.* New York: United Nations Children's Fund.

UNICEF. 1999b. *Women in Transition.* The MONEE CEE/CIS Baltics monitoring report 6. New York: United Nations Children's Fund.

UN. 1993. *Declaration on the Elimination of Violence against Women.* General Assembly. New York: United Nations.

UN. 1994. *Demographic Yearbook Special Issue: Population Ageing and the Situation of Elderly Persons.* New York: United Nations.

UN. 1995. *Population and Development: Programme of Action Adopted at the International Conference on Population and Development* (ST/ESA/SER.A./ 149). New York: United Nations.

UN. 1996. *Levels and Trends of Contraceptive Use as Assessed in 1994.* New York: United Nations.

UN. 1998. *World Population Monitoring 1996: Selected Aspects of Reproductive Rights and Reproductive Health* (ST/ESA/SER.A/156). New York: United Nations.

UN. 1999. *Key Actions for the Further Implementation of the Program of Action of the International Conference on Population and Development*. New York: United Nations.

UNRISD. 1997. *Working towards a more gender equitable macro-economic agenda*. Geneva: United Nations Research Institute on Social Development.

Uplekar, M. W. 2000. Private health care. *Social Science and Medicine* 51: 897–904.

Uplekar, M. W. and R. A. Cash. 1991. The private GP and leprosy: A study. *Leprosy Review* 62: 410–419.

Uplekar, M. W. and D. S. Shepard. 1991. Treatment of tuberculosis by private general practitioners in India. *Tubercle and Lung Diseases* 72: 284–290.

U.S. Bureau of the Census. 1998. *Statistical abstract of the United States: 1998*, 118th ed. Washington, DC: U.S. Bureau of Census.

U.S. Department of Justice. 1998a. *Prevalence, Incidence, and Consequences of Violence Against Women: Findings from the National Violence Against Women Survey*. Washington, DC: U.S. Department of Justice.

U.S. Department of Justice. 1998b. *Violence by Intimates. Analysis of Data on Crimes by Current or Former Spouses, Boyfriends and Girlfriends*. Washington, DC: Bureau of Justice Statistics.

U.S. Surgeon General. 1964. *Smoking and Health: Report of the Advisory Committee to the Surgeon General of the Public Health Service*. Washington, DC: U.S. Department of Health, Education, and Welfare.

Ustun, T. B. and N. Sartorius. 1995. *Mental Illness in General Health Care: An International Study*. Geneva: Wiley on behalf of the World Health Organization.

Vågerö, D. and E. Lahelma. 1998. Women, work, and mortality: An analysis of female labor participation. In *Women, Stress, and Heart Disease*, eds. K. Orth-Gomér, M. Chesney, and N. K. Wenger. Hillsdale, NJ: Lawrence Erlbaum.

Valkonen, T. and Martikainen, P. 1995. Unemployment and mortality. Causation or selection? In *Adult Mortality in Developed Countries. From Description to Explanation*, eds. A. Lopez, G. Caselli, and T. Valkonen. Oxford: Oxford University Press.

Van der Gaag, J. and T. Barham. 1998. Health and health expenditures in adjusting and non-adjusting countries. *Social Science and Medicine* 46(8): 995–1009.

Van der Straten, A., King, R., Grinstead, O., Serufilira, A., and S. Allen. 1995. Couple communication, sexual coercion and HIV risk reduction in Kigali, Rwanda. *AIDS* 9(8): 935–944.

Vandemoortele, J. 2000. *Absorbing Social Shocks, Protecting Children and Reducing Poverty*. UNICEF staff working paper (EPP-00-001). New York: United Nations Children's Fund.

Vandiver, V. L. 1998. Quality of life, gender and schizophrenia: A cross-national survey in Canada, Cuba and U.S.A. *Community Mental Health Journal* 34: 501–511.

Vera, H. 1993. The client's view of high quality care in Santiago, Chile. *Studies in Family Planning* 24: 40.

Verbrugge, L. M. 1976a. Females and illness: Recent trends in sex differences in the United States. *Journal of Health and Social Behavior* 17: 387–403.

Verbrugge, L. M. 1976b. Sex differentials in morbidity and mortality in the United States. *Social Biology* 23(4): 275–296.

Verbrugge, L. M. 1985. Gender and health: An update on hypotheses and evidence. *Journal of Health and Social Behavior* 26: 156–182.

Verbrugge, L. M. 1989. The twain meet: Empirical explanations of sex differences in health and mortality. *Journal of Health and Social Behavior* 30(3): 282–304.

Vezina, N., Tierney, D., and K. Messing. 1992. When is light work heavy? Components of the physical workload of sewing machine operators working at piecework rates. *Applied Ergonomics* 23(4): 268–276.

Vlassoff, C. 1994. Gender inequalities in health in the third world: Uncharted ground. *Social Science and Medicine* 39(9): 1249–1259.

Vlassoff, C. and E. Bonilla. 1994. Gender-related differences in the impact of tropical diseases on women: What do we know. *Journal of Biosocial Science* 26: 37–53.

von Schirnding, Y. E. R. 1999. Addressing health-and-environment concerns in national planning. *Urban Health and Development Bulletin* 2: 59–61.

Wagstaff, A., van Doorslaer, E., and F. Ruter. 1993. *Equity in the Finance and Delivery of Health Care: An International Perspective*. New York: Oxford University Press.

Wajcman J. 1994. Delivered into men's hands? The social construction of reproductive technology. In *Power and Decision. The Social Control of Reproduction*, eds. G. Sen and R. Snow. Cambridge: Harvard Center for Population and Development Studies with Harvard University Press.

Walberg, P., McKee, M., Shkolnikov, V., Chenet, L., and D. A. Leon. 1998. Economic change, crime and mortality crisis in Russia: Regional analysis. *British Medical Journal* 317: 312–318.

Waldron, I. 1976. Why do women live longer than men? *Social Science and Medicine* 10: 349–362.

Waldron, I. 1986. What do we know about the causes of sex differences in mortality? *Population Bulletin of the United Nations* 18: 59.

Waldron, I. 1991. Effects of labour force participation on sex differences in mortality and morbidity. In *Women, Work and Health: Stress and Opportunities,* eds. M. Frankenhauser, U. Lundberg, and M. Chesney. New York: Plenum Press.

Waldron, I., Weiss, C. C., and M. E. Hughes. 1998. Interacting effects of multiple roles on women's health. *Journal of Health and Social Behaviour* 39: 216–236.

Walsh, J. A. 1988. *Establishing Health Priorities in the Developing World.* New York: United Nations Development Program.

Walsh, J. A. and K. S. Warren. 1979. Selective primary health care: An interim study for disease control in developing countries. *New England Journal of Medicine* 301: 967–974.

Walt, G. and K. Buse, eds. 1999. Special Issue: Managing external resources in the health sector: Lessons from SWAps. *Health Policy and Planning* 14(3).

Walt, G., Pavignani, E., Gilson, L., and K. Buse. 1999. Managing external resources in the health sector: Are there lessons for SWAPs? *Health Policy and Planning.* 14(3): 273–284.

Walters, V. 1993. Stress, anxiety and depression: Women's accounts of their health problems. *Social Science and Medicine* 36(4): 393–402.

Walters, V. and N. Charles. 1997. "I just cope from day to day": Unpredictability and anxiety in the lives of women. *Social Science and Medicine* 45(11): 1729–1739.

War on Want. 2000. Tobin tax update. A digest of news for the UK Tobin tax campaign network. www.waronwant.org.

Wardlaw, T. and D. Maine. 1999. Process indicators for maternal mortality programmes. In *Safe Motherhood Initiatives: Critical Issues,* eds. M. Berer and T. K. S. Ravindran. London: Reproductive Health Matters.

Watkins, K. 1998a. *Cost Recovery and Equity in the Health Sector: Issues for Developing Countries.* UK and Ireland Oxfam Policy Department. Oxford: Oxfam UK.

Watkins, K. 1998b. Cost-recovery and equity: The case of Zimbabwe. Paper prepared for World Institute for Development Economics Research, Oxfam UK.

Watts, C., Ndlovu, M., and E. Keogh. 1997. The magnitude and health consequences of violence against women in Zimbabwe. Musasa project report. Unpublished document.

Weinberg, D. H. 1996. A brief look at postwar U.S. income inequality. Current population reports P60-191. Washington, DC: U.S. Government Printing Office.

Weinstein, M. C. and W. B. Stason. 1976. *Hypertension: A Policy Perspective.* Cambridge: Harvard University Press.

Weiss, E. and G. Rao Gupta. 1998. *Bridging the Gap: Addressing Gender and Sexuality in HIV Prevention.* Washington, DC: International Research Center on Women.

Weissman, J. S. and A. M. Epstein. 1994. *Falling Through the Safety Net: Insurance Status and Access to Health Care.* Baltimore: Johns Hopkins University Press.

Welbourn, A. 1992. Rapid rural appraisal, gender and health: Alternative ways of listening to needs. *IDS Bulletin* 23: 1.

Welbourn, A. 2000. *Gender, Sex and HIV: How to Address Issues that No-One Wants to Hear About.* Tant qu'on a la Sante (DDC/UNESCO/IUED). Geneva: Universitaire d'Etude sur le Développment, Université de Genève.

Wells, C. K. and A. R. Feinstein. 1988. Detection bias in diagnostic pursuit of lung cancer. *American Journal of Epidemiology* 128: 1016.

West, S. K., Munoz, B., Turner, V. M., Mmbaga, B. B., and H. R. Taylor. 1991. The epidemiology of trachoma in central Tanzania. *International Journal of Epidemiology* 20(4): 1088–1092.

West, C. 1993. Reconceptualizing gender in physician-patient relations. *Social Science and Medicine* 36(1): 57–66.

Whitaker, C. N. C. 1996. The impact of women's participation in an income-generation program in southwestern Tanzania. Ph.D. dissertation, Johns Hopkins University.

Whiteford, L. 1993. Child and maternal health and international economic policies. *Social Science and Medicine* 37(11): 1391–1400.

Whitehead, M., Dahlgren, G., and L. Gilson. 2001. Developing the policy response to inequities in health: A global perspective. In *Challenging Inequities in Health: From Ethics to Action,* eds. T. Evans, M. Whitehead, F. Diderichsen, A. Bhuiya, and M. Wirth. New York: Oxford University Press.

WHO. 1981. *Social Dimensions of Mental Health.* Geneva: World Health Organization.

WHO. 1984. *Biomass Fuel Combustion and Health* (EFP/84.64). Geneva: World Health Organization.

WHO. 1990. *Working Group on Psychological Effects of Nuclear Accidents: Summary Report* (EUR/ICP/CEH 093(S)). Copenhagen: WHO Regional Office for Europe.

WHO. 1991a. Creating common ground: Women's perspectives on the selection and introduction of fertility regulation technologies. Report of a meeting between women's health advocates and scientists, Geneva, February 20–22.

WHO. 1991b. *Obstetric Fistulae: A Review of Available Information* (WHO/MCH/MSM/91.5) Geneva: World Health Organization.

WHO. 1992. *Epidemiological, social and technical aspects of indoor pollution from biomass fuel* (WHO/EHG/92.3A). Geneva: World Health Organization.

WHO. 1994a. *Mother and Baby Package: Implementing Safe Motherhood in Countries* (WHO/FHE/MSM/94.11). Geneva: World Health Organization.

WHO. 1994b. *Assessment of Fracture Risk and Its Application to Screening for Postmenopausal Osteoporosis.* WHO technical report series 843. Geneva: World Health Organization.

WHO. 1995. *World Health Report 1995: Bridging the Gap.* Geneva: World Health Organization.

WHO. 1996a. *Groups at Risk: WHO Report on the Tuberculosis Epidemic.* Global tuberculosis programme. Geneva: World Health Organization.

WHO. 1996b. *Linkage Methods for Environment and Health Analysis* (WHO/ UNEP/USEPA WHO/EHG/95.26). Geneva: World Health Organization.

WHO. 1996c. *Violence Against Women. WHO Consultation* (FRH/WHD/ 96.27). Geneva: World Health Organization.

WHO. 1997a. *Global and Regional Estimates of Incidence of and Mortality due to Unsafe Abortion with a Listing of Available Country Data,* 3rd ed. (WHO/ RHT/MSM/97.16). Geneva: World Health Organization.

WHO. 1997b. *Coverage of Maternity Care. A Listing of Available Information.* (WHO/RHT/MSM/96.28). Geneva: World Health Organization.

WHO. 1997c. Department for prevention and control of communicable diseases. Fact sheet 164. Geneva: World Health Organization.

WHO. 1997d. *Health and Environment in Sustainable Development* (WHO/ EHG/97.8). Geneva: World Health Organization.

WHO. 1997e. *Intersectoral Action for Health: Addressing Health and Environment Concerns in Sustainable Development* (WHO/PPE/PAC/97.1). Geneva: World Health Organization.

WHO. 1997f. *Violence Against Women. A Health Priority Issue* (FRH/WHD/ 97.8). Geneva: World Health Organization.

WHO. 1998a. *DALYs and Reproductive Health: Report of an Informal Consultation* (WHO/RHT/98.28). 27–28 April. Geneva: World Health Organization.

WHO. 1998b. *Gender and health: Technical paper* (WHO/FRH/WHD/98.16). Geneva: World Health Organization.

WHO. 1998c. *Communicable Disease Cluster (CDS).* Geneva: World Health Organization.

WHO. 1998d. *Global Programme on Tuberculosis.* Geneva: World Health Organization.

WHO. 1998e. *Report of the Technical Consultation on Safe Motherhood.* Geneva: World Health Organization.

WHO. 1998f. *Methods for Health Impact Assessment in Environmental and Occupational Health* (WHO/EHG/98 ILO/OSH/98.1). Geneva: World Health Organization.

WHO. 1998g. *The World Health Report, 1998. Executive Summary.* Geneva: World Health Organization.

WHO. 1999a. *Interpreting Reproductive Health* (WHO/CHS/RHR/99.7). Geneva: World Health Organization.

WHO. 1999b. Task force for osteoporosis. Interim report and recommendations. *Osteoporosis International* 10: 259–264.

WHO. 1999c. *The World Health Report 1999*. Geneva: World Health Organization.

WHO. 1999d. *Health 21: The Health for All Policy for the WHO European Region, 21 targets for the 21st century*. Copenhagen: World Health Organization Regional Office for Europe.

WHO. 1999e. *WHO Multi-Country Study of Women's Health and Domestic Violence. Core Protocol* (WHO/EIP/GPE/99.3). Geneva: World Health Organization.

WHO. 1999f. *Putting Women's Safety First: Ethical and Safety Recommendations for Research on Domestic Violence Against Women* (WHO/EIP/GPE/99.2). Geneva: World Health Organization.

WHO. 1999g. *Injury. A Leading Cause of the Global Burden of Disease* (WHO/HSC/PVI/99.11). Geneva: World Health Organization.

WHO. 2000a. *World Health Report*. Geneva: World Health Organization.

WHO. 2000b. *Global Prevalence and Incidence of Selected Curable Sexually Transmitted Diseases: Overview and Estimates*. Geneva: World Health Organization.

WHO 2000c. WHO Violence Against Women Database.

WHO-ICPE (World Health Organization and International Consortium of Psychiatric Epidemiology). 2000. Cross-national comparisons of mental disorders. *Bulletin of the World Health Organization* 78: 413–426.

WHO, UNFPA, and UNICEF. 1997. *Action for Adolescent Health: Towards a Common Agenda—Recommendations from a Joint Study Group* (WHO/FRG/ADH/97.9) Geneva: World Health Organization.

WHO, UNICEF, and UNFPA. 2001. Maternal mortality in 1995: Estimates developed by WHO, UNICEF and UNFPA (CWHO/RHR/01.9). Geneva: World Health Organization.

Wikander, U. 1992. Shared work, shared power: Women's subordination at and through work. A historical essay. In *Contract in Crisis,* eds. G. Åström and Y. Hirdman. Stockholm: Carlssons Bokförlag [in Swedish].

Wilkinson, R. G. 1992. Income distribution and life expectancy. *British Medical Journal* 304: 165–168.

Wilkinson, R. G. 1996. *Unhealthy Societies: The Afflictions of Inequality*. London: Routledge.

Williams, A. 1999. Calculating the global burden of disease: Time for a strategic reappraisal? *Health Economics* 8(1): 1–8.

Williams, D. R. 1997. Race and health: Basic questions, emerging directions. *Annals of Epidemiology* 7: 322–333.

Williams, K. and D. Umberson. 2000. Women, stress and health. In *Women and Health,* eds. M. Goldman and M. Hatch. New York: Academic Press.

Wingo, P. A., Ries, L. A., Giovino, G. A., Miller, D. S., Rosenberg, H. M., Shopland, D. R., Thun, M. J., and B. K. Edwards. 1999. Annual report to the nation on the status of cancer, 1973–1996, with a special section on lung cancer and tobacco smoking. *Journal of the National Cancer Institute* 91(8): 675–690.

Wingwood, G. M. and R. J. DiClemente. 1997. Child sexual abuse, HIV sexual risk and gender relations of African-American women. *American Journal of Preventive Medicine* 13: 380–384.

Wolf, S. L., Barnhardt, H. X., and N. G. Kuntner. 1996. Reducing frailty and falls in older persons: An investigation of tai chi and computerized balance training. Atlanta FICSIT Group. Frailty and Injuries: Cooperative studies of intervention techniques. *Journal of the American Geriatrics Society* 44: 489–497.

Wolfe, B. L. 1994. Reform of health care for the non-elderly poor. In *Confronting poverty: Prescriptions for Change,* eds. S. Danziger, G. Sandefur, and D. Weinberg. Cambridge: Harvard University Press.

Wolfensohn, J. 1999. Coalitions for Change. Address to the Board of Governors of the World Bank, Washington, DC.

Wolff, E. N. 1995. *Top Heavy: A Study of the Increasing Inequality of Wealth in America.* New York: Twentieth Century Fund Press.

Women in Europe for a Common Future. 1999. Persistent organic pollutants and reproductive health. Background document for the International POPs Elimination Network workshop on Women, POPs and Reproductive Health, Geneva.

Women in Europe for a Common Future. 2000. Gender, health and environment: Best practices of European women. Background document for ECE regional preparatory meeting on the 2000 review of the implementation of the Beijing Platform for Action, Geneva, February 19–21.

Women's Aid. 1999. *Violence Against Women as a Health Issue. Responding to Abuse of Women by Male Partners: A Resource for Training in Accident and Emergency Units.* Dublin, Ireland: Women's Aid.

Women's Environment and Development Organization. 1999. *Risks, Rights and Reforms: A 50-Country Survey Assessing Government Actions Five Years after the International Conference on Population and Development.* New York: Women's Environment and Development Organization.

Wood, K. and R. Jewkes. 1997. Violence, rape, and sexual coercion: Everyday love in South Africa. *Gender and Development* 5(2): 23–30.

Wood, K., Maforah, F., and R. Jewkes. 1998. "He forced me to love him": Putting violence on adolescent sexual health agendas. *Social Science and Medicine* 47: 233–242.

World Bank. 1993. *World Development Report: Investing in Health.* New York: Oxford University Press.

World Bank. 1995a. *World Development Report 1995.* Appendix 3. New York: Oxford University Press.

World Bank. 1995b. *Improving Women's Health in India.* Washington, DC: World Bank.

World Bank. 1997. *World Development Report 1997: The State in a Changing World*. Washington, DC: World Bank.

World Bank. 1998a. *Global Development Finance*. Washington, DC: World Bank.

World Bank. 1998b. *World Development Indicators* Washington, DC: World Bank.

World Bank. 2000a. *"Consultations with the Poor"*: A Study to Inform the World Development Report 2000/2001 on Poverty and Development. Washington, DC: World Bank.

World Bank. 2000b. *World Development Report 2000/2001*. Washington, DC: World Bank.

World Water Council. 2000. *World Water Vision. Results of the Gender Mainstreaming Project: A Way Forward*. The Hague: World Water Forum.

Worth, D. 1989. Sexual decision-making and AIDS: Why condom promotion among vulnerable women is likely to fail. *Studies in Family Planning* 20(6): 297–307.

Wratten, E. 1993. Poverty in Tanzania. Report prepared for the Overseas Development Administration, London.

Wyshak, G. 1981. Hip fracture in elderly women and reproductive history. *Journal of Gerontology* 36(4): 424–427.

Wyshak, G. and R. E. Frisch. 1994. Carbonated beverages, dietary calcium, the dietary calcium/phosphorous ratio and bone fractures in girls and boys. *Journal of Adolescent Health* 15(3): 210–215.

Wyshak, G., Frisch, R. E., Albright, T. E., Albright, N. L., Schiff, I., and J. Witschi. 1989. Non-alcoholic carbonated beverage consumption and bone fractures among women former college athletes. *Journal of Orthopedic Research* 7(1): 91–99.

Xu, L., Lu, A., Zhao, X., Chen, X., and S. R. Cummings. 1996. Very low rates of hip fracture in Beijing, People's Republic of China: The Beijing osteoporosis project. *American Journal of Epidemiology* 144(9): 901–907.

Yip, S. K., Chung, T. K., and T. S. Lee. 1997. Suicide and maternal mortality in Hong Kong. *Lancet* 350(9084): 1103.

Yodanis Carrie, L. and A. Godenzi. 1999. *Report on the Economic Costs of Violence Against Women*. Fribourg, Switzerland: University of Fribourg.

Yousefi, V. O. 1999. Agrochemicals in South Africa. *African Newsletter* (1).

Yumkella, F. 1996. *Women, Onchocerciasis and Ivermectin in Sierra Leone*. Published by the special programme on research and training in Tropical Diseases. Geneva: World Health Organization.

Zakrewski, S. F. 1997. *Principles of Environmental Toxicology*. ACS Monograph 190. Washington, DC: American Chemical Society.

Zeitlin, J. 1997. The impact of women's work on their health: Theoretical approaches with empirical tests from India and Indonesia. Ph.D. dissertation, Harvard School of Public Health, Harvard University.

Zierler, S. and N. Krieger. 1997. Reframing women's risk: Social inequalities and HIV infection. *Annual Review of Public Health* 18: 401–436.

Zierler, S., Feingold, L., and D. Laufer. 1991. Adult survivors of childhood sexual abuse and subsequent risk of HIV infection. *American Journal of Public Health* 83: 572–575.

Zunzunegui, M. V., Beland, F., Llacer, A., and V. Leon. 1998. Gender differences in depressive symptoms among Spanish elderly. *Social Psychiatry and Psychiatric Epidemiology* 33: 195–205.

Zwi, A. and A. Mills. 1995. Health policy in less developed countries. *Journal of International Development* 7(3): 299–347.

Contributors

Jill Astbury is a psychologist with a Ph.D. from the University of Melbourne, where she is Associate Professor and Deputy Director of the Key Centre for Women's Health in Society, Faculty of Medicine, Dentistry, and Health Sciences, and a WHO Collaborating Center in Women's Health. She developed the first postgraduate courses in women's health in a medical faculty in Australia. Her research interests are the epistemological aspects of theories on women's mental health and links among gender, social position, life and reproductive events, and mental health outcomes. Professor Astbury is the author of *Crazy for You: The Making of Women's Madness* (Oxford University Press, 1996).

Maggie Bangser holds an M.A. in Public and Private Management from Yale University. She is based in Tanzania where she is Director of the Women's Dignity Project, a regional initiative in east Africa that addresses obstetric fistula within the context of gender and health equity and human rights. Previously, she was a Research Affiliate at the Harvard Center for Population and Development Studies, Coordinator of a fistula program in Tanzania, Program Officer for the Ford Foundation in east and southern Africa, and Program Officer for Asia at the International Women's Health Coalition in New York.

Nancy Breen is an economist and the Health Disparities Research Coordinator in the Applied Research Program (ARP), U.S. National Cancer Institute. She earned her Ph.D. in economics at the New School for Social Research in New York City. The mission of ARP is to improve cancer monitoring systems in the United States by extending them across the cancer control continuum. Research in health disparities focuses on monitoring and understanding how cancer risks, barriers to health services, and the burden of cancer are differentially distributed in the United States. Dr. Breen's area of responsibility includes investigating how race, social class, gender, community factors, and health service diffusion shapes cancer control and cancer outcomes.

Maureen Butter is an environmental biologist. Since 1984 she has been Director of the Science Shop for Biology at the University of Groningen. The Science Shop aims to improve social justice by providing research requested by civil society groups. Research is carried out on a low-cost or no-cost basis with the help of students who receive credits for doing community-based research. In 1997

Dr. Butter published her Ph.D. thesis on women's emancipation and sustainable development at the University of Groningen. Since then she has been involved in consulting and political advocacy on gender and environment issues at national, regional, and global levels.

Jane Cottingham   has an M.Sc. in Population Sciences from the Harvard School of Public Health. In 1976 she cofounded ISIS, Women's International Information and Communication Service, and served as the organization's director in Geneva for eleven years. She is currently Technical Officer for Women's Perspectives and Gender Issues at the Department of Reproductive Health and Research at WHO in Geneva, a post she has held since 1991. She works with women's health groups, policy makers, and scientists to ensure that women's rights and gender perspectives are integrated into the reproductive health research agenda.

Claudia García-Moreno   is a physician with an M.A. in Community Medicine from the London School of Hygiene and Tropical Medicine. She has over twenty years' experience working in public health in Africa, Latin America, and some parts of Asia. Since 1990 her work increasingly focused on women's health and gender in health. She was Chief of the Women's Health Program at WHO from 1994 to 1998 and developed WHO's work on violence against women. She is coordinator of the WHO Multi-Country Study on Women's Health and Domestic Violence Against Women and works on mainstreaming gender in WHO's work.

Asha George   has an M.Sc. in Population and International Health from the Harvard School of Public Health. She is a Doctoral Candidate at the Institute of Development Studies, University of Sussex and Research Fellow at the Harvard Center for Population and Development Studies. Before this she was a project manager for UNIFEM and UNFPA in Mexico for funding related to the social mobilization around the Beijing women's and Cairo population conferences. Her research interests include the political economy of international health, reproductive health, and health systems analysis.

Kara Hanson   holds a D.Sc. in Health Economics from Harvard University. She is a Lecturer in Health Economics and works with the Health Economics and Financing Program at the London School of Hygiene and Tropical Medicine. Her research interests include health system financing and organization, equity and efficiency implications of private sector involvement in financing and delivering health services, operation of markets for essential public health commodities, and economics of malaria interventions. She has worked extensively in sub-Saharan Africa.

Pamela Hartigan   has a Ph.D. in Developmental Psychology. She joined the Pan American Health Organization (PAHO) to spearhead an initiative supporting joint action between governments and nongovernment offices, and in 1994 she began to lead PAHO's Women, Health, and Development Program. She left PAHO in 1997 to work with WHO as Manager of the Task force on Gender-Sensitive Interventions of the Special Program on Research and Training in Tropical Diseases; in 1998 she was appointed Director of the Department of Health Promotion. In October 2000 she left WHO to head the Schwab Foundation for Social Entrepreneurship based in Geneva.

Aditi Iyer   has studied sociology and has an M.A. in Social Work from the Tata Institute of Social Science, Bombay. She has undertaken multidisciplinary research in the field of health with the Foundation for Research in Community Health and with the Center for Enquiry into Health and Allied Themes. As Research Consultant at the Indian Institute of Management Bangalore, her work primarily focuses on gender, operational, and equity issues in health and health care in India. She was awarded the Goran Sterky Fellowship at the Division of International Health Care at the Karolinska Institute in 1998.

Cynthia Myntti   received her Ph.D. in Social Anthropology from the London School of Economics and her M.P.H. from Johns Hopkins University. For nearly a decade she worked as a reproductive health program officer for the Ford Foundation in Cairo and Jakarta. She taught and conducted research while working at the London School of Hygiene and Tropical Medicine, Sanaa University in Yemen, Humphrey Institute at the University of Minnesota, and American University of Beirut in Lebanon. She has also worked as a consultant for international organizations. Most recently she wrote *Interpreting Reproductive Health* for WHO.

Piroska Östlin   is a medical sociologist with a Ph.D. in Medical Science from the University of Uppsala in Sweden. She is Senior Researcher at the Karolinska Institute and Research Associate at the Harvard Center for Population and Development Studies. Her research concerns methodological problems in occupational epidemiology, as well as the significance of the work environment on women's and men's health. Before the Karolinska Institute, she was Secretary of the Swedish National Public Health Commission, where she was responsible for defining public health targets and suggesting strategies to reduce social inequalities in health.

Janet Price   trained as an M.D. at the University of Sheffield. She is an Honorary Research Fellow at the Liverpool School of Tropical Medicine. Before this she worked with women's organizations in India and as Research Fellow in International Health at the Liverpool School of Tropical Medicine. With her work with the Gender and Health group at Liverpool, her research interests include feminist theory, the body, and disability.

Gita Sen   has a Ph.D. in Economics from Stanford University and is Sir Ratan Tata Chair Professor at the Indian Institute of Management, Bangalore, and Adjunct Lecturer at the Harvard School of Public Health. She is a founding member and research coordinator for the feminist network DAWN. She works with several organizations in a consultative and/or advisory capacity, including among others, HealthWatch (India), UN Research Institute for Social Development, WHO Advisory Committee on Health Research, International Women's Health Coalition (USA), and MacArthur Foundation. She received the Volvo Environment Prize in 1994 and an honorary doctorate from the University of East Anglia in 1998.

Jacqueline Sims   studied International Relations in Geneva and Social Anthropology at Harvard University. She worked for WHO for twenty years on various aspects of environmental health, including food safety, environmental pollution, and rural and urban development. A major focus was on linkages between women, health, and environment issues, particularly with respect to household energy supply and use. Her current work with the Department of Health and Development focuses on gender dimensions of health and poverty.

Rachel Snow   is a reproductive biologist with a D.Sc. in Population Studies from the Harvard School of Public Health. She is Unit Head for Reproductive Health at the Institute for Tropical Hygiene at the University of Heidelberg Medical School in Germany. She is a founding editor of the *African Journal of Reproductive Health*. She served on WHO Human Reproduction Program's (HRP) Advisory Committee for Technology Development, HRP's gender advisory panel, and Coordinating Committee of the International Training Initiative in Gender and Reproductive Health. Her research concerns measurement of the reproductive health burden and development and assessment of appropriate reproductive health technologies.

Hilary Standing   is a social scientist–social anthropologist with a Ph.D. from London University, School of Oriental and African Studies. Her areas of interest include social development and micro and macro social analysis, with particular reference to the health sector; gender issues in development; qualitative methodologies for applied and intervention research, including organizational development techniques; reproductive health; and gender and social impacts of economic transformation. She has done field work in both rural and urban India. Formerly Senior Lecturer at the University of Sussex, she is a Fellow of the Institute of Development Studies, University of Sussex.

Rachel Tolhurst   has an M.A. in Gender Analysis in Development from the School of Development Studies at the University of East Anglia. She is Research Associate at the Liverpool School of Tropical Medicine, where her concerns are gender and equity issues in health, focusing on health sector reform and malaria control. Earlier she worked as a research assistant with the Gender and Health Group at the Liverpool School of Tropical Medicine, developing Guidelines for the Analysis of Gender and Health.

Index

Aårhus Convention, 218
Abortion, 85, 96–98, 104, 106–108, 122, 328–329, 331, 357
Access to health care, 6, 26, 53, 59, 102–103, 106–107, 124, 164–165, 235–237, 240–243, 285, 295, 329, 334, 364
Accidents, 67, 70, 71, 209–210, 341. *See also* Injuries
Action Health, Inc., 269
Adolescent Health and Information Project, 269
Adolescents
female, 22, 26, 30, 85, 96, 106, 115, 122, 125, 357, 364
male, 89, 125, 131
AFDC (Aid to Families with Dependent Children), 231, 234–235
Aging, 18
and cancer, 246–247
and disability-adjusted life-years, 337
and falling, 180–182
and hip fractures, 169–179
and isolation, 179–180
and Medicare, 237–240
Agriculture
and the Aral Sea, 206–207
and ergonomics, 209–210
hazards, 199–200
and pesticides, 74, 199, 210–212
and water quality, 208–209

women in, 73–74, 202, 261
workers, 12, 261
AIDS, 329, 331. *See also* HIV
and community norms, 91
risk of, 49–53
Alameda County Study, 224–225, 247–248
Alcohol
dependence, 151–153
and domestic violence, 130
Anemia, 14, 320
Antenatal or prenatal health, 23, 26, 27, 91, 94, 99, 102, 107, 121
Anxiety, 152–153
Aral Sea, 206–207
Argentina, 263
Armenia, 207
Assembly line production, 75–76
Australia, 71, 116
Autoimmune conditions, 204

Bamako initiative, 353–354
Bangladesh, 16, 31, 55, 116, 130, 270
Rural Advancement Committee (BRAC), 31, 270
Barbados, 115
Batterer intervention programs (BIPs), 131–132
Behavior
change, 60, 66, 131–132, 134

Behavior (cont.)
  health risks of, 6–7, 16, 50–51, 60,
    66, 88, 91, 95–96, 121, 125, 212–
    213, 225–226, 334, 340–341
Bias
  clinical trial, 14, 23–25
  data, 19–22, 58–59, 163–164,
    324–325, 333, 342
  diagnosis, 17–18, 24, 28–29, 55,
    146, 149, 152
  treatment, 21–22, 24, 28–29, 137–
    138, 325–326
Bilbao, 157
Biology and gender, 2–4, 8–9, 12–
  13. *See also* Gender
  and communicable diseases, 46–47,
    56–58
  and depression, 157–162
  and employment, 65–66
  and health consequences of disease,
    331–332
  and hip fractures, 169–179
  and mental health, 147–151
  and occupational hazards, 73–78
Birth control. *See* Contraception
Bone mineral density (BMD), 167,
  172–179, 183–184
  and gender, 189–191
  and osteoporosis, 186–187
Brazil, 262
Breast cancer, 236, 248–251, 251–
  252
Breast milk, 205–207
Bretton Woods Institutions. *See* International Monetary Fund (IMF);
  World Bank

Calcium, 183–184
Cambodia, 335–336
Canada, 114, 116, 118, 182, 186,
  212, 262
Cancer
  breast, 236, 248–251, 251–252
  cervical, 41, 49
  endometrial, 174
  esophageal, 200

liver, 200
lung, 246, 247–248
prostate, 248–251
and race, 250–251
screening, 240–241
and smoking, 247–248
social discrimination in, 246–247,
  251–252
urinary tract, 200
Carbon monoxide, 340
Carbonated cola beverages, 184
Carcinogens, 72, 76, 200
Cardiovascular system, 149, 226–227
and depression, 164
epidemiology, 24
and overtime work, 77
Care burdens, 39, 91, 179–180,
  235–236, 327, 337, 356–357
Caste, 1, 2–3, 283–284. *See also* India; Race
Central African Republic, 115
Cervical cancer, 41, 49
Chad, 263
Chemical pollution, 200, 203–207
Childhood diseases, 37, 38
  health care of, 265
Children
  abuse of, 124–125
  and chemical pollution, 203–204
  and communicable diseases, 37, 38,
    40, 56–58
  sexual abuse of, 115, 120
  and user fees on health care, 265
  and violence against women, 122–
    123, 124–125
  witnessing violence, 129–130
Chile, 116, 118, 157
China, 15, 178, 184
Client-Oriented, Provider-Efficient
  (COPE) methodology, 30
Clinical trials, 14, 23–25, 59, 187–188
Colombia, 116
Colonialism, 43
Comorbidity, 13–15, 122–123, 126,
  144, 145, 151, 152–153, 156, 164,
  171, 185, 333

Confidentiality in health care, 55
Conflict tactics scale (CTS), 113–114
Congenital anomalies and malformations, 23, 72, 74, 95, 210
Contextual-situational frameworks in health care reform, 366–370
Contraception, 52, 85, 91–92, 103–104
Convention on the Elimination of all Forms of Discrimination Against Women, 139
Coronary heart disease, 2
Cost-effectiveness, 126, 337–339, 343, 355

Data
  bias, 19–22, 58–59, 324–325, 333, 342
  domestic violence, 136–138
  gaps, 136–137, 146, 156, 196
  reliability, 19–20
DDT, 205, 211
Death. *See* Mortality
Denmark, 170
Dental care, 241
Depression, 143–144, 146, 151–153, 157–162. *See also* Disorders
  and gender, 157–162
  postpartum, 101, 149
  and poverty, 154–155
  and relationships, 158–159
  and reproduction, 147–148
  and social position, 159, 161
  and socialization, 161–162
  and violence, 120, 123, 159–160
  and the workplace, 77–78, 161–162
Diagnosis bias, 17–18, 24, 28–29, 55, 146, 149
Diarrheal diseases, 37, 38, 40, 56–57
Disability-adjusted life expectancy (DALEs), 316–317. *See also* Health Measures
Disability-adjusted life-years (DALYs), 39–40, 54, 94–98, 313–314, 316,

317–323, 325–326, 337, 343, 356. *See also* Health Measures
Discrimination in health care, 21–22, 28–30, 226–227
  and cancer, 246–247, 251–252
  and clinical and drug research, 23–25
  and economic disparities in the United States, 235–237
Diseases. *See also* Disorders
  and approaches to measuring ill health, 314–317
  classification of, 39
  and disability-adjusted life-years, 325–327
  measures, 325–326
  and nonfatal health states, 334–337
  risk factors for, 339–342
  and social position, 39, 77–78, 223–224
  underreported, 328–330
Disorders. *see also* Depression; Diseases
  affective, 12–13, 70, 73, 120, 143–144, 145, 151
  antisocial, 145
  bipolar (manic-depressive), 145, 148, 153
  menstrual, 4, 13, 23–24, 72, 95, 147
  skin, 67, 74–75, 77
Domestic violence. *See* Violence against women
Donors, 215, 259, 264, 268, 274, 278, 359–360
Drugs
  in India, 296–298
  for prevention of hip fractures, 187–189
  research, 23–25

Ebola virus, 42
Educational status, 92, 103, 132–133, 224–227, 272–273
Egypt, 83, 116
Elderly. *See* Aging

Employment. *See* Labor
Endocrine disruptors, 204
Ergonomics, 76, 209–210
Ethiopia, 98–99, 100, 210
Euroqol, 315

Falling, 180–182
Family planning. *See* Abortion; Contraception; Reproduction
Fat tissue, 23
Female genital mutilation, 90, 93, 112, 333
Female headed households, 156, 235, 364
Finland, 171, 182
First intercourse, 49, 104, 115
Fistula, 100–101
Forensic medicine, 139
France, 157, 180, 260

Gambia, 64, 175–177, 186, 210
Gender Development Index (GDI), 154, 156
Genetics
  and hip fractures, 175–179, 190
  research, 168–169, 178–179
Germ theory, 37, 44
Germany, 16, 260
Ghana, 58, 71–72, 262
  Health Assessment, 315
Girls' Power Initiative, 269
Global burden of disease (GBD), 41, 94–98, 313–314, 316
  and disability-adjusted life-years, 325–327
  and underreported diseases, 328–330
  and valuation of nonfatal health states, 334–337
  worldwide, 317–323
Global poor, 1, 3, 8, 14–16, 26, 37, 41–42, 61, 71–72, 320–323
Global rich, 1, 3, 28–29, 42, 61, 71, 223–224, 323
Globalization
  and disease, 41–42, 195
  and domestic violence, 131

Great Britain, 43–44, 117, 119, 157, 170, 176, 180, 185, 186–187, 248, 355
Greece, 171, 262

Hazards
  agricultural, 12, 73–74, 199–200
  modern, 195, 197–199, 209–210
  occupational, 12, 63–78, 199–200
  traditional, 48, 56, 65–66, 66, 69, 72–73, 207–208, 340–341
Health care. *See also* Research
  and consequences of violence against women, 120–125
  costs, 107, 124, 126, 281, 289–292, 295–297, 302–305, 337–339, 355, 357
  decentralization, 357–358
  effect of debt service and disinvestment on, 262–266
  and environmental health, 11, 197–201
  expenditures, 30, 263–264, 287–288, 349–351, 358
  funding and resources, 26–27
  and gender, 6–8, 10, 47–49, 55–56, 69–70, 168–169
  and globalization, 41–42, 195
  programming, 27–29, 266–273
  and structural adjustment programs, 351–353
  system policies, 25–32, 44–45, 78–80, 92–94, 106–108, 133–140, 162–163, 214–217
  and tropical medicine, 44
  and violence against women, 124, 134–136
  of women, 4–5, 10–19, 124, 265, 354
Health impact assessments (HIAs), 214
Health insurance, 26, 237–243, 358
Health maintenance organizations (HMOs), 241
Health measures
  disability-adjusted life expectancy (DALE), 316–317

disability-adjusted life years (DALYs), 39–40, 54, 94–98, 313–314, 316, 317–325, 317–326, 327, 343, 356
Euroqol, 315
Ghana health assessment, 315
health-related quality of life (HRQL), 315
McMaster Health Index Question-naire, 315
Nottingham health profile, 315
quality-adjusted life years (QALYs), 315
years of life lost (YLLs), 316, 317, 318
Health-related quality of life (HRQL), 315
Health workers
auxiliary nurse midwife, 293
nurse, 135, 356
provider, 28–30, 102–103, 105, 106, 135, 284–285
Health Workers for Change, 30
Heavily Indebted Poor Countries (HIPCs), 259–260, 278
Hepatitis C, 37, 39
History, 4
HIV, 37, 39, 49, 86, 98–100, 329, 331
and comorbidity, 14
risk of, 49–53
and social factors, 14
Homemakers, 71–73, 207–208, 229, 351–352
Homicide, 95, 112, 123–124
Hong Kong, 171, 180, 184
Hormones
and chemical pollution, 203–204
and hip fractures, 174–175, 187–188
Hormone replacement therapy (HRT), 187–188
Human Development Index (HDI), 154
Human Development Reports, 257–258

Human papilloma virus (HPV), 14, 41, 49
Human rights framework, 25–26, 139–140
Humiliation, 158–159
Hypertension, 243–244
Hysteria, 12–13, 147

Iceland, 170
Illness. *See* Morbidity
Immunizations, 240, 354
Income gaps, 1
Incontinence, 100
India, 15, 31, 55, 106, 116, 118, 219, 269. *See also* Castes
cost of health care in, 302–305
economic class differences in, 286–289
gender bias in, 285–286
health care system in, 281–284
prescription drugs in, 296–298
private health services in, 293–297, 299–305
public health services in, 292–293, 299–305
public-private mix of health care services in, 289–292
rural and urban differences in health services in, 284–285
untreated morbidity in, 305–308
Indian Systems of Medicine, 285
Indonesia, 64, 100
Indoor air pollution, 207–208
Industrial Revolution, the, 43–44
Infant and child mortality, 16, 40, 56–57, 58, 67, 101, 122–123, 149, 208, 264, 333, 351
Infertility, 46, 74, 95, 98, 108, 147, 149, 327, 330, 333, 335
Infrastructure development, 200
Injuries, 72, 77, 120–121, 209–210, 341. *See also* Accidents
International Classification of Impair-ment, Disease and Handicap (ICIDH), 95, 327

International Conference on Population and Development (ICPD), 83, 84–86, 102, 107
International Monetary Fund (IMF), 259–260
Intersectoral approaches to health policy, 30–31, 84–86, 104–105, 138, 268–271

Japan, 157, 177–178, 180, 182, 260, 326

Kazakhstan, 206
Kenya, 58, 116, 269
Kenya Rural Enterprise Program/Population Council, 269
Kongwa Women's Credit Programme/Helen Keller Worldwide, 269
Korea, Republic of, 116, 178

Labor. *see also* Occupational health
  and assembly line production, 75–76
  and depression, 77–78, 161–162
  effect on gender and health, 64–68, 77–78, 341
  and employment hierarchies, 228–230
  and ergonomics, 76, 209–210
  gender segregation of, 68–70, 73–78, 203, 207–208, 216, 228–230
  and hazards at work, 63–78, 340
  and hip fractures, 182–183
  and household earnings, 230–231
  and indoor air pollution, 77, 207–208, 340–341
  market participation of women, 26, 63–64, 228–229, 341
  and medical insurance coverage, 237–240
  racial segregation of, 228–230
  and unemployment, 231–235
  unions, 70, 79, 229
  and work-related fatalities, 76
Lebanon, 105

Legislation, 64, 70, 78–79, 85, 87, 92–94, 106, 111, 138–140, 295
Leprosy, 49, 332
Life expectancy, 15–16, 66, 179–180, 326
  disability-adjusted, 316–317
  and hip fractures, 171–173, 179
  of men, 333–334
  sex gap in, 155, 331, 333–334
  of women, 333–334
Life Vanguards, 269
Low birthweight, 95, 123, 208, 210, 331, 341, 351

Macroeconomic policies, 41–42, 52, 216, 278, 348
Mahila Sarvangeen Utkarsh Mandal, 269
Malaria, 7, 14, 20, 37, 38, 39–40, 44, 45, 46, 72, 326, 330
  and bed nets, 58
Malawi, 263
Mali, 263
Mastectomy, 248
McMaster Health Index Questionnaire, 315
Medicaid, 237, 243
Medical insurance, 237–243
Medicare, 237–240
Men
  and AIDS, 49–53, 98–100
  and batterer intervention programs (BIPs), 131–132
  and bone mineral density (BMD), 167, 172–175
  and community norms for sexual behavior, 90
  domestic violence against, 131
  and falling, 180–182
  and gender division of labor, 68–70
  and the global burden of disease, 317–325, 330
  and hip fractures, 170, 172–179, 182–183
  and HIV, 49–53, 98–100, 331
  as homemakers, 229

and isolation, 179–180
life expectancy of, 16, 333–334
and morbidity, 16
and muscle mass, 76, 173–174, 183
and nutrition, 183–184
and preventive health services, 18
and prostate cancer, 248–251
and schizophrenia, 149–150, 153–154
and sex differences in consequences of disease, 331–332
and sexually transmitted infections (STIs), 49–53
and social welfare, 234–235
and stress, 77–78
and tuberculosis (TB), 53–56
and unemployment, 66
violence against, 111–112, 120
and work-related fatalities, 76
Mental health, 12–13, 73
Mexico, 116, 118, 128, 200
Micro-credit, 31, 270, 358
Morbidity, 281, 288–289
and approaches to measuring ill health, 314–317
and children, 56
and hip fractures, 169–170
in India, 285–288, 305–308
and poverty, 224
untreated, 305–308
and women, 17, 96–101, 121–124, 209–210, 333
Mortality
and abortion, 106–107
breast cancer, 248–249
cancer, 246–252
and communicable disease, 37, 39–41
data, 327–328
and domestic violence, 123–124, 328–329
due to hip fractures, 170–171
due to pesticides, 211
and income, 252–253
infant and child, 16, 40, 56–57, 58, 101, 122–123, 149, 208, 264, 333, 351

lung cancer, 246, 247–248
male, 16, 123
maternal, 96–98, 105
and poverty, 224
premature, 15–16
and sexually transmitted infections (STIs), 94–101
and socioeconomic factors, 16
and violence against women, 121–124
work-related, 76
Movimento Manuela Ramos, 272–273
Mozambique, 263
Mycotoxins, 200

National Academy of Science, 129
National Water Act, South Africa, 218
Nepal, 269
Netherlands, the, 28, 116, 180, 213, 325
New Zealand, 182
Nicaragua, 114, 116, 118, 123, 130, 263
Niger, 263
Nigeria, 100, 269, 358
Nonfatal health states, 334–337
Nottingham Health Profile, 315
Nutrition, 183–184, 340

Obesity, 225
OEDCD/DAC work on gender equality, 214–215
Oral rehydration therapy (ORT), 29, 56–57
Osteoporosis, 186–187
Outer Hebrides, 157

Pakistan, 100
Pan American Health Organization (PAHO), 138
Papua New Guinea, 116, 205
Paraguay, 116
Persistent organic pollutants (POPs), 204

Person Trade-Off (PTO) method, 334–337
Peru, 64
Pesticides, 73–74, 199, 210–212
Philippines, 66, 116
Planned Parenthood Association of South Africa, 269
Pollution
  air, 11, 72, 198, 207–208
  chemical, 200, 203–207
  cooking, 207–208
  industrial, 11–12, 72, 198–199, 203–204, 216, 340
  microbiological, 38–39, 41, 198, 205–207
Population growth, 83, 85, 93, 101, 108
Postpartum depression, 101, 149
Poverty, 1, 3, 224–227
  and abortion, 107
  and communicable diseases, 37, 39–41, 56–58, 60–61, 351
  and debt service and disinvestment, 262–266
  and depression, 157–158
  and domestic violence, 126, 136
  and environmental health, 196–201, 202–203, 215–216
  and gender, 8, 14–16, 89–90, 154–155, 169, 202–203, 270, 351, 360–361, 362
  and the global burden of disease, 319–324
  and globalization, 41–42
  and health care policy, 258–261, 266–273
  and health insurance, 237–240
  and hip fractures, 179, 185
  in India, 282
  and intimate and family relationships, 89–90
  and medical care, 266–268
  and mental health, 154–157
  and morbidity and mortality, 224
  and race, 159, 224, 235–236
  and social welfare, 234–235
  and structural adjustment programs, 351–353
  and user fees or cost sharing, 107, 265–266
  and violence against women, 125–126, 270
  and water quality, 208–209, 264, 270
  and women's health, 14–15, 65–66, 257–258
Power and gender, 7–8, 14, 52
  and environmental health, 203
  and policy programming, 270
  and sexual relationships, 89–90
  and violence against women, 112–114, 127–131
Premenstrual syndrome (PMS), 4, 147
Preventive health services, 18, 91–92, 164–165, 236, 265
  and cancer, 246–247, 248–251
Primary health care, 39, 45, 106, 289, 355
Privatization of health services, 281, 293–297, 299–305, 359
Prostitution, 115, 120
Puerto Rico, 117, 118

Quality-adjusted life years (QALYs), 315

Race, 2, 226–227. *See also* Castes
  and cancer, 250–251
  and colonialism, 43
  and environmental racism, 201
  and health status, 243, 245
  and hip fractures, 175–178
  and household earnings, 230–231
  and medical insurance, 237–243
  and pollution, 201
  and poverty, 159, 224, 235–236
  and smoking and hypertension, 243–244
  and social discrimination in health care, 21–22, 251–255, 359
  and workforce segregation, 228–230

Rape, 7, 114–120
Reemerging diseases, 38
Regulations, 74, 76, 77, 78–79, 107,
    216, 294
Repetitive strain injuries, 76
Reproduction
    and chemical pollution, 203–207
    and communicable diseases, 47
    and health care, 4, 12–13, 29–30,
        84–88, 91–92, 101–106, 272
    health conditions related to, 96–101
    legislation and public policy affect-
        ing, 92–94
    and mental health, 14, 147
    and morbidity, 17
    and mortality, 96–98
    and pesticides, 74
    and population growth, 83
    and reproductive tract infections
        (RTIs), 10, 25
Rural vs. urban populations, 41–42,
    43–44, 100–101, 103, 171, 284–
    285, 302–304
Russia, 16, 155, 206
Rwanda, 115, 117, 118, 263

Sanitation, 56
Schistosomiasis, 14, 46, 48
Schizophrenia, 149–150, 153–154
Sector-wide approaches to health care
    reform, 359–361
Segregation of labor, gender, 68–70,
    73–78, 203, 207–208, 216, 228–
    230
Self-assessment, 213
Self Employed Women's Association
    (SEWA), 219
Sex vs. gender, 2, 168. *See also* Biol-
    ogy and gender
    and hip fractures, 172–179
Sexual abuse, 7, 114–120, 129
Sexuality
    and communicable diseases, 47, 49
    and first intercourse, 49, 104, 115
    and intimate and family relation-
        ships, 88–90

    and sexually transmitted infections
        (STIs), 50–53
    unsafe, 95–96
Sexually transmitted infections (STIs),
    42, 44, 85, 91, 94–101, 104–105
    prevalence of, 329–330
    risk of, 49–53
    and violence against women, 121–
        124
Shelters, 125, 133
Singapore, 171
Smoking, 243–244, 247–248
Social class. *See* Social position; Socio-
    economic groups
Social position, 1, 2–3, 7, 16, 20–22,
    64. *See also* Castes; Gender; Race;
    Socioeconomic groups
    and depression, 159, 161
    and disease, 39, 77–78, 223–224,
        340–341
    and domestic violence, 128–129,
        150–151
    and mental health, 148, 154–157
    and mortality, 16
    and race, 28
    and work, 21, 80
Social Security, 64, 165
Socialization and gender, 6–8, 20,
    83–86, 85–86
    and communicable diseases, 47–49
    and depression, 152, 161–162
    and domestic violence, 85–86, 127–
        131, 132–133
    and intimate and family relation-
        ships, 88–90
    and mental health, 152, 154–157
Society for Women's Action and
    Training Initiative, 269
Sociobiology, 25, 83, 86–88, 108–
    109, 168
Socioeconomic groups, 2, 5, 7
    and breast cancer, 251–252
    effect on health status, 63–78, 223–
        227, 252–253
    and gender, 20–22, 132–133
    and health insurance, 241, 243

Socioeconomic groups (cont.)
and hip fractures, 179–185, 189–192
in India, 284–289
and infectious diseases interventions, 56–58
and intimate and family relationships, 89–90
and life expectancy, 326
and medical insurance, 240–243
and mental health, 154–157
and morbidity, 288
and sexually transmitted infections (STIs), 52
and social discrimination in health care, 251–255
South Africa, 106–107, 115, 117, 175–176, 202, 218, 269
Spain, 157
Sri Lanka, 15
State institutions and reproductive health, 92–94
Stepping Stones, 60
Stress, 12, 226
and depression, 157–158
and unemployment, 66
work-related, 77–78
Structural adjustment programs (SAPs), 259–260, 261, 349–353
Structural violence, 112–114
Sudan, 100, 211
Suicide, 67, 123, 125, 126
Survey of Income and Program Participation (SIPP), 227–228
Sweden, 1, 12, 21, 66, 75, 77, 123, 210, 262
Switzerland, 115, 117, 119

Tanzania, 261, 263, 264, 267, 269, 325
Tetrachlorodibenzo-p-dioxin, 206–207
Thailand, 20, 49, 99, 105, 117
Trachoma, 48
Traditional healers, 30, 55, 355

Treatment bias, 21–22, 24, 28–29, 137–138, 325–326
Tropical medicine, 44
Tuberculosis (TB), 2, 37, 38, 39, 45, 49, 320
diagnosis and treatment for, 53–56
Turkey, 100

Uganda, 117, 205, 257
Ukraine, 117
Underreported diseases, 328–330
UNICEF, 264
United Kingdom, 117, 119, 157, 170, 176, 180, 185, 186–187, 248, 260
United Nations Declaration on the Elimination of Violence Against Women, 113
United States, 114, 117, 119, 122–123, 124, 170, 171, 206
access to health care in the, 235–237
distribution of wealth and citizenship in the, 227–228
employment hierarchies, 228–230
household earnings, 230–231
and the International Monetary Fund (IMF), 260
medical insurance in the, 237–243
and social discrimination in health care, 251–255
social discrimination in the, 226–227
unemployment in the, 231–235
Untreated morbidity, 281, 288–289, 305–308
Urbanization, 41–42, 43–44, 131, 183, 184, 195
Urinary tract infection (UTIs), 100
User fees, 107, 265–266, 273

Vaginitis, 100
Vietnam, 55, 105
Vitamins, 183–184

War, 115
Water quality and environmental
   health, 208–209, 264, 270
Welfare, social, 234–235
West Bank, Gaza Strip, 117, 119
Whitehall Study, 224–225
Women's Health Action Research
   Centre, 269
World Bank (WB), 63, 114, 259–
   260, 265, 274, 313, 316
World Conference on Human Rights
   (Vienna, 1993), 111
World Conference on Women, 139
World Development Report, 63, 313,
   316
World Health Organization (WHO),
   11
World Health Reports, 15, 317
World Neighbors, 269

Years of life lost (YLLs), 316, 317,
   318
Yugoslavia, 115

Zambia, 64, 106, 263, 352, 358
Zero tolerance, 85, 134, 165
Zimbabwe, 52, 72, 114, 119, 157,
   160, 263, 265, 276